I0569227

Sustainability Assessments of Buildings

Special Issue Editor
Umberto Berardi

MDPI • Basel • Beijing • Wuhan • Barcelona • Belgrade

Special Issue Editor
Umberto Berardi
Ryerson University
Canada

Editorial Office
MDPI AG
St. Alban-Anlage 66
Basel, Switzerland

This edition is a reprint of the Special Issue published online in the open access journal *Sustainability* (ISSN 2071-1050) from 2016–2017 (available at: http://www.mdpi.com/journal/sustainability/special_issues/assessments_buildings).

For citation purposes, cite each article independently as indicated on the article page online and as indicated below:

Author 1; Author 2. Article title. *Journal Name* **Year**, *Article number*, page range.

First Edition 2017

ISBN 978-3-03842-598-4 (Pbk)
ISBN 978-3-03842-599-1 (PDF)

Photo courtesy of Umberto Berardi

Table of Contents

About the Special Issue Editor

Umberto Berardi, PhD, is an Associate Professor at Ryerson University in Toronto (ON, Canada). His main research interests and contributions are related to the study of building systems that incorporate new materials. In the first years of his career, Dr. Berardi often worked on natural materials for acoustic applications and on sustainable design through natural materials. Recently, he has been focusing on integrating innovative materials such as nanotechnologies into building systems. He has mainly focused on organic PCMs and on granular and monolithic aerogel. Dr. Berardi has an extensive publication record with over 80 peer-reviewed journals, most of which in top journals. Many of his papers have received high appreciation and have been awarded among the most read and most cited papers of the journals in which they appeared. Dr. Berardi was awarded the ISSNAF award in Washington DC, as the most brilliant Italian Engineer under 40 in North America and the Applied Energy award as the author of one of the most cited papers in Applied Energy in 2016. Dr. Berardi was the International Committee Chair of the ICSDEC 2016 in Tempe (AZ), the Technical Program and Leadership Committee co-Chair of ICSDEC 2015 in Chicago (IL), and will be the chair the IAQVEC 2019. Dr. Berardi serves as associate editor or editorial member of several journals. Dr. Berardi has a body of funded research comprising over $1.5 M in government and private sector sponsored research (included a CFI-JELF; NSERC Discovery Grant; Early Research Award from the MRI from Ontario).

Preface to "Sustainability Assessments of Buildings"

It is my great pleasure to present you this book which contains recently published papers in the Special Issue about Sustainability assessments of buildings. The demand for this Special Issue raised from the floor, as more and more papers dealing with this topic were submitted to Sustainability in the last few months. The need to collect the recent research in this field became evident.

International research has confirmed that the built environment is the most promising sector for a rapid transition to sustainability. In this scenario, many examples of sustainable urban environments are showing the advantages of sustainability. Meanwhile, an increasing request for tools to assess their sustainability is recorded. The assessment of sustainability of the built environment is an essential step toward its promotion. However, large difficulties exist creating useful and measurable assessment indicators since sustainability is time- and location-dependent. Meanwhile, the need to assess both products and processes for sustainabile buildings has been considered particularly important for a sector as inertial as that of the built environment.

Moreover, recent literature has discussed the importance to go beyond the sustainability assessment of single buildings and to enlarge the assessment scale to communities to meet all the different aspects of sustainability (see the really interesting Chapter 8 by Wu et al. for discovering a new hybrid evaluation method based on analytical hierarchy process (AHP)-entropy weight and the cloud modelto evaluate community sustainability). There is evidence that significant achievements in sustainability assessments have been done through the introduction of rating systems for the urban design. These increase the assessment scale and allow consideration of aspects not accounted for at the building scale. Requests to go beyond the building-centric approach in sustainability assessments have favored the discussion about new possible areas of sustainability assessment within the built environment.

This book opens with the interesting chapter by Bernardi et al. that reviews the many existing rating systems for assessing the environmental impact of buildings established in recent years, each one with its peculiarities and fields of applicability. The work is motivated by an interest in emphasizing such differences among systems to better understand current rating systems and extract the main implications to building design.

The second chapter discusses the development of indicators for assessing green interior design of new residential buildings in China, grounded in the socio-technical systems approach. This research show that the boundaries of green interior design with respect to performance, methodology and stakeholders, affect the assessment.

Then, a series of chapters analyze sustainability building practices in specific countries follow. For example Jiang and Li present a Decomposition and Decoupling Analysis of Life-Cycle Carbon Emission in China's Building Sector (Chapter 3) while Siva et al. reflect on the phenomenon of Green Buildings in Singapore and use a Sectoral Innovation System approach to analyze the current building practice in Singapore (Chapter 4).

An absolute interesting topic in sustainability assessements deals with the implications of uncertainties in input variables (Chapters 5 and 6). Unfortunately, these uncertainities are quite often not identified, quantified, or included in building simulations results. For example, the chapter by Amoako-Attah and B-Jahromi considers climatic deterministic, uncertainty, and sensitivity analysis through energy assessments. The chapter analyses the variability of comparable weather data set to identify the most influential weather parameters that contribute to thermal comfort implications for dwellings. Along the same topic, Yao and Zheng discusses the implications of Manual Solar Shades on the Building Energy Performance assessment (Chapter 6). The stochastic characteristics of building occupant modelling is clearly beyond the scope of this book, nevertheless it is important to remind the importance to consider building assessments within their inevitable uncertianities and inaccuracies.

Following Chapters (7 to 9) offer an interesting tool to assess new ways to assess building sustainability. For example, Zhao and Zhengnan propose to develop a rating system for the building energy efficiency based on in situ measurement, and test their model for office buildings in China's cold zone.

Finally, as well investigated in chapter 10 by Lombardi et al. ("Multicriteria Spatial Decision Support Systems for Future Urban Energy Retrofitting Scenarios") issue Nowadays, there is an increasing concern about sustainable urban energy development taking into account national priorities of each city. Many cities have started to define future strategies and plans to reduce energy consumption and greenhouse gas emissions. Urban energy scenarios involve the consideration of a wide range of conflicting criteria, both socio-economic and environmental ones. Moreover, decision-makers require proper tools that can support their choices in a context of multiple stakeholders and a long-term perspective. In this context, Multicriteria Spatial Decision Support Systems are often used in order to define and analyze urban scenarios since they support the comparison of different solutions, based on a combination of multiple factors.

While buildings are striking the paradigm shift of being more and more energy efficient, to the point that zero energy buildings represent the target for policies in many countries, building sustainability keeps gaining a significant momentum. As energy efficient buildings accomplish one of the demand for building sustainability, this last target requires much more. In particular, the local requirements of sustainability prevents to define rigid solutions, and challenge the building sector to customize sustainable solutions to each and every case.

These are just some of the questions that this book tries to address.

I wish you a pleasant reading.

Umberto Berardi

Special Issue Editor

Article

An Analysis of the Most Adopted Rating Systems for Assessing the Environmental Impact of Buildings

Elena Bernardi [1,2], Salvatore Carlucci [1,*], Cristina Cornaro [2] and Rolf André Bohne [1]

[1] Department for Civil and Environmental Engineering, Faculty of Engineering, Norwegian University of Science and Technology, NTNU, 7491 Trondheim, Norway; elenabernardi.eb@gmail.com (E.B.); rolf.bohne@ntnu.no (R.A.B.)

[2] Department of Enterprise Engineering, University of Rome 'Tor Vergata', 00133 Rome, Italy; cornaro@uniroma2.it

* Correspondence: salvatore.carlucci@ntnu.no; Tel.: +47-735-946-34

Received: 22 April 2017; Accepted: 8 July 2017; Published: 13 July 2017

Abstract: Rating systems for assessing the environmental impact of buildings are technical instruments that aim to evaluate the environmental impact of buildings and construction projects. In some cases, these rating systems can also cover urban-scale projects, community projects, and infrastructures. These schemes are designed to assist project management in making the projects more sustainable by providing frameworks with precise criteria for assessing the various aspects of a building's environmental impact. Given the growing interest in sustainable development worldwide, many rating systems for assessing the environmental impact of buildings have been established in recent years, each one with its peculiarities and fields of applicability. The present work is motivated by an interest in emphasizing such differences to better understand these rating systems and extract the main implications to building design. It also attempts to summarize in a user-friendly form the vast and fragmented assortment of information that is available today. The analysis focuses on the six main rating systems: the Building Research Establishment Environmental Assessment Methodology (BREEAM), the Comprehensive Assessment System for Built Environment Efficiency (CASBEE), the *Deutsche Gesellschaft für Nachhaltiges Bauen* (DGNB), the *Haute Qualité Environnementale* (HQE[TM]), the Leadership in Energy and Environmental Design (LEED), and the Sustainable Building Tool (SBTool).

Keywords: rating systems; building environmental impact; sustainability; BREEAM; CASBEE; DGNB; HQE; LEED; SBTool

---

1. Introduction

Rachel Carson's book *Silent Spring* (1962), in which she describes the powerful—and often negative—effect humans have on the natural world, gave birth to the modern environmental movement. Initially, the environmental movement was mostly concerned about toxics such as Dichlorodiphenyltrichloroethane (DDT) and other pesticides. Later, the focus shifted to air pollution, such as acid rain, and there is a current focus on the continued global warming and the accumulation of plastics in the oceans. Awareness of the damage being done to the planet has gradually pushed scientists and policy-makers to struggle with the problem of climate change (among other issues) because of anthropic activity. In this regard, the concepts of sustainable development [1] and sustainability, which are closely related to each other, were introduced into public discussion. However, the definition of sustainable development introduced by the Brundtland Report has been criticized for its focus on continued economic growth in a limited world [2,3], in opposition to the theories on *limits to growth* [4,5]. So far, economic growth has been almost directly correlated with the exergy from fossil fuel combustion [6]. Thus, continued industrialization and technological development, conceived as human triumph over nature [7], has led to a rapid overexploitation of natural resources without ensuring a maximum long-term use. Continued economic growth has led to an overuse of environmental resources. Global warming is an example of the overuse of waste sinks, as greenhouse gases are wastes (i.e., an unwanted product from the burning of fossil fuel) emitted into the atmosphere. In this context, it is of paramount importance that all economic sectors contribute to ensuring a long-term ecological balance that fosters an exploitation of the natural resources aligned with the restoring capacity of the planet. This is the foundation of sustainability that, in technical terms, is commonly examined through three dimensions: the effect of a phenomenon or system on society (often referred to as *social sustainability*), its impact on the environment (often referred to as *environmental sustainability*), and its economic implications (often referred to as *economic sustainability*). This threefold depiction (Figure 1) is called the triple bottom line (TBL) of sustainability; it was first introduced by Elkington [8] in 1994 and is still used nowadays.

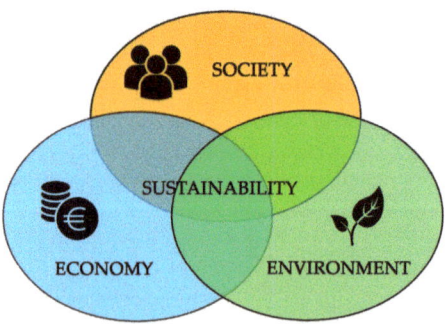

Figure 1. Triple bottom line of sustainabiliy. Source: [8].

The aim of the TBL is to consider the impact of resource consumption and the value creation in terms of integration among the three dimensions, assuming that each of them is equally important.

According to the Western Australia Council of Social Services [9], *social sustainability* is the capacity to provide a good quality of life by creating healthy and livable communities based on equity, diversity, connectivity, and democracy. This *moral capital* requires the maintenance and the replenishment of shared values and equal rights. Human capital is accepted today as part of economic development [10]. In this regard, it is necessary to define *economic sustainability* as the optimal employment of existing resources, so that a responsible and beneficial balance can be achieved over the long-term to reach the preservation of the capital. Economic sustainability concerns the real economic impact that a society has on its economic environment. The final definition to complete the triad of the TBL is *environmental sustainability*. It is defined as the capacity to use natural resources without exceeding their regenerative capacity and protecting the "natural capital" to prevent harm to humans and the environment. This means constraining the scale of the human economic system within the biophysical limits of the overall ecosystem on which it depends; therefore, environmental sustainability is inherently linked with the concepts of sustainable production and sustainable consumption [9].

Going into the details of the TBL framework, and based on the three sustainability dimensions, a wide variety of rating systems have been developed for assessing the environmental performance of buildings, and these are currently available on the market.

These tools have been proposed by different research institutions and have been shaped to reflect specific needs. Crawley and Aho [11] provided the first comparison between some of the major environmental assessment methods in 1999. They focused on the building sector and assessed the environmental sustainability specifically by comparing the scopes of four schemes and identifying general trends. Later, a milestone in categorizing tools was carried out in 2008 by Haapio and

Viitaniemi [12] in which the schemes are classified by building types, users, phase of the life cycle, databases accessed, and the form in which the results are presented, such as graphs, tables, grades, certificates, and reports. In the same year, Ding [13] proposed an overview of the role of the building assessment methods in developing a sustainability index that might be used for assessing projects and then for setting out a conceptual framework for appraising projects. Recent works have been published by Berardi [14,15], Todd, et al. [16], Abdalla, et al. [17], and provide a discussion on the topic from different perspectives.

The scope of this paper is to collect the widest range of available information from technical manuals and official websites and via direct relationships with agents on the boards of companies or institutions that created these assessment tools. The main contributions offered by this paper are the analysis of many rating systems for buildings that were collected from different sources, the reconstruction of their chronological evolution and geographical distribution worldwide, and the thorough comparison and analysis of the six most studied and adopted rating systems. Moreover, the scoring mechanisms of these six rating systems are presented.

The paper is divided into six sections. The first describes the concepts underlying the environmental assessment schemes. The second section summarizes the two main approaches for assessing building sustainability performance: rating systems and life cycle assessment. Appendix A collects a large number of schemes and tools and provides information about their year of introduction, promoting countries, and owners/administrators. The list of rating systems listed in Appendix A may not be exhaustive, although a wide range is included. The material and methods adopted to develop this paper are presented in Section 3. After the establishment of four selection criteria, six rating systems were selected and are presented in detail in Section 4. Section 5 is dedicated to the analysis and comparison of the six selected schemes based on several criteria such as project type, building type, life cycle phase, and scopes, arranged considering all the aspects involved in environmental performance evaluation. A summary of the primary contributions of this paper is presented in the last section.

2. Overview of Environmental Assessment Schemes for Buildings

During the last 20 years, there have been significant developments in the investigation of the impact of buildings on the environment. The common tendency has been to establish an objective and comprehensive methodology for assessing a broad range of environmental impacts caused by a building or even a group of buildings. The purpose of these schemes is to measure the environmental sustainability of a built environment in a consistent and comparable manner, with respect to pre-established standards, guidelines, factors, or criteria [18]. The two main approaches that have been used to design environmental assessment schemes for buildings are life cycle assessment (LCA) and building assessment methods or rating systems. In some applications, both of these approaches were combined [11,16].

In this paper, we only focus on the analysis of rating systems and do not carry out an in-depth investigation of LCA tools that are mostly designed to estimate the embodied energy or equivalent emissions related to materials and products. Brief information on both rating systems and LCA tools are presented in the subsequent two sections.

2.1. Life Cycle Assessment

The life cycle assessment is a method for examining the environmental impact of a material, product, or process throughout its whole life cycle [19,20]. This procedure of assessment—in some cases considered more objective than others—appraises in a quantitative way all the exchange flows between the products and the environment in all the transformation processes involved. It can be applied to a wide spectrum of fields, including the building industry.

LCA is distinguishable in two approaches that are called *attributional LCA* and *consequential LCA*. *Attributional LCA* focuses on the analysis of the physical environmental impact from a life cycle perspective, while *consequential LCA* analyzes how this environmental impact will change in response to possible decisions [20]. In both approaches, LCA can be implemented in a wide range of software available on the market, and the type of assessment to be done will dictate which software is used [21]. LCA has been used since 1990, and specifically, current regulations introduce the *cradle-to-grave* as the common way to state the attributional LCA. For instance, the international standard ISO 14040 declares: "LCA studies the environmental aspects and potential impact throughout a product's life (i.e., cradle-to-grave) from raw material acquisition through production, use and disposal. The general categories of environmental impacts needing consideration include resource use, human health, and ecological consequences" [22]. LCA is, hence, a systematic analysis that can be used to evaluate the alternatives for environmental improvement as a support for the decision-making process. The system boundaries of the building's LCA can be of three types: *cradle-to-grave*, *cradle-to-gate*, and *gate-to-gate*. The *cradle-to-gate* approach is an assessment of a partial life cycle of a product, from resource extraction to the factory gate, before the product is transported to the consumer. It is usually used as a basis for the environmental product declaration [23]. The *gate-to-gate* approach is a partial analysis that looks at only one process in the entire production chain. Information about each gate-to-gate module can be linked accordingly in a product chain, including information about the extraction of raw materials, transportation, disposal, and reuse, to provide a full cradle-to-gate evaluation. The *cradle-to-grave* approach is the most used because it starts from the pre-use phase, including raw material acquisition, goes through manufacturing and transportation to site, and terminates with the end-of-life phase, which includes demolition, recycling potential, landfill, and reuse [24].

In recent years, the consequential LCA has been increasingly used in the building industry and construction sector, but this study concentrates on the rating systems for assessing the environmental performance of buildings, so both attributional and consequential LCA approaches are outside its scope.

2.2. Rating Systems for Assessing the Environmental Performance of Buildings

The rating systems for assessing the environmental performance of buildings are intended to establish an objective and comprehensive method for evaluating a broad range of environmental performance. The aim of these schemes is to measure the performance of a building in a consistent and harmonized manner with respect to pre-established standards, guidelines, factors, or criteria. Scoring methods [25] have been used the most to create rating systems for assessing the environmental sustainability of buildings and are based on four major components:

- *Categories*: these form a specific set of items relating to the environmental performance considered during the assessment;
- *Scoring system*: this is a performance measurement system that cumulates the number of possible points or credits that can be earned by achieving a given level of performance in several analyzed aspects;
- *Weighting system*: this represents the relevance assigned to each specific category within the overall scoring system;
- *Output*: this aims at showing, in a direct and comprehensive manner, the results of the environmental performance obtained during the scoring phase.

This structure is used by all rating systems for assessing the environmental impact of buildings, but when the details are examined specific adaptations may diverge in several significant parts.

2.3. Rating Systems for Assessing the Environmental Impact of Buildings in the World

The Building Research Establishment Environmental Assessment Method (BREEAM) was the first scheme aimed at assessing the environmental impact of a building. It was introduced in 1990 [26,27], and, since then, the field of the rating systems for assessing the environmental impact of buildings has been subject to a rapid increase in the number of schemes developed and introduced on the market worldwide [12]. This phenomenon seems to have reached stabilization in the last few years (Figure 2).

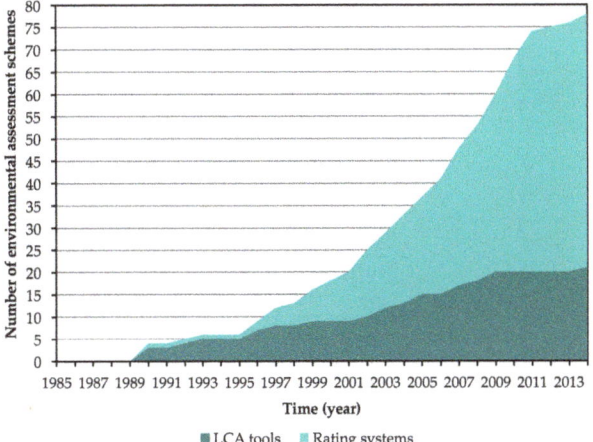

Figure 2. Trend of the schemes used for assessing the environmental impact of buildings presented worldwide from 1990 to 2014. LCA: life cycle assessment.

Table A1, shown in Appendix A, lists more than 70 sustainable building assessment systems released worldwide, including LCA schemes and the rating systems, and provides additional information. Figures 2 and 3 graphically represent the data collected in Table A1, exploiting their temporal evolution and their geographical distribution. The highest rate of introduction of new schemes was registered between 1995 and 2010. After 2010, the rate went down. The rating systems represent the larger share of all schemes presented worldwide and show a logistic growth. Conversely, the trend of the LCA schemes develops quite linearly.

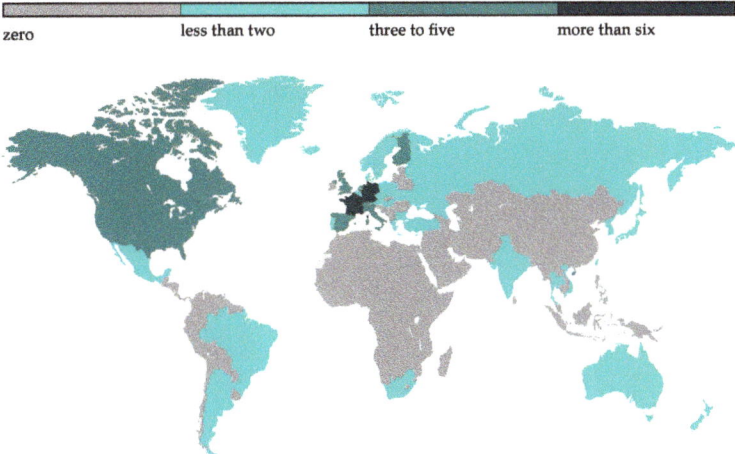

Figure 3. Number of rating systems for assessing the environmental impact of buildings available per country.

The geographical distribution of the collected tools is as follows: 54 schemes in Europe, 15 in Asia, 8 in North America, 3 in both Oceania and South America, and almost 0 in Africa and Middle Eastern countries. Furthermore, some schemes (e.g., the Sustainable Building Tool (SBTool) and SPeAR) cannot be attributed to any specific country or continent. However, the three schemes available in South America are just a customization of frameworks originally developed in other continents.

3. Methodology

As already mentioned, this paper focuses on the rating systems. The great majority of data used in this study was acquired directly from the official technical manuals for the rating schemes. Additional material was collected from the official homepages of the certification organizations or from previous scientific review papers. However, the literature concerning the schemes and their structure and content is rather limited and most of the proposed reviews only pertain to applications of the schemes to local case studies. In this paper, the selected schemes were not applied and tested on case studies and the analysis exclusively focuses on the elaboration and evaluation of the officially declared attributes of the frameworks.

For this study, only environmental rating systems for assessing the environmental performance of buildings have been considered and no benchmarking or evaluation software (e.g., ATHENA, BeCost, BEES, Eco-Quantum, Envest 2, EQUER, LEGEP®, PAPOOSE, ABCplanner, Green Globe 21, BEAT, PLACE3S, SCALDS, SPARTACUS) has been further analyzed. An analysis of a few evaluation tools can be found in [12]. Moreover, among all the rating systems available worldwide, only those that meet all the following four criteria were considered in the subsequent analyses:

1. An exclusive focus on buildings;
2. Scientific interest: cited in at least 20 papers reflected in the *Elsevier's Scopus* database; the search was executed on article titles, abstracts, and keywords.
3. Widespread adoption: more than 500 certified projects;
4. A consolidated development state: more than 5 years of service.

As shown in Table 1, only six rating systems met the four selection criteria, and will be described in Section 4:

1. Leadership in Energy and Environmental Design (LEED®), United States;
2. Building Research Establishment Environmental Assessment Methodology (BREEAM), United Kingdom;
3. Comprehensive Assessment System for Built Environment Efficiency (CASBEE), Japan;
4. SBTool, international;
5. *Haute Qualité Environnementale* (HQE™), France;
6. *Deutsche Gesellschaft für Nachhaltiges Bauen* (DGNB), Germany.

Table 1. Evaluation of rating systems against the identified four selection criteria.

Rating System	Research Keys in Elsevier's Scopus (5 April 2017)	Citations in Scopus	Certified Projects	Years of Development
LEED	leed OR "leadership in energy and environmental design" AND sustainable AND building AND (assessment OR evaluation)	256	89,600	19
BREEAM	breeam OR ("bre environmental assessment method" OR "building research establishment environmental assessment methodology") AND sustainable AND building AND (assessment OR evaluation)	132	>559,000	26
CASBEE	casbee OR "comprehensive assessment system for built environment efficiency" AND sustainable AND building AND (assessment OR evaluation)	47	>14,000 [a]	11
SBTool	sbtool AND sustainable AND building AND (assessment OR evaluation)	28	<2000	21
HQE™	hqe OR ("haute qualité environnementale" OR "High environmental quality") AND sustainable AND building OR (assessment OR evaluation)	24	380,000 [b]	23
DGNB	dgnb OR "deutsche gesellschaft für nachhaltiges bauen" AND sustainable AND building AND (assessment OR evaluation)	24	>718	8
Green Star	"green star" AND sustainable AND building AND (assessment OR evaluation)	19	1450	9
GreenGlobes	greenglobes OR "green globes" AND sustainable AND building AND (assessment OR evaluation)	10	1200	17
Green Mark	"green mark" AND sustainable AND building AND (assessment OR evaluation)	6	3000	12
NABERS	nabers OR "national australian built environment rating system" AND sustainable AND building AND (assessment OR evaluation)	5	15,000	16
EEWH	eewh AND sustainable AND building AND (assessment OR evaluation)	5	4300	18
TERI-GRIHA	teri-griha OR "teri green rating for integrated habitat assessment" AND sustainable AND building AND (assessment OR evaluation)	0	875	10
BEAM Plus	"beam plus" AND sustainable AND building AND (assessment OR evaluation)	6	467	21
LEnSE	lense AND sustainable AND building AND (assessment OR evaluation)	4	N/A	9
PromisE	promise AND finland AND sustainable AND building AND (assessment OR evaluation)	0	N/A	11
ESCALE	escale AND sustainable AND building AND (assessment OR evaluation)	0	N/A	16
Ökoprofil	okoprofil OR ecoprofil AND sustainable AND building AND (assessment OR evaluation)	0	N/A	18
SICES	sices OR "sustainability index of a community energy system" AND sustainable AND building AND (assessment OR evaluation)	0	N/A	N/A
SPeAR®	spear OR "sustainable project appraisal routine" AND sustainable AND building AND (assessment OR evaluation)	3	N/A	17
LiderA	lidera OR "liderar pelo ambiente para a construção sustentável" AND sustainable AND building AND (assessment OR evaluation)	5	24	12
CEPAS	cepas OR "comprehensive environmental performance assessment scheme" AND sustainable AND building AND (assessment OR evaluation)	1	N/A	15
SBAT	sbat OR "sustainable building assessment tool" AND sustainable AND building AND (assessment OR evaluation)	14	N/A	15
GHEM	ghem OR "Green home evaluation manual" AND sustainable AND building AND (assessment OR evaluation)	0	N/A	N/A
GOBAS	gobas OR "green olympic building label" AND sustainable AND building AND (assessment OR evaluation)	0	N/A	14
ESGB	esgb OR "evaluation standard for green building" AND sustainable AND building AND (assessment OR evaluation)	12	N/A	11
LOTUS	lotus OR "sustainable building assessment system" AND sustainable AND building AND (assessment OR evaluation)	3	12	10

[a] updated in 2015; [b] updated in 2016; N/A: not available; LEED: Leadership in Energy and Environmental Design; BREEAM: Building Research Establishment Environmental Assessment Methodology; CASBEE: Comprehensive Assessment System for Built Environment Efficiency; HQE: *Haute Qualité Environnementale*; DGNB: *Deutsche Gesellschaft für Nachhaltiges Bauen*; SBTool: Sustainable Building Tool.

Next, these six schemes are thoroughly analyzed in Section 5 to explore similarities and differences between them and to, eventually, identify implications for the design of buildings. To this purpose, the selected rating schemes are grouped into homogeneous categories, and data is compared regarding geographical coverage, design purpose, and requirements, etc. Finally, some general conclusions are drawn.

4. Description of the Selected Rating Systems

The six selected rating systems are described in this section. Exploitation of categories, scoring, weighting and outputs, the structure, and the main features of each system are presented.

4.1. Building Research Establishment Environmental Assessment Methodology (BREEAM)

Conceived in the UK in 1988 by the Building Research Establishment, the Building Research Establishment Environmental Assessment Methodology (BREEAM) was launched in 1990. Currently it has been used in around 556,600 certified buildings all around the world and more than two million buildings have been registered for assessment since its launch in 1990.

The scheme is composed of ten categories describing sustainability through 71 criteria in total. A percentage-weighting factor is assigned to each category, and the overall number of 112 available credits is proportionally assigned. However, there are some constraints on the credit assignment: indeed, a minimum achievement is required for the categories *Energy and CO_2* and *Water and Waste*, which are reported in Table 2 where the categories for each scheme are listed.

Table 2. BREEAM: categories for each scheme.

Rating System	Energy and CO_2 emissions	Water	Materials	Surface Water Run-Off	Waste	Pollution	Health and Wellbeing	Ecology	Management	Governance	Social and Economic Wellbeing	Resource and Energy	Land Use and Ecology	Transport and Movement	Innovation	Landscape and Heritage	Integrated Design	Stakeholders	Resilience
BREEAM Communities 2012											●	●	●	●	●	●			
BREEAM New construction 2016	●	●	●		●	●	●			●			●	●			●		
BREEAM In-use 2015	●	●	●		●	●	●			●			●	●					
BREEAM Infrastructure 2016	●	●	●		●	●	●						●	●	●	●	●	●	●
BREEAM Nondomestic refurbishment 2015	●	●	●		●	●	●			●			●	●			●		
EcoHomes	●	●	●		●	●	●			●			●	●			●		
Code for sustainable homes	●	●	●	●	●	●	●	●		●									

4.2. Comprehensive Assessment System for Built Environment Efficiency (CASBEE)

The Comprehensive Assessment System for Built Environment Efficiency, usually referred to by the acronym CASBEE, is the Japanese sustainability rating system for buildings. It was developed in 2001 by the Japan Sustainable Building Consortium (JSBC), which is a nongovernmental organization comprising the Japanese government, academic partners, and industry [28]. In 2005, it was launched on the international market and, since 2011, it has become mandatory in 24 Japanese municipalities. CASBEE is structured to have several schemes that depend on the size of a building and address the four main building life phases:

- CASBEE for Predesign, for use in site selection and building planning;
- CASBEE for New Construction, to be used in the first three years after building completion;

- CASBEE for Existing Buildings, to be used after at least one year of operation;
- CASBEE for Renovation, which is intended to support a building refurbishment.

To fulfill the specific purposes, CASBEE also features a huge batch of supplementary rating systems that are relevant when the basic version cannot be used, such as *detached houses, temporary constructions, heat island effect, urban development,* and *cities and market promotions*.

CASBEE assesses a building project using a metric called *building environmental efficiency (BEE)*, which is given by the ratio between the two metrics *built environmental quality (Q)* and *built environmental load (LR)*

$$BEE = \frac{Q}{LR}$$

Q calculates the "improvement in everyday amenities for the building users, within the virtual enclosed space boundary" and LR quantifies the "negative aspects of environmental impact that go beyond the public environment" [29]. Q and LR range between 0 to 100 and are computed based on three subcategories, tabulated on a score sheet, as reported in Table 3.

Table 3. CASBEE's score sheet.

Scoring for Q	Scoring for LR
Q1: Indoor environment	LR1: Energy
Q2: Quality service	LR2: Resources and materials
Q3: Outdoor environment on site	LR3: Off-site environment

BEE is expressed as the gradient of a line on a graph that has LR on the *x*-axis and Q on the *y*-axis. Based on the BEE value, a level of performance (i.e., S, A, B+, B−, and C) is associated with a given project. For additional details, see the CASBEE official website [30]. The values calculated in each category are represented on a radar chart. The assessment results sheet analyses and applies weights, using coefficients for each item and the Q and LR values and produces, as a last step, an overall score conveyed through the BEE index [31]. This index is used to assess the six categories covered by the CASBEE evaluation: *indoor environment, quality of service, outdoor environment (on-site), energy, resources and materials,* and *off-site environment*.

4.3. Deutsche Gesellschaft für Nachhaltiges Bauen

The *Deutsche Gesellschaft für Nachhaltiges Bauen*, referred to by the abbreviation DNGB, was developed by the *Deutsche Gesellschaft für Nachhaltiges Bauen* (German Sustainable Building Council), which was founded in 2007, with the collaboration of the Federal Ministry of Transport, Building and Urban Affairs. The DNGB was lunched in 2009 with the aim of promoting building sustainability in Germany and developing a German certificate for sustainable buildings [32]. The DGNB refers to the Environmental Product Declaration developed according to the standards ISO 14025 [33] and EN 15804 [34] and is mostly based on quantitative measures calculated using the life cycle assessment approach. This evaluation system is flexible and can be applied to national and international environmental assessment, including 13 different building types and, since 2011, entire urban districts. The evaluation is based on 63 criteria, subdivided into six categories that are weighted by a specific weighting factor (Table 4). The sum of the points obtained in all the categories provides the overall score for the building. Each criterion can receive a maximum of 10 points. Four categories (*ecological quality, economical quality, socio-cultural and functional quality,* and *technical quality*) have equal weight in the assessment, while *process quality* is less important (see weights in Table 4); thus, the DGNB system gives the same importance to the economic, ecological, sociological, and technical aspects of an intervention.

Table 4. DGNB: categories, weights and category descriptions.

Category	Weighting Factor	Description
Ecological quality	22.5%	Ecological impacts on local and global environment of the building's construction, utilization of renewal resources, waste, water and land use.
Economical quality	22.5%	Life cycle cost and monetary values.
Socio-cultural and functional quality	22.5%	Health, comfort, user satisfaction, cultural backgrounds, functionality and assurance of design quality.
Technical quality	22.5%	Fire and noise protection, quality of the building shell and ease of maintenance.
Process quality	10.0%	Quality of planning and design, construction process, building use and maintenance and quality of the construction activities.
Quality of the location	Rated independently	Transport-related topics, risks and image of location.

There are some specific minimum requirements that must be considered, such as the *indoor air quality* and the *Design for all* requirements included in the *socio-cultural and functional quality* criterion, and the *legal requirements for fire safety and sound insulation* included in the *technical quality* criterion. It is necessary to achieve a minimum required level in each quality section to obtain the evaluation.

4.4. Haute Qualité Environnementale (HQE^{TM})

The *Haute Qualité Environnementale* standard, referred to by its abbreviation HQE™, was developed in 1994 in France by the HQE™ association [35]. This association supports stakeholders, designers, partners, developers, and users during a project's phases and aims to guarantee a high environmental quality of buildings. The HQE™ Association has developed many schemes, exploitable in France and abroad. It is structured to have three organizations in charge of delivering national evaluations (Certivèa, Cerqual, and Cèquami) and one for supporting the evaluation across the world (Cerway) [36]. HQE™ covers buildings throughout their life cycle, that is, throughout their design, construction, operation, and renovation. It is addressed to nonresidential and residential buildings, and detached houses. Furthermore, a specific scheme for the management system of urban planning and development projects is also available. The environmental performance requirements are organized into four topics that together include 14 categories. Topics are almost the same for all building types, but the targets are arranged differently for residential buildings and nonresidential buildings (i.e., commercial, administrative, and service buildings) (Tables 5 and 6, respectively).

Table 5. HQE^{TM}: distribution of targets for residential buildings.

Environment	Energy and Savings	Comfort	Health and Safety
Target 1: Building's relationship with its immediate environment	Target 4: Energy management	Target 8: Hygrothermal comfort	Target 12: Quality of spaces
Target 2: Quality of components	Target 5: Water management	Target 9: Acoustic comfort	Target 13: Air quality and health
Target 3: Sustainable worksite	Target 7: Maintenance management	Target 10: Visual comfort	Target 14: Water quality and health
Target 6: Waste management		Target 11: Olfactory comfort	

Table 6. HQE^{TM}: Distribution of targets for commercial, administrative and service buildings.

Environment	Energy	Comfort	Health
Target 1: Building's relationship with its immediate environment	Target 4: Energy management	Target 8: Hygrothermal comfort	Target 12: Quality of spaces
Target 2: Quality of components		Target 9: Acoustic comfort	Target 13: Air quality and health
Target 3: Sustainable worksite		Target 10: Visual comfort	Target 14: Water quality and health
Target 5: Water management		Target 11: Olfactory comfort	
Target 6: Waste management			

A building project obtains an assessment for each target expressed according to three ordinal levels: *basic, performing,* and *high Performing*. To be certified, a building must achieve the *high performing* level in at least three categories and the *basic* level in a maximum of seven categories. This rating system does not weight each category by a weighting factor, because they are considered to have the same importance throughout the assessment framework.

4.5. Leadership in Energy and Environmental Design (LEED)

The first Leadership in Energy and Environmental Design Pilot Project Program, referred to as LEED® Version 1.0, was launched in the USA in 1998 by the US Green Building Council (USGB), a nongovernmental organization that includes representatives from industry, academia, and government [37]. Since that time, the LEED® system has undergone some revisions, integrations, and national customizations. The LEED® Version 4.0 was released in 2016 and is currently in use. The LEED® Green Building Rating Systems are voluntary and are intended to evaluate the environmental performance of the whole building over its life cycle. Different schemes are designed for rating new and existing commercial, institutional, and residential buildings. Each scheme has the same list of performance requirements set out in five categories, but the number of credits, prerequisites, and available points change considerably according to the specific area of interest and the building type. Table 7 provides a description of the categories included in the LEED® environmental rating scheme.

Table 7. LEED®'s categories and description.

Category	Description
Sustainable sites	This section examines the environmental aspects linked to the building site. The goal is to limit the construction impact and verify meteoric water outflow.
Water efficiency	The section is linked to the water use, management and disposal in the buildings. The reduction of water consumption and meteoric water reuse are promoted.
Energy and atmosphere	In this section building energy performance improvement, the use of renewable sources and the energy building performance control are promoted.
Materials and resources	In this area the environmental subjects associated to the material selection, the reduction of virgin material use, the garbage disposal and the environmental impact due to transport are considered.
Indoor environmental quality	The themes considered in this section cover indoor environmental quality, taking into account for example healthiness, comfort, air renewal and air pollution control.
Innovation in design	The aim of this section is to identify the design aspects that improve on the sustainability operations in the building construction.
Regional priority	This area has the objective of encouraging the design groups to focus the attention on the local characteristics of the environment.

Almost all schemes present mandatory prerequisites and noncompulsory credits, which can be selected according to the objectives that is to be achieved. The summation of points for each credit generates the evaluation outcome. All the credits receive a single weight according to a precisely defined scoring system.

The scoring system has a maximum score of 100 points, plus there are up to 10 additional bonus points for complying with two special categories. Out of the possible total of 100 points, a minimum of 40 points should be obtained to pass the basic evaluation.

4.6. SBTool

In 1996, the international Green Building Challenge initiative, which was later named the Sustainable Building Challenge, set the goal of establishing energy and environmental performance standards that would be suitable in both international and national contexts. It was therefore necessary to identify assessment tools that, through different methodological bases, would be able to objectively assess the requirements of the environmental, economic, and social impacts of a building during its entire life cycle.

Developed by the work of representatives from 20 countries, this process led to the so-called SBMethod that was designed to offer, besides a common international standard, an easy customization with respect to individual national contexts. This method is continually updated by a technical committee managed by the International Initiative for a Sustainable Built Environment (iiSBE). The SBMethod covers the three aspects of sustainability (i.e., environmental, economic, and social impacts) from the building perspective and can be used to assess every design concept or existing building independently from its prevalent use and geometrical extension, according to the four phases: predesign, design, construction, and operation.

Originating from the SBMethod, the Green Building Tool (GBTool), as it was initially called, was later renamed the Sustainable Building Tool (SBTool). The SBTool is a generic framework for rating the environmental performance of a building by assigning scores and credits for a number of areas [38]. The method is structured in a way that means that each parameter is defined with a weight. It is a weighted assessment where the weighting factors are different for different building types, such as single buildings, residential buildings, commercial buildings, new-builds and existing constructions, or a mix of the two. The performance issues and the phases of the life cycle used for the assessment are listed in Table 8.

The system provides separate modules for the *site and building* assessments, carried out in the predesign phase, and the *building* assessments, done in the design, construction, or operation phases [39]. The performance framework of SBTool is organized into four levels, namely: (1) performance issues, (2) performance categories, (3) performance criteria, and (4) performance subcriteria [40]. Each performance issue contains categories that represent the domain in a more detailed and specific manner.

Table 8. The SBTool's issue area expressed per each phase of a building's life cycle. Adapted from [40].

Issue area	Predesign	Design	Construction	Operation
Site location, available services and site characteristics	•			
Site regeneration and development. Urban design and infrastructure		•		•
Energy and resource consumption		•	•	•
Environmental loadings		•	•	•
Indoor environmental quality		•	•	•
Service quality		•	•	•
Social, cultural and perceptual aspects		•	•	•
Cost and economic aspects		•	•	•

5. Comparative Analysis of the Selected Rating Systems

As already mentioned, the number of rating systems for assessing the environmental impact of buildings is high, and the goal of this section is to give insights into the subject by the analysis and comparison of a selection of existing schemes. Table 9 summarizes some information about the six schemes selected. How the schemes' categories, similarities, and differences can be exploited is displayed. In the following tables, the schemes are classified according to the following categories:

Table 9. Summary of the main features of the selected rating systems.

Rating System	Launch Year	Launch Country	Certification Body	International Versions and National Adaptations	Weighting System	Rating Levels
BREEAM	1990	UK	BRE	*International versions:* • Nondomestic refurbishment • In-use • New construction: buildings *National adaptations:* • United Kingdom • USA • Germany • Netherlands • Norway • Spain • Sweden • Austria	Applied to each category	• Unclassified • Pass • Good • Very good • Excellent • Outstanding
CASBEE	2004	Japan	JSBC	N/A	Complex weighting system applied at every level	• S • A • B+ • B− • C
DGNB 2014	2008	Germany	DGNB	*International version* • Core 14 *National adaptation:* • Austria • Bulgaria • China • Denmark • Germany • Switzerland • Thailand	Applied to each category	• Bronze * • Silver • Gold • Platinum
HQE™	1997	France	• Certivéa • Cerqual • Céquami • Cerway	*International versions* • Non-residential building in operation 2015 • Infrastructures 2015 • Habitat and environment • Nonresidential building under construction 2015 • Residential building under construction 2015 • Management system for urban planning projects 2016	N/A	• Pass • Good • Very good • Excellent • Exceptional

Table 9. *Cont.*

Rating System	Launch Year	Launch Country	Certification Body	International Versions and National Adaptations	Weighting System	Rating Levels
LEED v.4	1998	USA	USGBC	*International versions:* • LEED v3.0 for new construction and major renovations • LEED for homes • LEED for core and shell • LEED for existing buildings: operations and maintenance • LEED for commercial interiors • LEED for schools • LEED for retail • LEED for healthcare • LEED for neighborhood development (in pilot stage) *National adaptations:* • Argentina • Brazil • Canada • Italy	All credits are equally weighted, but the number of credits related to each issue is different	• Certified • Silver • Gold • Platinum
SBTool 2016	2002	International	iiSBE	*National adaptations:* • Czech Republic (SBToolCZ) • Portugal (SBToolPT) • Italy (Protocollo Itaca) • Spain (Verde)	Applied to each category	• −1 • 0 • 1 • 3 • 5

* Level available only for existing buildings.

- Type of intervention (Table 10);
- Building type (Table 11);
- Phase of the building's life cycle (Table 12);
- Scopes (Table 13).

The first analysis aims at contrasting the selected six rating systems for assessing the environmental impact of buildings with respect to the type of intervention (Table 10). While BREEAM, CASBEE, DGNB, HQE™, and LEED® have dedicated subschemes or modules to cover all the four types of intervention, the SBTool does not provide assessment tools for building refurbishment and urban planning.

Table 10. Type of intervention covered by the selected schemes.

Rating System	New Buildings	Existing Buildings	Buildings under Refurbishment	Urban Planning Projects
BREEAM	•	•	•	•
CASBEE	•	•	•	•
DGNB	•	•	•	•
HQE™	•	•	•	•
LEED®	•	•	•	•
SBTool	•	•		

Rating schemes can be used to certify the environmental performances of different types of buildings, such as residential, office, commercial, industrial, and educational buildings, and all other buildings that do not fit into any of these building types are grouped in the field called Other types of buildings. It can be seen in Table 11 that BREEAM, CASBEE, DGNB, and HQE™ can be used with all building types. LEED® and SBTool do not include industrial buildings in their evaluation. Regarding the life cycle phase of a building, BREEAM, CASBEE, DGNB, and HQE™ cover all the four considered life cycle phases of a building. LEED® does not evaluate *predesign* or *design*, and the SBTool does not cover the *use/maintenance* phase.

Table 11. Building type assessed by the selected schemes.

Rating System	Residential Buildings	Office Buildings	Commercial Buildings	Industrial Buildings	Educational Buildings	Other Type of Buildings	Urban Planning
BREEAM	•	•	•	•	•	•	•
CASBEE	•	•	•	•	•	•	•
DGNB	•	•	•	•	•	•	•
HQE™	•	•	•	•	•	•	•
LEED®	•	•	•	N/A	•	•	•
SBTool	•	•	•	N/A	•	N/A	N/A

Table 12. Life cycle phase of the building assessed by the selected schemes.

Rating System	Predesign and Design	Construction	Post-Construction	Use/Maintenance
BREEAM	•	•	•	•
CASBEE	•	•	•	•
DGNB	•	•	•	•
HQE™	•	•	•	•
LEED®	N/A	•	•	•
SBTool	•	•	•	N/A

As a matter of fact, regarding the original categories, different items in two or more schemes often refer to the same field and, sometimes, similar denominations do not assess exactly the same attributes. We have therefore identified eight major scopes, in which the characteristic elements of all the categories have been grouped. According to this analysis, the categories that are the ones most assessed by the schemes are *energy performance* and *solid waste management*. Other important categories are *materials, water, waste water management*, and *ecology and environmental quality*, which are assessed by the great majority of schemes. The scopes that are assessed the least are those related to *resistance to natural disasters*, which are considered only by CASBEE, DGNB, and HQE^TM. Similarly, the category *olfactory comfort* is considered only by the schemes in HQE^TM, while, in the other systems, it is included in the more general category *air quality*. Finally, the *building information and users guide* is considered only by the schemes of the BREEAM collection and in some isolated cases by a few subschemes in LEED®, HQE^TM, and DGNB. In Figure 4, to support the results, the scopes distribution among the schemes is presented graphically.

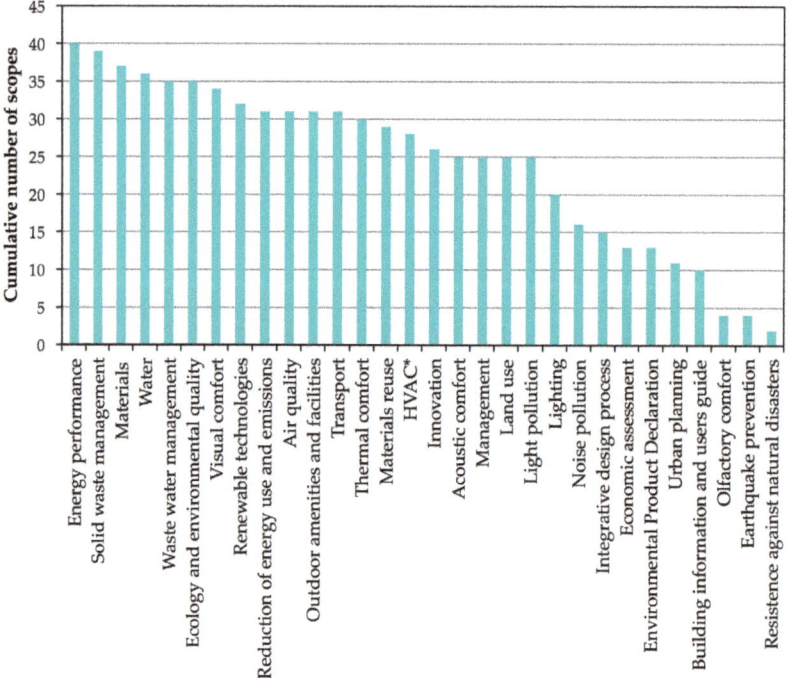

Figure 4. Scopes distribution among the analyzed rating schemes (* HVAC: heating, ventilation, and air-conditioning).

Table 13. Comparison of the scopes and criteria of the six selected rating schemes used for evaluating the sustainability of buildings.

Scope	Criteria	BREEAM Europe Commercial 2009	BREEAM In-use international 2016	BREEAM New construction: infrastructure 2016 (pilot)	BREEAM International new construction 2016	BREEAM UK Domestic refurbishment 2014	BREEAM Nondomestic refurbishment 2015	BREEAM UK Datacenters 2010	BREEAM Communities 2012	Code for sustainable homes 2010	CASBEE for home (detached houses) 2007	CASBEE for building (new construction) 2014	CASBEE for market promotion (offices and retail) 2014	CASBEE for urban development 2014	CASBEE for cities 2012
Energy	Energy Performance	●	●	●	●	●	●	●		●	●	●	●		
	Renewable Technologies	●	●		●					●	●	●			
	HVAC	●	●		●					●					
	Lighting	●	●		●		●			●		●	●		
	Reduction of Energy Use and Emissions		●	●		●		●		●				●	●
Indoor Environmental Quality	Olfactory Comfort														
	Visual Comfort	●	●		●							●	●		
	Thermal Comfort	●	●		●							●	●		
	Acoustic Comfort	●	●		●				●			●	●		
	Air quality	●	●		●							●	●		
Innovation	Innovation	●	●		●				●			●			
Management	Management	●	●		●	●	●	●	●			●			
	Building information and Users Guide	●	●		●		●		●						
	Economic assessment	●	●		●			●						●	●
Materials and Resources	Integrative Design Process	●	●		●										
	Materials Reuse	●	●		●				●			●	●	●	●
	Environmental Product Declaration		●		●										
	Materials	●	●		●		●		●			●		●	●
	Water	●	●		●	●	●	●	●			●	●	●	●
Pollution and Waste	Land Use	●	●		●		●		●	●		●		●	●
	Noise Pollution	●	●		●		●		●	●		●	●		
	Light Pollution		●		●		●					●			
	Waste Water Management	●	●		●		●		●	●		●	●	●	
	Solid Waste Management	●	●		●	●	●		●	●		●		●	
Resistance Against Natural Disasters	Earthquake Prevention											●	●	●	
	Resistance against Natural Disasters				●										
Site Quality	Outdoor Amenities and Facilities	●	●		●				●			●		●	●
	Transport	●	●		●	●	●		●					●	●
	Urban Planning													●	●
	Ecology and Environmental Quality	●	●		●	●	●		●	●		●		●	●

17

Table 13. *Cont.*

Scopes →	Energy					Indoor Environmental Quality					Innovation	Management				Materials and Resources					Pollution and Waste				Resistance Against Natural Disasters		Site Quality			
Rating System	Energy Performance	Renewable Technologies	HVAC	Lighting	Reduction of Energy Use and Emissions	Olfactory Comfort	Visual Comfort	Thermal Comfort	Acoustic Comfort	Air quality	Innovation	Management	Building information and Users Guide	Economic assessment	Integrative Design Process	Materials Reuse	Environmental Product Declaration	Materials	Water	Land Use	Noise Pollution	Light Pollution	Waste Water Management	Solid Waste Management	Earthquake Prevention	Resistance against Natural Disasters	Outdoor Amenities and Facilities	Transport	Urban Planning	Ecology and Environmental Quality
DGNB																														
DGNB Core 14	●	●	●	●			●	●	●	●	●	●	●	●	●	●		●	●	●	●		●	●			●	●	●	●
HQE™																														
NF Maison individuelle neuf 2013	●	●	●	●	●	●	●	●	●	●		●						●	●	●	●	●	●	●		●		●	●	●
NF Maison rénovée 2014	●	●	●	●		●	●	●	●	●								●	●	●	●	●	●	●		●		●	●	●
NF Logement habitat neuf	●					●	●	●	●	●								●	●		●	●	●	●					●	●
NF Qualité environnementale des bâtiments 2015	●		●			●	●	●	●	●								●	●	●	●	●	●	●					●	●
NF Bâtiment durable 2014	●				●		●	●	●	●				●		●		●	●	●	●		●	●			●	●	●	●
HQE™ Nonresidential building in operation 2015	●		●					●	●	●			●	●							●			●			●	●		●
HQE™ Infrastructures 2015				●	●	●		●	●	●								●	●		●		●	●				●	●	●
Habitat & Environnement	●	●	●									●				●		●	●										●	●
HQE™ Non-residential building under construction 2015	●	●	●	●	●	●	●	●	●	●		●	●	●		●		●	●	●	●	●	●	●		●	●	●	●	●
HQE™ Residential building under construction 2015	●	●			●		●	●	●	●									●		●			●						●
HQE™ Management system for urban planning projects 2016	●				●							●	●	●				●	●	●	●	●	●	●			●	●	●	●

Table 13. Cont.

Rating System	Energy					Indoor Environmental Quality					Innovation	Management				Materials and Resources					Pollution and Waste				Resistance Against Natural Disasters		Site Quality			
	Energy Performance	Renewable Technologies	HVAC	Lighting	Reduction of Energy Use and Emissions	Olfactory Comfort	Visual Comfort	Thermal Comfort	Acoustic Comfort	Air quality	Innovation	Management	Building information and Users Guide	Economic assessment	Integrative Design Process	Materials Reuse	Environmental Product Declaration	Materials	Water	Land Use	Noise Pollution	Light Pollution	Waste Water Management	Solid Waste Management	Earthquake Prevention	Resistance against Natural Disasters	Outdoor Amenities and Facilities	Transport	Urban Planning	Ecology and Environmental Quality
LEED®																															
LEED v4 for Homes Design and Construction — Multifamily mid-rise 2010	●	●	●		●					●		●			●			●	●	●			●	●			●			●
Homes and multifamily low-rise 2010	●	●	●		●					●		●			●			●	●	●			●	●			●			●
LEED v4 for Interior Design and Construction — Commercial interiors and hospitality	●	●	●	●	●		●			●	●	●			●	●	●	●	●			●		●			●		●	●
Retail	●	●	●	●	●		●			●	●	●			●	●	●	●	●			●		●			●		●	●
LEED v4 for Operation and Maintenance — Existing buildings and schools	●	●	●		●		●			●	●	●				●		●				●	●	●			●	●	●	●
Retail, data centers, hospitality, warehouses and distribution centers, multifamily	●	●	●		●		●			●	●	●						●				●	●	●				●	●	●

Table 13. *Cont.*

Scopes		LEED v4 for Building Design and Construction					SBTool
Category	Item	Schools	Healthcare	Core and shell	New construction, retail, data centers, warehouses and distribution centers, hospitality	Neighborhood development	SBTool 2012
Energy	Energy Performance	•	•	•	•	•	•
	Renewable Technologies	•	•	•	•	•	
	HVAC	•	•	•	•		
	Lighting						•
	Reduction of Energy Use and Emissions	•	•	•	•		
Indoor Environmental Quality	Olfactory Comfort						•
	Visual Comfort	•	•	•	•		•
	Thermal Comfort	•	•	•	•		•
	Acoustic Comfort	•	•	•	•		•
	Air quality	•	•	•	•		•
Innovation	Innovation	•	•	•	•	•	
Management	Management						
	Building information and Users Guide		•				
	Economic assessment						•
	Integrative Design Process	•	•	•	•		
Materials and Resources	Materials Reuse	•	•	•	•		
	Environmental Product Declaration	•	•	•	•		
	Materials	•	•	•	•		•
	Water	•	•	•	•		•
	Land Use	•	•	•	•		
Pollution and Waste	Noise Pollution	•					•
	Light Pollution	•	•	•	•		
	Waste Water Management	•	•	•	•		•
	Solid Waste Management	•	•	•	•		•
Resistance Against Natural Disasters	Earthquake Prevention						
	Resistance against Natural Disasters						
Site Quality	Outdoor Amenities and Facilities	•	•	•	•		•
	Transport	•	•	•	•		•
	Urban Planning		•	•			•
	Ecology and Environmental Quality	•	•	•	•		•

6. Conclusions

In this paper, an overview of the available rating systems for assessing the environmental impact of buildings is presented. The rating systems for assessing the environmental impact of buildings are technical instruments that have been developed with the specific purpose of evaluating the environmental performances of buildings. In the last decade, a growing interest in sustainability and sustainable development has been registered due to the urgent requirement for a worldwide reduction in greenhouse gas emissions for the safety of our planet and the health of global society. This has had a remarkable impact on the building and construction industry and, consequently, a wide array of rating schemes has been developed with different purposes and features to enhance buildings' sustainability.

The core of this work is a comparative analysis of six widespread and consolidated schemes that are the most cited in the scientific literature. The present study is motivated by the need to identify differences in the rating schemes to better understand their main features and identify their possible implications. After carrying out a survey of more than 70 schemes for assessing the environmental impact of buildings, the following six schemes were selected and analyzed in depth: the Building Research Establishment Environmental Assessment Methodology (BREEAM), the Comprehensive Assessment System for Built Environment Efficiency (CASBEE), the *Deutsche Gesellschaft für Nachhaltiges Bauen* (DGNB), the *Haute Qualité Environnementale* (HQE™), the Leadership in Energy and Environmental Design (LEED®), and the SBTool.

Data was collected from technical manuals and official websites and, sometimes, through direct relationships with agents on the technical or administrative board of the companies creating these systems. In this regard, we should point out that some challenges were faced during the data acquisition process. User manuals are not always available, and information, even though it is usually publicly disclosed, often appears to be fragmentary or is only available in local languages.

We also noticed that a systematic comparison of the schemes is difficult, sometimes even prohibitive. As a matter of fact, different rating schemes have been developed for different purposes and hence a precise comparison of categories and subcategories is often not achievable.

The analysis has been carried out considering several aspects, and we discovered the following:

- All rating systems for assessing the environmental impact of buildings are suitable for both new and existing buildings and, apart from the SBTool, cover the refurbishment of buildings as well;
- BREEAM, CASBEE, DGNB, and HQE™ can be used to assess all types of buildings, while LEED® does not cover industrial buildings and the SBTool is the most limited since it does not cover urban planning projects, and building types other than residential, office, commercial, and educational buildings;
- BREEAM, CASBEE, DGNB, and HQE™ cover all the life cycle phases of a building;
- SBTool is the only system that has also been designed for certifying a low performance level of a building;
- Regarding the categories assessed by the schemes, *energy performance, solid waste management, material,* and *water* are the most considered categories from a quantitative perspective;
- The categories that are considered less are *resistance against natural disasters, earthquake prevention,* and *olfactory comfort.*

In conclusion, it should be noted that these schemes have been largely accepted and widely used in the building sector. Regarding future development of these schemes, desirable features are:

- Completeness, that is, analyzing in an appropriate way all the elements characterizing a building and its life cycle;
- Representing in a clear way the weighting system and supporting the scoring system with sound evidence.

Acknowledgments: This work was partially funded by the European Union's Horizon 2020 Research and Innovation Programme under grant agreement 680529, often referred to by the acronym QUANTUM. The sole responsibility for the content of this article lies with the authors. It does not necessarily reflect the opinion of the European Commission (EC). The EC is not responsible for any use that may be made of the information this article contains.

Author Contributions: The work presented in this article is the result of a collaboration of all authors. Elena Bernardi, Salvatore Carlucci, and Cristina Cornaro analyzed the literature on the subject, contributed to writing the manuscript, and edited the document. Salvatore Carlucci, Cristina Cornaro, and Rolf André Bohne critically reviewed the article. All authors contributed to the discussion and conclusions of this research.

Conflicts of Interest: The authors declare no conflict of interest.

Appendix A

Table A1. Rating systems assessing the environmental impact of buildings in use worldwide. Adapted from [41].

Region	Country	Name	Owner/Management	Year	Type of Method	References
Africa	South Africa	Green Star SA	South Africa GBC	2008	Rating system	[41,42]
		SBAT	CSIR	2002	Rating system	[43,44]
Asia	China	GHEM	China Real Estate Chamber of Commerce	N/A	Rating system	[41]
		GOBAS	Minister of Science & Technology	2003	Rating system	[41,45]
		DGNB	DGNB China	2009	Rating system	[32,41,46]
		ESGB	Ministry of Housing and Urban-Rural Construction	2006	Rating system	[41,47]
	Hong Kong	BEAM Plus	HK-BEAM Society	1996	Rating system	[41,48]
		CEPAS	HK Building Department	2002	Rating system	[41]
	India	TERI-GRIHA	The Energy & Research Institute (TERI)	2007	Rating system	[41,49]
		LEED® India	Indian GBC	2011	Rating system	[41,49,50]
	Japan	CASBEE	Japan Sustainable Building Consort.	2004	Rating system	[51,52]
		NIRE-LCA	National Institute for Resource and Environment	1996	LCA tool	[53]
	Korea	GBCC	Korean Korea Institute of Energy Research	1997	Rating system	[54]
	Singapore	Green Mark	Singapore Building & Construction Authority	2005	Rating system	[55]
	Taiwan	EEWH	Architecture and Building Research Institute	1999	Rating system	[56]
	Thailand	DGNB	ARGE—Archimedes Facility—Management GmbH, Bad Oeynhausen & RE/ECC	2010	Rating system	[46]
	Vietnam	LOTUS	Vietnam GBC	2007	Rating system	[57]
Europe	Austria	BREEAM AT	DIFNI	N/A	Rating system	[58]
		DGNB	ÖGNI	2009	Rating system	[46]
	Belgium	LEnSE	Belgian Building Research Institute	2008	Rating system	[41]
	Bulgaria	DGNB	Bulgarian GBC	2009	Rating system	[46]
	Czech Republic	DGNB	DIFNI	2011	Rating system	[46]
		SBToolCZ	iiSBE International, CIDEAS	2010	Rating system	[59]
	Denmark	BEAT 2002	SBI	2002	Rating system	[12,60]
		DGNB	Denmark GBC	2011	Rating system	[32,46]
	Finland	PromisE	VTT	2006	Rating system	[41]
		BeCost	VTT	N/A	LCA tool	[12]
		KCL-ECO	VTT	1992	LCA tool	
	France	HQE™ Method	HQE™	1997	Rating system	[41]
		ELODIE	CSTB's Environment division	2006	LCA tool	[41]
		TEAM™	Ecobilan	1995	LCA tool	[12,61]
		EQUER	École des Mines de Paris, Centre d'Énergétique et Procédés	1995	LCA tool	[12,61]
		ESCALE	CSTB and the University of Savoie	2001	Rating system	[12,62]
		PAPOOSE	TRIBU Architects	N/A	LCA tool	[12,61]
	Germany	DGNB	German Sustainable Building Council	2008	Rating system	[46]
		BREEAM DE	DIFNI	2011	Rating system	[58]
		GABI	IKP University of Stuttgart, PE Product Engineering GmbH	1990	LCA tool	
		GEMIS	Oeko-Institut (Institute for applied Ecology)	1990	LCA tool	
		LEGEP®	LEGEP Software GmbH	2001	LCA tool	[12]
		OpenLCA	GreenDeltaTC GmbH	2013	LCA tool	

Table A1. *Cont.*

Region	Country	Name	Owner/Management	Year	Type of Method	References
		Umberto	Ifu Hamburg GmbH	-	LCA tool	
	Greece	DGNB	DIFNI	2010	Rating system	[46]
	Hungary	DGNB	DIFNI	2010	Rating system	[46]
		LEED® Italia	Italy GBC	2006	Rating system	[63]
	Italy	*Protocollo ITACA*	iiSBE Italia	2004	Rating system	[41]
		eVerdEE	ENEA	2004	LCA tool	
	Luxembourg	BREEAM LU	DIFNI	2009	Rating system	[58]
		BREEAM-NL	Dutch GBC	2011	Rating system	[41,58,64]
	Netherlands	SIMAPRO	Pre Consultants	1990	LCA tool	[65]
		Eco-Quantum	IVAM	2002	LCA tool	[12]
	Norway	BREEAM-NOR	Norwegian GBC	2012	Rating system	[12,58]
		Økoprofil	SINTEF	1999	Rating system	[66]
	Poland	DGNB	DGNB International	2013	Rating system	[46]
	Portugal	LiderA	*Instituto Superior Técnico, Lisbon*	2005	Rating system	[41]
Europe		SBToolPT	iiSBE Portugal, LFTC-UM, ECOCHOICE	2007	Rating system	[67]
	Russia	DGNB	DGNB International	2010	Rating system	[46]
		VERDE	Spanish GBC	2006	Rating system	[41]
	Spain	DGNB	N/A	2011	Rating system	[46]
		BREEAM ES	*Fundacion Instituto Technològico de Galicia*	2010	Rating system	[58,68]
	Sweden	EcoEffect	Royal Institute of Technology	2006	Rating system	[69]
		BREEAM SE	Swedish GBC	2008	Rating system	[58]
		BREEAM CH	DIFNI	N/A	Rating system	[58]
	Switzerland	DGNB	SGNI	2010	Rating system	[46]
		Eco-Bat	University of Applied Science of Western Switzerland	2008	LCA tool	[70]
		REGIS	Sinum AG	1993	LCA tool	
	Turkey	DGNB	-	2010	Rating system	[46]
	Ukraine	DGNB	DGNB International	N/A	Rating system	[46,71]
		BREEAM	BRE	1990	Rating system	[12,58,72]
	United Kingdom	CCaLC Tool	The University of Manchester	2007	LCA tool	
		Envest 2	BRE	2003	LCA tool	[12,73]
		LEED® Canada	Canada GBC	2009	Rating system	[41,74]
	Canada	GreenGlobes	ECD Canada	2000	Rating system	[41,75]
North America		Environmental Impact Estimator	ATHENA Sustainable Material	2008	LCA tool	
		ATHENA™	ATHENA Sustainable Material Institute	2002	LCA tool	[12,73,76]
	Mexico	SICES	Mexico GBC	N/A	Rating system	[41]
		LEED®	United States GBC	1998	Rating system	[12,41]
	United States	BEES 4.0	NIST	1998	LCA tool	[12,73,77]
		GreenGlobes	Green Building Initiative	2004	Rating system	[41,75]
	Australia	Green Star	Australian GBC	2003	Rating system	[78,79]
Oceania		NABERS	NSW Office of Environment and Heritage	2001	Rating system	[80,81]
	New Zealand	Green Star NZ	New Zealand GBC	2007	Rating system	[82,83]
	Argentina	LEED® Argentina	Argentina GBC	N/A	Rating system	[68,84]
South America		LEED® Brazil	Brazil GBC	2007	Rating system	[39,85]
	Brazil	HQE™	*Fundação* Vanzolini	2014	Rating system	[35]
Generic		SBTool	iiSBE	2002	Rating system	[38,67]
		SPeAR	Ove Arup Ltd.	2000	Rating system	[86]

References

1. Brundtland, G.H.; Khalid, M. *Report of the World Commission on Environment and Development: Our Common Future*; Oxford University Press: Oxford, UK, 1987.
2. Clayton, R. Is sustainable development an oxymoron? *Process Saf. Environ. Prot.* **2001**, *79*, 327–328. [CrossRef]
3. Choi, J.S.; Pattent, B.C. Sustainable development: lessons from the paradox of enrichment. *Ecosyst. Health* **2001**, *7*, 163–178. [CrossRef]
4. Meadows, D.H.; Meadows, D.L.; Randers, J. *The Limits to Growth*; Universe Books: New York, NY, USA, 1972.
5. Ayres, R.U. Cowboys, cornucopians and long-run sustainability. *Ecol. Econom.* **1993**, *8*, 189–207. [CrossRef]
6. Ayres, R.U.; Ayres, L.W.; Warr, B. Exergy, power and work in the US economy, 1900–1998. *Energy* **2003**, *28*, 219–273. [CrossRef]
7. Hopwood, B.; Mellor, M.; O'Brien, G. Sustainable Development: Mapping Different Approaches. *Sustain. Dev.* **2005**, *13*, 38–52. [CrossRef]
8. Elkington, J. *Cannibals with Forks—The Triple Bottom Line of 21st Century Business*; New Society Publishers: Gabriola, BC, Canada, 1997.
9. Goodland, R. The Concept of Environmentl Sustainability Annu. *Rev. Ecol. Syst.* **2005**, *26*, 1–24. [CrossRef]
10. World Bank. *Environmental Assessment Sourcebook*; World Bank: Washington, DC, USA, 1992.
11. Crawley, D.; Aho, I. Building environmental assessment methods_applications and development trends. *Build. Res. Inf.* **1999**, *27*, 300–308. [CrossRef]
12. Haapio, A.; Viitaniemi, P. A critical review of building environmental assessment tools. *Environ. Impact Assess. Rev.* **2008**, *28*, 469–482. [CrossRef]
13. Ding, G.K. Sustainable construction: The role of environmental assessment tools. *J. Environ. Manag.* **2008**, *86*, 451–464. [CrossRef] [PubMed]
14. Berardi, U. Sustainability Assessment in the Construction Sector: Rating Systems and Rated Buildings. *Sustain. Dev.* **2012**, *20*, 411–424. [CrossRef]
15. Berardi, U. Beyond Sustainability Assessment Systems: Upgrading Topics by Enlarging The Scale of Assessment. *Int. J. Sustain. Build. Technol. Urban Dev.* **2011**, *2*, 276–282. [CrossRef]
16. Todd, J.A.; Crawley, D.; Geissler, S.; Lindsey, G. Comparative assessment of environmental performance tools and the role of the Green Building Challenge. *Build. Res. Inf.* **2010**, *29*, 324–335. [CrossRef]
17. Abdalla, G.; Maas, G.; Huyghe, J.; Oostra, M. Criticism on Environmental Assessment Tools. In Proceedings of the 2nd International Conference on Environmental Science and Technology, Belgrade, Serbia, 28 September–2 October 2016.
18. Poveda, C.A.; Lipsett, M.G. A Review of Sustainability Assessment and Sustainability/Environmental Rating Systems and Credit Weighting Tools. *J. Sustain. Dev.* **2011**, *4*, 36–55. [CrossRef]
19. Guinée, J. Handbook on life cycle assessment operational guide to the ISO standards. *Int. J. Life Cycle Assess.* **2002**, *7*, 311–313. [CrossRef]
20. Finnvedern, G.; Hauschild, M.Z.; Ekvall, T.; Guinée, J.; Heijungs, R.; Hellweg, S.; Koehler, A.; Pennington, D.; Suh, S. Recent developments in Life Cycle Assessment. *J. Environ. Manag.* **2009**, *91*, 1–21. [CrossRef] [PubMed]
21. Rice, G.; Clift, R.; Burns, R. Comparison of currently available european LCA software. *Int. J. Life Cycle Assess.* **1997**, *2*. [CrossRef]
22. ISO. *ISO 14040: Environmental Management—Life Cycle Assessment—Principles and Framework*; International Organization for Standardization: Geneva, Switzerland, 2006.
23. Puettmann, M.E.; Bergman, R.; Hubbard, S.; Johnson, L.; Lippke, B.; Oneil, E.; Wagner, F.G. Cradle-to-gate life-cycle inventory of US wood products production: CORRIM Phase I and Phase II products. *Wood Fiber Sci.* **2010**, *42*, 15–28.
24. Ortiz, O.; Castells, F.; Sonnemann, G. Sustainability in the construction industry: A review of recent developments based on LCA. *Constr. Build. Mater.* **2009**, *23*, 28–39. [CrossRef]
25. Podvezko, V. The Comparative Analysis of MCDA Methods SAW and COPRAS. *Eng. Econ.* **2011**, *22*, 134–146. [CrossRef]
26. Sev, A. A comparative analysis of building environmental assessment tools and suggestions for regional adaptations. *Civ. Eng. Environ. Syst.* **2011**, *28*, 231–245. [CrossRef]

27. Retzlaff, R. Green buildings and building assessment systems: A new area of interest for planners. *J. Plan. Lit.* **2009**, *24*, 3–21. [CrossRef]

28. Wong, S.-C.; Abe, N. Stakeholders' perspectives of a building environmental assessment method: The case of CASBEE. *Build. Environ.* **2014**, *82*, 502–516. [CrossRef]

29. CASBEE. Green Book Live. Available online: http://www.greenbooklive.com/page.jsp?id=1 (accessed on 26 June 2017).

30. CASBEE. CASBEE Homepage. Available online: http://www.ibec.or.jp/CASBEE/english/overviewE.htm (accessed on 26 June 2017).

31. IBEC. *CASBEE for New Construction. Technical Manual;* Institute for Building Environment and Energy Conservation (IBEC): Tokyo, Japan, 2008.

32. DGNB. DGNB Official Web Page. Available online: http://www.dgnb-system.de/en/system/international/China.php (accessed on 26 June 2017).

33. ISO. *Environmental Labels and Declarations—Type III Environmental Declarations—Principles and Procedures;* ISO: Geneva, Switzerland, 2006; p. 25.

34. CEN. *EN 15804:2012 + A1:2013. Sustainability of Construction Works—Environmental Product Declarations—Core Rules for the Product Category of Construction Products;* European Committee for Standardization (CEN): Bruxelles, Belgium, 2012/2013.

35. HQE. Haute Qualitè Environnementale. Available online: http://www.behqe.com (accessed on 26 June 2017).

36. Cerway. *HQE™ Management System for Urban Planning Projects. Requirements Scheme for the Management System of Urban Planning and Development Projects—HQE™ Certified by Cerway;* Cerway: Paris, France, 2014.

37. USGBC. *LEED for New Construction and Major Renovation;* US Green Building Council: Washington, DC, USA, 2009.

38. iiSBE. International Initiative for a Sustainable Built Environment Homepage. Available online: http://iisbe.org/sbtool-2012 (accessed on 26 June 2017).

39. USGBC. US Green Building Council Homepage. Available online: http://www.usgbc.org/DisplayPage.aspx?CMSPageID=220S (accessed on 26 June 2017).

40. Larsson, N. *User Guide to the SBTool Assessment Framework;* iiSBE: Ottawa, ON, Canada, 2012.

41. Loftness, V.; Haase, D. *Sustainable Built Environments—Selected Entries from the Encyclopedia of Sustainability Science and Technology;* Springer: New York, NY, USA, 2013; Volume XIV, p. 746.

42. GBC. Green Building Council South Africa. Available online: https://www.gbcsa.org.za/green-star-sa-rating-system/ (accessed on 26 June 2017).

43. CSIR. CSIR eNews Official Web Page. Available online: http://www.csir.co.za/enews/2008_mar/be_02.html (accessed on 26 June 2017).

44. Gibbert, J.T. Sustainable building assessment tool: Integrating sustainability into current design and building process. In Proceedings of the World Sustainable Building Conference, Melbourne, Australia, 21–25 Setpember 2008.

45. Borong, L.; Qin, O.; Daojin, G.; Lei, T. Assessment practices of Gobas in China. In Proceedings of the 2005 World Sustainable Building Conference, Tokyo, Japan, 27–29 September 2005.

46. DGNB. DNGB International Application. Available online: http://www.dgnb-system.de/en/system/international/ (accessed on 26 June 2017).

47. Wang, Z.Q.; Hu, Q. The Comparative Study on the Sustainable Sites Indicators between ESGB and LEED. *Appl. Mech. Mater.* **2012**, *253–255*, 249–253. [CrossRef]

48. HKGBC. Hong Kong Green Building Council. Available online: https://www.hkgbc.org.hk/eng/BEAMPlus_NBEB.aspx (accessed on 26 June 2017).

49. Korkmaz, S.; Erten, D.; Syal, M.; Potbhare, V. A review of green building movement timelines in developed and developing countries to build an international adoption framework. In Proceedings of the Fifth International Conference on Construction in the 21st Century: Collaboration and Integration in Engineering, Management and Technology, Istanbul, Turkey, 20–22 May 2009; pp. 20–22.

50. IGBC. Indian Green Building Council. Available online: https://igbc.in/igbc/ (accessed on 26 June 2017).

51. CASBEE. CASBEE Official Web Page. Available online: http://www.ibec.or.jp/CASBEE/english/ (accessed on 26 June 2017).

52. Aotake, N.; Ofuiji, N.; Miura, M.; Shimada, N.; Niwa, H. Comparison among results of various comprehensive assessment systems-a case study for a model building using CASBEE, BREEAM and LEED. In Proceedings of the Sustainable Building Conference (SB05), Tokyo, Japan, 27–29 September 2005.
53. Research Center for Life Cycle Assessment. AIST-LCA Ver.4. Available online: https://www.aist-riss.jp/old/lca/cie/activity/software/aist/outline.html (accessed on 13 March 2017).
54. KGBCC. Korean Green Building Certification Criteria. Available online: http://wfi.worldforestry.org/media/posters/kt_park.pdf (accessed on 26 June 2017).
55. BCA. Building and Construction Authority Official Web Page. Available online: http://www.bca.gov.sg/greenmark/green_mark_buildings.html (accessed on 26 June 2017).
56. EEWH. EEWH Assessment System for Building Renovation. Available online: http://twgbqanda.com/english/e_tgbr.php?Type=2&menu=e_tgbr_class&pic_dir_list=0 (accessed on 26 June 2017).
57. CEC. CEC Green Building Library. Available online: http://www3.cec.org/islandora-gb/en/islandora/object/greenbuilding%3A100 (accessed on 26 June 2017).
58. BREEAM. BREEAM Official Web Page. Available online: http://www.breeam.org (accessed on 26 June 2017).
59. SBToolCZ. Národní Nástroj pro Certifikaci Kvality Budov. Available online: http://www.sbtool.cz (accessed on 26 June 2017).
60. Forsberg, A.; von Malmborg, F. Tools for environmental assessment of the built environment. *Build. Environ.* **2004**, *39*, 223–228. [CrossRef]
61. Nibel, S.; Rialhe, A. Implementation and comparison of four building assessment tools. In Proceedings of the Sustainable Building Conference, Maastricht, The Netherlands, 22–25 October 2000.
62. Gerard, C.; Chantagnon, N.; Achard, G.; Nibel, S. ESCALE: A method for assessing the environmental quality of buildings at design stage. In Proceedings of the 2nd International Conference on Decision Making in Urban and Civil Engineering, Lyon, France, 9–11 October 2000.
63. GBC. Green Building Council Italia. Available online: http://www.gbcitalia.org/page/show/-leed-leadership-in-energy-and-environmental-design (accessed on 26 June 2017).
64. BREEAM-NL. BREEAM Netherlands Official Web Page. Available online: https://epeaswitzerland.com/fr/2014/10/breeam-nl/ (accessed on 26 June 2017).
65. Castro, M.; Remmerswaal, J.A.; Reuter, M.A. Life cycle impact assessment of the average passenger vehicle in the Netherlands. *Int. J. Life Cycle Assess.* **2003**, *8*, 297–304. [CrossRef]
66. Pettersen, T.D.; Strand, S.M.; Haagenrun, S.E.; Krigsvol, G. EcoProfile—A Simplistic Environmental Assessment Method Experiences and New Challenges. Available online: http://globe2.thaicyberu.go.th/node/2405724 (accessed on 26 June 2017).
67. Mateus, R.; Braganca, L. Sustainability assessment and rating of buildings: Developing the methodology SBTool PT–H. *Build. Environ.* **2011**, *46*, 1962–1971. [CrossRef]
68. Larsson, N.K.; Cole, R.J. Green Building Challenge: the development of an idea Build. *Res. Inf.* **2001**, *29*, 336–345. [CrossRef]
69. Glaumann, M. EcoEffect—A holistic tool to measure environmental impact of building properties. In Proceedings of the International Conference Sustainable Building, Maastricht, The Netherlands, 22–25 October 2000; pp. 1–3.
70. Favre, D.; Citherlet, S. Eco-Bat: A Design Tool for Assessing Environmental Impacts of Buildings and Equipment. *Build. Simul.* **2008**, *1*, 83–94. [CrossRef]
71. EGS-plan. EGS-plan Ingenieurgesellschaft für Energie, Gebäude und Solartechnik mbH. Available online: http://www.stz-egs.de/home/?lang=en (accessed on 26 June 2017).
72. Grace, M. BREEAM—A practical method for assessing the sustainability of buildings for the new millennium. In Proceedings of the Sustainable Building Conference, Maastricht, The Netherlands, 22–58 October 2000.
73. DOE. Energy Efficiency and Renewable Energy, Building Energy Software Tool Directory. Available online: http://www.eere.energy.gov/buildings/tools_directory (accessed on 26 June 2017).
74. CAGBC. Canada Green Building Council—Every Building Greener. Available online: https://www.cagbc.org (accessed on 26 June 2017).
75. GreenGlobes. Green Globes Official Web Site. Available online: http://www.greenglobes.com/home.asp (accessed on 26 June 2017).
76. Meil, J.K. Building materials in the context of sustainable development: an overview of forintek's research program and model. *Life Cycle Anal.* **1995**, *8*, 79–92.

77. Trusty, B.W.; Horst, S. Integrating LCA Tools in Green Building Rating Systems. Available online: https://www.irbnet.de/daten/iconda/CIB2759.pdf (accessed on 26 June 2017).
78. GBCA. Green Building Council of Australia. Available online: https://www.gbca.org.au/green-star/ (accessed on 26 June 2017).
79. Roderick, Y.; McEwan, D.; Wheatley, C.; Alonso, C. Comparison of energy performance assessment between LEED, BREEAM and Green Star. In Proceedings of the Eleventh International IBPSA Conference, Glasgow, Scotland, 27–30 July 2009; pp. 1167–1176.
80. NABERS. National Australian Built Environment Rating System. Available online: http://www.nabers.gov.au/public/WebPages/Home.aspx (accessed on 26 June 2017).
81. Cole, R.J.; Howard, N.; Ikaga, T.; Nibel, S. Building Environmental Assessment Tools: Current and future roles. In Proceedings of the World Sustainable Building Conference, Tokyo, Japan, 27–29 September 2005.
82. NZGBC. New Zealand Green Building Council. Available online: http://www.nzgbc.org.nz (accessed on 26 June 2017).
83. Byrd, H.; Leardini, P. Green buildings: Issues for New Zealand. *Procedia Eng.* **2011**, *21*, 481–488. [CrossRef]
84. GBC, A. Argentina Green Building Council. Available online: http://www.argentinagbc.org.ar/leed/ (accessed on 26 June 2017).
85. GBCB. Green Building Council Brazil. Available online: http://www.gbcbrasil.org.br (accessed on 26 June 2017).
86. Arup. Ove Arup Official Web Page. Available online: http://www.arup.com/Projects/SPeAR.aspx (accessed on 26 June 2017).

 *sustainability*

Article

Exploring Socio-Technical Features of Green Interior Design of Residential Buildings: Indicators, Interdependence and Embeddedness

Yan Ning [1,*], Yadi Li [1], Shuangshuang Yang [1] and Chuanjing Ju [2]

[1]   Department of Construction and Real Estate, Southeast University, Nanjing 210096, China;
      liyd_seu@126.com (Y.L.); yangss95@163.com (S.Y.)
[2]   Department of Business Administration, Southeast University, Nanjing 210096, China;
      101012004@seu.edu.cn
*   Correspondence: ningyan@seu.edu.cn

Academic Editor: Umberto Berardi
Received: 23 August 2016; Accepted: 12 December 2016; Published: 27 December 2016

Abstract: This research aims to develop indicators for assessing green interior design of new residential buildings in China, grounded in the socio-technical systems approach. The research was carried out through a critical literature review and two focus group studies. The results show that the boundaries of green interior design were identified with respect to three dimensions, namely performance, methodology and stakeholders. The socio-technical systems approach argues for the recognition of the interdependence between the systems elements and the feature of embeddedness. The interdependence of the systems elements exists within each of these three dimensions and across them. It is also found that the socio-technical systems of green interior design are embedded in the social, regulatory and geographic context. Taking interior design of residential buildings as the empirical setting, this study contributes to the literature of green building assessment by presenting a socio-technical systems approach.

Keywords: environmental impact assessment; green interior design; green building; socio-technical systems; embeddedness; China

1. Introduction

Green development has become the national strategy for economy development and the topmost governmental agenda in China. The Chinese government initiated five principles for national development in the fifth Plenary Session of the 18th the Communist Party of China Central Committee in 2015. These are innovation, coordination, green, openness and sharing. According to the BP Statistical Review of World Energy, in 2012, China accounted for 21.9% of total worldwide primary energy consumption. The building sector consumes about 27.0% of the country's total energy. The building sector has accounted for approximately 43% of China's total energy consumption from the life-cycle perspective [1]. Thus, achieving green in the building sector will significantly contribute to a reduction in overall use of carbon and energy.

The Chinese Government has announced a series of action targets and roadmaps for achieving green buildings. For example, the Ministry of Finance (MOF) and the Ministry of Housing and Urban-Rural Development (MOHURD) jointly announced the 'Implementation Plan for Accelerating Green Building Development' that set the targets for creating 1 billion m² of new green building areas by 2015, constituting at least 30% of new building areas by 2020. In 2014, the Central Government and State Council initiated the "New National Urbanization Plan 2014–2020" in which 50% of new building are projected to reach the green building standards by 2020. The 'Evaluation Standard for Green

Building' (ESGB) was published and updated in 2006 and 2014 respectively [2]. All these regulatory contexts motivate the entire industry to strive for a green building paradigm shift.

Increasing studies also shade light on energy/carbon reduction in the building sector in China [3,4], either for commercial [5,6] or for residential buildings [7]. Studies also focused on specific stages of green building delivery, for instance design [8], construction [9] and retrofit [10]. Policies for addressing problems with respect to green building delivery were also extensively examined [4], in terms of challenges and opportunities [3,11,12].

However, the interior design of new residential buildings is rarely examined in China. Although pollution control and indoor environmental standards associated with interior design of residential buildings have been sparsely addressed, there is a lack of established tools for assessing their environmental impacts. This gap in knowledge is significant given that the interior design and construction constitute a considerable market share in the construction sector, and green interior design is of vital importance to the green building delivery.

This study aims to develop indicators for assessing green interior design of new residential buildings. This study argues for a socio-technical systems approach [3], which emphasizes that green interior design is characterized by systems and embeddedness features. The systems feature embraces the interdependence among the systems element [13,14] and the embeddedness feature implies that green interior design is embedded into the social, regulatory and geographic context. This study focuses on new residential buildings as they have distinct features from other building types (e.g., office and hotels) and existing residential buildings.

The paper is organized as follows. Section 2 presents a literature review of green interior design and socio-technical systems approach, followed by a conceptual framework for defining the boundaries of green interior design (Section 3). Section 4 reports on the research method of focus group studies. The key results of the indicators for assessing green interior design and discussion of the socio-technical systems features are presented in Section 5. Conclusions and recommendations for future studies are shown at the end.

2. Literature Review

2.1. Green Interior Design of Residential Buildings

People spend 90% of their time indoors [15]. However, it is found that levels of indoor pollutants are usually two to five times higher than outdoor levels [16], which could be detrimental to the health and well-being of occupants [17]. Thus, improving the indoor environment is of great importance to their well-being [18]. However, in classical interior design, designers often prioritize on meeting the aesthetic and functional needs of the clients, rendering environmental issues less important [19].

Prior studies have fallen short of providing a cohesive description of the boundaries of green interior design of residential buildings thus far. In a simple manner, studies argued that green interior design intends to cover a wider scope than the classical approach. These include material, aesthetic qualities, environmental and health impacts, availability, ease of instalment and maintenance, and life-cycle cost [20]. Kang and Guerin [18] defined environmentally sustainable interior design practice as three aspects: global sustainable interior design, interior materials, and quality indoor environments.

In the green building standards for new construction or renovation, e.g., Leadership in Energy and Environmental Design (LEED), and the Building Research Establishment Environmental Assessment Method (BREEM), parts of the assessment credits are associated with interior design. In addition, six aspects of indoor environment are assessed in ISO 16813:2006. These are indoor air quality, thermal comfort, acoustical comfort, visual comfort, energy efficiency and HVAC system controls. These are applicable to environment design for new construction and the retrofit of existing buildings. However, it mainly deals with the indoor environment, referring less to space performance and material savings.

In addition, the LEED for Homes Design and Construction (LEED BD + C: homes and multi-family low-rise; LEED BD + C: Multifamily Midrise) specified the requirements on location and transportation, sustainable sites, water efficiency, energy and atmosphere, materials and resources, indoor environmental quality, innovation and regional priorities. It defined broader requirements for achieving green interior design, such as credits assigned to location and transportation, sustainable sites and outdoor water use. These aspects might not be applicable to the China's context as these aspects are dealt with by architectural designers and fixed prior to the interior design. Similarly, the local assessment tool ESGB comprises energy savings, land savings, water savings, material savings, environment protection, and building functional requirements during the complete building life cycle. Notwithstanding these evaluation tools, there is a lack of well-established tools, specifically with respect to assessing green interior design of new residential buildings.

Research has examined green interior design of offices and commercial buildings [21]. The LEED and BCA (Building and Construction Authority) Green Mark initiated assessment tools for offices and commercial interiors. The BCA published the "BCA Green Mark for Office Interior" [22]. It comprises energy efficiency, water efficiency, sustainable management and operation, indoor environmental quality, other green features [22]. LEED for commercial and institutional interiors addressed sustainable sites, energy and atmosphere, materials and resources, and indoor environmental quality [23]. The BREEAM UK non-domestic building refurbishment and fit-out schemes have four assessment parts. These are building fabric and structure, core services, local services and interior design. Refurbishment and fit-out projects can be assessed against one or all of the four parts, or any combination [24]. However, the indicators developed in these tools, while providing valuable inspiration for assessing green interior design of residential buildings, would not be applicable to the residential building in China.

2.2. Socio-Technical Systems Approach

Socio-technical systems are referred to as "a somewhat abstract, functional sense as the linkages between elements necessary to fulfill societal functions" [25] (p. 898). The socio-technical systems approach not only focuses on achieving interior design at the design and construction stages, but also on functionality at the occupancy phase.

The systems approach highlights that system elements are tightly interrelated and interdependent with each other [25]. Open systems are another important feature of the socio-technical systems approach. Although sustainable building is increasingly recognized as involving complex socio-technical systems [3,14], studies rarely investigate their features. Drawing on the analytical framework [25,26], green interior design is considered to have complex socio-technical systems. Aside from the indicators for green interior design being developed, this study examined the socio-technical systems features of green interior design of residential buildings.

2.3. Empirical Context of Green Interior Design in China

Given the open system feature of the socio-technical systems, the economic, social and regulatory contexts of green interior design of residential buildings in China are elaborated in detail. These contextual factors together shape the development of green interior design of residential buildings.

2.3.1. Economic Context of Green Interior Design

Due to with rapid urbanization, the decorating industry has huge development potential. The capital of the decorating industry reached 3160 billion CNY in 2014, as compared to 1180 billion CNY in 2005 (see Figure 1). Residential decoration constitutes almost half of this capital. The growth rate in these years was kept stable around 10% [27]. This indicates there is a great market potential in interior design and construction.

Figure 1. Total capital of the decoration industry and growth rate. Source: MOHURD [27].

Two significant drivers of this growth could be identified. The first is the political incentive of fine decoration (whereby the developer undertakes the decoration work) in the building sector. In the last decade, the majority of residential buildings were handed over without fine decoration; the interior design and construction is entirely left to the buyers. However, increasing studies found that this delivery system resulted in a huge amount of waste and environmental problems [28]. As a consequence, the policy now is re-oriented to incentivize fine decoration. According to MOF and MOHURD [29], all new residential buildings are suggested to be handed over with fine decoration already complete. The second driver is the booming market of the refurbishment of existing residential buildings. The first mass construction of residential buildings in China took place in the late 1990s. It was gradually observed that these buildings underwent varying degrees of refurbishment.

2.3.2. Social Context of Green Interior Design

Contractor registration heads in China comprise three categories, namely general contractors, specialist contractors and labor subcontractors. Construction firms that undertake decoration work belong to one type of these specialists. Their work scope covers decoration work and directly related supporting works [30]. There were around 140,000 firms that undertook decoration work in 2014.

The old registration system was transformed from a three-class grade to two-class grade (i.e., first and second Class) in 2014 [30]. Grades are classified in accordance with financial capability, personals and track record. Firms in the class one have no limits in tender amount, whereas those in class two are limited to a contract amount below 20 million CNY. For design firms, there are three grades (see Table 1).

Table 1. Design and construction firm categories in residential decoration.

Firm Types	Grades	Registration Criteria
Design firm	Class one	Financial capability and track record
	Class two	Personals
	Class three	Technology and management systems
Construction firm	Class one	Financial capability
	Class two	Personals
		Track record

Source: MOHURD [30,31].

2.3.3. Regulatory Context of Green Interior Design

Regulations of relevance to interior design fall into three levels, namely national, industrial and provincial levels. The former two are applicable to all regions, whereas the latter refers to local regulations coming into effect in a specific province. A review of the existing regulations, codes and rules in China was carried out. The national and industrial regulations cover one aspect and multiple aspects are presented in Supplementary Materials Annex 1 and 2 respectively. Provincial-level regulations are presented in the similar manner (see Annex 3 and 4). From these tables, three patterns could be observed.

First, existing rules and regulations are closely associated with interior design. Thus, the development of green interior design should be compatible with the existing regulations. Specifically, green interior design should comply with the civil building regulations. This is because buildings are classified into two types in China, namely industrial and civil building (see Figure 2); residential buildings belong to the latter category. In any case, rules and regulations are highly localized. Developing indicators for green interior design thus requires a contextualized plan.

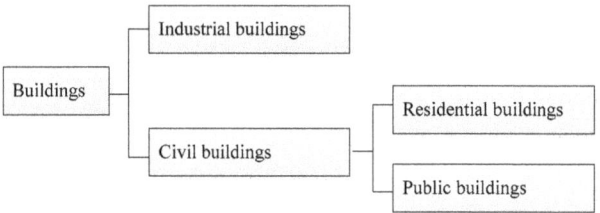

Figure 2. Building type classification in China. Source: adapted from Li & Yao [3].

Second, a lack of well-established assessment tool for green interior design is observable at national, industrial or provincial levels. Such a deficiency might severely hinder the green transformation of the interior design and construction for residential buildings.

Third, green interior design practices face complex and intricate regulation systems. Ye et al. [32] found that contents in most standards largely overlap; some mandatory provisions in local standards are unnecessary. Besides, green interior design could be controlled and monitored by multiple governmental entities. Thus, to promote such practices through regulations would require coordination among multiple governmental entities. Lack of such coordination would impose great obstacles to practice uptake and implementation.

3. Conceptual Framework of Green Interior Design for Residential Buildings

This study adopted the framework of Ju, Ning and Pan [33] to initially define green interior design of residential buildings. It deals with three dimensions, which are performance, methodology and stakeholders (see Table 2). The former two present the technical aspect, whereas the latter portrays the social aspect.

(1)   The performance of green interior design comprises five aspects. These are effective space utilization, healthy indoor environment, energy saving, water conservation and material saving. These five aspects were initially identified from the extant literature and further verified through focus groups;

(2)   The methodology deals with the temporal and spatial dimensions. The temporal dimension includes workflow and material flow. Work flow covers design, material selection, construction, maintenance and end-of-life. Although this study deals with green design, it is recognized that design solutions have great impacts on construction, maintenance stages. The material dimension deals with the material flow of the cradle-to-grave life cycle. The spatial dimension describes the location of physical subjects. It has to properly deal with the component of interior design, compatibility with architectural and mechanical, electrical and plumbing (MEP) design and outdoor environment;

(3)   The stakeholder dimension refers to the actors who play a role in achieving green interior. These include developers, contractor, designers, suppliers, end-users, the government and industrial organizations.

Table 2. Boundaries of green interior design of residential buildings.

Systems	Dimension		Indicator
Technical systems	Performance		Space performance, indoor environmental quality, energy efficiency, water conservation and material savings
	Methodology	Temporal dimension: workflow	Design, material selection, construction, operation, maintenance and end-of-life
		Temporal dimension: material flow	Raw material extraction, Transportation from extraction site to factory, manufacturing, transportation from factory to building site, construction installation, operation, renovation, deconstruction and recycling/landfill site
		Spatial dimension	Components of interior design, architectural design, MEP design and outdoor environment
Social systems	Stakeholders		Developers, contractors, designers, suppliers, end-users, government and industrial organizations

Source: Adapted from Pan and Ning [14] and Ju et al. [33]. MEP: mechanical, electrical and plumbing.

4. Research Methods

4.1. Focus Group Studies

This study adopted focus groups to develop indicators for and explore the socio-technical systems feature of green interior design of residential buildings in China. Focus groups are useful for exploring a particular topic [34]. The purpose of the first-round focus group was to derive the indicators, and verify five categories in the conceptual framework as well as interdependence and embeddedness features. The second focus group aimed to validate the indicators and socio-technical systems features obtained in the first round.

Participants were selected using purposive sampling. Participants from a wide range of organization types were targeted. In the end, seven participants were invited in the first round. Detailed background information is shown in Table 3. In the second round, another two participants from environmental assessment firms and construction firms were invited, together with six participants from the first round. The reason for inviting the same participants in two rounds is because they would help to closely validate the framework derived from the first round. Each focus group lasted for three hours.

Following the suggestion of Cyr [34], at the start of first focus group, participants were requested to: (1) comment on proposed definition (Table 2); (2) suggest specific indicators under each aspect and comment on the appropriateness of the five aspects; (3) discuss why the aspects and associated indicators are essential for interior design; and (4) comment on the socio-technical systems features.

Table 3. Profiles of focus group participants.

Participants	Organization	Designation	Round 1	Round 2
1	Government organization	Director	Yes	Yes
2	Government organization	Deputy director	Yes	Yes
3	Governmental organization	Officer	Yes	Yes
4	Environmental assessment firm	Director	Yes	Yes
5	Research institute for building science	Director	Yes	Yes
6	Construction group	Vice general manager	Yes	Yes
7	Academia	Associate professor	Yes	-
8	Environmental assessment firm	Engineer	-	Yes
9	Construction firm	Chief Executive Officer	-	Yes
Total			7	8
Duration			3 h	3 h

4.2. Data Analysis

Data analysis was carried out following the rules of systematic combining approach [35]. Two types of unit of analysis were adopted, namely individual and interaction levels [34]. The individual level unit of analysis was used to triangulate the proposed indicators and socio-technical systems feature; the interactive unit of analysis was appropriate for exploring the indicator development and socio-technical systems features.

Themes (i.e., the five categories) and indicators identified from the literature review were verified from the focus groups, relying on labels that could represent similar descriptions across different participants. In the end, indicators of green interior design were identified. Emerged aspects were compared with the existing findings. Through going back and forth between framework, data sources and analysis, this step fulfilled the match between theory and data in systematic combining [35].

5. Results and Discussion

5.1. Importance of Green Interior Design and Socio-Technical Perspective

Participants agreed that developing indicators for assessing green interior design of residential buildings is of vital importance for green building delivery in China. They summarized three reasons. Firstly, the regulatory context of considering green building delivery as a national strategy in China has been widely accepted. Developing a standard for green interior design could well fit with the national policy vision. In addition, a green building paradigm shift requires concerted efforts from all parties throughout the building cycle. The interior design is an essential stage.

Secondly, in practice, there exists a considerable market demand for delivering green interior. Participants commented that end-users in China expressed enormous concern on the environmental pollution caused by the interior decoration. Thus, there is a strong demand for green interior design. However, the market still failed to fully meet the end-users' requirements.

Thirdly, participants acknowledged the importance of the systems approach in addressing green interior design. Existing standards and regulations prescribe some aspects of interior works, for example, the indoor air quality and energy efficiency. However, no tools are available for articulating green interior design in a systems approach.

5.2. Aspects of Green Interior Design

Participants agreed with the presentation of the five key aspects of green interior design and suggested specific indicators under each aspect (see Table 4).

Table 4. Indicators for green interior design for residential buildings.

Aspects	Indicators	Description
Space performance	Efficient use of space (SP1)	• Properly-configured functions (SP11) • Multiple functions-oriented (SP12)
	Adaptive use (SP2)	• Adaptive use and consideration of potential future needs (SP21) • Space flexibility and adjustable when new requirements arise (SP22)
	Compatibility with architectural and MEP design (SP3)	• Compatibility with the architecture design (SP31) • Compatibility with the MEP design and configuration (SP32)
Indoor environmental quality	Acoustic (IEQ1)	• Sealing of gaps around windows and doors, openings of high sound conduction (IEQ11) • Use of materials for increasing sound absorption and insulation (IEQ12) • Reduction of vibration noise arising from water flows in pipes (IEQ13)
	Lighting (IEQ2)	• Maximization of the use of natural daylight through openings without impairing the structure (IEQ21) • Use of light-colored interiors that reflect light from windows or skylights (IEQ22) • Use of high performance artificial lights and appropriate configuration (IEQ23) • Avoid using materials with high surface reflectance (IEQ24)
	Thermal comfort (IEQ3)	• Increase air tightness through air barriers around windows and doors (IEQ31) • Use of passive technologies, shading, reflection, absorption devices (IEQ32) • Humidity control (IEQ33)
	Indoor air quality (IEQ4)	• Proper mechanical flushing of indoor pollutant sources (IEQ41) • Air purification filters to prevent outdoor pollution (IEQ42) • Improving air circulation (IEQ43) • Prevent interior pollution migration (IEQ44) • Selection of low-pollutant materials (IEQ45) • Air quality monitoring systems (IEQ46) • Removal of sources of water or moisture (IEQ47)
Energy efficiency	Envelope (EE1)	• Energy-saving windows and door treatments (EE11) • Use of insulation in interior walls (EE12) • Choice of appropriate shading devices (EE13)
	Lighting and daylight (EE2)	• Selection of high performance lighting and control devices (EE21) • Selection of lighting supported by renewable energies (EE22) • Implementation of a flexible lighting control systems with plug and play components such as wall controls, sensors, and dimming ballasts (EE23) • Smart controls such as occupancy sensors and daylight dimming (EE24)
Water conservation	Water conservation (WC)	• Selection of water-efficient appliances, fixtures and fittings (WC1) • Installation of devices to monitor water leakage (WC2) • Reduction in the volumes of sewage (WC3) • Water usage monitoring (WC4) • Recycling of domestic wastewater (WC5)

Table 4. *Cont.*

Aspects	Indicators	Description
Material-saving	Ease of maintenance (MS1)	• Selection of high performance decoration materials and products (MS11) • Ease of maintenance finishes, materials and products (MS12)
	Environmental friendly materials (MS2)	• Use materials salvaged from waste (MS21) • Selection of recyclable materials (MS22) • Selection of localized materials (MS43)
	Buildability (MS3)	• Plan material use (MS31) • Use of standard sizes of materials and products (MS32) • The technical interface (MS33) • Selection of industrial modules produced off-site (MS34)
	Life-cycle cost optimization (MS4)	• Consideration of different component service lives in order to achieve lowest life-cycle cost (MS41)

5.2.1. Space Performance (SP)

Participants indicated that the major concern of end-users is to maximize the interior space use. To enhance space performance, interior design should embrace occupants' behaviors and requirements. Three indicators were developed for guiding effective space utilization. These are proper space planning (SP1), adaptive use (SP2) and compatibility with the architecture and MEP design (SP3).

Efficient use of space (SP1). The interior space should be properly configured (SP11), enabling a smooth activity flow. When planning the room spaces, multiple function purposes (SP12) should be taken into account, which would help to maximize space use for different functions. To achieve this, it is important to investigate the true requirements of users.

Adaptive use (SP2) indicates the consideration of future needs (SP21) and ensures space flexibility which presents adjustability when new requirements arise (SP22). Flexible designs aim to meet occupants' unforeseen requirements. Along with the rapid technological change as well as possible alteration of the function and workflows in the room, occupants may need more flexible and adaptable interiors to accommodate these unforeseen changes. One example is to maximize the user's control of the environment, for instance mobile furniture, or building utilities that are reconfigurable and expandable.

Compatibility with the architecture and MEP design (SP3). As interior design is fully based on existing architectural design (SP31) and develops in tandem with the MEP design (SP32), it is important to ensure design elements are compatible with each other. The interior design needs to fully make use of the existing conditions imposed by the architectural design. The design team should be familiar with the base architecture in order to achieve unified scale and compatibility.

5.2.2. Indoor Environmental Quality

The results show that achieving indoor environmental quality (IEQ) was manifested by acoustic (IEQ1), lighting (IEQ2), thermal comfort (IEQ3) and indoor air quality (IEQ4).

Acoustic performance (IEQ1). Three strategies were proposed to enhance acoustic performance. These are sealing gaps around windows, doors and openings (IEQ11), selecting materials with high sound absorption and insulation (IEQ12) and reducing noise vibrations arising from water flows in pipes (IEQ13). Proper selection of the absorptive surfaces would help to eliminate noise disturbance.

Lighting performance (IEQ2). To improve indoor lighting performance, passive strategies are helpful, such as maximizing the use of natural daylight through openings (IEQ21). This should also improve the daylight use efficiency through light-colored interiors that reflect light from windows or skylight (IEQ22). This is consistent with prior studies that conclude that internal reflectance of materials and finishes affect daylighting [36]. It might be necessary to avoid using materials of high surface reflectance (IEQ24). In addition, it is important to select high performance artificial lights and deploy appropriate configurations (IEQ23).

Thermal comfort (IEQ3). To achieve thermal comfort, several strategies could be adopted, such as increasing air tightness through air barriers around windows and doors (IEQ31). It is also recommended to adopt various effective passive technologies, such as shadings, reflections and absorption devices (IEQ32). Lastly, humidity control technologies could be adopted (IEQ33) in certain period in Jiangsu Province.

Indoor air quality (IEQ4). Participants commented that indoor air quality is the most serious concern in interior design and construction. The topmost strategy is to select low pollution materials (IEQ45), such as green labelling materials. Selecting low pollution materials will reduce the pollutants brought into the building. The second strategy is to improve air circulation (IEQ43), and adopt proper mechanical flushing of indoor pollutant sources (IEQ41). Quite often homes that are poorly ventilated will have high levels of biological contaminants arising from mould growth on damp surfaces. It is important to prevent interior pollution migration (IEQ44), for example preventing cooking smoke migrating from the chicken.

As haze is currently a serious concern in the north China, air purification filters to prevent outdoor pollution (IEQ42) and air quality monitoring systems (IEQ46) are considered to be a solution. The last strategy is to remove sources of water or moisture that encourage fungal growth (IEQ47). This needs to avoid external and internal leaks and adopt proper humidity control devices.

5.2.3. Energy Efficiency (EE)

For interior design, energy efficiency could be achieved by improving envelope (EE1) and lighting and daylight (EE2). It is worth noting that the selection of air-conditioner and water heater is often decided by the end-users rather than the developer or the interior designers in China. Thus these two energy consumption sources were excluded.

Improve envelope (EE1). It is common to adopt energy saving window and door treatments (EE11). Another strategy is to use high-insulation interior walls (EE12). Exterior insulation walls are excluded here because they are often included in the main structure construction work package rather than the interior work. It is also recommended to use internal shading devices (EE13).

Lighting and daylight (EE2). High performance lighting and control devices (EE21) are suggested, to uptake lighting by renewable energies (EE22), and to implement a flexible lighting control system with plug and play components (e.g., wall controls, sensors, and dimming ballasts) (EE23). Various smart controls such as occupancy sensors and daylight dimming are preferable (EE24).

5.2.4. Water Conservation (WC)

Through the focus group, five strategies were proposed to reduce water consumption. Two are of relevance to technological aspects, such as selecting water-efficient appliances, fixtures and fittings (WC1), and reducing the volumes of sewage (WC3). Two strategies are particular to monitoring water usage (WC4) and water leakage (WC2). The last strategy is to recycle domestic wasted water (WC5).

5.2.5. Material-Saving

In order to save materials, four strategies would be helpful. These are use of materials with ease of maintenance (MS1), selection of environmentally-friendly materials (MS2), increase in buildability (MS3) and optimization of life-cycle cost (MS4).

Ease of maintenance (MS1). To save materials, it is necessary to design for ease of maintenance. A first suggestion is to select materials that are of low maintenance (MS11). Using easily maintained finishes will be critical. Another useful method is to select high performance fittings and products (MS12). Extra consideration should be given to products used in heavy-use areas and specific functional areas.

Environmentally-friendly materials (MS2). The environmentally-friendly materials indicate that there is life-cycle optimization, with respect to raw materials, manufacturing, transportation, installation, use and disposal or reuse. It is suggested to use materials salvaged from wastes (MS21) and use recyclable (MS22) and local materials (MS23). Using materials containing recycled content is also preferable. As the carbon labeling is currently on promotion in China, carbon labeling materials are suggested.

Buildability (MS3) is another important assessment criterion from the life-cycle perspective. In order to enhance buildability, it is helpful to use materials and products of standard sizes (MS32) and properly deal with the technical interface between products assembling (MS33). One important strategy is to promote industrial modules produced off-site (MS34). This would largely reduce the on-site waste. Lastly, it is better to draw a material use plan in advance (MS31). This would largely reduce waste and rework.

Life-cycle costing (MS4). It is also recognized that short-term solutions, although less expensive, do not necessarily produce cost savings in the long run. Therefore, a life-cycle costing approach should be materialized in the green interior design. One important strategy is to systematically consider the life span of different components in order to optimize life-cycle cost (MS41). It is important to prepare a fine match of different finishes and products [37].

5.3. Socio-Technical Feature of Green Interior Design

Participants reached a consensus about the socio-technical systems feature of green interior design. These are two-layer system feature and embeddedness feature (see Figure 3).

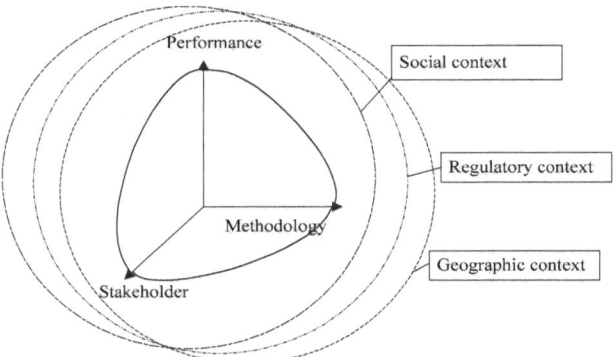

Figure 3. The socio-technical systems features of green interior design.

5.3.1. Two-Layer Systems Features

Systems feature implies the necessity of examining interdependence among elements of the socio-technical systems. Three dimensions of green interior design, namely performance, methodology and stakeholders, are multifaceted and interwoven with each other. The former two present the technical aspect, whereas the latter has the feature of social systems. To achieve green interior design, it is important to properly deal with the interdependence of the socio-technical systems.

In the first layer, interdependence exists between performance, methodology and stakeholders. It is recognized that achieving green interior design is highly technical and requires technological advancement and various passive design solutions. However, mere reliance on the technologies is often found to be limited, which requires the complements from the social aspect. The social aspects refers to the collective endeavors of the key stakeholders. Participants commented that parties' interests are often not well aligned. This would further impede the technology adoption and implementation in green interior design and construction.

In the second layer, interdependence exists within each dimension. With regards to the temporal dimension, the green design solutions will influence the buildability and maintenance in the later stages. Feedbacks collected from the construction and maintenance will inform the design decision making. Within the performance dimension, it is found that independence exists among five aspects. For example, materials show multiple functions (e.g., buildability, maintenance, life-cycle cost and environmental impacts), which will influence the five aspects of interior design to a varying extent. In addition, some finishes may provide satisfactory durability, yet have limitations in the ease of maintenance. This leads to conflicts in the durability and level of maintenance.

5.3.2. Embeddedness Feature of the Socio-Technical Systems

Embeddedness, considering green interior design as an open system, is another feature of the socio-technical systems of green interior design. Embeddedness feature could be interpreted in relation to the social, regulatory and geographic context.

(1) Social context of green interior design

Firstly, the interior design reflects the needs of the occupants who have inherent habit and preferences. Technical specifications thus need to be customized to the occupants' requirements. This is consistent with Li & Yao [3] who argued that it is important to understand building users' demands, expectations and behavior/lifestyle and this requires socio-technical knowledge. Thus, designers' skills for understanding the needs of end-users are desirable. Interior designers' behavioral intentions associated with the green interior design is determined by their attitude, subjective norms, and perceived behavioral control [38]. This indicates that it is hard to isolate the technical interior design solutions from the social settings.

In addition, persuading the client to accept green ideas is often difficult. This is consistent with the results from the survey of green building technology adoption in China which found that stakeholders' reluctance to use was the largest barrier [12]. High upfront investment and inertia might be possible reasons [39]. Thus, it is necessary to inform end-users on the long term value of green interior design.

Secondly, the green interior design practices are socially contextualized in the project setting. Although it is recognized that designer's knowledge of green interior design is of great importance to the implementation, they may not always put it into practice [40]. Project scheduling pressure might be one obstacle.

Thirdly, apart from designers and end-users, achieving green interior design requires the participation of other parties. For instance, interior design requires coordination with structural, mechanical, and electrical engineers. This entails an integrated approach. Key to achieving an integrated approach is open communication and early involvement [41,42]. These two strategies would help to avoid common errors, mistakes and rework.

Lastly, it is essential to investigate the cultural beliefs and customs. Many nationalities and religions attach significance to certain colors, patterns and materials. For instance, most Western cultures consider black the color of mourning. Eastern/Oriental cultures associate white with mourning.

(2) Regulatory context of green interior design

The articulation of the socio-technical systems of green interior design varies from one context to another due to regulatory differences. The regulatory context is manifested through two aspects. Firstly, green interior design must comply with current regulations. Secondly, it is recognized that the achieving green interior design involves co-option of various standards. For example, in the US, green interior design may be of relevance to selecting ENERGY STAR appliances and low-flow plumbing fixtures [23]. In Singapore, adoption of water efficient fittings covered under the Water Efficiency Labelling Scheme [22] is encouraged.

Participants expressed their concern of regulatory deficiencies for motivating practitioners to adopt green interior design in China. They compared the achievement of green interior works to green building in terms of political impacts. They commented that practitioners now have great motivation to invest in green building solutions because the ESGB exists for legitimating such behaviors and the government also provides momentary incentives. However, for the green interior works, no such policies could be used to recognize the green efforts. This could deter adoption and diffusion.

(3) Geographic context of green interior design

Weather conditions are one facet of the geographic context. China has five climate zones. These are Severe Cold, Cold, Hot Summer and Cold Winter, Hot Summer and Warm Winter, and Mild Zone [3]. This study examined interior design in the Jiangsu Province in the middle of China where the weather conditions is Hot Summer and Cold Winter. Purification filters would be suggested in the green interior because the outdoor air quality suffers due to severe haze pollution. But, in the South China, there may be high levels of humidity. This would require use of an air dryer.

Local climatic conditions are important criterion when selecting materials and finishes. Special maintenance requirements would be required for heavy snow or rain, very arid or humid climates, unusual soil conditions and sand and high level of sun exposure.

6. Conclusions

This study aimed to develop indicators for and explore the socio-technical systems of green interior design of residential buildings in China, grounded in the socio-technical systems approach. The study was carried out through a combination of a critical literature review and two focus group studies.

One important result is the conceptual framework for defining the boundaries of green interior design for residential buildings. Consistent with prior studies [33], it deals with three dimensions, namely performance, methodology and stakeholders. The performance dimension comprises space performance, indoor environmental quality, energy efficiency, water conservation and material saving. The methodology dimension deals with the temporal (i.e., work and material flow) and spatial dimensions. The stakeholder dimension refers to the actors who have a role in achieving green interior design. This framework provides a system understanding of the boundary of green interior design for new residential buildings.

Another finding is that this study verified proposed five aspects of performance (i.e., space performance, indoor environmental quality, energy efficiency, water conservation and material saving, see Table 3) and developed indicators for each aspect. The systems framework was verified to be valid.

The last finding is the identification of the socio-technical systems features of green interior design. Although prior studies argued for a socio-technical systems approach in green building delivery [3], this is rarely examined in a systems approach. Distinct from prior systems approaches that examine indicators in isolation, this systems approach focuses on three dimensions (e.g., performance, methodology and value) and emphasizes the interdependence between the systems elements. Interdependence exists both within and across each aspect. Crucial to the green interior design is their feature of being embedded into the social, geographic and regulatory context.

Taking interior design of new residential buildings in China as the empirical setting, this study contributes to the knowledge by presenting two features of socio-technical systems approach, namely the interdependence and embeddedness. The practical implication is that practitioners and policy makers should recognize the socio-technical systems feature of the green interior and take the one-fits-all green strategies with caution. This is because these strategies often take the end-users to be passive recipients, whereas the socio-technical system features argue for active and collective participation of the key stakeholders. In addition, practitioners and policy makers could customize the indicators developed in this study to their specific projects with considerations of the social, regulatory and geographic contexts.

This study only examined the green interior design in China, grounded in the socio-technical systems approach. To reinforce the socio-technical features of green interior design, comparative

Sustainability **2017**, *9*, 33

studies among different nations are recommended. Additional research design (e.g., case studies, interview, questionnaire survey) could be employed to further validate the key findings.

Another recommendation for future studies is to adopt larger scale surveys to further gauge the extent to which green interior design has been implemented in various geographic contexts. Despite the development of indicators for assessing green interior design, parameters for each indicator are worth further in-depth examination. For example, although internal shading devices at windows (EE13) are recommended to increase energy efficiency, the specific parameters of the shading devices are still not known. Further studies in this regard are thus recommended.

Supplementary Materials: The following are available online at www.mdpi.com/2071-1050/9/1/33/s1, Annex 1: Code and regulations of relevance to green interior design for residential building at the national and industrial level (1), Annex 2: Code and regulations of relevance to green interior design for residential building at the national and industrial level (2), Annex 3: Code and regulations of relevance to green interior design for residential building in Jiangsu province (1), Annex 4: Code and regulations of relevance to green interior design for residential building in Jiangsu province (2).

Acknowledgments: This research was supported by the National Science Foundation of China (71502032; 71602031), and the Priority Academic Program Development of Jiangsu Higher Education Institutions. Reviewer's constructive comments are highly appreciated.

Author Contributions: Yan Ning and Chuanjing Ju conceived and designed the research. Yadi Li and Shuangshuang Yang collected and analyzed the data and contributed the policy review.

Conflicts of Interest: The authors declare no conflict of interest.

References

1. Zhang, Y.; He, C.Q.; Tang, B.J.; Wei, Y.-M. China's energy consumption in the building sector: A life cycle approach. *Energy Build* **2015**, *94*, 240–251. [CrossRef]
2. Ministry of Housing and Urban-Rural Development (MOHURD). *Evaluation Standard for Green Building*; MOHURD: Beijing, China, 2014.
3. Li, B.; Yao, R. Building energy efficiency for sustainable development in China: Challenges and opportunities. *Build. Res. Inf.* **2012**, *40*, 417–431. [CrossRef]
4. Zhang, Y.; Wang, Y. Barriers' and policies' analysis of China's building energy efficiency. *Energy Policy* **2013**, *62*, 768–773. [CrossRef]
5. Chen, H.; Lee, W.L. Energy assessment of office buildings in China using LEED 2.2 and BEAM Plus 1.1. *Energy Build.* **2013**, *63*, 129–137. [CrossRef]
6. Jiang, P.; Keith, T.N. Opportunities for low carbon sustainability in large commercial buildings in China. *Energy Policy* **2009**, *37*, 4949–4958. [CrossRef]
7. Gong, X.; Akashi, Y.; Sumiyoshi, D. Optimization of passive design measures for residential buildings in different Chinese areas. *Build. Environ.* **2012**, *58*, 46–57. [CrossRef]
8. Yu, J.; Yang, C.; Tian, L. Low-energy envelope design of residential building in hot summer and cold winter zone in China. *Energy Build.* **2008**, *40*, 1536–1546. [CrossRef]
9. Shi, Q.; Zuo, J.; Huang, R.; Huang, J.; Pullen, S. Identifying the critical factors for green construction—An empirical study in China. *Habitat Int.* **2013**, *40*, 1–8. [CrossRef]
10. Xu, P.; Chan, E.H.W. ANP model for sustainable Building Energy Efficiency Retrofit (BEER) using Energy Performance Contracting (EPC) for hotel buildings in China. *Habitat Int.* **2013**, *37*, 104–112. [CrossRef]
11. Cai, W.G.; Wu, Y.; Zhong, Y.; Ren, H. China building energy consumption: Situation, challenges and corresponding measures. *Energy Policy* **2009**, *37*, 2054–2059. [CrossRef]
12. Du, P.; Zheng, L.Q.; Xie, B.C.; Mahalingam, A. Barriers to the adoption of energy-saving technologies in the building sector: A survey study of Jing-jin-tang, China. *Energy Policy* **2014**, *75*, 206–216. [CrossRef]
13. Morrison-Saunders, A.; Pope, J. Conceptualizing and managing trade-offs in sustainability assessment. *Environ. Impact Assess. Rev.* **2013**, *38*, 54–63. [CrossRef]
14. Pan, W.; Ning, Y. The dialectics of sustainable building. *Habitat Int.* **2015**, *48*, 55–64. [CrossRef]
15. Environmental Protection Agency (EPA). Question about Your Community: Indoor Air. 2013. Available online: http://www.epa.gov/region1/communities/indoorair.html (accessed on 20 March 2016).

16. Environmental Protection Agency (EPA). Buildings and Their Impact on the Environment: A Statistical Summary. 2009. Available online: http://www.epa.gov/greenbuilding/pubs/gbstats.pdf (accessed on 20 March 2016).

17. Kubba, S. Chapter 5—Design Strategies and the Green Design Process. In *LEED Practices, Certification, and Accreditation Handbook*; Butterworth-Heinemann: Boston, MA, USA, 2010.

18. Kang, M.Y.; Guerin, D.A. The state of environmentally sustainable interior design practice. *Am. J. Environ. Sci.* **2009**, *5*, 179–186. [CrossRef]

19. Mazarella, F. Interior Design. 2011. Available online: http://www.wbdg.org/design/dd_interiordsgn.php (accessed on 20 March 2016).

20. Hayles, C.S. Environmentally sustainable interior design: A snapshot of current supply of and demand for green, sustainable or Fair Trade products for interior design practice. *Int. J. Sustain. Built Environ.* **2015**, *4*, 100–108. [CrossRef]

21. Fadeyi, M.O.; Taha, R. Provision of Environmentally Responsible Interior Design Solutions: Case Study of an Office Building. *J. Archit. Eng.* **2012**, *19*, 58–70. [CrossRef]

22. Building and Construction Authority (BCA). *BCA Green Mark for Office Interior*; version 1.1; BCA: Singapore, 2012.

23. Leadership in Energy and Environmental Design (LEED). *LEED Reference Guide for Green Interior Design and Construction for the Design, Construction and Renovation of Commercial and Institutional Interiors Projects*; U.S. Green Building Council: Washington, DC, USA, 2009.

24. Building Research Establishment Environmental Assessment Method (BREEM). *BREEAM International Refurbishment and Fit-out*; BREEAM: London, UK, 2015.

25. Geels, F.W. From sectoral systems of innovation to socio-technical systems: Insights about dynamics and change from sociology and institutional theory. *Res. Policy* **2004**, *33*, 897–920. [CrossRef]

26. Murphy, J.T. Human geography and socio-technical transition studies: Promising intersections. *Environ. Innov. Soc. Transit.* **2015**, *17*, 73–91. [CrossRef]

27. Ministry of Housing and Urban-Rural Development (MOHURD). *Statistic Yearbook of Chinese Docoration Industry*; MOHURD: Beijing, China, 2015.

28. Li, Z.; Kong, S. Mass production of fine decoration. *Constr. Econ.* **2013**, *3*, 66–69.

29. Ministry of Finance (MOF); Ministry of Housing and Urban-Rural Development (MOHURD). *Notices on Implementation Suggestions for Accelerating the Promotion of Green Buildings*; MOF; MOHURD: Beijing, China, 2012.

30. Ministry of Housing and Urban-Rural Development (MOHURD). *Contractor Registration Head Standard*; MOHURD: Beijing, China, 2015.

31. Ministry of Housing and Urban-Rural Development (MOHURD). *Registration Standards for Engineering Firms*; MOHURD: Beijing, China, 2007.

32. Ye, L.; Cheng, Z.; Wang, Q.; Lin, H.; Lin, C.; Liu, B. Developments of green building standards in China. *Renew. Energy* **2015**, *73*, 115–122. [CrossRef]

33. Ju, C.; Ning, Y.; Pan, W. A review of interdependence of sustainable building. *Environ. Impact Assess. Rev.* **2016**, *56*, 120–127. [CrossRef]

34. Cyr, J. The Pitfalls and Promise of Focus Groups as a Data Collection Method. *Sociol. Methods Res.* **2014**, *45*, 231–259. [CrossRef]

35. Dubois, A.; Gadde, L.E. Systematic combining: an abductive approach to case research. *J. Bus. Res.* **2002**, *55*, 553–560. [CrossRef]

36. Yeh, A.G.; Yuen, B. Introduction. In *High-Rise Living in Asian Cities*; Springer: Dordrecht, The Netherlands, 2011; pp. 1–8.

37. Grant, A.; Ries, R. Impact of building service life models on life cycle assessment. *Build. Res. Inf.* **2013**, *41*, 168–186. [CrossRef]

38. Lee, E.; Allen, A.; Kim, B. Interior design practitioner motivations for specifying sustainable materials: Applying the theory of planned behavior to residential design. *J. Inter. Des.* **2013**, *38*, 1–16. [CrossRef]

39. Jensen, O.M. Consumer inertia to energy saving. In *ECEEE 2005 Summer Study*; Panel 6; ECEEE: Stockholm, Sweden, 2005; pp. 1327–1334.

40. Bacon, L. Interior Designer's Attitudes toward Sustainable Interior Design Practices and Barriers Encountered When Using Sustainable Interior Design Practices. 2011. Available online: http://digitalcommons.unl.edu/archthesis/104/ (accessed on 20 March 2016).
41. Häkkinen, T.; Belloni, K. Barriers and drivers for sustainable building. *Build. Res. Inf.* **2011**, *39*, 239–255. [CrossRef]
42. Mollaoglu-Korkmaz, S.; Swarup, L.; Riley, D. Delivering sustainable, high-performance buildings: Influence of project delivery methods on integration and project outcomes. *J. Manag. Eng.* **2011**, *29*, 71–78. [CrossRef]

 *sustainability*

Article

Decomposition and Decoupling Analysis of Life-Cycle Carbon Emission in China's Building Sector

Rui Jiang and Rongrong Li *

School of Economic & Management, China University of Petroleum (Huadong),
No. 66 West Changjiang Road, Qingdao 266580, China; 15275240289@163.com
* Correspondence: lirr@upc.edu.cn; Tel.: +86-532-8698-1324

Academic Editor: Umberto Berardi
Received: 10 April 2017; Accepted: 8 May 2017; Published: 10 May 2017

Abstract: With accelerating urbanization, building sector has been becoming more important source of China's total carbon emission. In this paper, we try to calculate the life-cycle carbon emission, analyze influencing factors of carbon emission, and assess the delinking index of carbon emission in China's building sector. The results show: (i) Total carbon emission in China's building industry increase from 984.69 million tons of CO_2 in 2005 to 3753.98 million tons of CO_2 in 2013. The average annual growth rate is 18.21% per year. Indirect carbon emission from building material consumption accounted to 96–99% of total carbon emission. (ii) The indirect emission intensity effect was leading contributor to change of carbon emission. The following was economic output effects, which always contributed to increase in carbon emission. Energy intensity effect and energy structure effect took negligible role to offset carbon emission. (iii) Delinking index show the status between carbon emission and economic output in China's building industry during 2005–2006 and 2007–2008 was weak decoupling; during 2006–2007 and during 2008–2010 was expansive decoupling; and during 2010–2013 was expansive negative decoupling.

Keywords: life-cycle; building sector; decomposition; delinking analysis; China

---

1. Introduction

According to National Economical Industry Classification (GB/T4754-2012) [1], the building industry includes: construction of buildings, civil engineering, renovation and decoration four categories. The energy consumption of building industry includes the energy consumed during occupancy in the various buildings. The sources of carbon emissions are distinguished as two scopes: (i) direct emissions, which refer to the CO_2 emissions from the consumption of energy of building industry; and (ii) indirect emissions, which refer to CO_2 emissions from the consumption of construction materials. Buildings accounted for 32% of total global final energy use (equal to 117 ExaJoules), 19% of energy-related GHG emissions, 51% of global electricity consumption, 33% of black carbon emissions, and an eighth to a third of F-gases emission (large differences in F-gases data are due to differing accounting conventions) [2–4]. In particular, the building energy consumption in China recently surpassed the US building consumption, and it is expected to increase significantly in the next decades, pushed by the demand for new residential buildings [5–8]. In 2009, the building sector was responsible for one fifth of China's total primary energy consumption and 18% of the overall Chinese GHG emissions.

China has experienced urbanization with an excessively large number of building projects in the past decades [9,10]. Even more, China's urbanization is projected to be accelerating in the future [11–13]. The accelerating urbanization will lead to a rapid growth of energy usage and material consumption, and a commensurate increase in carbon emission, which means carbon emission from building industry will become more important source of China's total carbon emission. Thus, curbing China's building sector carbon emission, and even China's total carbon emission, requires a better understanding of carbon emission from China's building industry.

Growth in building energy use poses a challenge for the Chinese government; in recent years, to curb energy consumption in buildings, the Chinese government has undertaken many actions at national level, as shown in Table 1. Other countries also face this problem and issue building codes and regulations for energy efficiency [8,14–17], as presented in Table 2.

In addition, a large number of scholars have studied carbon emission from building industry at global-level [2,3,18–20], national-level [8,17,21–29], sub-national-level [30–34], etc. What attracted these scholars are three issues: (i) they usually conducted empirical analysis to estimate or predict carbon emission in building industry; (ii) they use quantitative model to quantify these influencing factors of carbon emission in building industry; and (iii) they use qualitative or quantitative model to explore the relationship between economic output and carbon emission in building industry.

In this paper, we try to calculate carbon emission in China's building industry, to explore its influencing factors, and to assess its decoupling status. To be more specific, we firstly estimate direct (fossil fuel combustion) and indirect (building material consumption) carbon emission in building industry, using China's official data and carbon emission coefficient from IPPCC. Then, we conduct a quantitative analysis of the key influencing factors of carbon emission in China's building industry, using the combination method of kaya identity and logarithmic mean Divisia index (LMDI) model. Finally, we assess the decoupling status between economic output and carbon emission in China's building industry, using Tapio method and decoupling effort index. Given that many developing countries have experienced, or will experience urbanization, which lead to building industry booming, and a commensurate rapidly increase in carbon emission [12,35], our work would bring some implications for carbon emission of building industry in some other developing countries.

Table 1. The actions of Chinese government to curb energy consumption in buildings.

Time	Action	Purpose and Specific Content
September 2005	"Circular of the general office of the State Council on further promoting the reform and popularization of wall materials"	Further promote the reform of wall materials and promote energy-efficient construction, effective protection of arable land and energy conservation.
November 2005	Civil building energy conservation management regulations	In order to strengthen the administration of energy conservation, improve the efficiency of energy utilization and improve the quality of indoor thermal environment, the Ministry of construction has formulated the regulations in accordance with the relevant laws and regulations.
August 2007	Measures for the administration of green building evaluation marks	These measures are formulated for the purpose of standardizing the work of green building evaluation and marking and guiding the healthy development of green buildings.
September 2007	Green construction guidelines	Green construction refers to the construction of the project, in ensuring the quality, safety and other basic requirements under the premise of scientific management and technological progress, to maximize the resources and reduce the negative impact on the construction activities of the environment to achieve energy saving, land, water, Materials and environmental protection.
August 2008	Civil building energy conservation regulations	This Ordinance is to strengthen the management of civil building energy conservation, reduce energy consumption in the use of civil buildings, improve energy efficiency.
October 2008	Interim Measures for the administration of financial subsidies for renewable energy efficient building materials	To support the Wenchuan earthquake construction waste treatment and recycling, national finance will arrange special funds to support the production of energy-saving building materials and recycling utilization.
December 2010	"National Green Building Innovation Award" and "National Green Building Innovation Award"	To do a good job in the management and evaluation of the National Green Building Innovation Award, and guide the healthy development of green building in China.
January 2011	On further deepening the northern heating area of existing residential building heating metering and energy conservation work notice	During the Twelfth Five-Year Guideline, the Ministry of finance, and department of housing and urban rural development will further intensify efforts to improve the relevant policies to carry out heating metering and energy conservation work.
December 2011	"Housing Ministry of Urban and Rural Construction on the implementation of the" State Council on the issuance of "the Twelfth Five-Year Guideline" energy-saving emission reduction comprehensive work program notice "implementation plan"	This program requires all levels of housing urban and rural construction departments to fully understand the housing urban and rural areas in the field of energy conservation and emission reduction work of the importance and urgency, establish a high degree of political responsibility and sense of mission, strengthen cooperation with relevant departments, solid work to ensure Complete the task of energy-saving emission reduction.
January 2013	Forward the development and reform of the Ministry of Housing and Urban Construction "Green Building Action Program" notice	In order to thoroughly implement the scientific concept of development, effectively transform the urban and rural construction mode and the development of the construction industry, improve the efficiency of resource utilization, achieve energy conservation and emission reduction targets, improve and actively respond to global climate change, build a resource-saving and environment-friendly society, Civilized level, improve people's quality of life.

Table 2. The buildings code and regulation for energy efficiency in different countries.

Time	Country	Action	Specific Content
April 1989	China	"Standardization law"	It stipulates development and supervision related to standardization laws. It also specifies the penalties on products, which fail to meet compulsory standards for production, sales, and imports.
March 2002	China	"Management Method of National Supervision and Random Inspection of Product Quality"	National supervision and random in section is one method of maintaining product quality by the State. Regular supervision and random inspections are conducted every quarter, and irregular supervision and inspections are conducted according to the status of the product quality.
January 1998	China	"Energy Conservation Law"	It regulates energy conservation management, energy utilization, improvement of energy conservation technologies, and legal liabilities.
2002	China	"Management Method of Energy Conservation Product Certification"	Product certifications adopt the principal of voluntarism. The method stipulates certification conditions, procedures, usage of energy conservation marks, and treatment after certification.
December 2004	China	"Medium and Long-term Energy Conservation Plan"	It promotes key energy conservation sectors during the "11th Five-Year Plan": industry, traffic and transportation, commercial and civil applications. The Plan also puts forward the organization and implementation of key energy conservation projects, such as modification of industrial coal-burning boilers, regional combined heat and power generation, utilization of excessive heat and pressure, saving and replacing oil, energy conservation of buildings, a green lighting project, establishment of energy conservation monitoring and a technical service system, etc.
2005	China	"China Buildings Program Strategy"	Its main goal is to promote building energy efficiency through appliance energy efficiency standards and building codes. It states that it is possible to do so using the following actions.
2005	China	"Design Standard for Energy Efficiency of Public Buildings"	More attention is paid to this particular Standard, as this is the only standard focusing on the energy efficiency of commercial buildings.
2010	China	The Chinese energy codes consist of three options for compliance	First, a prescriptive path which contains detailed specifications for individual components, second, an alternative to the prescriptive approach allowing trade-offs between envelope components, and third, a performance path that requires that the energy consumption of the proposed new building does not exceed energy consumption of a reference building [36].
2007	India	Energy Conservation Building Code (ECBC)	This code is designed to control building energy consumption and applies to commercial buildings with a connected load of 100 kW or 120 kVA.
2010	US	The building energy codes in the U.S. become more stringent	The U.S. building energy program started to focus on compliance and developed a plan to achieve 90% compliance with the model energy code by 2017, which requires active training and enforcement programs as well as annual measurement of the rate of compliance.
2015	Italy and Europe	The building energy codes in the U.S. become more stringent	Provide an overview on EPBD implementation in Europe and a Geocluster Italian distribution of BERCs in order to show their geographical distribution and their influence on the construction sector practices, focusing in particular on the region of Lombardy, describe the methodology followed for the definition of BERCs in nine municipalities in the same region and present the practical application of one of the nine BERCs to a NZEB residential case study as an example of what the EBPD recast define as NZEB.

2. Methods and Data

2.1. Methodologies

2.1.1. Method for Calculating CO_2 Emission

According to National Economical Industry Classification (GB/T4754-2012), the building industry includes: construction of buildings, civil engineering, and renovation and decoration four categories. Based on the previous studies [29,37–41] and the IPCC method of carbon emission inventories [2], we build the CO_2 emission calculation model for China's building industry. The CO_2 emission calculation of building industry includes two parts: first part is the direct CO_2 emissions and second part is indirect CO_2 emissions shown in the following equation:

$$C = C_{dir} + C_{ind} \tag{1}$$

where C represents total carbon emissions in China's building industry; C_{dir} represents the direct CO_2 emissions, which refer to the CO_2 emissions from the consumption energy of building industry; and C_{ind} represents indirect CO_2 emissions, which refer to CO_2 emissions from the consumption construction materials.

$$C_{dir} = \sum_i E_i \times F_i \tag{2}$$

where E_i is the i-th energy consumption, and F_i (kgCO$_2$/kg or kgCO$_2$/m^3 or kgCO$_2$/kWh) indicates the total energy consumption and the total CO_2 emission coefficient of i-th energy, which is shown in Tables 3 and 4.

$$C_{ind} = \sum_j M_j \times \beta_j \tag{3}$$

where M_j is the quantity of j-th kind of consumption construction materials, and β_j represents the CO_2 emission coefficient of j-th kind of consumption construction materials, which is shown in Table 5 [42].

Table 3. The carbon coefficients of different kinds of energy.

Energy	Default Value of Carbon Content	Carbon Oxidation Rate	Average Lower Heating Value	Carbon Coefficient
	tC/TJ	%	kJ/kg or kJ/m^3	kg CO$_2$/kg or kgCO$_2$/m^3
Raw Coal	26.37	98%	20,908	1.981
Washed coal	25.41	98%	26,344	2.405
Other washed coal	25.41	98%	10,454	0.955
Coal products	33.6	98%	17,793	2.148
#: briquette	33.6	90%	17,584	1.950
coal water slurry	33.6	98%	19,854	2.397
Pulverized coal	33.6	98%	20,933	2.527
Coke	29.5	93%	28,435	2.860
Natural Gas	15.3	99%	389,310	2.1622
Liquefied natural gas	15.3	100%	51,498	2.889
Crude Oil	20.1	98%	41,816	3.020
Gasoline	18.9	98%	43,070	2.925
Kerosene	19.6	98%	43,070	3.033
Diesel Oil	20.2	98%	42,652	3.096
Fuel Oil	21.1	98%	41,816	3.170
Liquefied petroleum gas	17.2	98%	50,179	3.101
Refinery Gas	18.2	98%	46,055	3.012
Other petroleum products	20.0	98%	35,168	2.527

Table 4. The carbon coefficients of electricity.

Year	The Ratio of Thermal Power (%)	The Ratio of Other (Water, Nuclear, Wind) (%)	Consumption Standard of Power (kgce/kW·h)	Carbon Coefficient (tCO$_2$/tce)
2005	81.89	18.11	0.343	6.264
2006	82.69	17.31	0.342	6.307
2007	82.98	17.02	0.332	6.144
2008	80.48	19.52	0.322	5.780
2009	80.3	19.7	0.32	5.731
2010	79.2	20.8	0.312	5.511
2011	81.34	18.66	0.308	5.588
2012	78.05	21.95	0.305	5.309
2013	78.19	21.81	0.302	5.262

Table 5. The carbon coefficients of consumption construction materials.

Building Material	Carbon Coefficient (kgCO$_2$/kg or Kg/m^3)
Cement	0.815
Steel	1.789
Glass	0.966
Wood	842.8
Aluminum	2.6

2.1.2. Logarithmic Mean Divisia Index Technique

IDA is an analytical tool originated from energy studies. Based on IDA, many specific decomposition methods can be developed and the LMDI approach introduced by Ang and Choi [43] has become the most popular IDA (Index Decomposition Analysis) methodology in the last decade among researchers [44]. The reasons are clear: its theoretical and practical advantages (demonstrated by Ang et al. [45]) make it superior to other alternatives. LMDI is an exhaustive (or refined) decomposition method, which ensures decompositions with identically null residual terms. The LMDI can be expressed as an extended Kaya identity, which was first proposed by Kaya [46]. Assume that V is an aggregate composed of n factors (x1, ... , xn), i.e., $V = \sum_i V_i$ and $V_i = x_{1,i} x_{2,i} \cdots x_{n,i}$ Further assume that from period 0 to T the aggregate changes from V^0 to V^T. The objective is to derive the contributions of the n factors to the change in the aggregate which can be expressed as [47]:

Additive form

$$\Delta V_{tot} = V^T - V^0 = \Delta V_{x1} + \Delta V_{x2} + \cdots + \Delta V_{xn} \tag{4}$$

Multiplicative form

$$D_{tot} = V^T / V^0 = D_{x1} D_{x2} \cdots D_{xn} \tag{5}$$

General Formulae of LMDI

$$\Delta V_{xk} = \sum_i L(V_i^T, V_i^0) \ln \left(\frac{x_{k,i}^T}{x_{k,i}^0} \right) \tag{6}$$

$$D_{xk} = \exp \left(\sum_i \frac{L(V_i^T, V_i^0)}{L(V^T, V^0)} \ln \left(\frac{x_{k,i}^T}{x_{k,i}^0} \right) \right) \tag{7}$$

where $L(a,b) = (a - b)/(\ln a - \ln b)$ is the logarithmic mean of a and b, and $L(a,b) = a$ Because Additive form is easy to understand and calculate, this article uses this form. The extended Kaya identity and LMDI is combined shown in the following formula:

$$C_t = C_{dir} + C_{ind} = \sum \frac{C_{it}}{E_{it}} \times \frac{E_{it}}{E_t} \times \frac{E_t}{Q_t} \times Q_t + \frac{C_{ind}}{Q_t} \times Q_t = \sum F_{it} \times S_{it} \times I_t \times Q_t + P_t \times Q_t \tag{8}$$

In this expression, we define the following variables, where

C_t represents the carbon emissions in the t year, the subscript i represents energy type; the superscript t represents year;

C_{it} is the carbon emissions from the i-th energy in the t year;

E_{it} is the consumption of the i-th energy in the t year;

E_t is total energy consumption in the t year;

Q_t is the economical outputs of building industry;

$F_{it} = \frac{C_{it}}{E_{it}}$ denotes the carbon coefficient of i-th energy;

$S_{it} = \frac{E_{it}}{E_t}$ illustrates the energy structure effect of i-th energy;

$I_t = \frac{E_t}{Q_t}$ represents energy intensity; and

$P_t = \frac{C_{ind}}{Q_t}$ is the effects of intensity of indirect carbon emission.

According to the LMDI method, the change of carbon consumption between a base year 0 and a target year t, is denoted by ΔC, and we use the additive decomposition to make further decomposition of Equation (8) to get the following formula:

$$\Delta C_t = C_t - C_0 = \Delta C_{Ft} + \Delta C_{St} + \Delta C_{It} + \Delta C_{Qt} + \Delta C_{Pt} \tag{9}$$

In this expression, we can consider the F_{it} is basically unchanged, so ΔC_{Ft} is 0. Thus, ΔC can be decomposed into the following determinant factors:

$$\Delta C_t = C_t - C_0 = \Delta C_{St} + \Delta C_{It} + \Delta C_{Qt} + \Delta C_{Pt} \tag{10}$$

where ΔC refers to the total changes in carbon emissions, which can be further decomposed into the following indictors: ΔC_{St} (the effect of energy structure: changes in the amount of CO_2 emissions caused by changes in the proportion of nine energy consumption in total energy consumption), ΔC_{It} (the effect of energy intensity: changes in the amount of CO_2 emissions caused by changes in the proportion of total energy consumption in the gross industrial output value), ΔC_{Qt} (the effect of industrial scale: changes in the amount of CO_2 emissions caused by changes in gross output value of construction industry;), and ΔC_{Pt} (the effect of indirect carbon emission intensity: changes in the amount of CO_2 emissions caused by the changes in the proportion of indirect carbon emissions and gross industrial output value). Equations (11)–(17) are used to calculate the changes in the amount of CO_2 emissions caused by the change of the factors of decomposition; based on the LMDI method, ΔC_{St}, ΔC_{It}, ΔC_{Qt}, ΔC_{Pt} can be expressed as follows:

$$\Delta C_{St} = \sum_{i=1}^{9} (w_{it}) \ln \frac{S_{it}}{S_{io}} \tag{11}$$

$$\Delta C_{It} = w_t \ln \frac{I_t}{I_o} \tag{12}$$

$$\Delta C_{Qt} = w_t \ln \frac{Q_t}{Q_o} + w_{ind} \ln \frac{Q_t}{Q_o} \tag{13}$$

$$\Delta C_{Pt} = w_{ind} \ln \frac{P_t}{P_o} \tag{14}$$

$$w_{it} = \frac{C_{it} - C_{io}}{\ln C_{it} - \ln C_{io}} \tag{15}$$

$$w_t = \frac{C_t - C_o}{\ln C_t - \ln C_o} \tag{16}$$

$$w_{ind} = \frac{C_{indt} - C_{indo}}{\ln C_{indt} - \ln C_{indo}} \qquad (17)$$

2.1.3. Decoupling Elasticity Model

The decoupling model is proposed by the Tapio model, which has been developed the OECD decoupling model, which has been widely used to analyze the relationship between economic growth and carbon emission [48,49]. In this paper, based on the additive decomposition results of CO_2 emission changes [50], the decoupling elasticity e can be formulated as follows:

$$e_{(C,GDP)} = \frac{\%C}{\%GDP} = \frac{\Delta C/C}{\Delta GDP/GDP} \qquad (18)$$

In this expression, e is the decoupling elasticity, %C is the percent change in carbon emissions, and %GDP is the percent change of economic output of building industry. Carbon emission is the carbon emission of construction for the current year, Δcarbon is the variation of carbon emission at the current time compared with the base period, GDP is the economic output of building industry in the current year, and ΔGDP is the variation of economic output of building industry at the current time compared with the base period. According to the values of e, there are eight logical possibilities [51,52], including weak decoupling, expansive decoupling, expansive negative decoupling, strong negative decoupling, weak negative decoupling, recessive coupling, recessive decoupling, and strong decoupling.

2.1.4. Decoupling Effort Index

In this paper, we identify the factors contributing to carbon emission of building industry in China using the Kaya identity and LMDI techniques; however, they cannot specifically and objectively measure the actual effects of energy conservation and pollution reduction efforts on CO_2 emissions. Effort is a general term referring to the actions that decrease the carbon emissions, both directly and indirectly, such as reducing energy intensity, improving energy efficiency, as well as optimizing the energy structure and excluding the expansion of economical outputs [53]. Thus, the effort in absolute terms or absolute effort during the period starting from the base year 0 to year t can be represented as the sum of the three factors identified [54]:

$$\Delta C_{ut} = \Delta C_t - \Delta C_{Qt} = \Delta C_{St} + \Delta C_{It} + \Delta C_{Pt} \qquad (19)$$

The decoupling effect index D from a base year 0 to a target year t takes the following values and is evaluated according to the standards below [54]:

$$D_t = -\frac{\Delta C_{ut}}{\Delta C_{Qt}} = -\left(\frac{\Delta C_{St}}{\Delta C_{Qt}} + \frac{\Delta C_{It}}{\Delta C_{Qt}} + \frac{\Delta C_{Pt}}{\Delta C_{Qt}} \right) = -(DS_t + DI_t + DP_t) \qquad (20)$$

$D_t \leq 0$, denotes no decoupling effort, carbon emissions increase faster than economic outputs because of inefficient emission reduction efforts [55]. $0 < D_t < 1$ denotes weak decoupling effort, the efforts of carbon emission reduction have only compensated for a small part of the carbon emissions from economic outputs growth. $D_t \geq 1$ denotes strong decoupling effort, the emission reduction achieved through various efforts was three or two times higher than the carbon emission increase.

2.2. Data Sources and Definition

The data of economic output and energy consumption in China's building industry are from China Energy Statistical Yearbook for the different sectors [56–58]. The unit of economic output is RMB (Yuan) at constant price of 2005. The unit of energy consumption is ton of coal equivalent (tce). The data of consumption of building materials and building industry output data are from China Statistical Yearbook on Construction [59–61]. The default value of carbon content, carbon oxidation rate, average lower heating value, and carbon coefficient for different kinds of energy are shown in

Tables 3 and 4, based on the GHG Protocol Tool for Energy Consumption in China [62]. It should be noted that the carbon coefficients of power sector vary due to the china's energy structure for power generation varying every year. The default value of the ratio of thermal power (%), the ratio of other (water, nuclear, and wind) (%), consumption standard of power and carbon coefficient is represented in Table 4 [17,63]. Carbon emission coefficients of building materials are shown in Table 5, according to the reference [64,65].

3. Result and Analysis

3.1. Estimation of CO_2 Emissions from China's Building Industry

Based on previous studies [17,29,37–40], carbon emissions from the building industry should include two parts: one is direct carbon emission from direct fossil fuel combustion in building industry and the other is indirect carbon from building material consumption.

3.1.1. Estimated Direct Carbon Emission

Using Equation (2) and carbon emission coefficients shown in Tables 3 and 4, we computed the direct carbon emission of China's building industry (see Figure 1). Total direct carbon emission of China's building industry increased from 32.06 million tons of CO_2 in 2005 to 50.12 million tons of CO_2 in 2013. The compound annual growth rate of direct carbon emission in China's industry was 5.74% during 2005–2013.

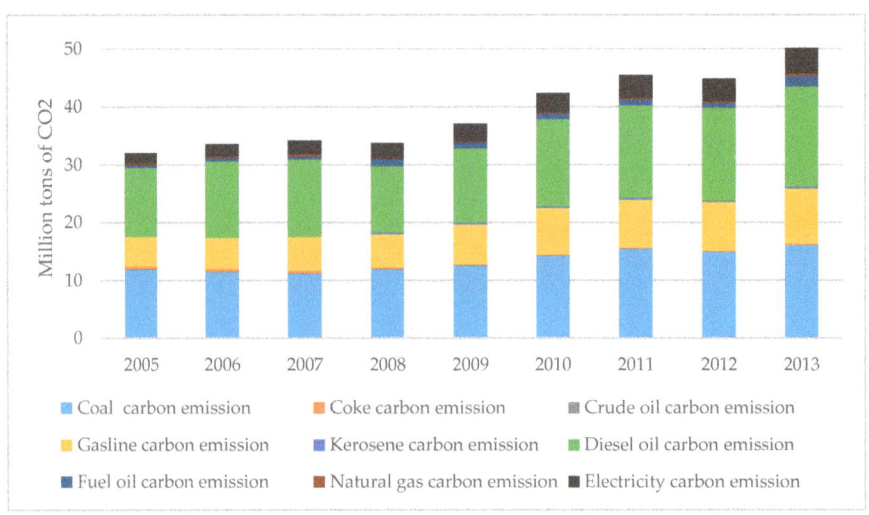

Figure 1. Direct carbon emission of China's building industry 2005–2013.

As shown in Figure 1, the direct carbon emission includes carbon emission from eight type of fuels (coal, coke, crude oil, fuel oil, gasoline, kerosene, diesel oil and natural gas) and electricity of building industry. The main sources of direct carbon emission in China's building industry are diesel oil coal, gasoline, and electricity. In 2005, burning diesel oil, coal, gasoline, and electricity consumption contributions to total direct carbon emission in China's building industry were 37.34%, 37.29%, 15.70% and 5.62%, respectively. In 2013, burning diesel oil, coal, gasoline, electricity consumption contributions to total direct carbon emission in China's building industry were 34.41%, 32.07%, 19.05% and 8.72%, respectively. Thus, burning diesel oil is the biggest source of direct carbon emission in China's building industry, followed by coal, gasoline, and electricity between 2005 and 2013.

3.1.2. Estimated Indirect Carbon Emission

Using Equation (3) and carbon emission coefficients shown in Table 5, we calculated the indirect carbon emission of China's building industry (see Figure 2). Total direct carbon emission of China's building industry increased from 86.61 million tons of CO_2 to 370.37 million tons of CO_2 between 2005 and 2013. The compound annual growth rate of direct carbon emission was 18.50% for this period. It should be noted that direct carbon emission was not always rising. Instead, direct carbon emission decreased from 518.56 million tons of CO_2 in 2012 to 370.37 million tons of CO_2 in 2013.

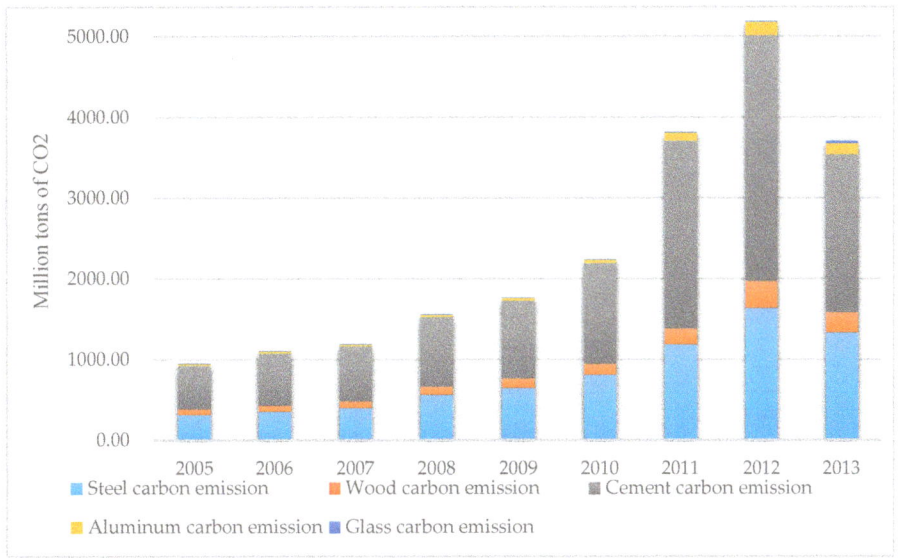

Figure 2. Indirect carbon emission of China's building industry 2005–2013.

The indirect carbon emission includes five types of building materials: cement, steel, wood, aluminum and glass. As shown in Figure 2, the dominant source of indirect carbon emission in China's building industry is the carbon emission from cement. Because the consumption of building materials is large and their carbon emission coefficient is high, the proportion of indirect carbon emissions is large.

In 2005, carbon emission from cement, steel, wood, aluminum and glass consumption produced 56.64%, 33.69%, 7.08%, 2.36% and 0.24% of total indirect carbon emission in China's building industry, respectively. In 2013, carbon emission from cement, steel, wood, aluminum and glass consumption contributed to total direct carbon emission in China's building industry were 52.80%, 35.91%, 6.86%, 3.62%, and 0.81%, respectively.

3.1.3. Estimated Total Carbon Emission

Total carbon emission in China's building industry was calculated using Equation (3). As shown in Figure 3, total carbon emission in China's building industry increased from 984.69 million tons of CO_2 in 2005 to 3753.83 million tons of CO_2 in 2013. The compound annual growth rate of total carbon emission was 18.21%, which was close to the compound annual growth rate of direct carbon emissions. The overwhelming dominant source of total carbon emission was indirect carbon emission, which accounted for 96–99% of total carbon emission from China's building industry during 2005–2013.

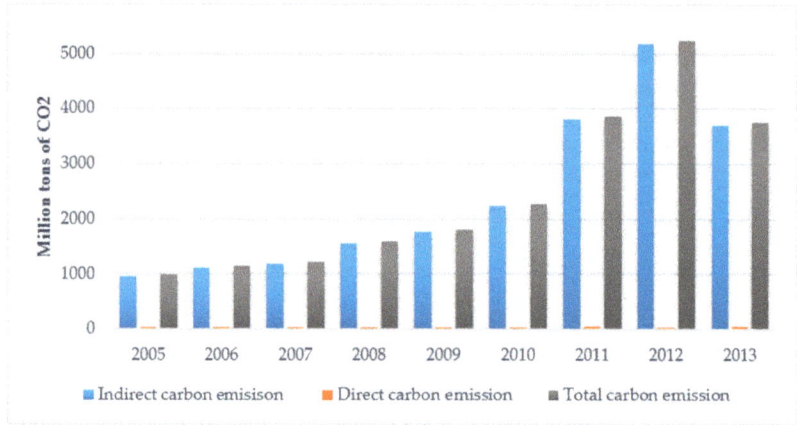

Figure 3. Direct, indirect and total carbon emission from China's building industry between 2005 and 2013.

3.2. Decomposition Analysis

Inspired by earlier studies [66–75], the total changes in carbon emissions ΔC is decomposed into the four indictors: ΔC_{St} (the effect of energy structure), ΔC_{It} (the effect of energy intensity), ΔC_{Qt} (the effect of industrial scale), and ΔC_{Pt} (the effect of indirect carbon emission intensity). Using Equations (11)–(17), we qualify effects of energy structure, energy intensity, economy, and indirect emission on change in total carbon emission from China's building industry between 2005 and 2013. The results are shown in Figure 4.

3.2.1. Economic Effects

As shown in Figure 4, economic effects (economic output from building industry) were the biggest contributor to the increase in carbon emission. During 2005–2013, economic effect contributed to increase carbon emission by 71.22%. Economic effects have always taken a positive role in increasing carbon emission. However, it should also be noted that economic effects became the second biggest contributor after indirect emission intensity since 2009.

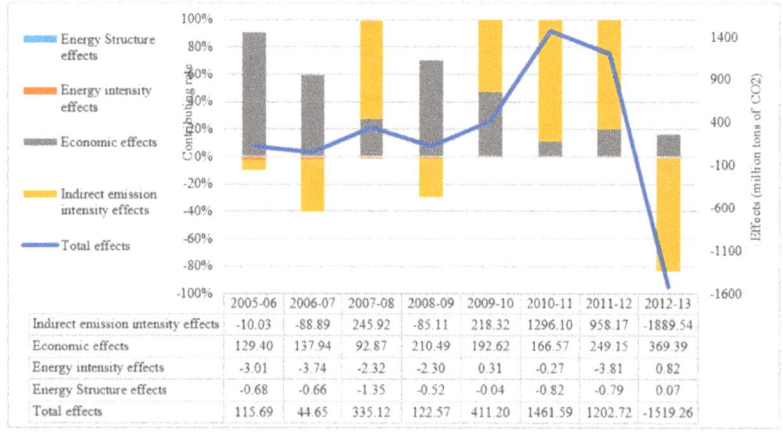

	2005-06	2006-07	2007-08	2008-09	2009-10	2010-11	2011-12	2012-13
Indirect emission intensity effects	-10.03	-88.89	245.92	-85.11	218.32	1296.10	958.17	-1889.54
Economic effects	129.40	137.94	92.87	210.49	192.62	166.57	249.15	369.39
Energy intensity effects	-3.01	-3.74	-2.32	-2.30	0.31	-0.27	-3.81	0.82
Energy Structure effects	-0.68	-0.66	-1.35	-0.52	-0.04	-0.82	-0.79	0.07
Total effects	115.69	44.65	335.12	122.57	411.20	1461.59	1202.72	-1519.26

Figure 4. Decomposition of carbon emission of building industry 2005–2013 unit: (million tons of CO_2).

3.2.2. Indirect Emission Intensity Effects

Generally, indirect emission intensity (indirect carbon emission economic output of building industry) effects are the second contributor to increase in total carbon emission of China's building industry. From 2005 to 2013, the accumulated contributing rate of indirect emission effects to increase total carbon emission reached 29.66%. However, the contribution from indirect emission intensity was not always positive. Indeed, indirect emission intensity effects offset the increase in carbon emission during 2005–2008, 2009–2010, and 2012–2013. During 2010–2012, indirect emission intensity offset became the leading contributor to increase in carbon emission. The change of indirect emission intensity effects might be related to the massive RMB 4 trillion (~US$0.6 trillion) infrastructure plan, which was proposed to deal with the 2008 global finance crisis in November 2008. Such rapid large-scale infrastructure investment might lead to inefficient material consumption. Indirect carbon emission intensity (indirect carbon emission per unit of GDP) increased from 0.96 $kgCO_2$/Yuan in 2009 to 1.07 kg CO_2/Yuan in 2010, to 1.66 kg CO_2/Yuan in 2011, and further to 2.05 kg CO_2/Yuan in 2012. Fortunately, the indirect carbon emission intensity decreased to 1.34 kg CO_2/Yuan in 2013. The indirect carbon emission intensity was reversed to leading contributor to offset the increase in carbon emission between 2012 and 2013.

3.2.3. Energy Intensity Effects and Energy Structure Effects

Both energy intensity effects and energy structure effects contributed to offset carbon emission. The accumulated contributing rate of energy intensity effects and energy structure effects to increase in carbon emission from 2005 to 2013 were −0.66% and −0.22%, respectively. This is closely related to the energy consumption structure in China's building industry. Coal and oil were the overwhelming dominant sources of energy consumption in China's building industry, whereas clean energy remained a smaller proportion. Given the energy consumption structure has not changed, the energy structure effects and energy intensity effects were minimal.

3.3. Decoupling Analysis

Based on former studies [49,54,76–87], we develop decoupling elasticity model and decoupling efforts model. Using Equations (18)–(20), we calculated the decoupling elasticity and decoupling efforts index. As illustrated in Figure 5, the growth rate of carbon emission and economical outputs, and the decoupling elasticity values of economic outputs are positive during the whole period. The values of Decoupling elasticity (e) is less than 0.8 in 2006 and 2008; the e is between 0.8 and 1.2 in 2007 and 2010; and the e is more than 1.2 in 2009 and 2011–2013. Consequently, the economic outputs decoupling states exhibit weak decoupling in 2006 as well as 2008, expansive decoupling in 2007 as well as 2010, and turn into expansive negative decoupling in 2009 and during 2011–2013. That means the growth rate of carbon emission is slower than the growth rate of economical outputs in 2006, 2008 and 2010, however, the growth rate of carbon emission is faster than the growth rate of economical outputs in 2007, 2009 and during 2011–2013, which is mainly attributed to the economy increase in China mainly depending on the infrastructure. The 2008–2009 Chinese economic stimulus plan is a US$586 billion stimulus package announced by the State Council of the People's Republic of China as an attempt to minimize the impact of the global financial crisis; in addition, China has experienced urbanization and industrialization. Its urbanization and industrialization has been accelerated in the past decade. The accelerating urbanization and industrialization led to booming of building industry, which means more energy were consumed and more building materials were used. Especially the indirect carbon emission from the building materials is the leading contributor of carbon emission, which is consistent with the estimated indirect carbon emission analysis.

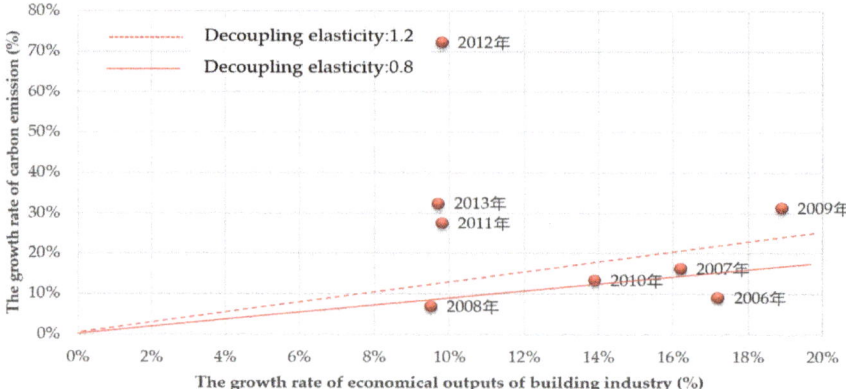

Figure 5. The change of decoupling elasticity of carbon emissions during 2006–2013.

We can see in Figure 6 that the change of decoupling effort indexes is consistent with the change of decoupling elasticity of carbon emissions. In addition, it is concluded that the reducing of intensity of indirect carbon emissions is a key factor in decoupling from the construction industry, however, the efforts of the energy structure effect and energy intensity are rarely small, which indicates the current status of unreasonable energy structure and energy intensive industry, and the energy supply is still dominated by high-carbon energy supply when the demand of energy is increasing while the supply of clean low-carbon energy supply cannot keep up with the economic development.

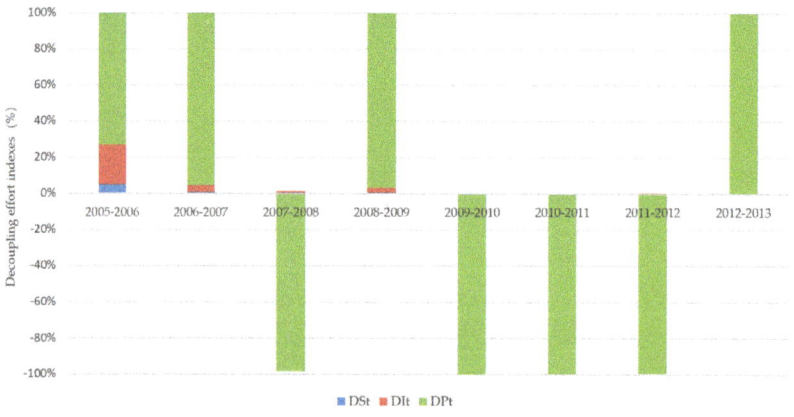

Figure 6. The change of decoupling effort indexes during 2006–2013.

4. Conclusions and Policy Implication

4.1. Conclusions

In this paper, we calculated the direct and indirect carbon emission in China's building industry from 2005 to 2013, then analyzed the drivers of carbon emission in China's building industry, and finally estimated the decoupling status of China's building industry. The main conclusions are as follows.

Using data of energy consumption and materials in China's building industry from China's official statistics, and carbon emission coefficient from IPCC, we calculated that the total carbon emission in China's building industry increased from 984.69 million tons of CO_2 in 2005 to 3753.98 million tons of CO_2 in 2013. The average annual growth rate is 18.21% per year. Indirect carbon emission from building material consumption accounted for 96–99% of total carbon emission.

Using LMDI technique, we qualify the four key influencing factors for carbon emission in China's building industry. The indirect emission intensity effect was leading contributor to change of carbon emission. It was followed by economic output effects, which always contributed to increase carbon emission. Energy intensity effect and energy structure effect took a negligible role to offset carbon emission.

The status between carbon emission and economic output in China's building industry during 2005–2006 and during 2007–2008 was weak decoupling; during 2006–2007 and during 2008–2010 was expansive decoupling; and during 2010–2013 was expansive negative decoupling. Indirect carbon intensity decoupling index was a leading contributor to the total decoupling index in China's building industry. It was followed by the energy structure and energy intensity decoupling index.

4.2. Policy Implication

Based on the above analysis, three policy recommendations are offered to decouple China's building industry from carbon emission (Figure 7).

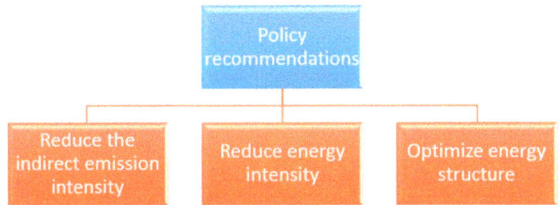

Figure 7. The suggestions based on the data analysis.

(1) Reducing the indirect emission intensity: Above all, the reduction of indirect emission intensity is a key to delinking economic output from carbon emission, given that indirect emission is the overwhelming dominant source of carbon emission in China's building industry. The measures to reduction of indirect emission intensity include, but are not limited to: (i) development of new building materials to reduce the consumption of traditional building materials, such as cement, steel, and aluminum; (ii) improving energy efficiency to lower carbon intensity of traditional building materials; and (iii) phasing out the low energy efficient building materials as soon as possible.

(2) Reducing energy intensity: As shown in our study, energy intensity effects were leading contributor to offset carbon emission in China's building industry. Improving energy efficiency is a cost-effective approach to decouple between economic output and carbon in China's building industry. The government should introduce policies and establish financial support systems to promote the development of low-carbon technologies, and encourage construction companies to adopt low-carbon construction technology to optimize building design, thereby improving energy efficiency and improving the suppression effect of energy intensity on carbon emission.

(3) Optimizing energy structure: We can fully develop the use of hydropower, wind energy, solar energy and other clean energy, reduce dependence on high-carbon energy, and establish a sound energy-saving emission reduction standard building system.

Acknowledgments: The current work is supported by "the Fundamental Research Funds for the Central Universities (27R1706019B)" and the Recruitment Talent Fund of China University of Petroleum (Huadong) (05Y16060020). We have received grants in support of our research work. The funds we have received covered the costs to publish in open access.

Author Contributions: Rui Jiang performed the experiments, analyzed the data, and contributed reagents/materials/analysis tools. Rongrong Li conceived and designed the experiments and wrote the paper. All authors read and approved the final manuscript.

Conflicts of Interest: The authors declare no conflict of interest.

References

1. National Bureau of Statistics of China. *National Economical Industry Classification*; China Statistics Press: Beijing, China, 2013; p. 2012. (In Chinese)
2. Allen, S.K.; Plattner, G.K.; Nauels, A.; Xia, Y.; Stocker, T.F. Climate Change 2013: The Physical Science Basis. In An Overview of the Working Group 1 Contribution to the Fifth Assessment Report of the Intergovernmental Panel on Climate Change (IPCC). 2014. Available online: http://www.ipcc.ch/report/ar5/wg1/ (accessed on 8 May 2017).
3. United Nations Environment Programme. *Buildings and Climate Change*; United Nations Environment Programme Sustainable Buildings & Climate Initiative: Paris, France, 2009.
4. Berardi, U. A cross-country comparison of the building energy consumptions and their trends. *Resour. Conserv. Recycl.* **2017**. [CrossRef]
5. Cubi, E.; Doluweera, G.; Bergerson, J. Incorporation of electricity GHG emissions intensity variability into building environmental assessment. *Appl. Energy* **2015**, *159*, 62–69. [CrossRef]
6. Herrera, J.C.; Chamorro, C.R.; Martín, M.C. Experimental analysis of performance, greenhouse gas emissions and economic parameters for two cooling systems in a public administration building. *Energy Build.* **2015**, *108*, 145–155. [CrossRef]
7. Chau, C.K.; Hui, W.K.; Ng, W.Y.; Powell, G. Assessment of CO_2 emissions reduction in high-rise concrete office buildings using different material use options. *Resour. Conserv. Recycl.* **2012**, *61*, 22–34. [CrossRef]
8. Wang, Q.; Li, R. Journey to burning half of global coal: Trajectory and drivers of China's coal use. *Renew. Sustain. Energy Rev.* **2016**, *58*, 341–346. [CrossRef]
9. Zhang, X.; Wang, F. Life-cycle assessment and control measures for carbon emissions of typical buildings in China. *Building Environ.* **2015**, *86*, 89–97. [CrossRef]
10. Wang, Q. China has the capacity to lead in carbon trading. *Nature* **2013**, *493*, 273. [CrossRef] [PubMed]
11. Wang, X.-R.; Hui, E.C.-M.; Choguill, C.; Jia, S.-H. The new urbanization policy in China: Which way forward? *Habitat Int.* **2015**, *47*, 279–284. [CrossRef]
12. Chauvin, J.P.; Glaeser, E.; Ma, Y.; Tobio, K. What is Different about Urbanization in Rich and Poor Countries? Cities in Brazil, China, India and the United States. *J. Urb. Econ.* **2016**. [CrossRef]
13. Wang, Q. China should aim for a total cap on emissions. *Nature* **2014**, *512*, 115. [CrossRef] [PubMed]
14. Chmutina, K. Building energy consumption and its regulations in China. In *China Policy Institute, School of Contemporary Chinese Studies, International House*; The University of Nottingham: Nottingham, UK, 2010.
15. Yu, S.; Evans, M.; Delgado, A. Building Energy Efficiency in India: Compliance Evaluation of Energy Conservation Building Code. *Curr. Politics Econ. North. West. Asia* **2015**, *24*, 119.
16. Salvalai, G.; Masera, G.; Sesana, M.M. Italian local codes for energy efficiency of buildings: Theoretical definition and experimental application to a residential case study. *Renew. Sustain. Energy Rev.* **2015**, *42*, 1245–1259. [CrossRef]
17. Wang, Q.; Chen, X. Energy policies for managing China's carbon emission. *Renew. Sustain. Energy Rev.* **2015**, *50*, 470–479. [CrossRef]
18. Qiang, W.; Li, R.; Hua, L. Toward Decoupling: Growing GDP without Growing Carbon Emissions. *Environ. Sci. Technol.* **2016**, *50*, 11435.
19. Dodman, D. Blaming cities for climate change? An analysis of urban greenhouse gas emissions inventories. *Environ. Urban.* **2009**, *21*, 185–201. [CrossRef]
20. Wang, Q.; Li, R. Impact of cheaper oil on economic system and climate change: A SWOT analysis. *Renew. Sustain. Energy Rev.* **2016**, *54*, 925–931. [CrossRef]
21. Wang, Q.; Li, R. Drivers for energy consumption: A comparative analysis of China and India. *Renew. Sustain. Energy Rev.* **2016**, *62*, 954–962. [CrossRef]
22. Acquaye, A.A.; Duffy, A.P. Input–output analysis of Irish construction sector greenhouse gas emissions. *Build. Environ.* **2010**, *45*, 784–791. [CrossRef]

23. Nässén, J.; Holmberg, J.; Wadeskog, A.; Nyman, M. Direct and indirect energy use and carbon emissions in the production phase of buildings: An input–output analysis. *Energy* **2007**, *32*, 1593–1602. [CrossRef]

24. Buchanan, A.H.; Honey, B.G. Energy and carbon dioxide implications of building construction. *Energy Build.* **1994**, *20*, 205–217. [CrossRef]

25. Ali, H.H.; Al Nsairat, S.F. Developing a green building assessment tool for developing countries—Case of Jordan. *Build. Environ.* **2009**, *44*, 1053–1064. [CrossRef]

26. Wang, Q.; Chen, X.; Jha, A.N.; Rogers, H. Natural gas from shale formation—The evolution, evidences and challenges of shale gas revolution in United States. *Renew. Sustain. Energy Rev.* **2014**, *30*, 1–28. [CrossRef]

27. Wang, Q.; Li, R. Sino-Venezuelan oil-for-loan deal–the Chinese strategic gamble? *Renew. Sustain. Energy Rev.* **2016**, *64*, 817–822. [CrossRef]

28. Rodríguez Serrano, A.; Porras Álvarez, S. Life Cycle Assessment in Building: A Case Study on the Energy and Emissions Impact Related to the Choice of Housing Typologies and Construction Process in Spain. *Sustainability* **2016**, *8*, 287. [CrossRef]

29. Zabalza, I.; Scarpellini, S.; Aranda, A.; Llera, E.; Jáñez, A. Use of LCA as a tool for building ecodesign: A case study of a low energy building in Spain. *Energies* **2013**, *6*, 3901–3921. [CrossRef]

30. Wang, Q.; Li, R.; Jiang, R. Decoupling and Decomposition Analysis of Carbon Emissions from Industry: A Case Study from China. *Sustainability* **2016**, *8*, 1059. [CrossRef]

31. Wang, Q. Effective policies for renewable energy—The example of China's wind power—Lessons for China's photovoltaic power. *Renew. Sustain. Energy Rev.* **2010**, *14*, 702–712. [CrossRef]

32. Han, M.; Chen, G.; Shao, L.; Li, J.; Alsaedi, A.; Ahmad, B.; Guo, S.; Jiang, M.; Ji, X. Embodied energy consumption of building construction engineering: Case study in E-town, Beijing. *Energy Build.* **2013**, *64*, 62–72. [CrossRef]

33. Zhang, X.; Shen, L.; Zhang, L. Life cycle assessment of the air emissions during building construction process: A case study in Hong Kong. *Renew. Sustain. Energy Rev.* **2013**, *17*, 160–169. [CrossRef]

34. Wang, Q.; Li, R. Natural gas from shale formation: A research profile. *Renew. Sustain. Energy Rev.* **2016**, *57*, 1–6. [CrossRef]

35. Duranton, G. Growing through cities in developing countries. *World Bank Res. Obs.* **2015**, *30*, 39–73. [CrossRef]

36. Evans, M.; Shui, B.; Halverson, M.; Delgado, A. Enforcing Building Energy Codes in China: Progress and Comparative Lessons. Available online: http://www.pnl.gov/main/publications/external/technical_reports/PNNL-19247.pdf (accessed on 8 May 2017).

37. Ortiz, O.; Castells, F.; Sonnemann, G. Sustainability in the construction industry: A review of recent developments based on LCA. *Constr. Build. Mater.* **2009**, *23*, 28–39. [CrossRef]

38. Hammond, G.P.; Jones, C.I. Embodied energy and carbon in construction materials. *Proc. Inst. Civ. Eng. Energy* **2008**, *161*, 87–98. [CrossRef]

39. Cabeza, L.F.; Barreneche, C.; Miró, L.; Morera, J.M.; Bartolí, E.; Fernández, A.I. Low carbon and low embodied energy materials in buildings: A review. *Renew. Sustain. Energy Rev.* **2013**, *23*, 536–542. [CrossRef]

40. Cabeza, L.F.; Rincón, L.; Vilariño, V.; Pérez, G.; Castell, A. Life cycle assessment (LCA) and life cycle energy analysis (LCEA) of buildings and the building sector: A review. *Renew. Sustain. Energy Rev.* **2014**, *29*, 394–416. [CrossRef]

41. Zhang, Z.H.; Liu, R.J. Carbon Emissions in the Construction Sector Based on Input-Output Analyses. Available online: http://en.cnki.com.cn/Article_en/CJFDTOTAL-QHXB201301010.htm (accessed on 8 May 2017).

42. Li, Z. Study on the Life Cycle Consumption of Energy and Resource of Air Conditioning in Urban Residential Buildings in China. Available online: http://www.globethesis.com/?t=1102360272977717 (accessed on 8 May 2017).

43. Ang, B.; Choi, K.-H. Decomposition of aggregate energy and gas emission intensities for industry: A refined Divisia index method. *Energy J.* **1997**, *18*, 59–73. [CrossRef]

44. González, P.F.; Landajo, M.; Presno, M. Tracking European Union CO_2 emissions through LMDI (logarithmic-mean Divisia index) decomposition. The activity revaluation approach. *Energy* **2014**, *73*, 741–750. [CrossRef]

45. Ang, B.W.; Zhang, F.Q.; Choi, K.H. Factorizing changes in energy and environmental indicators through decomposition. *Energy* **1998**, *23*, 489–495. [CrossRef]

46. Kaya, Y. Impact of Carbon Dioxide Emission Control on GNP Growth: Interpretation of Proposed Scenarios. Available online: http://www.ipcc.ch/ipccreports/sres/emission/index.php?idp=48 (accessed on 8 May 2017).

47. Ang, B.W. The LMDI approach to decomposition analysis: A practical guide. *Energy Policy* **2005**, *33*, 867–871. [CrossRef]

48. Gray, D.; Anable, J.; Illingworth, L.; Graham, W. Decoupling the Link between Economic Growth, Transport Growth and Carbon Emissions in Scotland. Available online: https://www.researchgate.net/publication/267221393 (accessed on 8 May 2017).

49. Tapio, P. Towards a theory of decoupling: Degrees of decoupling in the EU and the case of road traffic in Finland between 1970 and 2001. *Transp. Policy* **2005**, *12*, 137–151. [CrossRef]

50. Zhao, J.; Shi-Ping, H.E. Research on the Vibration Characteristics of Simply Supported Plate Covered by a Decoupling Layer and Immersed in Water. Available online: http://en.cnki.com.cn/Article_en/CJFDTOTAL-JCKX201302005.htm (accessed on 8 May 2017).

51. Arrow, K.; Bolin, B.; Costanza, R.; Dasgupta, P. Economic growth, carrying capacity, and the environment. *Science* **1995**, *268*, 520. [CrossRef] [PubMed]

52. De Bruyn, S.M.; van den Bergh, J.C.; Opschoor, J.B. Economic growth and emissions: Reconsidering the empirical basis of environmental Kuznets curves. *Ecol. Econ.* **1998**, *25*, 161–175. [CrossRef]

53. Lu, Q.; Yang, H.; Huang, X.; Chuai, X.; Wu, C. Multi-sectoral decomposition in decoupling industrial growth from carbon emissions in the developed Jiangsu Province, China. *Energy* **2015**, *82*, 414–425. [CrossRef]

54. Diakoulaki, D.; Mandaraka, M. Decomposition analysis for assessing the progress in decoupling industrial growth from CO_2 emissions in the EU manufacturing sector. *Energy Econ.* **2007**, *29*, 636–664. [CrossRef]

55. Wang, Z.; Yang, L. Delinking indicators on regional industry development and carbon emissions: Beijing–Tianjin–Hebei economic band case. *Ecol. Indic.* **2015**, *48*, 41–48. [CrossRef]

56. China Statistics Press. *China Energy Statistical Yearbook*; China Statistics Press: Beijing, China, 2005. (In Chinese)

57. China Statistics Press. *China Energy Statistical Yearbook*; China Statistics Press: Beijing, China, 2010. (In Chinese)

58. China Statistics Press. *China Energy Statistical Yearbook*; China Statistics Press: Beijing, China, 2013. (In Chinese)

59. China Statistics Press. *China Statistical Yearbook on Construction*; China Statistics Press: Beijing, China, 2005. (In Chinese)

60. China Statistics Press. *China Statistical Yearbook on Construction*; China Statistics Press: Beijing, China, 2010. (In Chinese)

61. China Statistics Press. *China Statistical Yearbook on Construction*; China Statistics Press: Beijing, China, 2013. (In Chinese)

62. United States Agency for International Development. GHG Protocol Tool For Energy Consumption in China. 2013. Available online: http://www.ghgprotocol.org/calculation-tools/all-tools/ (accessed on 8 May 2017).

63. HE Ai-zhong, L.P. Factor decomposition and decoupling analysis on CO_2 emissions: Evidence from China's circulation sector. *China Environ. Sci.* **2015**, *35*, 953–960.

64. Fan, Y.; Liu, L.-C.; Wu, G.; Tsai, H.-T.; Wei, Y.-M. Changes in carbon intensity in China: Empirical findings from 1980–2003. *Ecol. Econ.* **2007**, *62*, 683–691. [CrossRef]

65. Feng, B.; Wang, X.Q. Research on Carbon Decoupling Effect and Influence Factors of Provincial Construction Industry in China. *China Popul. Resour. Environ.* **2015**, *25*, 28–34.

66. Ren, S.; Yin, H.; Chen, X.H. Using LMDI to analyze the decoupling of carbon dioxide emissions by China's manufacturing industry. *Environ. Dev.* **2013**, *9*, 61–75. [CrossRef]

67. Voigt, S.; Cian, E.D.; Schymura, M.; Verdolini, E. Energy intensity developments in 40 major economies: Structural change or technology improvement? *Energy Econ.* **2014**, *41*, 47–62. [CrossRef]

68. Xu, S.C.; He, Z.X.; Long, R.Y. Factors that influence carbon emissions due to energy consumption in China: Decomposition analysis using LMDI. *Appl. Energy* **2014**, *127*, 182–193. [CrossRef]

69. Ang, B.W. LMDI decomposition approach: A guide for implementation. *Energy Policy* **2015**, *86*, 233–238. [CrossRef]

70. Wang, Q. China's citizens must act to save their environment. *Nature* **2013**, *497*, 159. [CrossRef] [PubMed]

71. Wang, Q.; Chen, X.; Yi-Chong, X. Accident like the Fukushima unlikely in a country with effective nuclear regulation: Literature review and proposed guidelines. *Renew. Sustain. Energy Rev.* **2013**, *17*, 126–146. [CrossRef]

72. Wang, Q.; Chen, X. Rethinking and reshaping the climate policy: Literature review and proposed guidelines. *Renew. Sustain. Energy Rev.* **2013**, *21*, 469–477. [CrossRef]

73. Raupach, M.R.; Marland, G.; Ciais, P.; Le, Q.C.; Canadell, J.G.; Klepper, G.; Field, C.B. Global and regional drivers of accelerating CO_2 emissions. *Proc. Natl. Acad. Sci. USA* **2007**, *104*, 10288–10293. [CrossRef] [PubMed]

74. Wang, Q. Time for commercializing non-food biofuel in China. *Renew. Sustain. Energy Rev.* **2011**, *15*, 621–629. [CrossRef]

75. Wang, Q. China needing a cautious approach to nuclear power strategy. *Energy Policy* **2009**, *37*, 2487–2491. [CrossRef]

76. Wang, Q.; Chen, X. China's electricity market-oriented reform: From an absolute to a relative monopoly. *Energy Policy* **2012**, *51*, 143–148. [CrossRef]

77. Wang, Q.; Chen, X. Regulatory failures for nuclear safety–the bad example of Japan–implication for the rest of world. *Renew. Sustain. Energy Rev.* **2012**, *16*, 2610–2617. [CrossRef]

78. Wang, Q.; Chen, X. Regulatory transparency—How China can learn from Japan's nuclear regulatory failures? *Renew. Sustain. Energy Rev.* **2012**, *16*, 3574–3578. [CrossRef]

79. Tapio, P. Disaggregative policy Delphi: Using cluster analysis as a tool for systematic scenario formation. *Technol. Forecast. Soc. Chang.* **2003**, *70*, 83–101. [CrossRef]

80. Tapio, P.; Banister, D.; Luukkanen, J.; Vehmas, J.; Willamo, R.; France, N. Energy and transport in comparison: Immaterialisation, dematerialisation and decarbonisation in the EU15 between 1970 and 2000. *Energy Policy* **2007**, *35*, 433–451. [CrossRef]

81. Rikkonen, P.; Tapio, P. Future prospects of alternative agro-based bioenergy use in Finland—Constructing scenarios with quantitative and qualitative Delphi data. *Technol. Forecast. Soc. Chang.* **2009**, *76*, 978–990. [CrossRef]

82. Wang, Q.; Chen, Y. Barriers and opportunities of using the clean development mechanism to advance renewable energy development in China. *Renew. Sustain. Energy Rev.* **2010**, *14*, 1989–1998. [CrossRef]

83. Qiang, W.; Qiu, H.N.; Kuang, Y. Market-driven energy pricing necessary to ensure China's power supply. *Energy Policy* **2009**, *37*, 2498–2504.

84. Wang, Q.; Jha, A.N.; Chen, X.; Dong, J.-F.; Wang, X.-M. The future of nuclear safety: Vital role of geoscientists? *Renew. Sustain. Energy Rev.* **2015**, *43*, 239–243. [CrossRef]

85. Andreoni, V.; Galmarini, S. Decoupling economic growth from carbon dioxide emissions: A decomposition analysis of Italian energy consumption. *Energy* **2012**, *44*, 682–691. [CrossRef]

86. Sorrell, S.; Lehtonen, M.; Stapleton, L.; Pujol, J.; Champion, T. Decoupling of road freight energy use from economic growth in the United Kingdom. *Energy Policy* **2012**, *41*, 84–97. [CrossRef]

87. Wang, Q. Nuclear safety lies in greater transparency. *Nature* **2013**, *494*, 403. [CrossRef] [PubMed]

Article

Green Buildings in Singapore; Analyzing a Frontrunner's Sectoral Innovation System

Vidushini Siva [1], Thomas Hoppe [2,*] and Mansi Jain [1]

1   Department of Technology and Governance for Sustainability (CSTM), Institute for Innovation and Governance Studies (IGS), Faculty of Behavioral, Management and Social Studies (BMS), University of Twente, P.O. Box 217, 7500 AE Enschede, The Netherlands; vidushini.siva@gmail.com (V.S.); m.jain-1@utwente.nl (M.J.)
2   Policy, Organisation, Law and Gaming (POLG), Department of Multi-Actor Systems (MAS), Faculty of Technology, Policy and Management (TPM), Delft University of Technology, Jaffalaan 5, 2628 BX Delft, The Netherlands
*   Correspondence: T.Hoppe@tudelft.nl; Tel.: +31-15-278-2783

Academic Editor: Umberto Berardi
Received: 29 March 2017; Accepted: 23 May 2017; Published: 31 May 2017

Abstract: The building sector in Singapore consumes up to half of the nation's total energy. The government has therefore been urging the transformation of the industry by targeting 80% of all buildings to be green-certified by 2030. Thus far, Singapore has done relatively well, and is widely viewed as frontrunner in this respect. This paper addresses the question: what are the benefits and limitations of Singapore's sectoral innovation system in spurring an energy transition in the building sector, in particular by up-scaling the use of green building technology? The Sectoral Innovation Systems (SIS) theoretical framework was used to analyze the Singapore case. Four SIS components were assessed: technological regime, market demand, actor interactions and networks, and institutional framework. The benefits of Singapore's sectoral innovation system identified in the analysis basically concern aspects of all of the four elements of SIS. Particular success factors concerned the launching of an integrated strategy to support green building innovations (i.e., the Green Mark policy scheme), implementing support policies, and setting up test beds. Furthermore, a masterplan to engage and educate end-users was implemented, knowledge exchange platforms were set up, regulations on the use of efficient equipment in buildings were issued, and standards and a certification system were adopted. The results also shed light on key barriers, namely, the reluctance of building users to change their habits, ineffective stakeholder collaboration, and green buildings innovation support coming from the government only. Measures in place have been moderately effective.

Keywords: energy transition; green certification; policy; sectoral innovation system; Singapore; green buildings

1. Introduction

The building sector is responsible for a significant share of energy-related carbon emissions across the world [1]. Tackling climate change by reducing Greenhouse Gases (GHG) emissions would require significant lowering of GHGs emitted by the construction sector. The "greening" of buildings is an important means which can contribute to this.

As one of the few countries in the world with a 100% urban population [2], Singapore's building sector consumes up to half the nation's total energy consumption [3]. In 2005, the Building Construction Authority (BCA) of Singapore launched the "Green Mark" scheme in an effort to impel the construction industry towards a more sustainable built environment. According to the BCA, the Inter-Ministerial Committee on Sustainable Development (IMCSD) has set a target of "at least 80% of the buildings in Singapore achieving the BCA Green Mark Certified rating by 2030" [4]. This will require a major transformation to change the way buildings in Singapore are designed, constructed, and operated.

At present, more than ten years after the introduction of the certification scheme, it is estimated that the number of green buildings in Singapore represent about 27% of the nation's total gross floor area [5]. If this type of growth persists, it is uncertain whether Singapore will be able to meet the IMCSD target. No academic studies have been conducted thus far that evaluate this approach. Therefore, we feel it is necessary to study the current support system for green buildings in Singapore and assess whether it is sufficient to spur the transformative change needed to fulfill the IMCSD target.

This study aims to further understanding of conditions that may spur large-scale energy transition in Singapore's building sector. For this reason, the focus of the analysis in this paper is on Singapore, a country that quite successfully addressed innovations of "green buildings" principles and succeeded to some extent in "greening" its built environment. In this study, the conditions are explored that spurred and hampered innovation in "green buildings", seeking to learn from the approach taken in Singapore.

The main research question posed in this paper is: What are the benefits and limitations of Singapore's sectoral innovation system in spurring energy transition in the building sector, in particular by upscaling the use of green building technology?

In this study, Singapore's innovation system can be characterized as the network of interactions between different elements of the building industry in Singapore—including but not limited to—producers, consumers, institutions, and government actors.

This paper is organized as follows: Section 2 provides a literature review of green buildings across the world and a survey of green buildings practices in Singapore. Section 3 presents the theoretical framework used in this study: the "Sectoral Innovation Systems" (SIS) framework. In Section 4, the research design and methodology are presented. Section 5 presents the results of this study. The results are then discussed in Section 6. Finally, the conclusions are presented in Section 7.

2. Background

2.1. Green Buildings

Green construction is generally accepted as the "practice of: (1) increasing the efficiency with which buildings and their sites use energy, water, and materials; and (2) reducing building impacts on human health and the environment, through better siting, design, construction, operation, maintenance, and removal—the complete building life cycle" [6]. This requires close cooperation between the multiple stakeholders involved in the development and operation of a building, including the architects, engineers, and end-users.

Typically, green buildings are designed to reduce the negative impacts of the built environment on human health and the natural environment. In Singapore, green buildings tend to have green features that are generally more energy efficient than those in conventional buildings. Some of the key features that might be commonly found in green buildings in Singapore are:

- Improved glass insulation to reduce solar heating through windows;
- Increased natural light, energy efficient lighting devices, and equipment to control lighting;
- Energy efficient cooling plants and ventilation systems for air conditioning;
- Building management systems to monitor and control equipment and optimize energy use; and
- The use of photovoltaic cells [7].

2.2. Promoting Energy Transition in the Building Sector

Countries across the world are attempting to promote the development of green buildings. They are trying to set up conditions under which green building innovations can develop, evolve—and when market demand is created—be scaled successfully. They can do this by setting up national innovation systems, that consist of four basic elements; viz., the government, research institutions, educational institutions and industry, in which research institutions and industrial firms are assumed to be the centers of the system [8]. However, the approach taken might vary across countries, as studies have shown that the government can also take a central role with just a few specialized firms playing a supporting role, while the majority of firms in the industry act passively [9]. In (national or sectoral) innovation systems (managerial and policy) attention can be awarded to phenomena that are considered the drivers of construction innovation, viz. environmental pressure, technological capability, knowledge exchange, and boundary spanning. These drivers are said to be active at the transfirm, intrafirm, and interfirm levels in the network of organizations in the construction sector [10]. Another important factor to be addressed in setting up green building innovation systems concerns the design and use of demonstration projects in supporting innovations [11].

For instance, the European building sector is undergoing major transformations due to the 2010/31/EU 'Energy Performance of Buildings' Directive (EPBD), which aims at the construction only of nearly-zero-energy buildings after 2020. At present, there is a substantial gap between current practices and the desired performance of buildings, which has to be bridged in a mere three years according to the directive, indicating the urgency of the energy transition of the building sector. Efforts to promote the development of green buildings have therefore increased substantially within countries and across the continent [12].

Studies show that technologies relating to green buildings are continually improving [13,14]. Much of such technology is readily available and can be quite cost effective, especially when considered over a longer time period to realize the benefits. Many studies demonstrate the economic and social benefits, and the potential of green buildings [15–19]. Nevertheless, progress towards sustainability has been particularly slow in the construction sector (e.g., [20,21]).

A fair amount of researchers have sought to identify the barriers that prevent the widespread uptake of green buildings [21–25]. In some cases, the adoption of green buildings has encountered considerable resistance due to the risks involved, as buildings are usually expensive and must stand for a long time [26]. Other studies show that economic and knowledge factors are important barriers to adoption (cf. [27]), as are social and psychological barriers [19].

Albino and Berardi [12] suggest that temporary relationships between the companies working on a single building project lead to a failure to develop sustainable construction principles [28–30]. They may even result in sustainable construction issues loosing priority on project agendas, which in turn might lead to poor sustainable performance of buildings when realized [31,32]. This can be related to the main building developers and suppliers involved in a building project being hesitant to invest in green technology as the financial benefits end up benefiting the end-users, and not themselves [33,34]. Although investment in sustainable construction, and more specifically in energy efficiency, is evident from a technical and economical point of view, business firms (but also public organizations) often do not undertake the necessary investment. This is also known as the "efficiency paradox" [35].

A study by Vermeulen and Hovens [20] revealed that end-users of buildings are often the final decision makers regarding the adoption of green building technology. They display a lack of knowledge of the perceived economic benefits of adopting new green building innovations, which poses a substantial barrier. Another study (also in the Netherlands: [21]) identified some of the key barriers that prevented the sustainable transition of the Dutch housing sector. They include poor demand for energy innovations, a fragmented knowledge base, and poor regulatory design.

Even in Sweden, where renewable energy sources account for more than half of the nation's energy production [36], several barriers were noted impeding the adoption of low energy buildings. One of the key barriers, as discovered in a study by Persson and Grönkvist [37], was risk aversion. Consumers prefer to choose experienced and proven technologies over new technologies. This is apparently so even when cheaper alternatives are available [27].

Across the world, retrofitting projects have tended to be hard to implement (when compared to the construction of new buildings) [23], and increased difficulties are experienced when introducing green and energy saving technologies in households [12].

In multiple studies, it was observed that retrofitting projects carry a huge risk in that the benefits, both energetic and monetary, will not be realized for many years after the work has been completed [38–40].

In 2009, Germany introduced an updated version of the "EnEV" (additional energy saving regulation), which mandates minimum standards for all new residential and non-residential buildings. This version contains stricter regulations for new buildings and buildings subject to refurbishment, and should therefore lead to improved energy efficiency in the German building sector. These measures have helped to make the results of green initiatives more transparent and accessible, which helps potential building buyers and tenants to make better informed decisions [41]. However, Germany does not rely on mandatory rules only; there are also other incentive schemes. One of these is by the "KfW bank", which is owned by the government and provides reduced interest rates for buildings with improved energy performance [42].

China can also be viewed as a potential growth market for green buildings. However, its government has been reluctant to incentivize this. The government has tried to promote building energy-efficiency through various policies, the most effective one for China being mandatory administration controls. However, its implementation requires more financial resources and consistent funding, which is at times unavailable [43]. In addition, policy enforcement is considered a problem. Due to complicated and bureaucratic administration, enforcement becomes rather ineffective [44].

A study in Hong Kong—a city with similar characteristics to Singapore in terms of its modernity and urbanization—explored the market readiness and policy implications of green buildings. The study revealed that sufficient technological expertise was available. Surveyed experts stated that legislation was considered important, stressing (and citing) the efforts made by the government [45]. Financial bonuses seemed to be the most sought-after incentive for building developers. One way to do this is through tax exemption. For example, the city of Baltimore in the USA offers tax credits for all new residential constructions that qualify for the minimum LEED Silver certification [46].

2.3. Green Building Rating Tools around the World

Several different types of assessment tools and certification schemes have been developed around the world to rate green (and monitor) buildings, such as LEED (US), BREEAM (UK), GBCA (Australia), Green Mark (Singapore), DGNB (Germany), CASBEE (Japan), and Pearl Rating System (Abu Dhabi). All these schemes are voluntary. They have been developed by local green building councils, and accredited by commissioned professionals. The World Green Building Council has been established as an international network organization for all the various local councils [23].

These schemes often follow a similar pattern in their assessment of different aspects of a building's degree of sustainability. Each scheme usually has a few "grades" of certification. Credits are awarded for different green features that have been integrated into a building or its design, and the total score reveals the "grade" of certification awarded. Schemes also contain different categories according to the building type and usage, e.g., offices, hotels, and hospitals, to ensure a fair comparison and assessment. The rating tools may differ for reasons that have to do with conditions that are specific to the location in which tools were developed (e.g., climate conditions).

2.4. Green Building Rating Tools in Singapore

In Singapore, the BCA has adopted the so-called "Green Mark" scheme. It has been described as the tropics' answer to the LEED scheme in the U.S. The Green Mark scheme differs from the aforementioned green building rating tools in three ways:

- It places greater emphasis on energy efficiency;
- It has been tailored for a tropical climate with the cooling of inner spaces using air-conditioning as a key consideration; and

- It has higher standards of measurement and verification, using more precise instruments to monitor equipment performance [47].

The "Green Mark" scheme was launched in January 2005 to encourage the construction of more environmentally friendly buildings by the Singapore industry. It has been endorsed and supported by a number of ministerial bodies in Singapore, such as the National Environment Agency. According to the BCA, "It provides a comprehensive framework for assessing the overall environmental performance of new and existing buildings to promote sustainable design, construction and operations practices in buildings. It is intended to promote sustainability in the built environment and raise environmental awareness among developers, designers and builders when they start project conceptualization and design, as well as during construction" [47].

The assessment system of the scheme awards points for specific energy efficient and pro-environmental features and practices that can be integrated into building projects and designs. These features must be more sustainable than the normal practice observed in conventional buildings. The total score provides an indication of the environmental friendliness of the building design and operation. Depending on the overall assessment and score, the building will be certified as having met the BCA Green Mark Platinum standard, the GoldPlus, Gold standard, or the Certified rating, with the Platinum certification being the highest [47].

In line with the Green Mark scheme, three strategic "Masterplans" have been rolled out by the BCA since 2005. In 2012, the Building Control Act was updated to include legislation on the certification of buildings. It stated that newly constructed buildings must at least achieve the minimum certification qualification. In 2013, it became mandatory on building owners to submit energy consumption data to the BCA. In 2014, it became mandatory for building owners to conduct periodic energy audits, and achieve the minimum Green Mark certification when updating or retrofitting their cooling system [48].

There is a requirement that Certified Green Mark buildings must be re-assessed every three years to maintain their Green Mark status. Newly constructed and certified buildings will subsequently be re-assessed under the existing building criteria. The initial certification for new buildings will be awarded based on design. However, after one year, assessment will be based on the building's actual performance [47].

2.5. Promoting Energy Transition in the Singaporean Building Sector

Although studies of green buildings in Singapore in general have been published [49], such studies tend to focus primarily on evaluating the Green Mark tool or the engineering and architectural aspects of green buildings [50].

In common with government agencies in other countries that seek to green their building sectors, the BCA deploys incentive schemes and initiatives in place. Examples include the "Green Mark Incentive Scheme for Existing Building and Premises" (GMIS-EBP), which co-funds up to 50% of the retrofitting cost of energy improvements; the "Building Retrofit Energy Efficiency Financing" scheme (BREEF), which helps to underwrite the risk of default on loans from participating financial institutions for implementing new technology; and the Green Mark Gross Floor Area scheme (GM GFA), which grants additional floor area to developers who seek to achieve at least the Green Mark Gold Plus certification. Aside from financial incentives, the BCA also promotes education through media and schools, and coordinates conferences and exhibitions [48].

3. Sectoral Innovation Systems

This study is interested in the systemic conditions that spur "green buildings" innovation. An innovation systems approach is warranted because we are not interested only in adoption of innovations as a decision-making process outcome (i.e., [32,51,52]), and we do not seek to explain for a sustainable transition (i.e., by using theories on socio-technical transitions, such as the Multi-Level Perspective [53] or Strategic Niche Management [54–57], although we acknowledge that the process of sustainable transition is ongoing in Singapore's building sector [58,59]), or focus on the effectiveness of (individual) support policies (e.g., [60–62]). Due to our interest at the system level, and conditions spurring innovations and the focus of this study on one economic sector (i.e., the built environment) we selected the Sectoral Innovation Systems (SIS) as the main theoretical framework for this study [21,63,64]. The framework was previously used to analyze green innovations emerging in domestic construction sectors in other countries (e.g., in the Netherlands [21], and in India [65]). We will now introduce the key concepts of the SIS framework.

Innovation is considered a key condition for fostering structural change. The concept of an innovation system (IS) has been developed to represent and understand the interactions between producers, users, institutions, and governments [66]. Sectoral innovation systems can be described as the collective emergent outcome of the co-evolutionary interactions between the core building blocks of a system or sectoral market [63,64,67].

SIS has four main dimensions; technological regime, market demand, agents, interactions and networks, and the institutional framework (cf. [21]). These dimensions are illustrated in Figure 1.

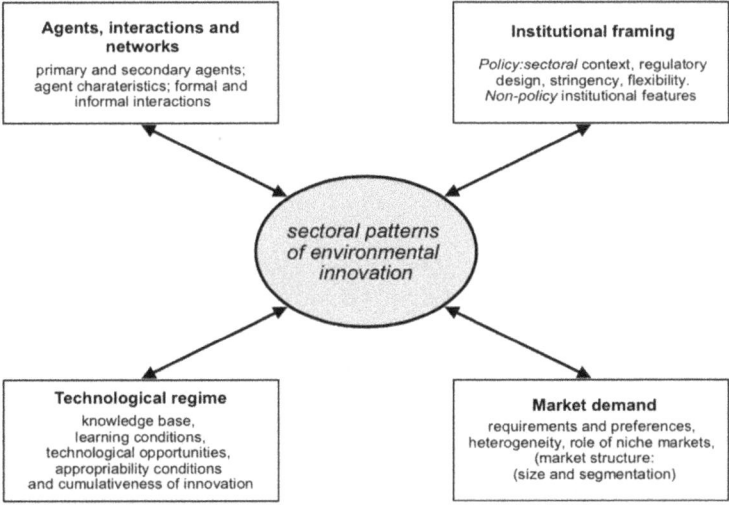

Figure 1. Graphical presentation of the SIS framework.

3.1. Technological Regime

Technologies are generally developed in a specific socio-technical context made up of tacit and explicit knowledge, sunk costs, learning conditions, complementarities, and interdependencies [64,68–70].
SIS consists of the following four main aspects.

- Technology: This refers to the new technologies available, the economic feasibility of these new technologies, and the extent to which implementing these new technologies was successful.
- Complementarities and interdependencies: This refers to whether new technology complements or replaces existing technology, and whether any technology is interdependent on another technology. This could be due to the convergence of previously separate products or the emergence of new demand from existing demand.
- Knowledge base: This refers to the extent of knowledge and the methods by which knowledge is disseminated and communicated.
- Learning conditions: This refers to both the internal and external learning processes, and opportunities.

3.2. Market Demand

Demand stems from the preferences of end-consumers, mostly revealed by actual consumer choices. It is valuable to understand the role of end-users in the innovation process by considering their perceptions in adopting certain technology, and how this translates into demand. Users can influence the innovation process, by "experimentally adopting certain technologies, or by gearing the technology to specific demand" [21]. In this study, it refers to the choices building owners and users make with regard to green technology, and how these preferences align with the perceptions of green buildings vis-à-vis the use of conventional buildings. Non-alignment of the two would typically slow down the uptake of green technology and hence, the development of green buildings in the construction sector.

3.3. Agents, Interactions and Networks

Agents include individuals as well as organizations, which interact through processes of communication, exchange, cooperation, competition, and command [63]. Agents can be divided into two sub-categories: primary and secondary agents. Primary agents perform core innovative activities, experiments, and capacity building [21]. Secondary agents play a supportive role through knowledge dissemination, financial support, regulations, and counseling.

The level of formal and informal interaction between the agents is also considered. Interactions can take place through platforms for networking and knowledge-sharing. Interactions in actor networks depend on both formal and informal rules. It is essential to understand how well these support innovations and the diffusion of innovations, i.e., green building technology.

3.4. Institutional Framework

Institutions include various formal and non-formal rules. Formal rules stem from government legislation, regulation, policies, and initiatives. Informal rules refer to routines, common habits, established practices, laws and standards. All of these shape agents' cognitions and actions, as well as inter-agent interactions [63,64]. They also have either a supportive or inhibitory role in the development of green buildings. For example, state laws can help influence the choices agents make through incentives, or even mandate the use of certain technology to ensure its uptake. Conversely, a society's natural habit can inhibit the uptake of technology; a risk-averse society might be hesitant to adopt emerging technology.

4. Methods

The research design of the study presented in this paper involves an in-depth case study of Singapore. A case study research design was chosen to investigate the phenomenon of an energy transition in the building sector in detail in its actual context in Singapore (cf. [71]) using a rich set of qualitative data.

Singapore was chosen as the case study for a variety of reasons, the key one being that Singapore is viewed as a frontrunner in the green building movement in the tropics and subtropics. Across Asia, Australia, and Africa, a total of 71 cities have adopted the Green Mark certification scheme. According to the BCA, "In 2010, the consulting firm Solidance had rated Singapore as the first in Asia for its green building policy. In early 2013, research by the McGraw Hill Construction found that out of 62 countries, Singapore was perceived the most highly involved country in the development of green buildings today" [7]. In line with this, and with the IMCSD's goal of having 80% of green buildings Green Mark certified by 2020, it is therefore valuable and interesting to explore the uptake of green buildings, and its contribution to the energy transition in the Singapore building sector. Singapore can possibly serve as a best practice, from which valuable lessons can be drawn. In terms of case selection on green building innovations in countries the selection of Singapore can be seen as "deviant case" or "extreme case" [72]. Therefore, it is useful to explore the reasons (and conditions) that account for successful green building innovation in this particular country.

4.1. Data Collection

Data collection involved eleven in-depth interviews with stakeholders, secondary data, participation in two conferences, and in a green building site tour. The interviews were divided into two sets: namely those with "primary actors" and those with "secondary actors", following the classification given in the SIS conceptualization. The first set of interviews involved six "primary actors", directly involved with green building projects. This group of interviewees consisted of building developers, architects, technology providers, and building occupants. The interviews provided primary knowledge regarding green building development in Singapore as the actors were directly involved in green building demonstration projects.

The actors mentioned above represent almost all the types of actors in the complex value chain of the building construction sector as identified by World Building for Sustainable Development [73]: viz. capital providers, developers, designers, engineers, contractors, materials and equipment suppliers, real estate agents, owners and users. In addition to the interviews conducted, information on these actors was also gathered using secondary data like reports from governments and other organizations, and information on them obtained via (other) interviewees.

The second set of interviews was conducted with five "secondary actors". This group consisted of government officials, representatives from consultancy agencies, non-profit organizations, and academic researchers. These interviews were done to further understand the dynamics between primary and secondary agents, and the role of the support system in facilitating green buildings niche formation.

Two sets of semi-structured questionnaires were prepared for interviews: one for actors classified as primary agents, and one for actors classified as secondary agents (see Appendix A for the questionnaires). The interviews included questions that were derived from the key theoretical components of the SIS framework. All the interviews were conducted face-to-face, with eight out of eleven having been audio recorded simultaneously. Recorded interviews were then transcribed into reports that were later used for treatment and analysis. Interviewing continued until data saturation was reached. However, interviews with representatives from financial sector actors (i.e., capital providers) were not possible due to non-availability of the selected interviewees at the time of data collection. For information about financial actors, secondary sources were used.

While it is acknowledged that there might be an overlap in the roles of some stakeholders, the study ensured that their roles were addressed separately. This was done by tailoring questions in a manner that was specific to the stakeholder's role in the building construction value chain. For example, when considering market demand, the aspect of consumer choice was phrased differently to different interviewees representing different types of building users. When interviewing a building developer, a question on market demand was raised such as "What choices and preferences do your clients and customers have?". However, to building users, the question was posed differently to better fit their role, i.e., "What preferences do you have in the building you choose to occupy?". Similarly, when institutional support was addressed, questions to a government agency representative were phrased such as "What type of grants do you offer?" or "Have you received feedback from grant receivers on the use of these grants?". To architects questions were raised such as "What types of government grants did you use?", "How do you appreciate them?", and "Do you think they are sufficient?". In this way, actor perspectives could be addressed while interviewing.

Secondary data used concerned news reports, BCA reports, government reports (e.g., on policy, energy savings realized, finance and public surveys), and data from the (academic and professional) literature.

4.2. Data Analysis

Qualitative data analysis software ("ATLAS.ti") was used to analyze the data collected. The program assisted in locating, organizing, and visualizing relations amongst the data found in the interview transcripts. A coding scheme was used in the program. The four different aspects of the SIS framework were used to assign codes. Their accompanying components, as outlined in the assessment framework, were assigned sub-codes. Quotes extracted from the interview transcripts were clustered under their relevant codes and sub-codes. This permitted systematic, comparative analysis. Both quantitative and qualitative interpretations of the data analysis were made; occurrences of the sub-codes were observed to understand the overall consensus among stakeholders, which was then substantiated by the information provided in the interviews, and other secondary data were then analyzed in detail. Conclusions were then drawn regarding each of the components of the SIS framework.

5. Results

This section presents the results, vis-à-vis the components of the SIS framework: (i) technological regime; (ii) market demand; (iii) actors, interactions and networks; and (iv) institutional framework.

5.1. Technological Regime

In conceptual terms, a technological regime has four sub-elements, viz.: technology, complementarities and interdependencies, a knowledge base, and learning process. The results with respect to these sub-elements are presented below.

5.1.1. Technology

The main green technologies popular in green buildings in Singapore are chiller plant systems, energy-efficient lighting systems, and solar panels. In terms of economic feasibility, all interviewees agreed that the cheapest technology is energy-efficient lighting systems. They usually have a short payback time of less than three years. For the other two, most interviewees admitted that they are rather expensive and have a long payback period (more than five years), but their feasibility is increasing due to advances in technology. High efficiency equipment can actually be made more compact, which has a lower impact on a building's sustainable footprint and increases retail space.

Given the (current) stable economic, political, and geographic conditions in Singapore, investors and companies foresee longevity in their businesses; hence, they foresee larger investments with longer payback periods, in which energy efficient equipment is preferred. They also foresee increased demand for renewable energy technology. Solar panels become more feasible in Singapore when one takes into account government subsidies to encourage the use of renewable energy sources; for instance, the prospect of feed-in tariff implementation.

With regards to chiller plant systems, a promising innovation is in the use of district cooling, in which chilled water is produced centrally and then distributed to buildings nearby via a piping network [74]. In fact, one of the world's largest district cooling plants, commissioned by the government, is housed completely underground at the Marina Bay district in Singapore. It is said that customers using it enjoy savings of more than 40%, an amount that could possibly support over 20,000 home apartment units. The chiller plant system helps to reduce space requirements and starting capital cost. Similar plants are being developed in Singapore, and the success of the Marina Bay plant could potentially pave the way for more cooling solutions [75]. Arguably, district cooling in Singapore could serve as a blueprint for energy efficient cooling of buildings in tropical regions.

Furthermore, the Government of Singapore supports the uptake of green technology through grant schemes promoted by the Green Building Innovation Cluster (GBIC). This scheme provides funding for experimentation, exhibition, and exchange of promising new energy efficiency solutions among industry stakeholders. The schemes have targeted future end-consumers to try and embrace these new technologies.

Despite these positive signs there are some substantial barriers. Aside from cost, eight of eleven stakeholders stated that a barrier was formed by a lack of change in the mindsets of actors throughout the value chain. First, managerial boards within construction companies do not prioritize sustainability. As long as financial growth is achieved and all equipment is operating in good condition, they are not motivated to optimize energy efficiency. Second, end-users themselves are averse to change on a broad cultural level. Simulating widespread use of new technology would involve awareness raising and education, while many people—especially the elderly—are unwilling to make efforts to learn how to adjust to, and use new technology. Furthermore, sustainability in itself is perceived an abstract concept with only long-term and far-fetched effects.

5.1.2. Complementarities and Interdependencies

Most interviewees indicated that green technology is starting to replace existing technology. With stricter rules from the BCA it is now mandatory for all buildings subjected to any sort of change to meet the minimum level of the Green Mark standard. This level of certification stipulates a certain level of efficiency that can only be achieved with water-cooled chillers. Hence, the use of air-cooled chillers is on the verge of being phased out of the market. The same scenario is prevalent when considering energy efficient lighting. LED lighting is replacing fluorescent and incandescent lighting.

Currently, the use of solar panels is only complementary to the use of conventional electricity from the grid as it is still considered quite expensive. However, it was reported in 2012 that grid parity had been achieved, so that electricity from the grid costs the same as installing and maintaining solar panels [76]. Solar PV companies were adopting the model of "solar leasing" to support consumers in offsetting the high start-up cost of investing in solar panels. Here, the consumers sign a contract to make their roof space available to solar panel companies to generate electricity and to pay for the energy they consume, at a discounted rate of 20 years. Additionally, the Housing and Development Board (HDB) called for a large solar-leasing tender in 2014, under which solar panels would be installed on the rooftops of over 500 residential buildings [77].

Alongside the installation of highly efficient technology, a surge occurred in the demand for building management systems, high sensitivity and high precision sensors that go along with the Green Mark certification. It requires strict monitoring of energy use by building appliances with highly accurate data collection. This serves as a good example of interdependency, as described by Malerba [64], where new demand emerges from existing demand.

5.1.3. Knowledge Base

There appears to be sufficient knowledge and technical expertise concerning green buildings and related technology. However, the availability of specific knowledge is limited, and it is kept by consultants and producers, without being shared voluntarily with consumers and end-users. Furthermore, most people look at the BCA guidelines and only implement technology that is (already) explicitly mentioned there. This appears to be related to a lack of knowledge on modeling energy systems in real-life applications. Under the third Masterplan by BCA, actions are undertaken to educate consumers in how to model their energy profile and simulate energy savings. In this way, they can not only implement new technology but also optimize the systems and appliances they already use.

5.1.4. Learning Process

There seems to be a substantial effort and openness coming from both primary and secondary agents to ensure coordinated knowledge exchange between projects, stakeholders, and the public. This is usually facilitated by the state government by organizing conferences, workshops, and seminars.

In terms of increasing their knowledge base, project developers in Singapore are keen to educate tenants and end-users. They provide guidebooks in collaboration with the BCA, called the "Green Lease Toolkit on sustainability practices". In 2015, a scheme was launched by BCA to encourage the certification of rental spaces, which would help to increase engagement and education of end-users. Moreover, buildings with high green building performance (typically Green Mark Platinum certified) are given public recognition by the BCA. These buildings are usually open to the public for guided educational tours.

There also appears to be a need to reorient the production of academic knowledge about green buildings. During one of the interviews, a university professor mentioned that a change is needed in the academic landscape. He argued that there should be more publications on incremental research and studies on actual testbeds and demonstration projects. This would highlight the performance of specific technologies, and opportunities to save energy in real-life practice.

5.2. Market Demand

Most of the interviewees ranked cost effectiveness as their highest priority, referring to buildings with low rent, and technology that has more benefits than cost. Technologies with low payback periods were preferred (i.e., under three years). The technologies perceived as the costliest in green buildings concerned energy efficient water-cooled chiller plants, which have payback periods between five to ten years, making them rather economically undesirable for consumers.

Consumers preferred well-established technologies that have proved to work in the past, and generally does not require any new level of knowledge to operate. Most interviewees agreed on the risk-averse nature of the Singaporean market, in which consumers are conservative in their choices and prefer not to be the first to try out experimental, unproven technology. However, some actors are currently taking measures to overcome this problem. For example, at a university, the first steps have been undertaken to implement emerging green building technologies. The site is in the university's own campus buildings (part of a program called "EcoCampus"). This not only allows new technologies to be tested in Singapore (to assess effectiveness, given the climate demands of high temperatures and high humidity conditions), but it also pairs researchers to the equipment to monitor and document the results carefully. Apart from this, the BCA also issued a pilot scheme called "BREEF" (Building Retrofit Energy Efficiency Financing), which helps to counter high upfront costs of investing in new technology by underwriting some of the risks when a company wishes to take out a loan to pay for the technology. These measures were considered effective in reducing risk aversion among investors and project developers.

Most interviewees considered sustainability a secondary (non-prioritized) factor. Typically, companies seek energy efficient measures to enhance their corporate social responsibility standpoint and brand marketing. Interviewees representing construction companies stated that striving to achieve sustainability goals is closely related to health and well-being of their employees. A green building is said to have a better overall office environment in terms of natural lighting, air quality, and comfortable temperature settings. This has also led building users to seek more green office spaces, especially for MNCs with higher financial capital. BCA recently released the Green Mark Portfolio Program, which seeks to certify tenant living spaces (as opposed to entire buildings) and optimize buildings' overall footprints. There is also a Green Lease Toolkit, which serves as a handbook for owners and tenants regarding good practices and sustainability targets.

Although more companies are seeking and using green office spaces, there seems to be a lack of effort on the part of retail space owners. Shopping malls and supermarket owners are opposed to the idea of energy efficiency because it perceived to have a negative impact on their sales. For instance, brightly lit malls with air-conditioning streaming out tend to attract customers. To increase air-tightness and prevent losses (as a solution), a greener mall could be designed having double doors. However, this usually reduces visual marketing and gross floor area. In supermarkets, refrigeration sections for frozen goods tend to be open to increase product visibility and increase sales, leading to extra energy losses. Another problem is related to a lack of legal provisions covering lighting and air-conditioning in shopping malls. However, the BCA recently started to pay more attention to the greening of shopping malls and retail spaces. Some public building managers have stressed that they want to set an example by achieving a higher Green Building performance than is required according to the Green Mark certification.

The BCA also has a role itself as "launching customer". Its headquarter is located in a Green Mark Platinum certified building, which concerns a "lifestyle mall" that combines shopping, residential use, and offices, all on the same site. At the time, more shopping malls were subjected to renovation with the aim of gaining a Gold Plus or Platinum rating to maintain competitiveness.

Despite all these efforts, a member of the Business Council for Sustainable Development conveyed that green buildings remain under-valued in the building market. They cannot be rented or sold at a premium, even when they are Green Mark certified. This would result in a lack of demand from investors. To address these and other issues, the BCA introduced a new scheme, called the Green Mark Gross Floor Area incentive scheme (GM GFA), in which buildings can afford increased GFA on the condition that substantial energy efficiency enhancements are made. Furthermore, policy makers are in the process of integrating energy efficiency in the assessment and appreciation of buildings in the scheme, so that energy efficient buildings can attain a higher market value than conventional ones.

5.3. Actors, Interactions, and Networks

5.3.1. Actors

A wide range of actors are involved in the building construction sector. Primary actors include architects, engineers, consultants, suppliers, technology providers, building owners, building developers, and tenants. Secondary actors include the BCA and other government agencies, green consultants, investors, non-profit organizations and councils, and research institutes (often academic).

Most interviewees agreed that BCA occupies the most influential position, some of them even stating that they are heavily dependent on the BCA. In Singapore, the state government has launched new regulations, and the industry follows its lead in adopting sustainable practices. Singapore tends to follow a top-down approach. When compared to other countries, the Singapore government is perceived to have a greater sense of understanding of what the market requires, which supports the creation of programmes and policies. These programmes and policies create conditions for innovation needed to bring about change in the building sector. Although different stakeholders can provide feedback on the standards, the BCA is said to have the last call and ensure that standards are being met.

5.3.2. Actor Interactions and Networks

The national government is very active in trying to forge interaction among the various stakeholders. Eight out of eleven stakeholders acknowledged that the government has done a good job in providing platforms for interaction. In the process of refreshing its masterplan and legislation, BCA calls upon an international panel of experts to provide their feedback and engages stakeholders through consultation sessions to review their plans and standards. However, the matter of who sets the agenda for those meetings is considered of great importance. More often than not, it is the BCA that decides the topic of discussion and it was (only) then, that the industry responds. The interaction between stakeholders proceeded mostly in only one direction; with few initiatives from the industry to approach the BCA. This was perceived to limit the effectiveness of such interactions, when concerns and ideas were not voiced in a multi-participant decision-making process.

Collaboration between stakeholders was regarded by the interviewees as poor. This was related to the absence of an approach using an integrative design. Different stakeholders come in at different stages of building projects, which often leads to a lack of coherence and sub-optimal design. This means that project goals could become diluted due to the temporal involvement of stakeholders. For example, an interviewee revealed that a project could have begun with the goal of installing an energy efficient chiller plant. However, the building developer (typically) splits the tendering process to different suppliers to provide different parts of the chiller system. In the end, its overall performance is neglected in favor of lower costs, and no single stakeholder is able to take responsibility for the integrated performance of the chiller plant.

Another interviewee suggested that a performance-based model could potentially counteract the problem of stakeholders coming in at different stages of the project resulting in communication. Currently, the Green Mark standard only stipulates what level of efficiency must be achieved, and it is up to the owner or user of the building to decide how to achieve it. However, a performance-based model could incentivize all parties to come together right from the start of a project, and deliberate how to design and optimize one or more buildings to achieve the desired "Green Building" performance.

5.4. Institutional Framework

5.4.1. Formal Institutions

The BCA uses several policy instruments and innovative approaches, e.g. grants as financial incentives. The BCA also recently issued a mandate for organizations to reveal energy performance data so that BCA can do more effective benchmarking. Companies performing well are given awards and recognition, which can help them boost their marketing. This has led numerous companies becoming more competitive and to strive for government endorsement. The BCA also approached "underperformers" to raise awareness, and provide information and guidance on how they can improve their energy performance. Besides this, the BCA offers many public education schemes to engage a wider audience.

In terms of effectiveness, six interviewees conceded that the efforts from the government have only been moderately effective, and that goal attainment was mostly related to the implementation and enforcement of strict laws and regulations. The 'Singapore Standards' document published by the government sets out the specifications for the "design, use or performance of materials, products, processes, services and systems" [78]. For instance, only chiller equipment that meet a minimum level of efficiency are allowed entry into the market. Interviewees from industrial parties considered this regulatory stipulation as, "quite demanding".

When considering grants, interviewees view the size of budgets granted as substantial. However, it was suggested that a better benchmarking method is needed to ensure that smaller companies with less financial capital can also benefit from the grants. Currently, they are fairly under-represented in the grant schemes. It was also observed that consultants and suppliers are usually reluctant to work on smaller projects, as it would earn them less money. Consequently, smaller companies are only marginally involved and often lag behind in their efforts to become more sustainable.

Although regulations are mostly considered as stringent, they are also perceived to have a fair level of flexibility. Stakeholders interviewed mentioned that the BCA takes feedback from industrial parties into account when updating the Green Mark scheme. However, this is less true of socio-cultural aspects (which are hardly mentioned in BCA's masterplans). For example, there is little attention to the aspect of human capital, which is related to the technology that is to be implemented. An interviewee suggested that the BCA should include this aspect in the educational programs and workshops, to foster a greater sense of team collaboration.

Recently, different government agencies joined forces to support the BCA in achieving its goals. However, these agencies do have their own agendas, which could occasionally lead to conflicting issues. For example, the Public Utilities Board has set goals to lower water consumption. This conflicts with BCA's guidelines to move towards water-cooled chiller systems, which increases water consumption in buildings using this technology. With improved communication and a more integrated policy-making approach involving all of the different government agencies, these kinds of issues can basically be addressed prior to the deployment of regulations.

5.4.2. Informal Institutions

In Singapore, very little support seems to come from NGOs and there is a sparse presence of community initiatives vis-à-vis green buildings. All of the interviewees agreed that from a cultural perspective, Singaporeans tend to be opposed to change. There is a generalized mindset on budgeting to only start fixing things once they are broken. This means that there is no initiative to optimize a system if its basic functionalities are perceived to be in good condition. In turn, people are typically risk-averse, and behave cautiously when deciding to adopt new technology.

However, the BCA has taken more action to provide incentives to change these cultural norms and habits. As mentioned previously, the GBIC program addresses the risk and uncertainties related to implementing new technology. Another measure is the 'Green Mark Pearl Award', which is given to building owners who demonstrate leadership in actively engaging tenants to shape their behavior and operational practices.

In addition, different media were being used to advertise green buildings, and public engagement efforts are also being made. The 'Green School Roadmap' gives younger generations of the public first-hand experience in the green building movement. In addition, a growing number of university courses are designed and dedicated to sustainable building design and green building technology. Overall, this movement is viewed by the interviewees as gaining momentum.

A summary of the results, with respect to the four aspects of SIS, is presented in Table 1.

Table 1. Results of the analysis using the SIS concepts.

SIS Component	Results
Technological regime	Technology: • Economic feasibility of green technology is improving as payback periods are reducing and people are looking for long-term equipment. • Risks involved in implementing new technology is unwritten by government through GBIC scheme. • There is an unwillingness l of change in people's mindsets as sustainability is considered an abstract concept; top-tier management staff are not interested. • There is no lack of technical expertise in Singapore; however, those with expertise are unable to influence mindset of the public and corporate management. Complementarities and interdependencies: • Green technology is replacing existing technology and will fully overthrow it in the near future. • Both the government and the private sector are promoting the use of solar panels. • There is a surge in demand for building management systems and high precious sensors due to the stringent Green Mark standards. Knowledge base: • There is sufficient knowledge and expertise about green buildings and related technology. • Knowledge is trapped within the industry, consultants and producers. • The Third Masterplan by the BCA seeks to educate tenants. Learning process: • Both internal and external learning process are taking place. • There are many platforms to support knowledge exchange, and to disseminate knowledge from the industry to consumers.
Market demand	Risk aversion to new technology • The EcoCampus project by Nanyang Technological University will serve as a test bed for new technology. • The BCA "BREEF" (Building Retrofit Energy Efficiency Financing) scheme will help to underwrite financial risk of implementing new technology; Sustainability is still not prioritized in the offices sector. • The Green Mark Portfolio Programme seeks to certify apartments to let for tenant (as opposed to entire buildings); The Green Lease Toolkit serves as a handbook for owners and tenants on good practices and sustainability targets. There is a hesitancy to move towards energy efficient technology in retail spaces: • Mandating the use of double door systems to prevent energy losses • Mandating the use of energy efficient lighting Undervaluation of green buildings: • The Green Mark Gross Floor Area (GM GFA) incentive scheme is implemented, in which buildings can be awarded increased gross floor area when the buildings undergo substantial energy performance improvements. • There are evaluation meetings to increase market value of green buildings so that investors might find it attractive to finance them.
Actors, networks, and interactions	Actors: • A wide range of primary and secondary actors is involved. • The BCA has the most influential role and many stakeholders rely on it. Interactions and Networks: • Multiple platforms support stakeholder interaction through conferences, workshops, and feedback sessions organized by the BCA. • There is much ineffective inter-stakeholder collaboration, which is related to a lack of communication and the absence an integrative (multi-stakeholder) design framework to be used in projects.

Table 1. *Cont.*

SIS Component	Results
Institutional framework	Formal institutions: • There are different government policies that are moderately effective. • Effectiveness is mostly related to the implementation and enforcement of strict regulations. • A grant scheme is in place, but can be improved to (also) target small- and medium-sized companies (which have poor access to capital to make investments independently). • There is flexibility in policies. • There are occasional conflicts between different governmental agencies involved in (different aspects of) Green Building projects. Informal institutions: • There is little support to, and involvement of, NGO and community groups. • Mandatory policies are received well by target group members; voluntary schemes only reach target groups poorly. • Media are intensively used to increase public engagement on Green Building issues. • Awareness has increased, in part related to courses being taught at universities and schools.

6. Discussion

The results give the impression that the current sectoral innovation system is supportive towards Green Buildings niche formation in Singapore. The case study revealed that the national government (via the BCA) took a central role in Singapore's Green Building innovation system. This observation is in line with results from a study by Bossink [9] on innovation systems in the Dutch construction, which revealed that government took a central role with just a few specialized firms in a supporting role, and with a majority of the firms in industry acting passively. This remarkable observation is in contrast with more commonly held views by innovation scholars (e.g., [8]) who claim that commercial firms and research institutions should have the lead, with the government playing a supporting role. Other factors deemed successful concerned the government setting up a stakeholder network for interaction, and the BCA setting the conditions under which demonstration could successfully operate. In line with Bossink [10], the Singapore case study revealed that the driving of innovation by organizing inter-stakeholder interaction via networks and platforms of interaction was successful. Regarding the demonstration projects, the scheme called "BREEF" (Building Retrofit Energy Efficiency Financing) was used to reduce risk aversion among investors and project developers. This observation is in line with the results from a study [11] in which the balancing of risks was found to be a critical factor to positively influence clean technology innovation in demonstration projects. Other factors also revealed in [11], were also observed in the Singapore case study vis-à-vis the demonstration projects, viz. experiential learning by participants; having policy, regulation, and legislation in favor of innovation; market demand creation for innovative products; positive communication; technology demonstration and deployment expenditure; and the use of innovation labels.

However, there are still substantial barriers that prevent the widespread uptake. In summary, they concern: (1) inflexible habits and mindsets; (2) the main push for green buildings coming predominantly from the government; and (3) ineffective collaboration.

The barriers found in the Singapore case are not unique; they also appear in other countries. For example, the inflexible habits and mindsets of end-users lead directly to a lack of demand for green innovations in the building sector. Lack of demand was also observed in the Netherlands [21]. The hesitancy consumers had to adopt green building technology has also been observed in the US and Korea [34]. Risk aversion also played a strong role in the inflexible habits of people, as was observed in Sweden [37]. More in general, the problem seems related to the so-called "efficiency paradox" [35]. Management of real estate corporations is unwilling or simply not interested to invest in energy efficient applications, despite the evident efficiency gains that can be made (also in monetary terms). Those who have (techno-economic) expertise were found to be unable to influence and persuade decision-makers in public and corporate management.

Regarding the ineffective collaboration in Singapore, it was noticed that the different stakeholders involved in building projects had not adopted integrative design approaches. This meant that they usually only came together to work on a project at scattered events along the project's timeline. This led to fleeting interactions, lack of coherence, difficult collaboration patterns and in the end to sub-optimal design of Green Buildings, which was also observed by Albino and Berardi [12] and Berardi [31] in other studies. In addition, approaches to foster integrated relationships between construction stakeholders (as suggested by Berardi [31]) were often absent. It is here that room for improvement lies.

This issue points to a certain shortcoming of the SIS framework (like many other conceptual frameworks in Innovation Studies, Transition Studies, economic models, innovation-diffusion models and policy frameworks): there is a lack of attention to the temporal dimension: i.e., to configurational dynamics in construction building processes that tend to differ over time, and that have a big impact on decision-making outcomes, and adoption of innovative energy appliance, a phenomenon found in several studies addressing decision-making processes in sustainable building projects [31,32,79]. However, the temporal dimension, as a problematic factor to adoption of innovative energy options in building construction processes, has also received attention in a more conceptual and methodological way. When explaining the outcomes of projects (when compared to initial goals that were set) [31,32,80], and when addressing in policy implementation or policy monitoring and evaluation, the temporal dimension is of great importance [62].

While different countries have adopted different strategies to overcome the barriers of Green Building market development, Singapore's strategy has been moderately effective. However, when compared to some measures mentioned in the literature, it can be seen that there is potential for improvement. Two examples of propositions would be the use of tax exemptions for new residential buildings that are LEED-Silver certified, as in the city of Baltimore, US [46], and the state-owned "KfW" bank in Germany, which provides loans at reduced interest rates for buildings with higher energy performance [42]. Since green buildings are under-appreciated in Singapore, tax exemptions and reduced interest rates might help to increase their market value.

There are also other strategies that the government of Singapore can employ to tackle key barriers. One of the problems confronting green building uptake in Australia [81] was the central government's inability to model the uptake of technology, and thus predict the effectiveness of policies targeting green building market introduction. Singapore is facing a similar problem. Currently, the BCA is considering the use of the EEB Policy modeling tool. This has been successfully used in other cities across the world. It can help model the building landscape according to the exact situational conditions of the city and simulate the effects of certain policies. This, it is believed, will enhance the effectiveness of policy schemes.

In line with Gou et al. [45], the BCA is perceived to be at the forefront of the Green Buildings movement, and it is continually taking steps to improve and evolve further. The Green Mark scheme has been adopted in 71 cities. Although Singapore is performing well within Asia Pacific region, it is not performing as well as it can on a best-practice level. This is because the standards tend to be too prescriptive, rather than performance based. The performance of a building is an aggregation of the performance of its components. Interviewees thus advised that Singapore should abandon the exact stipulation of what type of technology and appliances must be used. Instead, a benchmarking system for energy performance could be considered for implementation, leaving end-users to design this for themselves, allowing for more creative solutions. Although prescriptive models are easier for authorities and developers, historically they are not progressive. More mature markets have moved away from prescriptive to performance-based models. For example, in the EU, the EPBD has adopted a performance-based model, which stipulates the performance required. Moreover, EU Member States have to try and achieve certain performance levels. With only the government pushing for green buildings in Singapore, the system becomes rigid and gives little impetus to creativity. A performance-based model could potentially encourage greater innovation from the industry and other stakeholders.

7. Conclusions

This paper set out to answer the following research question: What are the benefits and limitations of Singapore's sectoral innovation system in spurring energy transition in the building sector, in particular by upscaling the use of green building technology?

The benefits of Singapore's sectoral innovation system identified concern aspects of all of the four key elements: the technological regime, market demand creation, agency, and the institutional framework. First, it was commitment by national government that set things in motion. The country's Building Construction Authority (BCA) launched the Green Mark policy scheme as an integrated strategy to spur green building innovation. In addition, many support policies were implemented and test beds were set up. A masterplan was developed to engage and educate building users, in particular tenants. Platforms were established to stimulate the exchange of best practices, expertise, and state-of-the-art knowledge. Strict regulations were issued to mandate the use of efficient equipment in new offices. In addition, Green Mark standards were developed. To attract investors, a scheme was implemented to cope with investment risks; incentive schemes and toolkits were made available, next to the government and the private sector running relevant renewable energy technology support programs of their own (e.g., solar panels). In addition, a certification scheme was developed. Finally, the schemes that were implemented were monitored, and evaluated regularly. In response, the government made sure policies remained flexible and could be adjusted in time.

As a result of this integrated approach, technical and techno-economic expertise of green buildings developed rapidly. The set of (both primary and secondary) actors involved in the green building niche increased, and so did interactions between them (e.g., facilitated by knowledge platforms), also stimulating internal and external learning processes. Furthermore, economic feasibility of green building technology improved as payback periods decreased and potential investors started to take more interest in looking for equipment with long term value. As a result, the Green Buildings niche matured, and green building technology started to gain a serious foothold in the conventional domestic building market.

Despite the benefits mentioned, the case study also revealed key barriers preventing the large-scale uptake of green building technology: (1) inflexible habits and mindsets of end-users; (2) the main push for green buildings coming predominantly from the government; and (3) ineffective inter-actor collaboration. Measures that were set in place by the government and other stakeholders to overcome these barriers were only considered moderately effective.

Despite the barriers exposed, the lessons from the Singapore case are worth disseminating to policy makers in other administrative entities who strive to green their buildings sector by adopting green buildings. Although the study presented in this paper sheds light on sectoral Green Buildings innovation in Singapore, the results should be understood with caution. Limitations of the study concern the use of a single case study design, making it hard to generalize results and to compare results with other cities and states. Moreover, the study presented was limited in terms of stakeholder representatives, i.e., by the number of interviews conducted. For future studies it would be recommended to make the study more inclusive by surveying a broader set of stakeholders, and hence presenting a wider set of perspectives. In addition, it could be valuable to explore the views, preferences and experiences vis-à-vis Green Building innovation systems with large sets of stakeholder group members. This could be studied by using quantitative surveys, which also allows for better generalization of results, than using a single case study research design only.

This paper has provided some valuable notions, particularly on the institutional dimension of the sectoral innovation system of the Singapore case (in particular Singapore's central government strategy, program, policy instruments, and certification systems used). However, it is important to note that more studies should be conducted in Singapore to gain further insights into the impact and effectiveness of policies that have been implemented, the outcomes of projects, and to map the changing dynamics of the building sector in Singapore and its influence on Green Buildings niche market formation. It is also encouraged that similar research concerning the (sectoral) innovation systems of Green Buildings in other cities and countries is conducted. This would allow for systematic comparative research, and might help to discern conditions that support innovation-diffusion.

Acknowledgments: The authors would like to express their gratitude to the interviewees who graciously permitted the first author to interview them for the study reported in this paper.

Author Contributions: Vidushini Siva, Thomas Hoppe and Mansi Jain conceived and designed the study. Vidushini Siva collected data. Vidushini Siva and Thomas Hoppe analyzed data. Vidushini Siva, Thomas Hoppe and Mansi Jain contributed to the data analysis. Vidushini Siva, Thomas Hoppe and Mansi Jain wrote the paper.

Conflicts of Interest: The authors declare no conflict of interest. The founding sponsors had no role in the design of the study; in the collection, analyses, or interpretation of data; in the writing of the manuscript, and in the decision to publish the results.

Appendix A

Table A1. Questionnaire.

Aspect of SIS	Primary Agents	Secondary Agents
Technological Regime	Technology • What are the dominant technologies used in green buildings? • What do you think about the economic feasibility of implementing these technologies (Are the costs high? especially for implementing them in existing buildings) • Have these technologies been successfully implemented? -If not, what were some barriers? What were the costs? Lack of expertise? Complementarities and interdependencies • Does the low-energy technology complement/align with existing technology in buildings or are they overthrowing/replacing existing technology? • Is there any technology that is dependent on any other? Knowledge base • What do you think about the existing pool of knowledge on green technology for green buildings in Singapore? (How big, how information is being disseminated, etc.) Learning After a project has been completed, whether successfully or not (e.g., the erection of a green building tower) • Primary learning: Are the learning outcomes shared amongst group members? • Secondary learning: Is the learning spread to a wider audience? (through conferences, workshops etc.)	Technology • What are the dominant technologies used in green buildings? • What do you think about the economic feasibility of implementing these technologies (Are the costs high? especially for implementing them in existing buildings) • Have these technologies been successfully implemented? -If not, what were some barriers? What were the costs? Lack of expertise? Complementarities and interdependencies • Does the low-energy technology complement/align with existing technology in buildings or are they overthrowing/replacing existing technology? • Is there any technology that is dependent on any other? Knowledge base • What do you think about the existing pool of knowledge on green technology for green buildings in Singapore? (How big, how much information is being passed around, etc.) • What is your role in enhancing technological innovations and knowledge of green buildings in Singapore? Learning After a project has been completed, whether successfully or not (e.g., the erection of a green building tower) • Primary level: Are the learning outcomes shared amongst group members? • Secondary level: Is the learning spread to a wider audience? (Through conferences, workshops, seminars etc.)

Table A1. *Cont.*

Aspect of SIS	Primary Agents	Secondary Agents
Market Demand	• Are green buildings prioritized amongst ___ (group that interviewee belongs to, e.g., building developers)? • In your experience, what kind of choices or preferences do owners/consumers/clients/end-users have? What kind of building designs and building features do they look for? What type of green technology interventions do they seek out? What is their main motivating factor? • How does this consumer preference fit in with green buildings—in terms of technology, design, etc.? Or do you think they align more with conventional types of buildings?	• Are green buildings prioritized amongst ___ (group that interviewee belongs to, e.g., building developers)? • In your experience, what kind of choices or preferences do owners/consumers/clients/end-users have? What kind of building designs and building features do they look for? What type of green technology interventions do they seek out? What is their main motivating factor? • How does this consumer preference fit in with green buildings—in terms of technology, design, etc.? Or do you think they align more with conventional types of buildings?
Agents, interaction and networks	**Actors** • To your knowledge, is there a wide range of actors involved in the development of green buildings in Singapore? Who are they, roughly speaking? • Do some actors play a more influential role than others? Which? How? **Interactions** • What is the level of formal and informal interaction between these actors? • Are there any platforms for knowledge-sharing and actor interaction? • How well do they support innovations and diffusion of green building technology? • Are you involved in participating/facilitating? • Are these supported or facilitated by the government or any other actor? • Do you feel dependent on any particular actor? **Networks** • What are the most important formal rules in the actor network regarding green buildings? • What are the most important informal rules in the actor network regarding green buildings?	**Actors** • To your knowledge, Is there a wide range of actors involved in the development of green buildings in Singapore? Who are they, roughly spoken? • Do some actors play a more influential role than others? Which? How? • What kind of support do you provide for green building developers/users/clients seeking certification? (e.g., financial—grant, loans, tax exemption, technical—training, maintenance, advisory, etc.) • Are you aware of any alternative sources of support? **Interactions** • What is the level of formal and informal interaction between these actors? • Do you offer any platforms for interaction? • Do you facilitate any networking sessions? If yes, how? • How well do they support innovations and diffusion of green building technology? • Do you know of any of these kind of platforms supported or facilitated by the government or any other actor? • Do you feel any actor is dependent on you (or vice versa)? **Networks** • What are the most important formal rules in the actor network regarding green buildings? • What are the most important informal rules in the actor network regarding green buildings?

Table A1. *Cont.*

Aspect of SIS	Primary Agents	Secondary Agents
Institutional Framework	Policy • To what extent are rules, regulations, policies, initiatives, and monitoring aligned towards the promotion of green buildings? • Is there sufficient support from government? Non-policy • How do informal institutions (such as common habits, beliefs, standards, established practices, etc.) support the development of green buildings? • How do informal institutions (such as common habits, beliefs, standards, established practice, etc.) inhibit development of green buildings?	Policy • Do you know what policy instruments are currently implemented to incentivize people to get their buildings certified/promote the transition to green buildings in Singapore? • How effective were these policies in terms of stimulating green buildings innovations? • What is the role of government in providing support for green building developers? • How stringent or flexible are policies/rules/institutions towards the development of green buildings? Non-policy • What are the non-policy tools being used? (For example, knowledge sharing platforms, private sector projects, NGO projects, market-based certification schemes, competitions, community projects, etc.). • What is your role in these non-policy mechanisms of promoting green buildings in Singapore?

References

1. EIA. *U.S. Energy Information Administration—EIA—Independent Statistics and Analysis*; U.S. Energy Information Administration—EIA: Washington, DC, USA, 2013.
2. Bank, W. *Urban Population (% of total)*; World Bank: Washington, DC, USA, 2013.
3. BCA. *BCA Building Energy Benchmarking Report 2014*; Building Construction Agency: Singapore, 2014.
4. BCA. *Annual Report 2012: Redefining the Built Environment and Industry*; Building Construction Authority: Singapore, 2013.
5. BCA. Build Green, 2015. Available online: https://www.bca.gov.sg/Publications/BuildGreen/others/BGreen_7_2015.pdf (accessed on 19 May 2017).
6. Howe, J.C. Overview of Green Buildings. Available online: https://sallan.org/pdf-docs/CHOWE_GreenBuildLaw.pdf (accessed on 19 May 2017).
7. BCA. *Singapore: Leading the Way of Green Buildings in the Tropics*; Building Construction Authority: Singapore, 2013.
8. Bartholomew, S. National systems of biotechnology innovation: Complex interdependence in the global system. *J. Int. Bus. Stud.* **1997**, *28*, 241–266. [CrossRef]
9. Bossink, B.A. Assessment of a national system of sustainable innovation in residential construction: A case study from The Netherlands. *Int. J. Environ. Technol. Manag.* **2009**, *10*, 371–381. [CrossRef]
10. Bossink, B.A. Managing drivers of innovation in construction networks. *J. Constr. Eng. Manag.* **2004**, *130*, 337–345. [CrossRef]
11. Bossink, B.A. Demonstration projects for diffusion of clean technological innovation: A review. *Clean Technol. Environ. Policy* **2015**, *17*, 1409–1427. [CrossRef]
12. Albino, V.; Berardi, U. Green buildings and organizational changes in Italian case studies. *Bus. Strategy Environ.* **2012**, *21*, 387–400. [CrossRef]
13. Butera, F.M. Climatic change and the built environment. *Adv. Build. Energy Res.* **2010**, *4*, 45–75. [CrossRef]
14. Xu, L.; Zhou, B.; Wang, C. Research on Design Technology of Green Building for Environmental Protection. Available online: https://www.google.com/url?sa=t&rct=j&q=&esrc=s&source=web&cd=1&ved=0ahUKEwiyrdDM34fUAhWQJFAKHSSoB74QFggiMAA&url=http%3A%2F%2Fwww.atlantis-press.com%2Fphp%2Fdownload_paper.php%3Fid%3D18006&usg=AFQjCNH5YrueJlza1iIFbq9coaMKUvpjBw&cad=rjt (accessed on 19 May 2017).

15. Svenfelt, Å.; Engström, R.; Svane, Ö. Decreasing energy use in buildings by 50% by 2050—A backcasting study using stakeholder groups. *Technol. Forecast. Soc. Chang.* **2011**, *78*, 785–796. [CrossRef]
16. Ries, R.; Bilec, M.M.; Gokhan, N.M.; Needy, K.L. The economic benefits of green buildings: A comprehensive case study. *Eng. Econ.* **2006**, *51*, 259–295. [CrossRef]
17. Von Paumgartten, P. The business case for high performance green buildings: Sustainability and its financial impact. *J. Facil. Manag.* **2003**, *2*, 26–34. [CrossRef]
18. Heerwagen, J.; Zagreus, L. *The Human Factors of Sustainable Building Design: Post Occupancy Evaluation of the Philip Merrill Environmental Center*; The Center for the Built Environment: Berkeley, CA, USA, 2005.
19. Hoffman, J.A.; Henn, R. Overcoming the social and psychological barriers to green building. *Organ. Environ.* **2008**, *21*, 390–419. [CrossRef]
20. Vermeulen, W.J.; Hovens, J. Competing explanations for adopting energy innovations for new office buildings. *Energy Policy* **2006**, *34*, 2719–2735. [CrossRef]
21. Faber, A.; Hoppe, T. Co-constructing a sustainable built environment in the Netherlands—Dynamics and opportunities in an environmental sectoral innovation system. *Energy Policy* **2013**, *52*, 628–638. [CrossRef]
22. Darko, A.; Chan, A.P. Review of Barriers to Green Building Adoption. *Sustain. Dev.* 2016. [CrossRef]
23. Zuo, J.; Zhao, Z.-Y. Green building research–current status and future agenda: A review. *Renew. Sustain. Energy Rev.* **2014**, *30*, 271–281. [CrossRef]
24. Hwang, G.B.; Tan, J.S. Green building project management: Obstacles and solutions for sustainable development. *Sustain. Dev.* **2012**, *20*, 335–349. [CrossRef]
25. Häkkinen, T.; Belloni, K. Barriers and drivers for sustainable building. *Build. Res. Inf.* **2011**, *39*, 239–255. [CrossRef]
26. Gluch, P. Building Green-Perspectives on Environmental Mangagement in Construction. Ph.D. Thesis, Chalmers University of Technology, Gothenburg, Sweden, June 2005.
27. Pinkse, J.; Dommisse, M. Overcoming barriers to sustainability: An explanation of residential builders' reluctance to adopt clean technologies. *Bus. Strategy Environ.* **2009**, *18*, 515–527. [CrossRef]
28. Shields, R.; Manseau, A. *Building Tomorrow: Innovation in Construction and Engineering*; Ashgate: Aldershot Hants, UK, 2005.
29. Williams, K.; Dair, C. What is stopping sustainable building in England? Barriers experienced by stakeholders in delivering sustainable developments. *Sustain. Dev. Bradf.* **2007**, *15*, 135.
30. Anumba, C.; Ren, Z.; Ugwu, O. *Agents and Multi-Agent Systems in Construction*; Routledge: Abingdon, UK, 2007.
31. Berardi, U. Stakeholders' Influence on the adoption of energy-saving technologies in Italian homes. *Energy Policy* **2013**, *60*, 520–530. [CrossRef]
32. Hoppe, T. Adoption of Innovative Energy Systems in Social Housing; Lessons from eight Large-Scale Renovation Projects in the Netherlands. *Energy Policy* **2012**, *51*, 791–801. [CrossRef]
33. Howarth, B.R.; Andersson, B. Market barriers to energy efficiency. *Energy Econ.* **1993**, *15*, 262–272. [CrossRef]
34. Son, H.; Kim, C.; Chong, W.K.; Chou, J.S. Implementing sustainable development in the construction industry: Constructors' perspectives in the US and Korea. *Sustain. Dev.* **2011**, *19*, 337–347. [CrossRef]
35. DeCanio, S.J. The efficiency paradox: Bureaucratic and organizational barriers to profitable energy-saving investments. *Energy Policy* **1998**, *26*, 441–454. [CrossRef]
36. SEA. *Electricity Supply and Use 2001–2014 (GWh). Statistics Sweden*; Swedish Energy Agency: Stockholm, Sweden, 2015.
37. Persson, J.; Grönkvist, S. Drivers for and barriers to low-energy buildings in Sweden. *J. Clean. Prod.* **2015**, *109*, 296–304. [CrossRef]
38. Techato, K.-A.; Watts, D.J.; Chaiprapat, S. Life cycle analysis of retrofitting with high energy efficiency air-conditioner and fluorescent lamp in existing buildings. *Energy Policy* **2009**, *37*, 318–325. [CrossRef]
39. Menassa, C.C. Evaluating sustainable retrofits in existing buildings under uncertainty. *Energy Build.* **2011**, *43*, 3576–3583. [CrossRef]
40. Ascione, F.; Bianco, N.; De Masi, R.F.; de'Rossi, F.; Vanoli, G.P. Energy retrofit of an educational building in the ancient center of Benevento. Feasibility study of energy savings and respect of the historical value. *Energy Build.* **2015**, *95*, 172–183.

41. Nelson, A.J.; Rakau, O.; Dörrenberg, P. Green Buildings: A Niche Becomes Mainstream. Available online: https://www.dbresearch.com/PROD/DBR_INTERNET_EN-PROD/PROD0000000000256216.pdf (accessed on 19 May 2017).

42. Schröder, M.; Ekins, P.; Power, A.; Zulauf, M.; Lowe, R. The KFW Experience in the Reduction of Energy Use in and CO2 Emissions from Buildings: Operation, Impacts and Lessons for the UK. Available online: https://www.igbc.ie/wp-content/uploads/2015/02/KfWFullReport.pdf (accessed on 19 May 2017).

43. Shen, L.; He, B.; Jiao, L.; Zhang, X. Research on the development of main policy instruments for improving building energy-efficiency. *J. Clean. Prod.* **2016**, *112*, 1789–1803. [CrossRef]

44. Huang, B.; Mauerhofer, V.; Geng, Y. Analysis of existing building energy saving policies in Japan and China. *J. Clean. Prod.* **2016**, *112*, 1510–1518. [CrossRef]

45. Gou, Z.; Lau, S.S.-Y.; Prasad, D. Market readiness and policy implications for green buildings: Case study from Hong Kong. *Coll. Publ.* **2013**, *8*, 162–173. [CrossRef]

46. Pippin, A.M. Survey of Local Government Green Building Incentive Programs for Private Development. Available online: http://digitalcommons.law.uga.edu/cgi/viewcontent.cgi?article=1010&context=landuse (accessed on 19 May 2017).

47. BCA. *BCA Green Mark Assessment Criteria and Online Application*; Building Construction Agency: Singapore, 2015.

48. BCA. *3rd Green Building Masterplan*; Building Construction Agency: Singapore, 2014.

49. Deng, Y.; Li, Z.; Quigley, J.M. Economic returns to energy-efficient investments in the housing market: Evidence from Singapore. *Reg. Sci. Urban Econ.* **2012**, *42*, 506–515. [CrossRef]

50. Li, Y.Y.; Chen, P.-H.; Chew, D.A.S.; Teo, C.C. Exploration of critical resources and capabilities of design firms for delivering green building projects: Empirical studies in Singapore. *Habitat Int.* **2014**, *41*, 229–235. [CrossRef]

51. Rogers, E.M. *Diffusion of Innovations*, 5th Revised Edition; Simon & Schuster Ltd.: New York, NY, USA, 2003.

52. Dieperink, C.; Brand, I.; Vermeulen, W. Diffusion of energy-saving innovations in industry and the built environment: Dutch studies as inputs for a more integrated analytical framework. *Energy Policy* **2004**, *32*, 773–784. [CrossRef]

53. Geels, F. Technological transitions as evolutionary reconfiguration processes: A multi-level perspective and a case-study. *Res. Policy* **2002**, *31*, 1257–1274. [CrossRef]

54. Raven, R.; van den Bosch, S.; Weterings, R. Transitions and strategic niche management: Towards a competence kit for practitioners. *Int. J. Technol. Manag.* **2010**, *51*, 57–74. [CrossRef]

55. Raven, R. *Strategic Niche Management for Biomass*; Technical University Eindhoven (TU/E): Eindhoven, The Netherlands, 2005.

56. Hoogma, R. *Experimenting for Sustainable Transport: The Approach of Strategic Niche Management*; Taylor & Francis: London, UK, 2002.

57. Kemp, R.; Schot, J.; Hoogma, R. Regime shifts to sustainability through processes of niche formation: The approach of strategic niche management. *Technol. Anal. Strateg. Manag.* **1998**, *10*, 175–198. [CrossRef]

58. Markard, J.; Raven, R.; Truffer, B. Sustainability transitions: An emerging field of research and its prospects. *Res. Policy* **2012**, *41*, 955–967. [CrossRef]

59. Markard, J.; Truffer, B. Technological innovation systems and the multi-level perspective: Towards an integrated framework. *Res. Policy* **2008**, *37*, 596–615. [CrossRef]

60. Murphy, L.; Meijer, F.; Visscher, H. A qualitative evaluation of policy instruments used to improve energy performance of existing private dwellings in the Netherlands. *Energy Policy* **2012**, *45*, 459–468. [CrossRef]

61. Tambach, M.; Visscher, H. Towards Energy-neutral New Housing Developments. Municipal Climate Governance in The Netherlands. *Eur. Plan. Stud.* **2012**, *20*, 111–130.

62. Hoppe, T.; Coenen, F.; van den Berg, M. Illustrating the use of concepts from the discipline of policy studies in energy research: An explorative literature review. *Energy Res. Soc. Sci.* **2016**, *21*, 12–32. [CrossRef]

63. Malerba, F. *Sectoral Systems of Innovation: Concepts, Issues and Analyses of Six Major Sectors in Europe*; Cambridge University Press: Cambridge, UK, 2004.

64. Malerba, F. Sectoral systems of innovation and production. *Res. Policy* **2002**, *31*, 247–264. [CrossRef]

65. Jain, M.; Hoppe, T.; Bressers, H. Analyzing Sectoral niche formation: The case of Net-Zero Energy Buildings in India. *Environ. Innov. Soc. Transit.* **2016**, in press. [CrossRef]

66. Edquist, C. Systems of innovation: Perspectives and challenges. *Afr. J. Sci. Technol. Innov. Dev.* **2011**, *2*, 14–43.

67. Malerba, F. *Sectoral Systems, The Oxford Handbook of Innovation*; Oxford University Press: Oxford, UK, 2005; pp. 380–406.

68. Dosi, G. Technological paradigms and technological trajectories: A suggested interpretation of the determinants and directions of technical change. *Res. Policy* **1982**, *11*, 147–162. [CrossRef]

69. Nelson, R.R.; Winter, S.G. *An Evolutionary Theory of Economic Change*; Harvard University Press: Cambridge, MA, USA, 2009.

70. Malerba, F.; Orsenigo, L. Technological regimes and sectoral patterns of innovative activities. *Ind. Corp. Chang.* **1997**, *6*, 83–118. [CrossRef]

71. Yin, R. *Case Study Research; Design and Methods*; Sage Publications: London, UK, 2003.

72. Gerring, J. *Case Study Research. Principles and Practices*; Cambridge University Press: Cambridge, UK, 2007.

73. World Business Council for Sustainable Development. *Energy Efficiency in Buildings: Business Realities and Opportunities*; World Business Council for Sustainable Development Geneva: Geneva, Switzerland, 2007.

74. Mulchand, A. S'pore has world's largest district cooling plant. In *The Traits Times*; Asia One; Singapore Press Holdings Ltd.: Singapore, 2013.

75. Othman, L. World's biggest underground district cooling network now at Marina Bay. *Today*, 31 May 2017.

76. Johnston, J.G. Singapore Reaches Retail Grid Parity For Solar. The 9 Billion, 2012. Available online: http://www.the9billion.com/2012/10/24/singapore-reaches-retail-grid-parity-for-solar/ (accessed on 19 May 2017).

77. Siau, M.E. HDB ramps up solar leasing with latest tender. In *Today Singapore*; Media Corp Press: Singapore, 2014.

78. NLB. *Singapore Standards*; National Library Board: Singapore, 2011.

79. Hoppe, T.; Bressers, H.; Lulofs, K. Energy conservation in Dutch housing renovation projects. In *The Social and Behavioural Aspects of Climate Change*; Martens, P., Ting Chiang, C., Eds.; Greenleaf: Sheffield, UK, 2010; pp. 68–95.

80. Hoppe, T.; Bressers, J.T.A.; Lulofs, K.R.D. Local government influence on energy conservation ambitions in existing housing sites—Plucking the low-hanging fruit? *Energy Policy* **2011**, *39*, 916–925. [CrossRef]

81. Higgins, A.; Syme, M.; McGregor, J.; Marquez, L.; Seo, S. Forecasting uptake of retrofit packages in office building stock under government incentives. *Energy Policy* **2014**, *65*, 501–511. [CrossRef]

 *sustainability*

Article

The Impact of Different Weather Files on London Detached Residential Building Performance— Deterministic, Uncertainty, and Sensitivity Analysis on CIBSE TM48 and CIBSE TM49 Future Weather Variables Using CIBSE TM52 as Overheating Criteria

Joseph Amoako-Attah and Ali B-Jahromi *

Department of Civil and Built Environment, School of Computing and Engineering, University of West London, London W5 5RF, UK; Joseph.Amoako-Attah@uwl.ac.uk
* Correspondence: ali.jahromi@uwl.ac.uk; Tel.: +44-0208-231-2270

Academic Editor: Umberto Berardi
Received: 18 August 2016; Accepted: 8 October 2016; Published: 22 November 2016

Abstract: Though uncertainties of input variables may have significant implications on building simulations, they are quite often not identified, quantified, or included in building simulations results. This paper considers climatic deterministic, uncertainty, and sensitivity analysis through a series of simulations using the CIBSE UKCIP02 future weather years, CIBSE TM48 for design summer years (DSYs), and the latest CIBSE TM49 DSY future weather data which incorporates the UKCP09 projections to evaluate the variance and the impact of differing London future weather files on indoor operative temperature of a detached dwelling in the United Kingdom using the CIBSE TM52 overheating criteria. The work analyses the variability of comparable weather data set to identify the most influential weather parameters that contribute to thermal comfort implications for these dwellings. The choice of these weather files is to ascertain their differences, as their development is underpinned by different climatic projections. The overall pattern of the variability of the UKCIP02 and UKCP09 Heathrow weather data sets under Monte Carlo sensitivity consideration do not seem to be very different from each other. The deterministic results show that the operative temperatures of the UKCIP02 are slightly higher than those of UKCP09, with the UKCP09 having a narrow range of operative temperatures. The Monte Carlo sensitivity analysis quantified and affirmed the dry bulb and radiant temperatures as the most influential weather parameters that affect thermal comfort on dwellings.

Keywords: building simulation; operative temperature; CIBSE overheating criteria; future weather; uncertainty and sensitivity analysis; CIBSE TM48; CIBSE TM49; CIBSE TM52

1. Introduction

There is a direct bearing of changes in climatic conditions on buildings in relation to buildings energy performance and thermal comfort. In building performance practice, it is imperative to secure reliable formatted multi-year weather files which have been prepared from reliable meteorological predictions to assess the energy performance and overheating risk in buildings [1–5].

In 2002, the Department for Environment, Food and Rural Affairs as part of the UK climate impacts program commissioned and funded the work on the UK climate projections, UKCIP02 [6]. This fourth generation of climate change is deterministic climate projection, which gives a single outcome for a specific variable at a given location [7]. The Climate Change Scenarios for the United Kingdom: The

UKCIP02 Scientific Report acknowledged that the UKCIP02 scenarios do not incorporate the entire range of possible future scenarios, as no probabilities were appended to the four climatic scenarios [6].

In 2009, the UK Climate Projections (UKCP09), the fifth and most comprehensive prediction of climate change projections was published by the United Kingdom Impacts Programme which has a collective contribution from the Met Office Hadley Centre, UK Climate Impacts Programme and over thirty different organisations [7] to provide practical support for effective adaptation to organisations whose work and functions are underpinned by climate change [7]. One of the key differences between the UKCIP02 and UKCP09 projections lies in the methodologies used in producing them. The UKCP09 scenarios are underpinned by probabilities of climate change based on quantification of the known sources of uncertainty. This aspect of the UKCP09 scenarios makes it supersede the UKCIP02 scenarios that are based only on a variant of one (Met Office) model [7].

The UKCP09 has deferring properties and characteristics when compared with UKCIP02. One key difference is that the UKCIP02 data generation is based on four of the six marker projected emission scenarios of the IPCC Special Report on Emission Scenarios (SRES) of high, medium-high, medium-low, and low, which underpin the United Kingdom's Meteorological Office Hadley Centre (MOHC) Climate Change Model (HadCM3) future global climate model (CIBSE 2009). On the other hand, the UKCP09 future projected emissions scenarios are underpinned by three of the six marker emission scenarios of the IPCC Special Report on Emission Scenarios of A1F1, A1B, and B1 scenarios, namely high, medium, and low emission scenarios, respectively [6,8,9].

In addition, the UKCIP02 variations are mapped to the MOHC HadRM3 regional climate models (RCM) to simulate climatic variations on a 50 km grid RCM spatial resolution [6]; UKCP09 scenarios, however, include pattern-scaling and down scaling uncertainty and have a greater RCM spatial resolution of 25 km, grid coupled with a 5 km resolution for a weather generator [7].

The output of climate models of the UKCIP02 and UKCP09 cannot be directly used in building simulation practice. Downscaling of annual, seasonal, or monthly outputs to hourly data is required. In 2008, the Chartered Institution of Building Services Engineers (CIBSE) released two sets of future weather files, the test reference years (TRYs) and the design summer years (DSYs) based on the UKCIP02 climate projections. The methodology used to produce the CIBSE future weather files was the 'morphing' time series adjustment [10] methodology that adjusted the historic weather files to the climate projection [8,11]. The first TRY typical year was based on direct observation of weather source baseline period of 1983–2004 [8]. These weather data sets are based on observed measurements and are deterministic in nature [11,12]. With the release of UKCP09 probabilistic climate projections, it was imperative to develop new methodologies that take cognisance of the probabilistic nature of the UKCP09 climate projections to advance the improvement of building simulation weather files. The Engineering and Physical Sciences Research Council (EPSRC) in 2008 funded four projects to utilize the probabilistic UKCP09 to produce weather files for building simulation analysis. CIBSE, on the other hand, have sought potential alternatives (with the morphing methodology in view) to offer weather files for building simulations based on the UKCP09 probabilistic climate projections [11].

The CIBSE TRY weather files as representative weather years for building energy performance analysis are not suitable for overheating analysis; hence, the DSY weather files were developed [13]. The method for developing the DSY weather files is simple when compared with that of the TRY weather files [13]. The CIBSE DSY is a single complete weather year which gives a near extreme weather year. CIBSE has currently developed a new methodology for producing DSYs based on the UKCP09 probabilistic climate projections for use in building simulations. This offers a better correlation between the likelihood of the DSY occurring and the likelihood of building overheating [14]. These new DSYs for London take into consideration the geographical location, the impact of the urban heat island effect, and future climate change, when performing building simulation summer overheating analysis for London [14,15]. The new DSY weather files for London include two additional weather stations of London Weather Centre (LWC) and Gatwick Airport (GTW). This offers different levels of overheating risk assessment for different locations in London, namely urban, intermediate urban, and suburban locations. Moreover, the new DSYs include the two additional years of 1976 (a year with two-week extreme heat wave) and 2003 (a year with more persistent warm summer) as the earlier DSY based on 1989 weather data from London Heathrow Airport (LHR) does not represent a sufficiently warm year for overheating risk assessment in buildings [14]. In addition, it considers three greenhouse emissions scenarios of high, medium, and low, three future periods of 2020s, 2050s, and 2080s, and differing levels of probabilities of 10th, 50th, and 90th percentiles [14,15].

1.1. Justification for the Choice of CIBSE Weather Files

Over the years, different approaches for developing weather data series for building performance analysis have been developed [7,16]. In the UK, basically two differing methodologies stand out in creating hourly weather files for use in building simulation practice; the 'morphing' methodology which is the current industrial standard by CIBSE, which adjusted the historic weather files to climatic projections, and the development of various probabilistic projections of hourly weather data sets by the use of the UKCP09 weather generator.

The UKCP09 weather generator is a stochastic tool that uses daily precipitation to create other weather outputs of daily and hourly variables on a 5 km grid for a historical period of 1961–1990 [7]. This offers an advantage due to greater spatial resolution. In addition, the weather generator is suitable for future TRY and DSY weather data sets for building performance analysis [11]. However, the CIBSE weather data sets developed using the morphing methodology are based on observed climatic periods and thus have limited uncertainties which could affect the baseline weather data [13]. Without the implementation of change factor corrections, the CIBSE weather data sets could result in overestimating future climate change variations due to changes in differences of climates reference points: 1961–1990 for the weather generator and 1983–2004 for the earlier CIBSE historic TRY and DSY weather files [11,13].

The choice of the CIBSE morphing methodology as against the weather generation data is based on its reliability [14]. The weather generator does not produce extreme events [11]. The weather generator output of weather data sets years is not as warm in terms of the Weighted Cooling Degree Hours (WCDH) criterion used in the historical data development of the new CIBSE DSYs. This is because the 'extremes of the temperature distribution are not clustered together into particular warm years to the extent as they are in the observed data' [14].

Although the monthly average climate over the years changes, one advantage of the morphing methodology in the non-variant underlying characteristics of the TRY and DSY weather data sets, which facilitates a direct comparison between the present and future building performance analyses. On the other hand, there are differences in basic weather characteristics such as the timing and severity of warm spells between the timelines in using the weather generator [11]. Furthermore, the current CIBSE DSY weather data sets for London consider the urban heat island effects in future weather files, whilst this consideration is absent in the UKCIP09 weather generator.

The use of the weather generator to statistically produce many thousands of historic and probabilistic future weather data at a high spatial resolution provides the significant advantage of a better idea of a complete data set for overheating risk assessment when compared with the observable weather data [17]. The weather generator has an advantage over the morphing methodology. It produces certain weather variables in place of missing data [11] when considering observed data independently. However, the many files generated pose a computational challenge to resources not readily available in building simulation practices [11,13].

A readily acceptable methodology should produce an output of weather data sets that is consistent with currently used data sets and augment the use of standardised weather data sets for use in building energy and thermal performance analysis. The weather generator's outputs of daily precipitation, partial vapour pressure, relative humidity, maximum temperature, minimum temperature, sunshine fraction, direct radiation, and potential evapotranspiration are insufficient for use within thermal simulation for building energy and thermal performance analysis. Key missing parameters such as wind speed, wind direction, atmospheric pressure, and cloud cover are essential in creating weather files of the same format, as is used in CIBSE weather data sets for building simulation software [11,13,17].

Although the weather generator method is more versatile than the morphing method, in terms of observed data and location, the large amount of weather data produced is of a disadvantage in simulation practice [16]. The CIBSE weather files based on the morphing methodology are used in this work due to the consistency between the present available observable historic weather files and those of the future files and a platform for direct comparison of standardised weather data sets for energy and thermal performance analysis. The majority of building performance simulators in the UK make use of CIBSE weather files as trusted consistently replicable weather data sets in their work, as it offers a single data set for a particular location, climatic period, emission scenario, and probability level for all designers to compare building performances [16,18]. This serves as the primary reason for the use of CIBSE weather data sets for this work.

This paper analyses the variability of the selected comparable CIBSE TM48 and CIBSE TM49 weather data set on internal operative temperatures to identify the most influential weather parameters that contribute to indoor operative temperatures in three locations in London. Uncertainty and sensitivity analysis of the CIBSE weather data sets based on the deterministic single projection of UKCIP02 and the CIBSE weather data sets based on the probabilistic UKCP09 projections is performed to ascertain the contrast between the two files. In addition, the 50th percentile central estimate weather files for Heathrow 1989 was used to provide comparable outputs in relation to the CIBSE's 2008 weather files. Moreover, the UKCP09 A1B (medium emission scenario) and the UKCIP02 A2 (medium-high emission scenario) are used for comparative analysis, as the two emission scenarios are closer in the chosen time period.

1.2. Monte Carlo Uncertainty and Sensitivity Analysis

The key to determining the target output of thermal comfort is a comprehensive building model and credible input variable information [19]. Though uncertainties of input variables may have significant implications on building simulations, they are quite often not identified, quantified, or included in building simulations [19]. Most simulation programs do not incorporate uncertainties in input and thus result in outputs of single estimates [19]. Uncertainties in building energy simulations are associated with the variability of the weather data, the thermo-physical properties of the buildings in relation to the building fabric and systems, and the associated internal heat gains coupled with variable occupant behaviour. The occurrence of uncertainties is attributed to incomplete specifications, inadequate knowledge of building characteristics, and a lack of specifications in operating conditions in relation to weather, internal heat gains, and system set points [19]. It may also relate to inherent simplifications of a model and a lack of sufficient input data information [20]. The impact of these input uncertainties influence the accuracy of building energy simulations in spite of the efficacy of the applied model [19]. Uncertainty analysis is thus used to determine a confidence limit for a model output [21].

1.3. Thermal Comfort

Thermal comfort is defined as that condition of mind that expresses satisfaction with the thermal environment [22]. It is one of the main criteria in accessing the overall post occupancy of building [23] and involves the interactions between the climate, the building with its services, and variable occupant behaviour [24]. Global thermal comfort models fall into two broad classes: the adaptive [25] and the rational [26]. Adaptive models are generally based on field investigations aimed to correlate acceptable indoor conditions as a function of the mean outdoor temperature [27]. On the contrary, the rational approach is based on the correlation of the thermal sensation with the heat balance equation on the human body [28], which is affected by the indoor microclimate (air temperature, mean radiant temperature, humidity, and air velocity) and personal parameters (activity and clothing thermophysical properties). For both approaches and under specific hypotheses in terms of the values of the main variables affecting the thermal sensation [26], the operative temperature can be used as an indicator of indoor comfort conditions.

Indoor operative temperature is a simplified measure of thermal comfort. Operative temperature can be calculated by averaging the air temperature with the mean radiant temperature with a weighting factor depending upon the air velocity [22]. Studies indicate that comfort temperature is closely related to the indoor operative temperature [29,30]. Too low or too high operative temperatures affect the thermal comfort of building occupants in general [31].

This paper focuses on using building simulation tools to produce indoor climatic data in the form of operative temperatures as a means of expressing thermal comfort based on CIBSE TM52 overheating criteria that is underpinned by the adaptive thermal comfort models. The CIBSE TM52 criteria is for naturally ventilated buildings [24].

2. Materials and Methods

In this work, Monte Carlo approaches are used in estimating climatic deterministic, uncertainty, and sensitivity analysis through a series of simulations using the UK Charted Institution of Building Services Engineers CIBSE UKCIP02 future weather years, CIBSE TM48 for design summer years (DSY), and the latest CIBSE TM49 DSY future weather data which incorporates the UKCP09 projections, to evaluate the variance in climatic projections and the impact of future climate change on the thermal comfort of a detached dwelling in the United Kingdom using the CIBSE TM52 overheating criteria. The global sensitivity analysis used in the study incorporates the standardised regression coefficient (SRC) and the partial correlation coefficient as sensitivity indices to identify the key parameters that contribute to thermal comfort implications in the dwellings due to climate change. In building simulation practices, it is acceptable for two different sensitivity analysis methods to be used to ascertain their robustness and further inspire confidence in the results [32].

The essence for the climatic sensitivity analysis is based on the following:

(1)   the limitations of the CIBSE TM48 morphing methodology in producing certain variables that independently have no relationship to the probabilistic consideration of the UKCP09 CIBSE TM49 weather series, making the output different from the latest weather data series;

(2)   differences in the baseline periods for the two climate projections: 1983–2004 and 1961–1990 baselines for the UKCIP02 and UKCP09 projections, respectively;

(3)   a consideration of the London urban heat island effect in the CIBSE TM49 weather files leading to the generation of three different weather data sets for London; and

(4)   a consideration of the extreme heat waves experienced in 1976 and 2003 years to examine overheating risk under different scenarios.

2.1. Thermal Analysis Simulation (TAS) 3D Modelling

It is generally recommended that for naturally ventilated buildings, the 50th percentile (best guess) projections and the medium greenhouse gas emission scenario has to be used in the building simulation analysis [33]. This choice of UKCP09 future weather file based on the 50th percentile of external temperature and 2050s emission scenarios was used because of its usage in other studies. For example, Mavrogianni et al. in 2012 used this criterion for their dynamic thermal simulation work for identifying factors that affect the high indoor summer temperatures in London dwellings [33]. The medium-high climate change emission scenario was chosen in the UPCIP02 weather file consideration. The CIBSE TM36, using dynamic thermal modelling, offered a quantitative assessment of the risks of overheating in 13 case study buildings comprising of houses, offices, and schools for three locations in the UK, using the UKCIP02 medium-high climate change scenario and the CIBSE Guide A (2006) [34] as the overheating criteria [35].

The various modelling and simulation parameters of Building Summary, Calendar, Building Elements, Zones, Internal conditions (which include thermostat set up, infiltration and ventilation, occupancy, lighting and equipment details), Schedule, and Aperture Types, which were used to populate and simulate each building, are maintained with the only variant being the weather data.

For details of the model, that is u-values, occupancy patterns, and other modelling and simulation assumptions and parameters, as well as the accuracy of the internal temperatures within the model, please see Appendix A.

A series of scenarios based on the current and the future climate variables on different timelines of 2020s, 2050s, and 2080s with their respective medium-high carbon scenarios for the CIBSE TM48 UKCIP02 weather files and similar time slice of 2020s, 2050s, and 2080s for CIBSE TM49 UKCP09 weather files are simulated for Gatwick Airport, London Weather Centre and Heathrow Airport.

2.2. Developing Multivariate Linear Regression

The case study is based on a building simulation and global sensitivity analysis that explores the analysis of uncertainties and sensitivities related to climate change variability. The IBM SPSS statistics Monte Carlo sensitivity analysis tool is used to identify the influential parameters that affect the internal operative temperature (thermal comfort) of dwellings.

The CIBSE weather data set used in the EDSL TAS simulation has seven key weather variables of global horizontal radiation, cloud cover, relative humidity, wind direction, wind speed, diffused horizontal radiation, and dry bulb temperature. Table 1 indicates the input parameters with their probability distributions for the uncertainty and sensitivity analysis for the climate change impact on thermal comfort. The CIBSE weather data sets used in this study are the design summer year (DSY) CIBSE TM48 UKCIP02 weather files and the CIBSE TM49 UKCP09 weather files for Gatwick Airport, London Weather Centre, and Heathrow Airport.

Table 1. Input parameters with their probability distributions for the uncertainty and sensitivity analysis for the climate change impact on thermal comfort.

Input Parameter	Acronym	Units	Probability Distribution
Global Radiation	GR	W/m^2	Normal
Diffused Radiation	DR	W/m^2	Normal
Cloud Cover	CC	(0–1)	Normal
External Temperature	ET	(°C)	Normal
External Humidity	EH	(%)	Normal
Wind Direction	WD	(°)	Normal
Wind Speed	WS	(m/s)	Normal
Average Radiation Temperature	ART	(°C)	Normal
Average Dry Bulb Temperature	ADBT	(°C)	Normal
Daily Hourly Exponentially Weighted Running Mean Temperature	DHEWRMT	(°C)	Normal

The detached dwelling used as the case study is 49 Carnation Drive, a 1995 three-bedroom house located at Bracknell, Berkshire, about 48 km from Central London, the closest weather station for CIBSE TM48 UKCIP02. For CIBSE TM49 UKCP09 weather files, the case study building location is located at 48.87 km, 48 km, and 18.71 km respectively from Gatwick Airport, London Weather Centre and Heathrow Airport.

EDSL TAS simulations were performed on variations of climate change as input parameters and consider uncertainties in various CIBSE DSY weather files in predicting indoor operative temperature as a thermal comfort indicative parameter. The EDSL TAS coupled with the developed Excel CIBSE TM52 overheating criteria historical data were then sent to IBM SPSS statistical software to create a multivariate linear regression XML model. The aim of this multivariate linear regression model was to capture the complex thermal interaction of parameters used in the EDSL TAS program. The uncertainty and sensitivity analysis on the multivariate linear regression model was then subsequently analysed using IBM SPSS statistics software.

2.3. Uncertainty and Sensitivity Analysis Due to Climate Change

This work employs the box and whiskers plot as one of the effective methods used in uncertainty analysis. The box and whiskers plot presents a summary of the important data set characteristics of the maximum and minimum values, the median, the dispersion, asymmetry, the extreme values, and the percentile rank analysis [36].

The purpose of sensitivity analysis in building performance modelling and simulation and observational study is to explore the uncertainty of the key input parameters that influence the prediction of the building performance parameters and to investigate the important varying contribution of different design parameters with respect to building performance [12,37]. The regression sensitivity analysis is mostly used in building performance analysis due to its computational and results interpretation simplicity [37].

The standardised regression coefficient (SRC) or the beta value method sensitivity analysis is widely used in the literature [12,37,38] and as it offers variability measure of independent input parameters in a linear regression model. The SRC offers a quantitative global sensitivity analysis index which is robust and easy to use [20]. It gives a quantitative measure of parameter sensitivity and influences the different input parameters on the output with the sign indicating the direction of the parameter sensitivity to the target parameter [38].

The standardised regression coefficient (SRC) and partial correlation coefficient (PCC) are chosen as regression sensitivity methods because they are appropriate for linear models [38]. The partial correlation assists in the examination of the relationship or association between two variables whilst controlling the other variables. Whilst the two methods may give the same results in the case of uncorrelated inputs, differences in results may show if there are correlated inputs as only PCC is appropriate for both correlated and uncorrelated inputs, but SRC is only suitable for uncorrelated inputs [38]. The standardised rank regression coefficient is not used, as it is only applicable for non-linear models [38].

Sensitivity analysis involves the changes in different design parameters to ascertain their relative influence on the target variable. The developed multivariate linear regression XML model is used to run the uncertainty and sensitivity analysis in the IBM SPSS statistical software. The Monte Carlo simulation was set to 100,000 iteration runs for each target parameter to provide adequate coverage of the solution space. The results of the uncertainty analysis are presented as box and whiskers plots. The box and whiskers plot also shows the variations in sensitivity measures for various input parameters. The IBM SPSS software is then used to calculate the standardised regression coefficient (SRC) and partial correlation coefficient (PCC) to ascertain the input parameters that are most sensitive and thus explain the high variability in the models.

3. Results

3.1. Deterministic Analysis

Figure 1 illustrates the deterministic analysis results in the form of histogram. The analysis compares the maximum, minimum, average, and range of internal operative temperatures using CIBSE TM52 as overheating criteria and of UKCIP02 Heathrow DSY medium-high and the UKCP09 Heathrow 1989 medium 50% probabilistic scenarios weather data sets.

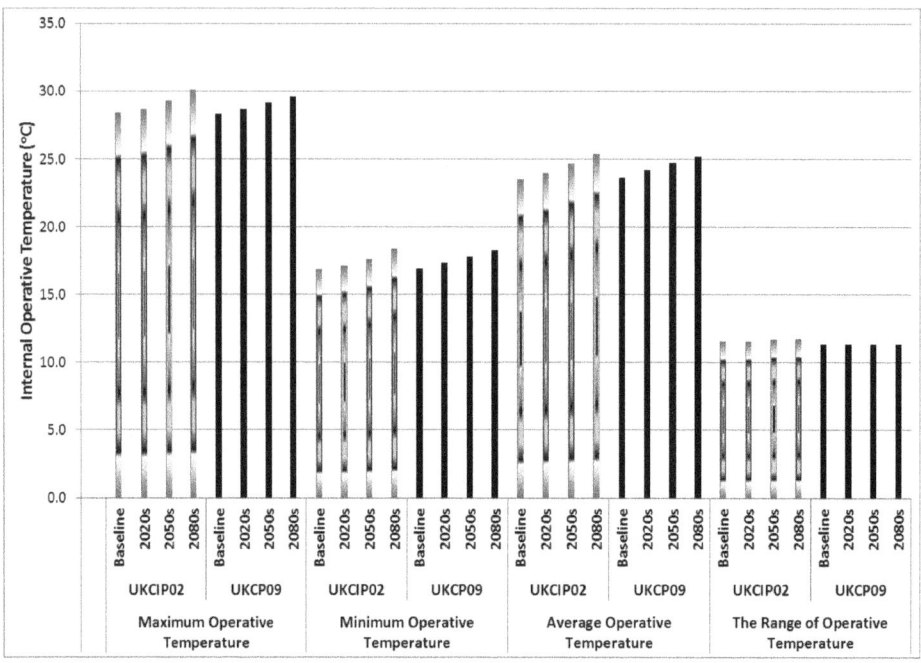

Figure 1. Internal operative temperatures for UKCIP02 Heathrow DSY medium-high and UKCP09 Heathrow 1989 medium 50% probabilistic scenarios.

There is a marginal difference in maximum operative temperatures for the Heathrow DSY medium-high and UKCP09 Heathrow 1989 medium 50% probabilistic scenarios for the baseline, 2020s, and 2050s weather data sets, with the former being slightly higher. For the 2080s scenarios, the difference in operative temperature for the two weather data sets is about 0.5 °C. The minimum operative temperature variability indicates a similar trend of marginal difference. The minimum operative temperatures for the UKCP09 Heathrow DSY 1989 medium 50% probabilistic scenarios' weather data sets for the baseline, the 2020s, and 2050s timelines show slightly higher temperatures in the range of about 0.1 °C for all respective comparative scenarios. The 2080s scenario variation is the opposite of that observed in other timelines with the UKCIP02 showing slightly higher minimum temperatures. The average internal operative temperatures for the two weather data sets' respective timelines show a strong similarity in the trend of average operative temperatures. The range operative temperatures for the UKCIP02 Heathrow DSY medium-high are slightly higher than their respective comparative timelines for the UKCP09 Heathrow 1989 medium 50% probabilistic scenarios, ranging from about 0.25 °C to 0.42 °C for the baseline and 2080s scenarios respectively.

Figures 2–5 illustrate the deterministic analysis results in the form of histogram analysis comparison of the maximum, minimum, average and range of operative temperatures of UKCP09 Heathrow DSY Medium 50% probabilistic scenarios for 1976, 1989 and 2003 and the time series analysis of internal operative temperatures using CIBSE TM52 as overheating criteria.

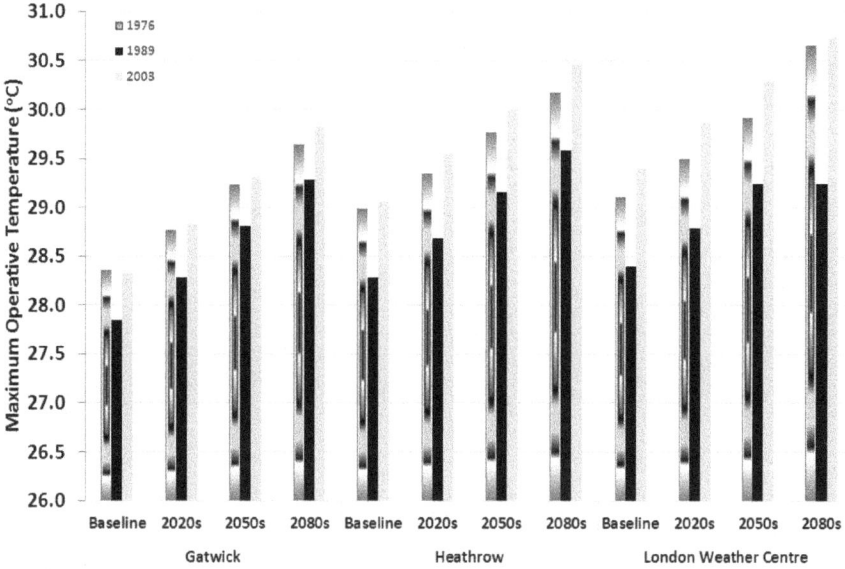

Figure 2. A comparison of maximum internal operative temperatures for Gatwick, Heathrow and London Weather Centre using UKCP09 1976, 1989 and 2003 medium 50% probabilistic weather data set scenarios with overheating analysis based on CIBSE TM52 adaptive thermal comfort criteria.

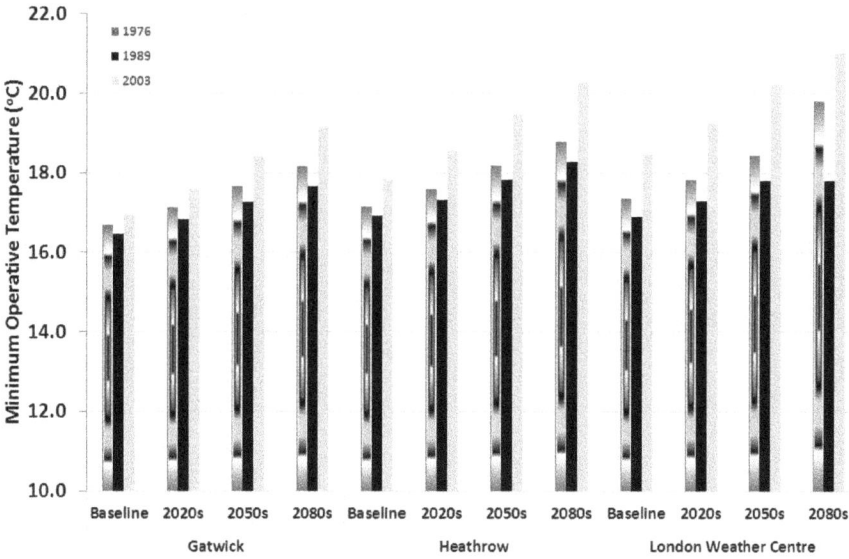

Figure 3. A comparison of minimum internal operative temperatures for Gatwick, Heathrow and London Weather Centre using UKCP09 1976, 1989 and 2003 medium 50% probabilistic weather data set scenarios with overheating analysis based on CIBSE TM52 adaptive thermal comfort criteria.

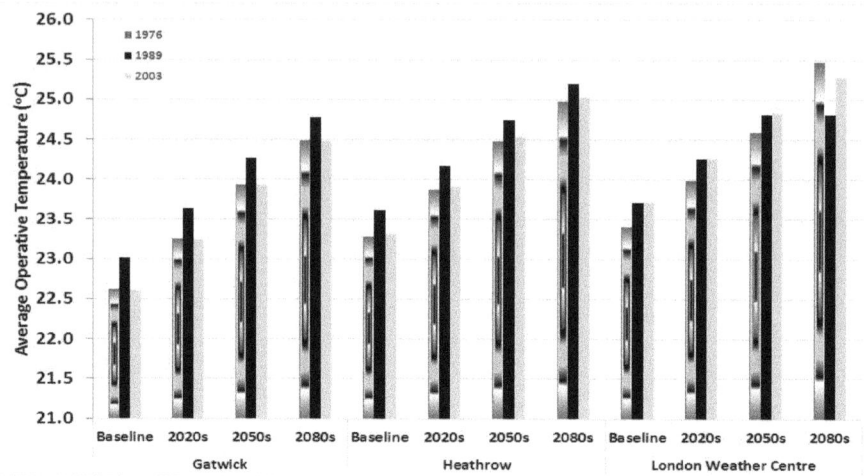

Figure 4. A comparison of average internal operative temperatures for Gatwick, Heathrow and London Weather Centre using UKCP09 1976, 1989 and 2003 medium 50% probabilistic weather data set scenarios with overheating analysis based on CIBSE TM52 adaptive thermal comfort criteria.

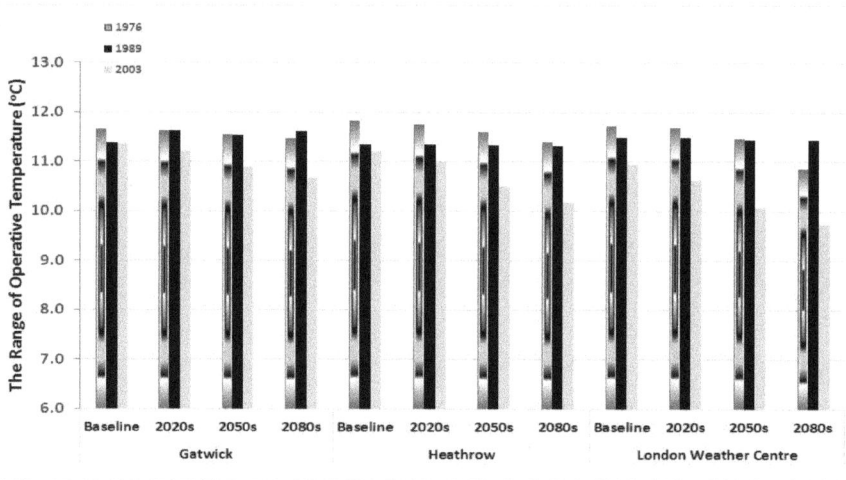

Figure 5. A comparison of the range internal operative temperatures for Gatwick, Heathrow and London Weather Centre using UKCP09 1976, 1989 and 2003 medium 50% probabilistic weather data set scenarios with overheating analysis based on CIBSE TM52 adaptive thermal comfort criteria.

As expected, there is a progressive increase in maximum internal operative temperatures for 1976 and 2003 for all timeline scenarios. Gatwick has the lowest maximum operative temperatures whilst London Weather Centre is observed to have the highest operative temperatures. The difference in the maximum operative temperatures between the various timeline scenarios of Gatwick when compared with Heathrow and London Weather Centre show a difference of about 0.6 °C and 1.0 °C for Heathrow and London Weather Centre respectively. The highest maximum operative temperatures for the London Weather Centre timelines could be attributed to the urban heat island effect. Similar trends are observed in Figure 3 which compares the minimum internal operative temperatures for the three locations using UKCP09 1976, 1989 and 2003 medium 50% probabilistic weather data set scenarios with overheating analysis based on CIBSE TM52 adaptive thermal comfort criteria.

The average operative temperatures for the three locations indicated as expected, with London Weather Centre having the highest average temperatures followed by Heathrow. Gatwick has the least average operative temperatures when compared to the other two locations. The 1989 medium 50% probabilistic weather data set appears to have slightly higher average operative temperatures of about 0.5 °C when compared to all scenarios of the 1976 and 2003 weather data sets. Comparison of the range operative temperatures shows the 2003 medium 50% probabilistic weather data set to have the lowest value when compared to the other years.

3.2. Uncertainty Analysis—Box and Whiskers Plots

Figure 6 illustrates the comparison of the UKCIP02 Heathrow DSY medium-high and UKCP09 Heathrow DSY 1989 medium 50% probabilistic weather data set effect on internal operative temperature to ascertain the impact of climate change on thermal comfort of residential buildings. The box and whiskers plot is a graphical method of representing data through their quartiles. The plots show the uncertainty associated with Monte Carlo simulation of overheating analysis with internal operative temperatures as the output parameter using the various weather scenarios indicated above as the only variants. The ten (10) input variables as displayed in Table 1 are used in the analysis and the same sample size of 3672 hourly data between 1 May and 30 September as specified in the CIBSE TM52 overheating criteria which were used in each analysis.

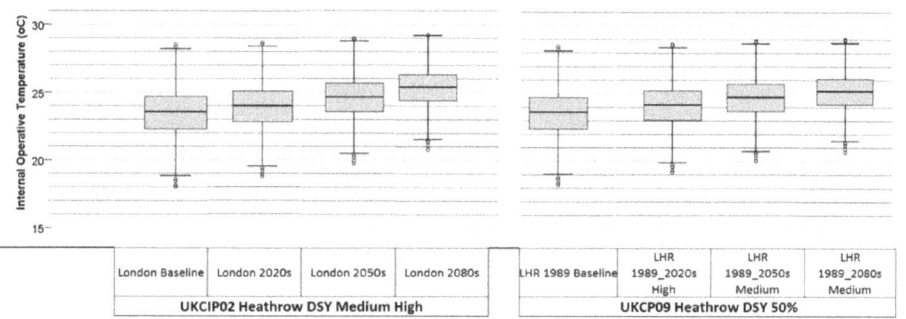

Figure 6. Box and whiskers plots of the UKCIP02 Heathrow DSY medium-high and UKCP09 Heathrow DSY 1989 medium 50% probabilistic weather data set.

A comparison of the median lines shows that the 50th percentiles of the UKCP09 for the 2020s and 2050s are slightly higher than that of the UKCIP02 weather projections, whilst the opposite is realised with regard to the 2080s weather data set. However, the overall pattern of variability of the two weather data sets seems to be not very different from each other as analysis of the UKCIP02 and UKCP09 results show that the median changes from 23.5 °C to 25.4 °C and 23.5 °C to 25.3°C respectively. Thus, there is no marked observable effect of change in internal operative temperatures in the two sets of the uncertainty analysis results.

The whiskers of the plots, indicated by the extended vertical lines above and below the plots and which show the variability of the internal operative temperatures outside the upper (75th percentiles) and lower quartiles (25th percentiles) to the 90th percentile and 10th percentile of the data sets respectively, also show symmetry pointing to the non-skewedness of the data. The whisker plots progressively decrease along the time lines of the two different weather data sets with the decrease in the UKCP09 Heathrow 1989 DSY Medium 50% probabilistic weather data sets slightly more pronounced than the UKCIP02 Heathrow DSY medium-high data sets.

The outliers showing the individual points outside the whiskers with 10% probability of occurrence are virtually similar when comparing the respective timeline scenarios of the two different weather data sets. The outliers for both the maximum and minimum values generally lie close to the whiskers' ends.

Figure 7 illustrates the box plots comparison of the internal operative temperatures reported in relation to the effect of the design summer year (DSY) medium 50% probabilistic scenarios of the 1976, 1989, and 2003 weather data sets of Gatwick, Heathrow, and London Weather Centre.

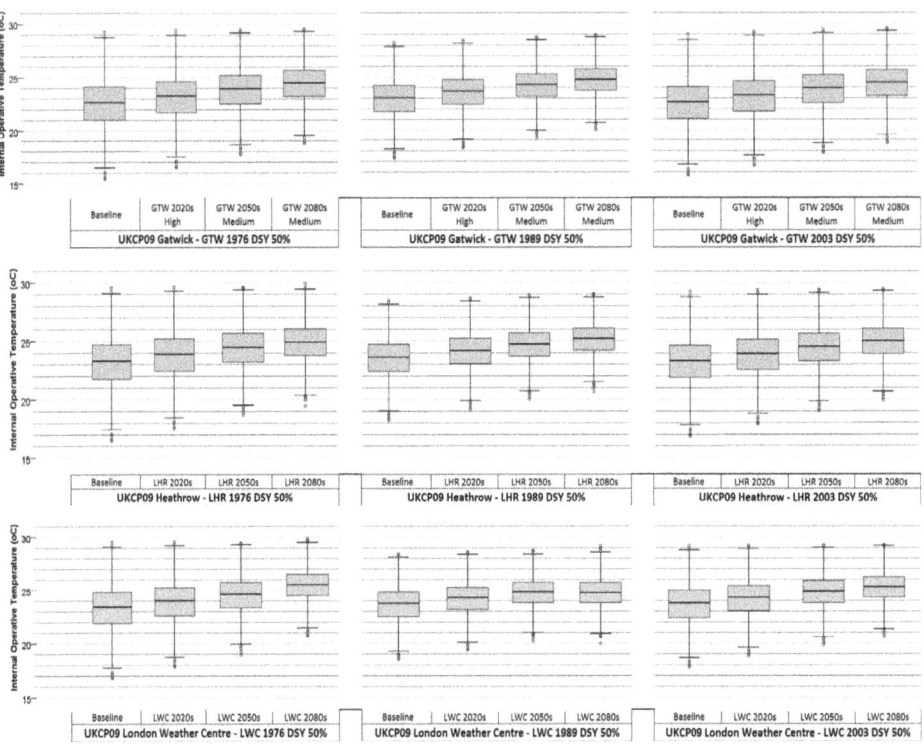

Figure 7. Box and whiskers plot comparison of the internal operative temperatures reported in relation to the effect of the design summer year (DSY) medium 50% probabilistic scenarios of the 1976, 1989, and 2003 weather data sets of Gatwick, Heathrow, and London Weather Centre.

In general, there is zero skewedness of the interquartile ranges and the whiskers. A progressive decrease of variability in the length of the interquartile ranges (IQR) is observed along the years, coupled with a progressive decrease in the whiskers. Thus, the baselines have larger dispersion for both the box and the whiskers and progressively decrease along the timelines.

Moreover, the variability of the interquartile range and the relative dispersion of the data set outer range are larger in the 1976 and 2003 scenarios than that of the 1989 scenario, indicating a clustering of parameters near the 25th and 75th percentiles and a further large dispersion of the outliers.

As expected, the medians of the 1989 scenarios of Gatwick, Heathrow, and London Weather Centre are comparatively lower than those of the 1976 and 2003 scenarios. In addition, the interquartile ranges and the whiskers are relatively smaller. This observation points to a relatively middle clustering of data about the medians, 25th percentiles, and the 75th percentiles of the 1989 timeline scenarios, indicating less uncertainty in the target variable of internal operative temperatures.

In general, the medians for the 2003 scenarios are higher than those of the 1976 scenarios. Furthermore, analysis of Figure 7 shows that the medians of the London Weather Centre timeline scenarios are higher than those of their comparative Heathrow timelines scenarios and even higher than those of the Gatwick timeline scenarios. This could be attributed to the urban heat effect in the city of London. As anticipated, the outliers of the 1976 and 2003 weather scenarios lie further away from the whiskers when compared with that of the 1989 data set point towards more extreme internal operative temperatures in those years' weather data sets.

3.3. Sensitivity Analysis with SRC and PCC as Sensitivity Indices

Figure 8 illustrates the comparison of the standardised regression coefficient (SRC) and the partial correlation coefficients (PCC) of the weather input variables for the UKCIP02 Heathrow and UKCP09 1989 Heathrow weather data sets. Figure 9 illustrates the comparison of the standardised regression coefficient (SRC) and the partial correlation coefficients (PCC) of the weather input variables for the UKCP09 1976 Gatwick, Heathrow and London Weather Centre weather data sets.

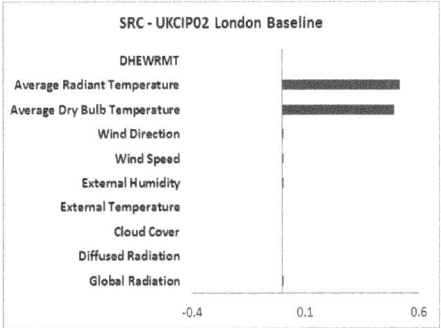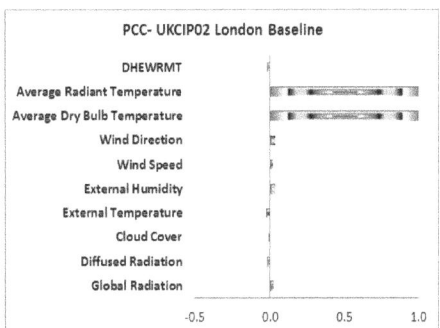
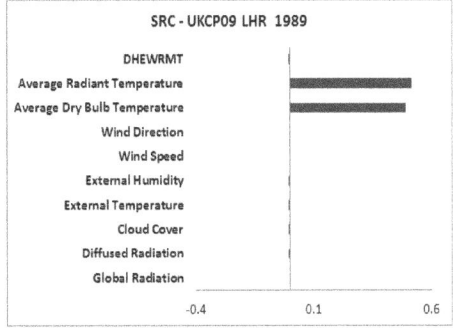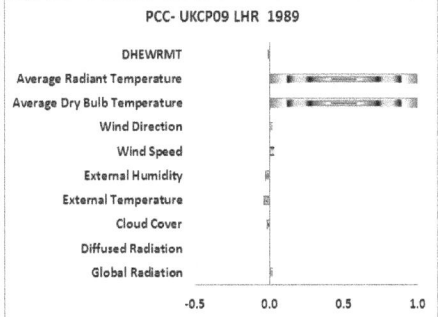

Figure 8. Comparison of the standardised regression coefficient (SRC) and the partial correlation coefficients (PCC) of the weather input variables for the UKCIP02 Heathrow and UKCP09 1989 Heathrow weather data sets.

All the sensitivity analysis results, when considering the variation of the weather data alone, indicate that the internal operative temperature of dwellings is mostly influenced by the radiant temperature and the dry bulb temperature. The other weather variables of wind direction, wind speed, external humidity, external temperature, cloud cover, diffused radiation, global radiation, and the daily hourly exponentially weight running mean temperature have a relatively small impact on the internal operative temperature. This observation is in consonance with the formulae used in predicting thermal comfort in CIBSE TM52 and BSI (2007) BS EN 15251, which combine the air and radiant temperatures to obtain the operative temperature.

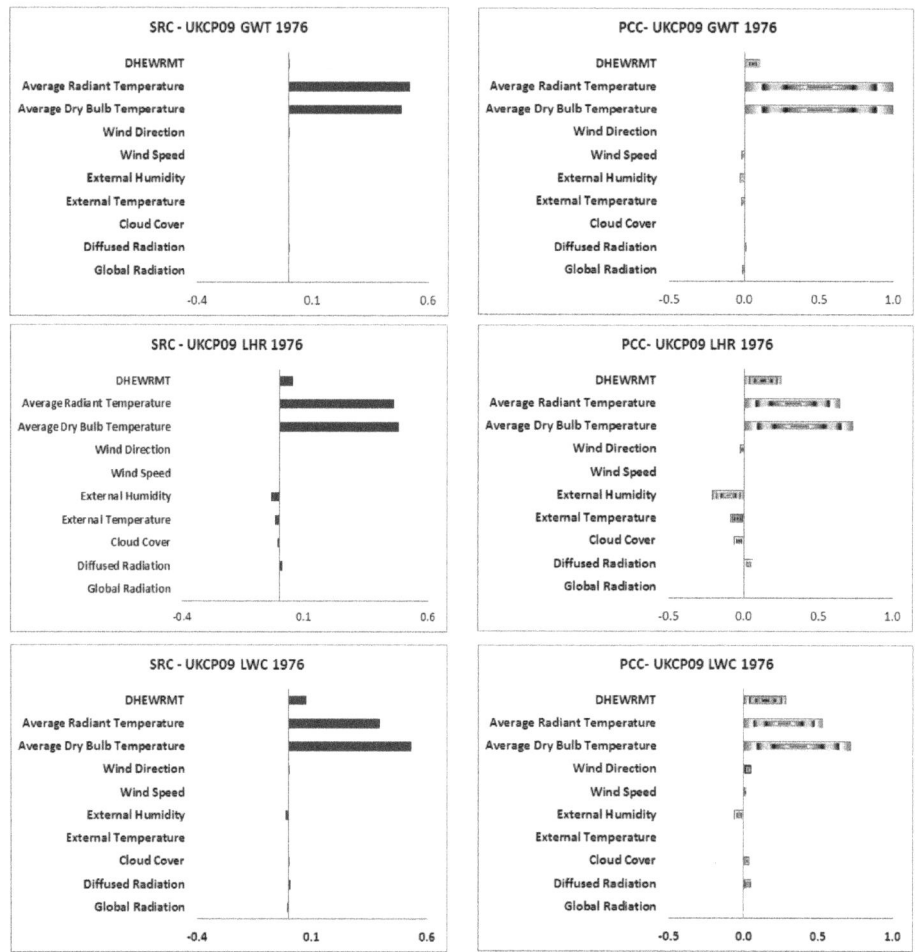

Figure 9. Comparison of the standardised regression coefficient (SRC) and the partial correlation coefficients (PCC) of the weather input variables for the UKCP09 1976 Gatwick, Heathrow and London Weather Centre weather data sets.

4. Discussion and Conclusions

This study investigated the impact of varying weather patterns on the thermal performance of dwellings. The work is underpinned by building simulation models in TAS coupled with the Monte Carlo global sensitivity analysis method using IBM SPSS to indicate that the proposed method can facilitate the analysis and prediction of sensitive weather parameters which influence the thermal comfort of residential buildings.

The deterministic analysis results of the UKCP09 Heathrow DSY Medium 50% probabilistic scenarios for 1976, 1989, and 2003 indicated a progressive increase in maximum internal operative temperatures for the 1976 and 2003 years for all timeline scenarios. Gatwick had the lowest maximum operative temperatures, whilst London Weather Centre was observed to have the highest operative temperatures. This affirmed the incorporation of the urban heat island effect of the London Weather Centre weather data sets of CIBSE TM49, as compared with the Heathrow and Gatwick weather files.

The Monte Carlo uncertainty analysis results of the median lines showed that the 50th percentiles of the UKCP09 for the 2020s and 2050s are slightly higher than that of the UKCIP02 weather projections, whilst the opposite is realised with regard to the 2080s weather data set. However, the overall patterns of variability of the two weather data sets do not seem to be very different from each other, as analysis of the UKCIP02 and UKCP09 results show that the median changes from 23.5 °C to 25.4 °C and 23.5 °C to 25.3 °C, respectively. Thus, there is no marked observable effect of change in internal operative temperatures in the two sets of the uncertainty analysis results. However, the deterministic results shows the operative temperatures of the UKCIP02 are slightly higher than those of UKCP09, with the UKCP09 having a narrow range of operative temperatures.

The Monte Carlo sensitivity analysis quantified and identified the dry bulb and radiant temperatures as the most influential weather parameters that affect thermal comfort on dwellings. This finding agrees with published literature (CIBSE TM52, 2013; CIBSE Guide A, 2006). These study results further indicate the marginal differences in maximum and minimum operative temperatures for the Heathrow DSY medium-high and UKCP09 Heathrow 1989 medium 50% probabilistic scenarios for the baseline, 2020s, and 2050s weather data sets, with the former being slightly higher. For the 2080s scenarios, the difference in maximum operative temperature for the two weather data sets was about 0.5 °C. Moreover, the time series analysis of internal operative temperatures using CIBSE TM52 as overheating criteria for the UKCIP02 Heathrow DSY medium-high and UKCP09 Heathrow DSY 1989 medium 50% probabilistic scenario weather data sets showed a very strong similarity in the respective timelines for the two weather data sets.

The standardised regression coefficient and the partial correlation coefficients are useful sensitivity indices for determining the relative importance of weather parameters that influence the indoor operative temperatures of dwellings. The work stresses the need for climate sensitive design, and knowledge of this could offer insight for efficient designs and retrofitting practice to improve the thermal comfort of dwellings. In addition, this work is useful in sustainable engineering practice, as it could be extended to the energy requirements of buildings.

For easy analysis and replicable of the methodology used in this work, it is recommended that building simulation software incorporate Monte Carlo and global sensitivity analysis as key standard functionalities of its modelling. This will enable simulation software to facilitate the analysis and predict key thermal performance parameters and further assess different energy conservation measures.

Author Contributions: Ali B-Jahromi conceived and designed the project; Joseph Amoako-Attah performed the experiments and analyzed the data. Joseph Amoako-Attah and Ali B-Jahromi wrote and reviewed the paper.

Conflicts of Interest: The authors declare no conflict of interest.

Appendix A

Table A1. Modelling and Simulation Parameters and Assumptions.

Building Fabric—Calculated area weighted average U-values	Wall	0.42 W/m²K
	Floor	0.46 W/m²K
	Roof	0.19 W/m²K
	Windows	3.29 W/m²K
	Door	2.74 W/m²K
	Garage door	1.77 W/m²K
Construction Data Base	NCM Construction—v5.2.tcd	
Occupancy levels; People density; Lux level	Bath	0.01873684 pers/m². 150 Lux
	Bed	0.01873684 pers/m². 100 Lux
	Circulation area	0.02293877 pers/m². 100 Lux
	Dining	0.0169163 pers/m². 150 Lux
	Kitchen	0.0237037 pers/m². 300 Lux
	Lounge	0.0187563 pers/m². 150 Lux
	Toilet	0.02431718 pers/m². 100 Lux
Fuel Source	Natural Gas	CO_2 Factor 0.216 Kg/kWh
	Grid Electricity	CO_2 Factor 0.519 Kg/kWh
Orientation	Latitude, longitude and time zone used in the modelling are 51.5 degrees North 0.4 degree East and UTC + 0.0 respectively to reflect the geographical and time parameters of London. Sheppey, Sheerness is 59.4 km from London, the closest weather station.	
Glazing	4-16-4 uncoated glass, air filled; solar energy transmittance of 0.76 and total (normal) light transmittance of 0.8	
Ventilation	Simple natural cross-ventilation in all directions. Window width is 10% less than wall external area. Openable window proportion 50% set in the manner of side openable windows. Set openable window temperature 20–21 °C (control zone dry bulb temperature). Openable window schedule 8 a.m. to 4 p.m.	
Weather data	DSY (CIBSE) for Gatwick, Heathrow and London Weather Centre. It includes Global Solar Radiation, Diffuse Solar Radiation, Cloud Cover, Dry Bulb temperature, Relative Humidity, Wind Speed and Wind Direction.	
Impact of shading	TAS simulation of "mean height of surroundings"	
Terrain type	City	
Ground reflectance	TAS default value of 0.2	
Calendar	NCM Standard	
Air Permeability	10 m³/hm²@50Pa	
Infiltration	0.500 ACH	
Lighting Efficiency	5.2 W/m² per 100 lux	
Average Conductance	172 W/K	

References

1. Palme, M.; Isalgue, A.; Coch, H. Avoiding the Possible Impact of Climate Change on the Built Environment: The Importance of the Building's Energy Robustness. *Buildings* **2013**, *3*, 191–204. [CrossRef]
2. Amoako-Attah, J.; B-Jahromi, A. Impact of Conservatory as passive solar design of UK dwellings. *Proc. Inst. Civ. Eng. J. Eng. Sustain.* **2016**, *169*, 198–213. [CrossRef]
3. Amoako-Attah, J.; B-Jahromi, A. Method comparison analysis of dwellings' temperatures in the UK. *Proc. Inst. Civ. Eng. J. Eng. Sustain.* **2015**, *168*, 16–27. [CrossRef]
4. Amoako-Attah, J.; B-Jahromi, A. Impact of standard construction specification on thermal comfort in UK dwellings. *Adv. Environ. Res.* **2014**, *3*, 253–281. [CrossRef]
5. Amoako-Attah, J.; B-Jahromi, A. Impact of future climate change on UK building performance. *Adv. Environ. Res.* **2013**, *2*, 203–227. [CrossRef]

6.   Hulme, M.; Jenkins, G.L.; Lu, X.; Turnpenny, J.R.; Mitchell, T.D.; Jones, R.G.; Lowe, J.; Murphy, J.M.; Hassel, D.; Boorman, P.; et al. *Climate Change Scenarios for the United Kingdom: The UKCIP02 Scientific Report*; Tyndall Centre for Climate Change Research, University of East Anglia: Norwich, UK, 2002.

7.   Jenkins, G.J.; Murphy, J.M.; Sexton, D.M.H.; Lowe, J.A.; Jones, P.; Kilsby, C.G. *UK Climate Projections: Briefing Report*; Met Office Hadley Centre: Exeter, UK, 2009.

8.   The Chartered Institution of Building Services Engineers. *The Use of Climate Change Scenarios for Building Simulation: The CIBSE Future Weather Years*; CIBSE TM48; Chartered Institution of Building Services Engineers: London, UK, 2008.

9.   Williams, D.; Elghali, L.; France, C.; Wheeler, R.C. Projecting building energy demand using probabilistic weather conditions accounting for climate change. In Proceedings of the CIBSE Technical Symposium, DeMontfort University, Leicester, UK, 6–7 September 2011.

10.   Belcher, S.E.; Hacker, J.N.; Powell, D.S. Constructing design weather for future climates. *Build. Serv. Eng. Res. Technol.* **2005**, *26*, 49–61. [CrossRef]

11.   Mylona, A. The use of UKCP09 to produce weather files for building simulation. *Build. Serv. Eng. Res. Technol.* **2012**, *33*, 51–62. [CrossRef]

12.   Tian, W.; de Wilde, P. Uncertainty and sensitivity analysis of building performance using probabilistic climate projections: A UK case study. *Autom. Constr.* **2011**, *20*, 1096–1109. [CrossRef]

13.   Eames, M.; Kershaw, T.; Coley, D. On the creation of future probabilistic design weather years from UKCP09. *Build. Serv. Eng. Res. Technol.* **2011**, *32*, 127–142. [CrossRef]

14.   The Chartered Institution of Building Services Engineers. *Design Summer Years for London*; CIBSE TM49; Chartered Institution of Building Services Engineers: London, UK, 2009.

15.   Virk, G.; Mylona, A.; Mavrogianni, A.; Davies, M. Using the new CIBSE design summer years to assess overheating in London: Effect of the urban heat island on design. *Build. Serv. Eng. Res. Technol.* **2015**, *36*, 115–128. [CrossRef]

16.   Gupta, R.; Gregg, M.; Du, H.; Williams, K. Evaluative application of UKCP09-based downscaled future years to simulate overheating risk in typical English homes. Structural Survey. *Struct. Surv.* **2013**, *32*, 231–252. [CrossRef]

17.   Smith, S.T.; Hanby, V.I. Methodologies for the generation of design summer years for building energy simulation using UKCP09 probabilistic climate projections. *Build. Serv. Eng. Res. Technol.* **2012**, *33*, 9–17. [CrossRef]

18.   Watkins, R.; Levermore, G.J.; Parkinson, J.B. Constructing a future weather file for use in building simulation using UKCP09 projections. *Build. Serv. Eng. Res. Technol.* **2011**, *32*, 293–299. [CrossRef]

19.   Dominguez-Munoz, F.; Cejudo-Lopez, J.M.; Carrillo-Andres, A. Uncertainty in peak cooling load calculations. *Energy Build.* **2010**, *42*, 1010–1018. [CrossRef]

20.   Rodriguez, G.C.; Carrillo-Andres, A.; Dominguez-Munoz, F.; Cejudo-Lopez, J.M.; Zhang, Y. Uncertainties and sensitivity analysis in building energy simulation using macroparameters. *Energy Build.* **2013**, *67*, 79–87. [CrossRef]

21.   Spitz, C.; Mora, L.; Wurtz, E.; Jay, A. Practical application of uncertainty and sensitivity analysis in building energy simulation using macro parameters. *Energy Build.* **2012**, *67*, 79–87.

22.   Handbook, A.F. Thermal Environmental Conditions for Human Occupancy, ASHRAE Standard 55-2010. In *American Society of Heating, Refrigerating and Air-Conditioning Engineers*; American Society of Heating, Refrigerating and Air-Conditioning Engineers: Atlanta, GA, USA, 2009.

23.   De Dear, R.J.; Akimoto, T.; Arens, E.A.; Brager, G.; Candido, C.; Cheong, K.W.D.; Li, B.; Nishihara, N.; Sekhar, S.C.; Tanabe, S.; et al. Progress in thermal comfort research over the last twenty years. *Indoor Air* **2013**, *23*, 442–461. [CrossRef] [PubMed]

24.   The Chartered Institution of Building Services Engineers. *The Limits of Thermal Comfort: Avoiding Overheating in European Buildings CIBSE TM52*; Chartered Institution of Building Services Engineers: London, UK, 2013.

25.   Nicol, F.; Humphreys, M.; Roaf, S. *Adaptive Thermal Comfort: Principles and Practice*; Routledge: London, UK, 2012.

26.   D'Ambrosio Alfano, F.R.; Olesen, B.W.; Palella, B.I.; Riccio, G. Thermal comfort: Design and assessment for energy saving. *Energy Build.* **2014**, *81*, 326–336. [CrossRef]

27.   De Dear, R.J.; Brager, G.S. Developing an adaptive model of thermal comfort and preference. *ASHRAE Trans.* **1998**, *104*, 145–167.

28. Fanger, P.O. Calculation of thermal comfort: Introduction of a basic comfort equation. *ASHRAE Trans.* **1967**, *73*, 1–20.

29. Nicol, J.F.; Raja, I.A.; Allaudin, A.; Jamy, G.N. Climatic variations in comfort temperatures: The Pakistan projects. *Energy Build.* **1999**, *30*, 261–279. [CrossRef]

30. McCartney, K.J.; Nicol, F. Developing an adapting comfort algorithm for Europe; results of the SCATS project. *Energy Build.* **2002**, *34*, 623–635. [CrossRef]

31. Ponni, M.; Baskar, R. A study of comfort temperature and thermal efficiency of buildings. *Int. J. Eng. Technol.* **2015**, *7*, 1469–1477.

32. Tian, W. A review of sensitivity analysis methods in building energy analysis. *Renew. Sustain. Energy Rev.* **2013**, *20*, 411–419. [CrossRef]

33. Mavrogianni, A.; Wilkinson, P.; Davies, M.; Biddulph, P.; Oikonomou, E. Building Characteristics as determinants of propensity to high indoor summer temperatures in London dwellings. *Build. Environ.* **2012**, *55*, 117–130. [CrossRef]

34. The Chartered Institution of Building Services Engineers. *CIBSE Guide A—Environmental Design*; Chartered Institution of Building Services Engineers: London, UK, 2006.

35. The Chartered Institution of Building Services Engineers. *Climate Change and the Indoor Environment: Impacts and Adaptation CIBSE TM36*; Chartered Institution of Building Services Engineers: London, UK, 2005.

36. Banacos, P.C. Box and Whiskers Plots for Local Climate Datasets: Interpretation and Creation Using Excel 2007/2010. Available online: http://www.weather.gov/media/erh/ta2011-01.pdf (accessed on 30 September 2016).

37. Storlie, C.B.; Swiler, L.P.; Helton, J.C.; Sallaberry, C.J. Implementation and evaluation of non-parametric regression procedures for sensitivity analysis computationally demanding modules. *Reliab. Eng. Syst. Saf.* **2009**, *94*, 1735–1763. [CrossRef]

38. Hygh, J.S.; DeCarolis, J.F.; Hill, D.B.; Ranji Ranjithan, S. Multivariate regression as an energy assessment tool in early building design. *Build. Environ.* **2012**, *57*, 165–175. [CrossRef]

Article

Stochastic Characteristics of Manual Solar Shades and their Influence on Building Energy Performance

Jian Yao * and Rongyue Zheng

Faculty of Architectural, Civil Engineering and Environment, Ningbo University, Ningbo 315211, China; rongyue@nbu.edu.cn
* Correspondence: yaojian@nbu.edu.cn

Received: 24 April 2017; Accepted: 19 June 2017; Published: 21 June 2017

Abstract: Occupant behavior has a significant impact on building energy performance. The purpose of this paper is to quantify the stochastic characteristics of manual solar shades and their influence on building energy performance. A co-simulation for occupants' stochastic control of manual solar shades was conducted and the statistic indicators (non-parameter tests and autocorrelation function) were calculated in order to identify potential occupant behavior patterns. The results show that occupants' stochastic shade control behavior among different seasons is not statistically different and that shade control behavior is not completely stochastic. Meanwhile, the trend in the fluctuation of Sc changes with time. Furthermore, a new index was introduced to evaluate the effectiveness of manual solar shades in terms of energy performance. The result shows that the effectiveness of manual solar shades is only between 39.8% and 81.3%, compared with automatically controlled shades, and there is a large potential for improving the effectiveness of manual solar shades in different seasons.

Keywords: stochastic model; manual solar shades; building energy performance; co-simulation; occupant behavior

---

1. Introduction

Buildings nowadays account for approximately 40% of the total energy consumption and thus architects around the world are looking for design solutions to improve the energy performance of buildings. During the building design stage, improving the thermal performance of the building envelope (such as the external wall [1], window materials [2]) plays a significant role in building energy saving. During the building operation stage, an integrated system for buildings' energy-efficient automation can also be used to achieve a significant decrease in building energy consumption [3].

Compared to energy efficient control systems, a high performance building envelope should be first considered by architects since it ensures a low energy demand at the beginning of a building's life span. Due to the increased window to wall ratio for an improved view to outside, heat loss through windows contributes to a large fraction of building energy consumption, which has been validated by Tomás et al. using multi-objective building energy optimization [4]. Solar shading devices provide a solution for enhancing window performance. The use of solar shading devices such as overhangs [5–7], side fins [8], fixed horizontal louvers [9], etc., has been investigated by researchers. However, these studies have focused on fixed shading devices that cannot be adjusted according to outdoor conditions, and thus these solutions have a disadvantage in balancing various aspects of indoor environmental quality including energy performance, discomfort glare, the view to outside, privacy, and thermal comfort [10].

Movable solar shading devices such as roller shades, curtains, and blinds can ensure a maximum energy saving while maintaining the best visual and thermal comfort and access to natural daylight. A number of research studies have reported the performance of movable solar shades. For example, Tzempelikos [11] assumed that roller shading devices were automatically closed when direct solar radiation is higher than 20 W/m^2, while Lee and Selkowitz [12] suggested a higher solar radiation of 94.5 W/m^2 for shades to be fully closed. Reinhart [13] assumed a similar control strategy where window blinds will be automatically closed as long as the direct solar radiance is above 50 W/m^2. These research studies all reported a significant improvement of building energy performance while maintaining a comfortable indoor thermal condition. Christopher et al. [14] compared the annual building energy consumption of five manual blind control algorithms. They found that the annual energy consumption differences ranged from 8.1% to 18.3% compared to buildings without manual shading devices. However, these studies not only crudely oversimplify occupants' control of solar shades, but also neglect the variability induced by the stochastic characteristics in occupant behavior [15].

To include the stochastic behavior in shade control, researchers such as Nicol [16] and Haldi [17,18] used logit regression to infer a probability distribution to describe occupants' shade action. However, there are some limitations in their models such as they merely considered two solar shading states (fully open and fully closed) and partly closed shades were not included, which was not in accordance with the real condition. Furthermore, occupants' stochastic behavior cannot be modeled in most building simulation programs (DOE-2 [19], EnergyPlus [20], TRNSYS [21], Esp-r [22], DeST [23,24]).To improve the accuracy of predicting occupants' solar shade control, the author developed a stochastic model for manual solar shades that considers partly shaded states and the performance of stochastic control can be quantitatively predicted by a coupling simulation [15]. The thermal, visual, and overall energy performances have been investigated in previous papers [15,25,26]. It was found that manual solar shades can improve indoor thermal comfort conditions by 154% compared to Low-E windows [25], and the Useful Daylight Index (UDI) can also be improved by about 30% with less daylight illuminance fluctuation and more comfortable daylight distribution due to the manual control of solar shades. In addition, the Daylight Glare Index (DGI) and Daylight Glare Probability (DGP) were used to assess the glare risks of manual solar shades, which demonstrated a significant reduction (about 22%) in intolerable glare compared to Low-E windows. Nevertheless, the results also found that occupants' action on solar shades was not always effective in minimizing glare risks, with about 12% of working hours experiencing intolerable glare [26]. A similar study on daylighting and the visual comfort performance of movable blinds has been conducted by Umberto Berardi and Taoning Wang [27], who recommended considering occupants' behavior to accurately evaluate the influence of the adjustment of shading devices on the building performance.

Thus, there is a need to further understand the stochastic characteristics of manual solar shades in order to improve the building performance of manual shades. Some research studies have conducted observations to analyze the characteristics of manual solar shades. Haldi et al. found that shade adjustment occurred mainly after arrival and/or before departure [17]. However, Rea reported contradicting findings. They found that the time of day had a negligible impact on shade actions [28]. Rubin et al. [29] reported that the seasonal effect on manual shade adjustment was not significant, while Zhang et al. found that window blinds varied seasonally for east, west, and south facades [30]. In addition, many studies reported that occupants adjust solar shades very infrequently (the shade movement rate is only about 1/day) or even never [25,31,32]. However, these studies did not give a detailed and statistical analysis of the stochastic characteristics of manual solar shades. Furthermore, the effectiveness of manual shades, an important index when analyzing building energy performance, has also not been quantitatively evaluated. Therefore, this paper uses statistical indicators to systematically evaluate the randomness of manual shade control and introduces an index to calculate the effectiveness of manual shades.

2. Methodology

2.1. Stochastic Model

This research is a continuation of previous research [15]. A Markov stochastic model for manual solar shades developed in the previous study was used in this paper [15]. This model was constructed based on field measurements and divided solar shades into five shading states (shade window area of 0%, 25%, 50%, 75%, and 100%, respectively). It is an improved model compared to other previous models [16,18], since it reflects occupants' real shade control behavior (windows were partly shaded). This model for solar shades was built in Building Controls Virtual Test Bed (BCVTB), a software environment developed by the Lawrence Berkeley National Laboratory [33], for co-simulation with EnergyPlus. A brief description of how this stochastic model is constructed and the co-simulation is conducted can be seen in Figure 1. More detailed information on this stochastic model and co-simulation can be found in a previous paper [15].

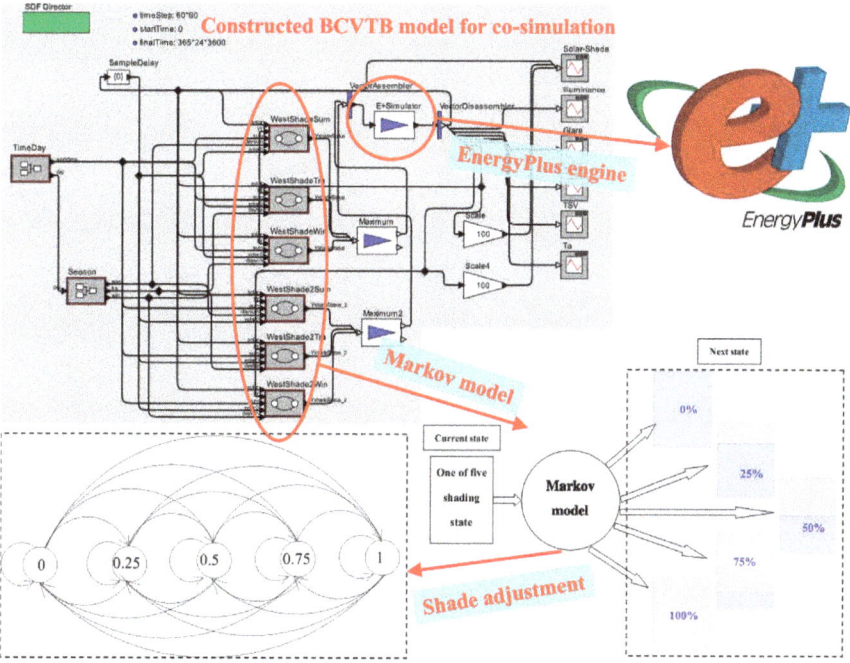

Figure 1. A graphic illustration of the developed method for the co-simulation of the performance of manual solar shades.

A typical office room in Ningbo (a typical city in a hot summer and cold winter zone of China) was selected. The details of the building, as well as other settings according to the design standard in this climate region, are listed in Table 1. This room was modeled in EnergyPlus and co-simulated in BCVTB. Manual solar shades were compared with automatically controlled ones which adopt a simple control strategy that assume occupants will bring sunlight into the interiors in winter and close shades in the summer to block excessive heat gains. A detailed description of this control strategy is given in Table 2.

Table 1. The dimension and setting of the building enveloped and HVAC etc.

Parameter	Value
Orientation	West
Dimension	Room: 4 × 4 × 3 m, Window: 3.8 × 2.8 m
Building envelope	U-value for external wall: 1 W/m²K, and adiabatic for internal walls, roof and floor; Two window settings for comparison: (1) clear double-pane window (U-value: 3.6 W/m²K) + manually controlled solar shades (MShade); (2) clear double-pane window (U-value: 3.6 W/m²K) + automatically controlled solar shades (AShade)
Work time	8:00–17:00
HVAC	Temperature: 20–26 °C, run time: 8:00–17:00
Interior heat generation	Light density: 11 W/m²; equipment: 20 W/m²
Fresh air	40 m³/h·p

Table 2. Solar shading control strategy for automated solar shades.

Season	Time	Shading Sate	The Aim of the Control
Summer	Daytime	Shade 2/3 of window area	Block excessive solar gain and keep enough daylight
	Nighttime	Fully open	Enable natural ventilation to decrease indoor temperature
Transition	All time	Shade 1/2 of window area	Try to get a balance between solar radiation and daylight
Winter	Daytime	Fully open	Admit solar heat to warm indoor space
	Nighttime	Fully closed	Reduce heat loss

2.2. Statistic Analysis

To analyze the stochastic characteristics of manual solar shades, the shading coefficient (Sc value, here it equals one minus the window shaded ratio. For example, if 25% of the window area is shaded, then Sc = 1 − 0.25 = 0.75), a commonly used index when evaluating solar shading performance, was considered in this paper. Thus, a lower Sc value indicates a higher shading performance and consequently a lower cooling demand. According to the distribution of the hourly variation and seasonal difference of Sc values for manual solar shades, the stochastic characteristics of occupants' behavior on solar shades can be inferred. In addition, statistical indicators (parameter and non-parameter tests) were used to quantitatively evaluate the potential difference of shade behavior among different seasons.

In addition, a mathematical index (autocorrelation function) for identifying repeating patterns (e.g., the presence of a periodic signal that has been buried under noise) was used in this paper to check whether occupants' stochastic control on shades was repeatable. Informally, it is the similarity between observations as a function of the time separation between them. In statistics, the autocorrelation function (ACF) of a random process (here, it is occupants' stochastic control on solar shades) describes the correlation between the process at different points in time. The ACF for lag k can be calculated as follows:

$$r_k = \frac{c_k}{c_0} \tag{1}$$

where $c_k = \frac{1}{T-1} \sum_{t=1}^{T-k} (y_t - \bar{y})(y_{t+k} - \bar{y})$ is the autocovariance function and c_0 is the sample variance of the time series. y is the sample value of the time series(here, it is the hourly Sc value), k is the time lag, and T is the length of the time series. The autocorrelation function (r_k) is one of the tools used to find patterns in the data. Specifically, the autocorrelation function reveals the correlation between points separated by various time lags.

The strength of using statistical indicators to evaluate the randomness of manual shade control is that statistical analysis is a universal method with which to assess the validity of a conclusion. Parametric tests involve specific probability distributions (such as the normal distribution) and the tests involve an estimation of the key parameters of that distribution from the sample data. Non-parametric tests are also called distribution-free tests since they are based on fewer assumptions. Thus, there is less of a possibility to reach incorrect conclusions because assumptions about the population are unnecessary. However, nonparametric tests are generally less powerful than their parametric counterparts. For this study, the selection between a parametric and non-parametric test will be based on the test of sample distribution.

To evaluate the energy performance, an index used to calculate the effectiveness of manual solar shade control will be introduced. This index is based on the cooling and heating energy demand and is compared with automatically controlled shades as described in Table 2. It can be expressed as:

$$E_{ff} = \frac{E_A}{E_M} \times 100\% \tag{2}$$

where E_{ff} is the effectiveness of Mshade, E_A is the energy demand for Ashade, and E_M is the energy demand for Mshade. Due to the stochastic characteristics of occupant behavior, manual shades are not always kept at optimal (or near optimal) positions with minimum heating or cooling energy demands. Therefore, E_M is usually higher than E_A. If manual shades are kept at the same near optimal positions as automatically controlled ones, E_M will be very close to E_A and E_{ff} will approach 100%, indicating a high effective control by occupants. Using Equation (2), one can easily assess the effectiveness of occupants' control on solar shades.

3. Results and Discussion

3.1. Sc Distribution

The hourly Sc distribution during the whole year is shown in Figure 2. Since the shade adjustment only occurs at working hours (8:00–17:00), the Sc values for other hours are not illustrated in this figure. It can be seen that the Sc value changes from 0 (fully shaded) to 1 (fully open), indicating that occupants may deploy shades to all possible positions. Meanwhile, high and low Sc values were observed in winter, summer, and transition seasons. However, no significant difference between seasons can be visually inspected.

Figure 3 further gives the histogram of the hourly Sc value distribution. The shape of the distribution looks like a normal distribution, with most Sc values falling in the range of 0.3–0.7. Occupants only kept their shades at two extreme positions (fully shaded and fully open) for about 7% of the working hours. This means that for most of the time, the windows were partially shaded by shades.

On the other hand, the daily average (10 working hours) Sc values are given in Figure 4. It can be seen that most Sc values fall in the range of 0.2–0.8 and the fluctuation of daily values is also significant. In addition, no daily average Sc equals 0 or 1, indicating that the fully open or fully closed position of shades will not be kept unchanged for a whole day (10 working hours). For seasonal comparison, no significant difference between seasons can be observed from this figure. The statistic analysis of seasonal difference will be further conducted in Section 3.3.

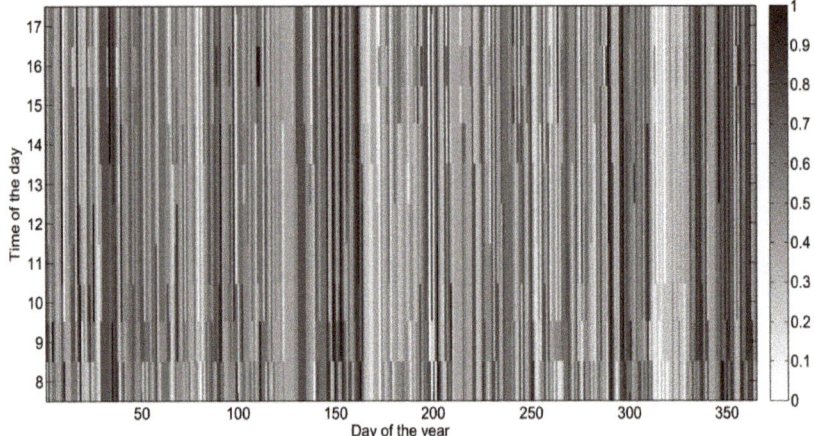

Figure 2. Hourly Sc distribution during the year.

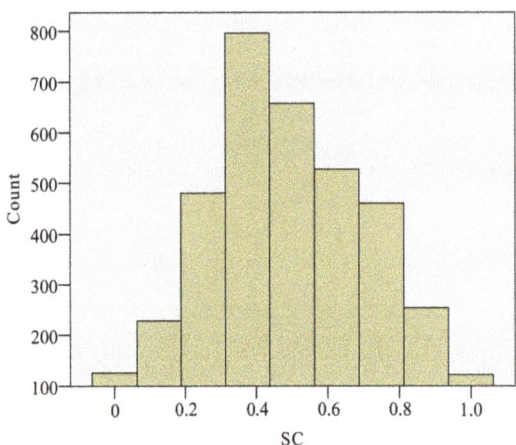

Figure 3. Histogram of the hourly Sc value distribution during the year.

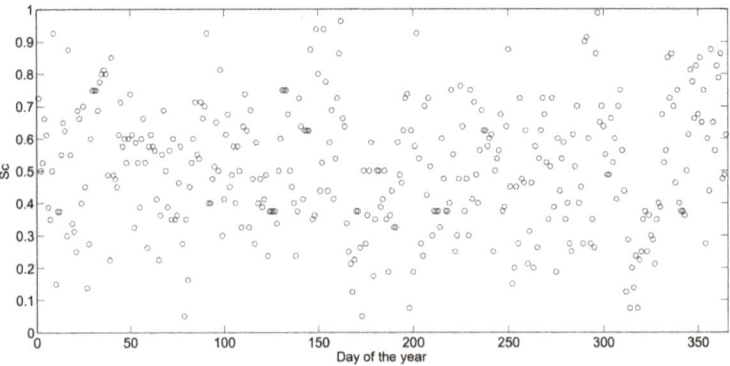

Figure 4. Daily average (10 working hours) Sc values.

3.2. Sc Change

Occupants change the shade positions infrequently, with more than 3000 h (90% of working hours) experiencing no movement of shades (see Figure 5). For most days, the Sc value only changes once during a day, indicating a daily shade change rate of about 1. Figure 6 gives the hourly change of the Sc value during the year. For a few days, no change in the Sc value was observed (the change of Sc equals 0). The largest change of Sc was less than 0.8 and most values (except 4 h) fall in the range of 0.1–0.5. This means that occupants usually adjust the shade position gradually with a small fraction (less than 50% of the window area) and are less likely to change shades from fully open to fully closed and vice versa (the change of Sc is 1). However, previous research or design standards assumed that shades were fully open when solar radiation falling on windows was not intensive and would be changed to fully closed when solar radiation was higher than a certain level. Therefore, the previous assumptions were not reasonable and would lead to a deviation of the energy performance of manual solar shades. This finding is important since it will improve the assumption about the possible shade change (Sc value change) when predicting the performance of manual solar shades.

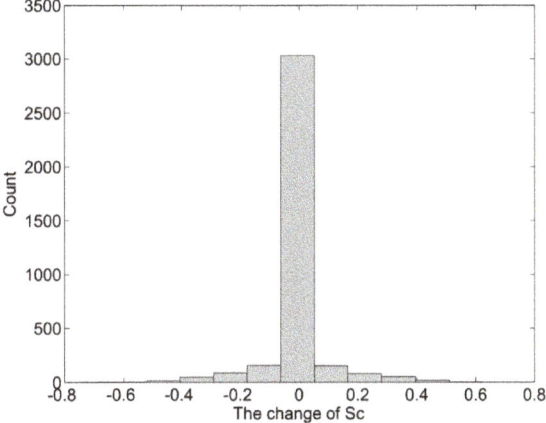

Figure 5. Histogram of the change of the Sc value during the year.

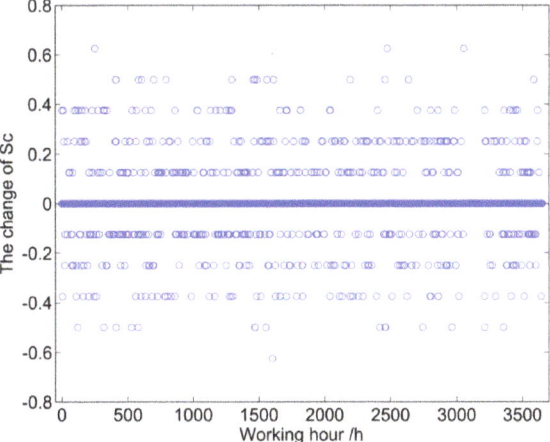

Figure 6. The hourly change of the Sc value during the year.

When solar shades will be adjusted is another important factor in determining shade control behavior. Figure 7 presents the frequency of Sc change at each time point during the year. It can be seen that shade change is about one times more frequent during 9:00–13:00 than other time points. The highest frequency is about 80, indicating that the shade change probability for this time point is about 22% (80/365) (or means that there will be a change of shade position at this time point during about 4.6 days (365/80)). The more frequent adjustment of solar shades in the morning than in the afternoon may be explained as follows: when solar radiation influences the west facade, occupants will adjust shades to block excessive radiation in order to avoid heat or glare problems and then keep shades at the same position for several hours, as long as the solar radiation is intensive.

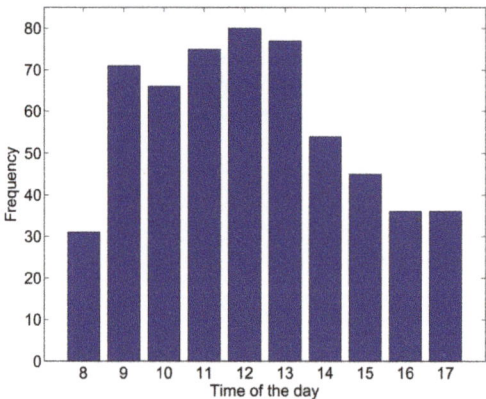

Figure 7. Frequency of Sc change at each time point during the year.

Figures 8 and 9 further illustrate the frequency of the Sc value increase and decrease at each time point during the year. The distribution shapes of these two figures at each time point are similar to that of Figure 7. Moreover, there is no significant difference between the Sc value increase and decrease. This reflects that occupants' shade control is stochastic and the probability of lowering or raising the shade position is very close for the whole year.

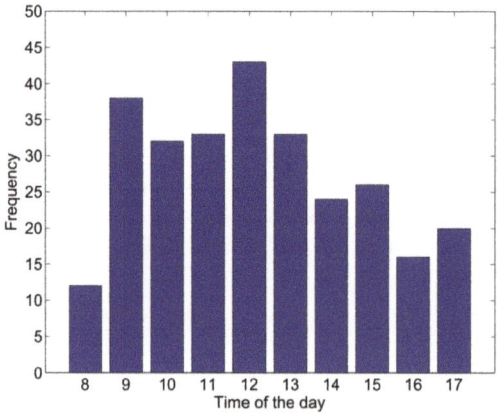

Figure 8. Frequency of Sc value increase at each time point during the year.

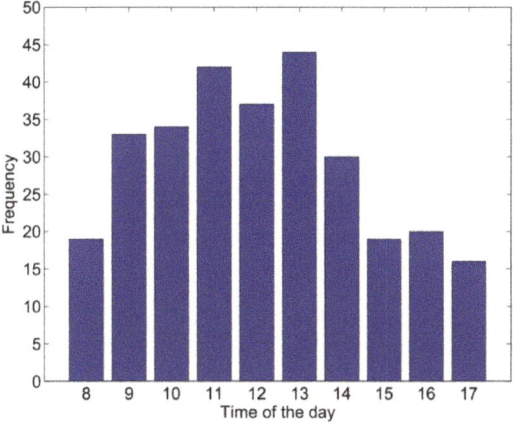

Figure 9. Frequency of Sc value decrease at each time point during the year.

3.3. Seasonal difference

In terms of the seasonal difference, three seasons were considered, with summer from days 152–273 (a total of 122 days), winter from days 1–58 and 334–365 (90 days), and the transition from days 59–151 and 274–333 (153 days). Thus, the number of hourly Sc values for the three seasons was different, with the transition season having (denoted as tra) 1530 h, summer (denoted as sum) 1220 h, and winter (denoted as win) 900 h. Figure 10 gives the hourly Sc distribution for the three seasons. The overall distributions of the Sc value for the three seasons are similar, with tra having more hours at almost each Sc value.

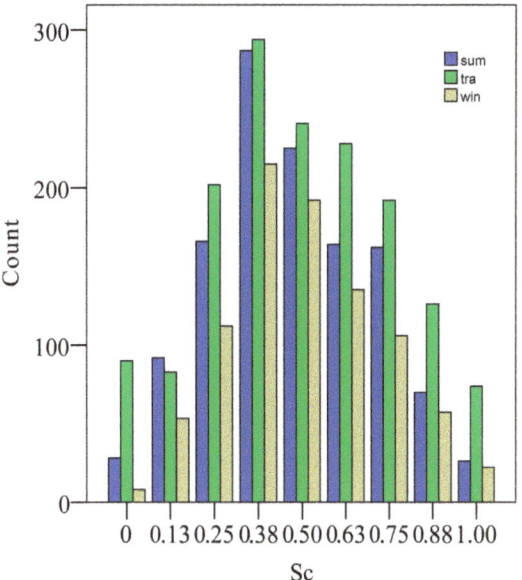

Figure 10. The hourly Sc distribution for the three seasons.

To further analyze the distribution of the Sc value in different seasons, a box plot of the hourly Sc values in the three seasons is illustrated in Figure 11. It can be seen that the average Sc values for the three seasons are very close (about 0.5). Meanwhile, sum and win have almost the same distribution, while tra has more Sc values higher than 0.6 compared to the other two seasons.

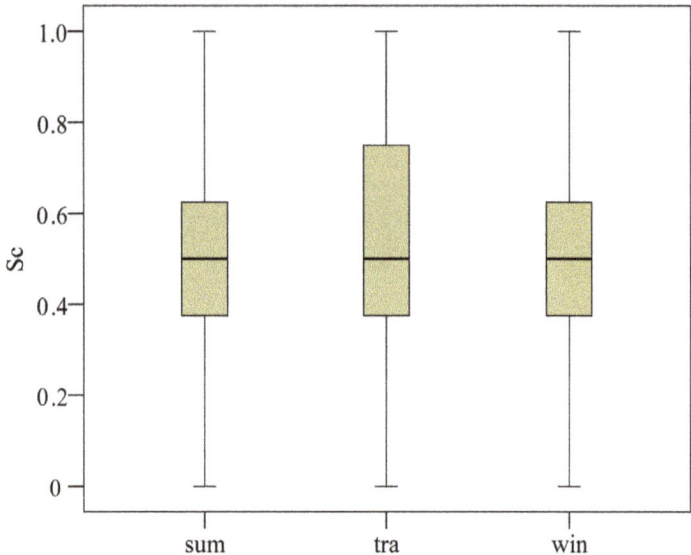

Figure 11. Box plot of hourly Sc values in three seasons.

To conduct the statistic analysis, the Kolmogorov-Smirnov test was used to check whether the Sc values in different seasons were of a normal distribution. The results showed that the asymptotic significance is 0.000 (<0.05, the significance level). This means that the null hypothesis should be rejected, indicating that the distribution of Sc does not resemble a normal distribution. Therefore, a parameter test (independent-samples t test) is not applicable since this test assumes sampling from normal parent populations. Instead, an independent-samples Kruskal-Wallis test, a non-parametric method for testing whether samples originate from the same distribution, was used since it does not assume that the data are normal. The independent-samples Kruskal-Wallis test shows that the asymptotic significance is 0.078 (>0.05, the significance level). It means that we should retain the null hypothesis, indicating that the distribution of the Sc value is the same across different seasons. Therefore, occupants' stochastic shade control behavior among different seasons is not statistically different, although there is little difference in the Sc distribution between seasons.

Figure 12 presents the ACF of hourly Sc values for different lag hours (here, 1–22 h were considered since they covered two days which were enough to check the daily periodic patterns of the Sc value). It can be seen from the figure that the ACF value decreases with increased lag hours. However, ACF drops to an almost constant value (no significant change when increasing lag hours) that falls out of their 95% confidence intervals (95%CI, U95: upper limit of 95%CI, L95: lower limit of 95%CI), which indicates that the series would not achieve a stationary condition. In other words, occupants' shade control behavior is not totally stochastic (such as a white noise) and shade adjustment at previous time steps influences current and future control. In addition, the trend of the fluctuation of Sc is not stable and changes with time.

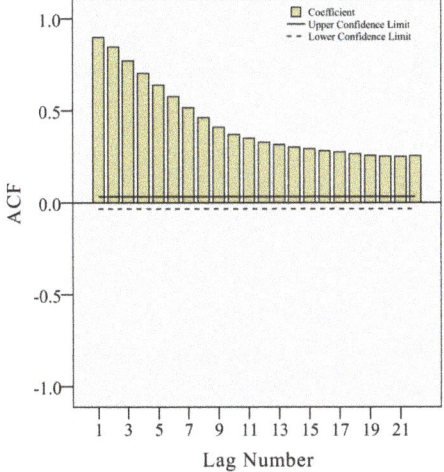

Figure 12. ACF of hourly Sc values.

3.4. Energy Performance

The cooling and heating energy performance of manual solar shades against automatically controlled ones is shown in Figures 13 and 14. It can be seen that Ashade performs better than Mshade for most of the time during the year, except for only a few hours. For the cooling demand, the big difference between Ashade and Mshade occurs in late afternoon in summer since this research focused on the west facade. The highest difference approaches 900 W at about 17:00, while at the beginning of the work day, the difference is only about 100–200 W. For the heating demand, Ashade performs better than Mshade in winter, while in the transition season, the situation is the opposite. This is because in the transition season, the window is assumed to be shaded by 50%, as described in Table 2. The largest heating difference is only about half of the largest cooling difference. Mshade has an annual cooling and heating increase of 536.3 kWh and 88.8 kWh compared to Ashade, respectively, corresponding to an increasing rate of 28.6% and 25.7%. That means that the cooling and heating energy performance would be overestimated by more than 25% if manual solar shades are considered as ideally controlled.

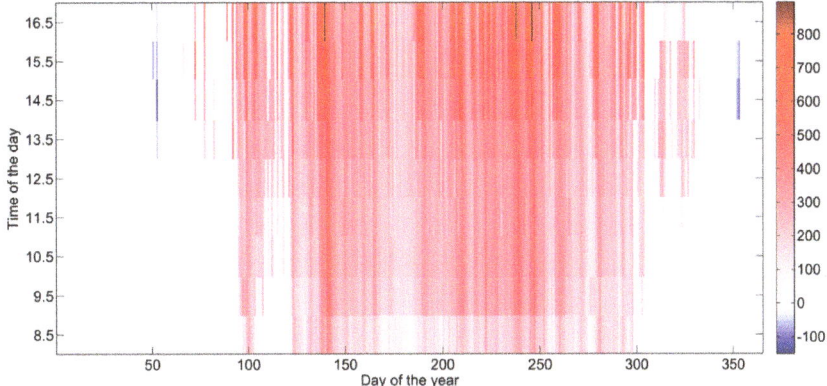

Figure 13. Cooling energy increase (W) of manual solar shades (Mshade) compared to automatically controlled ones (Ashade).

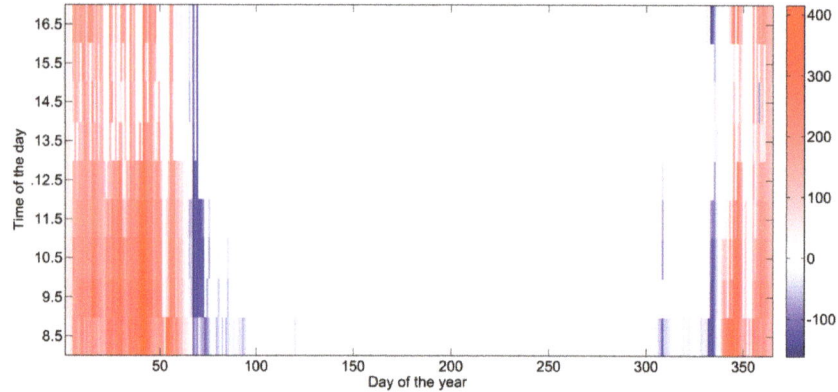

Figure 14. Heating energy increase (W) of manual solar shades (Mshade) compared to automatically controlled ones (Ashade).

To further investigate the overestimated energy performance, the ratios (E_{ff}) of the cooling and heating energy consumption of Ashade to Mshade are illustrated in Figures 15 and 16. It can be seen that during the hot summer period, this ratio reaches above 0.8, while in the transition season, this ratio drops significantly from 0.8 to near 0. This indicates that Mshade is more effective in summer than in the transition season. Due to the significant fluctuation of E_{ff} at each time point, the effectiveness of Mshade will be evaluated on a seasonal basis. According to these two figures, E_{ff} for cooling is 81.3% for summer and 46.4% for the transition season. E_{ff} for heating is much lower than cooling and it is only 51.9% for winter and 39.8% for the transition season. Therefore, there is a large potential for improving the effectiveness of Mshade in winter for the heating demand, as well as in the transition season for both heating and cooling.

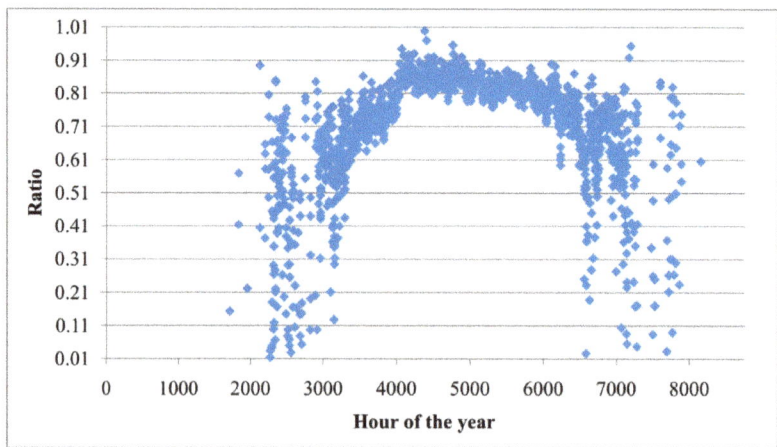

Figure 15. Ratio of cooling energy consumption of automatically controlled solar shades (Ashade) to manual shades (Mshade).

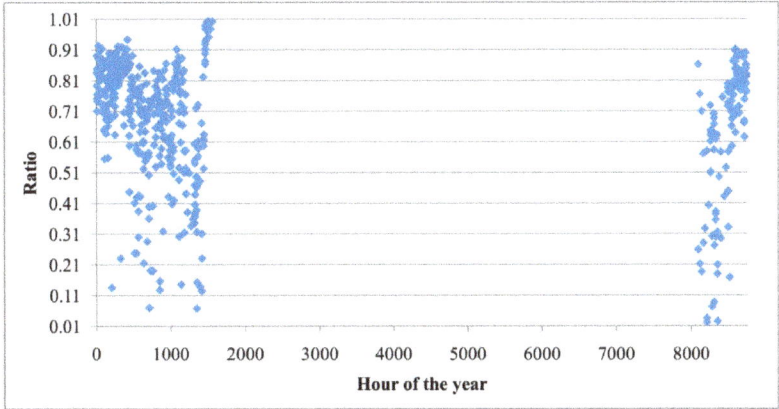

Figure 16. Ratio of heating energy consumption of automatically controlled solar shades (Ashade) to manual shades (Mshade).

4. Conclusions

This paper investigates the stochastic characteristics of manual solar shades and their influence on building energy performance. A stochastic model for manual solar shades developed by the author was used in this paper and a co-simulation-based occupant behavior analysis was conducted. An in-depth analysis on the shading performance of manual solar shades was performed by using non-parameter tests and the autocorrelation function in order to identify the potential occupant behavior patterns. The results show that occupants' stochastic shade control behavior among different seasons is not statistically different, although there is a little difference in the Sc distribution between seasons. In addition, the shade control behavior is not totally stochastic and shade adjustment at previous time steps influences current and future control. Meanwhile, the trend of the fluctuation of Sc changes with time. Furthermore, a new index was introduced to evaluate the effectiveness of manual solar shades in terms of energy performance. Using this index, the energy performance of manual solar shades was compared with automatically controlled ones. The result shows that the effectiveness of manual solar shades is between 39.8% and 81.3%, and there is a large potential for improving the effectiveness of manual solar shades in winter for the heating demand, as well as in the transition season for both heating and cooling.

Further studies, including questionnaire surveys and field measurements, are needed to better understand shade control behavior in order to explain why there is no seasonal difference in shade adjustment and how previous shade control influences current actions. Meanwhile, occupants' adaptation to an indoor microclimate (thermal and visual comfort and air quality etc.) may also influence shade control behavior. Thus, an investigation of the interactions between occupants and acceptable comfort conditions will help understand the specific reasons for stochastic shade control and allow for identifying potential measures to improve the effectiveness of manual solar shades.

Acknowledgments: This work was supported by National Key Technology R&D Program of the Ministry of Science and Technology under Grant 2013BAJ10B06 and Foundation of Ningbo University (XKl15D230), and the authors would like to thank the K.C. Wong Magna Fund in Ningbo University.

Author Contributions: Jian Yao designed the study and wrote the manuscript. Rongyue Zheng helped revise the manuscript.

Conflicts of Interest: The authors declare no conflict of interest.

References

1. Tzifa, V.; Papadakos, G.; Papadopoulou, A.G.; Marinakis, V.; Psarras, J. Uncertainty and method limitations in a short-time measurement of the effective thermal transmittance on a building envelope using an infrared camera. *Int. J. Sustain. Energy* **2017**, *36*, 28–46. [CrossRef]
2. Zheng, R.; Yao, J. The optimum energy saving measures for retrofitting residential buildings. *Open House Int.* **2016**, *41*, 88–92.
3. Marinakis, V.; Doukas, H.; Karakosta, C.; Psarras, J. An integrated system for buildings' energy-efficient automation: Application in the tertiary sector. *Appl. Energy* **2013**, *101*, 6–14. [CrossRef]
4. Echenagucia, T.M.; Capozzoli, A.; Cascone, Y.; Sassone, M. The early design stage of a building envelope: Multi-objective search through heating, cooling and lighting energy performance analysis. *Appl. Energy* **2015**, *154*, 577–591. [CrossRef]
5. Raeissi, S.; Taheri, M. Optimum overhang dimensions for energy saving. *Build. Environ.* **1998**, *33*, 293–302. [CrossRef]
6. Valladares-Rendón, L.G.; Lo, S. Passive shading strategies to reduce outdoor insolation and indoor cooling loads by using overhang devices on a building. *Build. Simul.* **2014**, *7*, 671–681. [CrossRef]
7. Ebrahimpour, A.; Maerefat, M. Application of advanced glazing and overhangs in residential buildings. *Energy Convers. Manag.* **2011**, *52*, 212–219. [CrossRef]
8. Aldawoud, A. Conventional fixed shading devices in comparison to an electrochromic glazing system in hot, dry climate. *Energy Build.* **2013**, *59*, 104–110. [CrossRef]
9. Datta, G. Effect of fixed horizontal louver shading devices on thermal perfomance of building by TRNSYS simulation. *Renew. Energy* **2001**, *23*, 497–507. [CrossRef]
10. Bakker, L.G.; Hoes-van Oeffelen, E.C.M.; Loonen, R.C.G.M.; Hensen, J.L.M. User satisfaction and interaction with automated dynamic facades: A pilot study. *Build. Environ.* **2014**, *78*, 44–52. [CrossRef]
11. Tzempelikos, A.; Athienitis, A.K. The impact of shading design and control on building cooling and lighting demand. *Solar Energy* **2007**, *81*, 369–382. [CrossRef]
12. Lee, E.S.; Selkowitz, S.E. The Design and Evaluation of Integrated Envelope and Lighting Control Strategies for Commercial Buildings. Available online: https://www.osti.gov/scitech/biblio/10107748 (accessed on 19 June 2017).
13. Sun, L.; Lu, L.; Yang, H. Optimum design of shading-type building-integrated photovoltaic claddings with different surface azimuth angles. *Appl. Energy* **2012**, *90*, 233–240. [CrossRef]
14. Dyke, C.; Van Den Wymelenberg, K.; Djunaedy, E.; Steciak, J. Comparing Whole Building Energy Implications of Sidelighting Systems with Alternate Manual Blind Control Algorithms. *Buildings* **2015**, *5*, 467–496. [CrossRef]
15. Yao, J. Determining the energy performance of manually controlled solar shades: A stochastic model based co-simulation analysis. *Appl. Energy* **2014**, *127*, 64–80. [CrossRef]
16. Nicol, J.F. Characterising Occupant Behaviour in Buildings: Towards a Stochastic Model of Occupant Use of Windows, Lights, Blinds, Heaters and Fans. Available online: http://www.ibpsa.org/proceedings/BS2001/BS01_1073_1078.pdf (accessed on 19 June 2017).
17. Haldi, F.; Robinson, D. On the behaviour and adaptation of office occupants. *Build. Environ.* **2008**, *43*, 2163–2177. [CrossRef]
18. Haldi, F.; Robinson, D. Adaptive actions on shading devices in response to local visual stimuli. *J. Build. Perform. Simul.* **2010**, *3*, 135–153. [CrossRef]
19. Birdsall, B.E.; Buhl, W.F.; Curtis, R.B.; Erdem, A.E.; Eto, J.H.; Hirsch, J.J.; Olson, K.H.; Winkelmann, F.C. The DOE-2 computer program for thermal simulation of buildings. *AIP Conf. Proc.* **1985**, *135*, 642–649. [CrossRef]
20. Crawley, D.B.; Lawrie, L.K.; Winkelmann, F.C.; Buhl, W.F.; Huang, Y.J.; Pedersen, C.O.; Strand, R.K.; Liesen, R.J.; Fisher, D.E.; Witte, M.J.; et al. EnergyPlus: creating a new-generation building energy simulation program. *Energy Build.* **2001**, *33*, 319–331. [CrossRef]
21. Beckman, W.A.; Broman, L.; Fiksel, A.; Klein, S.A.; Lindberg, E.; Schuler, M.; Thornton, J. TRNSYS The most complete solar energy system modeling and simulation software. *Renew. Energy* **1994**, *5*, 486–488. [CrossRef]
22. Strachan, P.A.; Kokogiannakis, G.; Macdonald, I.A. History and development of validation with the ESP-r simulation program. *Build. Environ.* **2008**, *43*, 601–609. [CrossRef]

23. Yan, D.; Xia, J.; Tang, W.; Song, F.; Zhang, X.; Jiang, Y. DeST—An integrated building simulation toolkit Part I: Fundamentals. *Build. Simul.* **2008**, *1*, 95–110. [CrossRef]

24. Zhang, X.; Xia, J.; Jiang, Z.; Huang, J.; Qin, R.; Zhang, Y.; Liu, Y.; Jiang, Y. DeST—An integrated building simulation toolkit Part II: Applications. *Build. Simul.* **2008**, *1*, 193–209. [CrossRef]

25. Yao, J.; Chow, D.H.C.; Zheng, R.Y.; Yan, C.W. Occupants' impact on indoor thermal comfort: A co-simulation study on stochastic control of solar shades. *J. Build. Perform. Simul.* **2016**, *9*, 272–287. [CrossRef]

26. Yao, J.; Chow, D.; Chi, Y. Impact of Manually Controlled Solar Shades on Indoor Visual Comfort. *Sustainability* **2016**, *8*, 727. [CrossRef]

27. Berardi, U.; Wang, T. Daylighting in an atrium-type high performance house. *Build. Environ.* **2014**, *76*, 92–104. [CrossRef]

28. Rea, M.S. Window blind occlusion: a pilot study. *Build. Environ.* **1984**, *19*, 133–137. [CrossRef]

29. Rubin, A.I.; Collins, B.L.; Tibbott, R.L. Window Blinds as a Potential Energy Saver: A Case Study. Available online: https://www.ncjrs.gov/pdffiles1/Digitization/64368NCJRS.pdf (accessed on 19 June 2017).

30. Zhang, Y.; Barrett, P. Factors influencing the occupants' window opening behaviour in a naturally ventilated office building. *Build. Environ.* **2012**, *50*, 125–134. [CrossRef]

31. Inoue, T.; Kawase, T.; Ibamoto, T.; Takakusa, S.; Matsuo, Y. The development of an optimal control system for window shading devices based on investigations in office buildings. *ASHRAE Trans.* **1988**, *104*, 1034–1049.

32. Inkarojrit, V. Balancing Comfort: Occupants' Control of Window Blinds in Private Offices. Available online: http://escholarship.org/uc/item/3rd2f2bg#page-1 (accessed on 19 June 2017).

33. BCVTB. Building Controls Virtual Test Bed. Available online: http://simulationresearch.lbl.gov/bcvtb (accessed on 19 June 2017).

Article

Developing a Rating System for Building Energy Efficiency Based on In Situ Measurement in China

Li Zhao and Zhengnan Zhou *

School of Architecture, Tsinghua University, Beijing 100084, China; li-zhao15@mails.tsinghua.edu.cn
* Correspondence: zznan@tsinghua.edu.cn; Tel.: +86-10-6277-3094

Academic Editor: Umberto Berardi
Received: 28 December 2016; Accepted: 24 January 2017; Published: 3 February 2017

Abstract: Building energy consumption in China recently surpassed the US building consumption, and it is expected to increase significantly in the next decade pushed by the continuous population and urbanization increase. In response to that situation, the Chinese government introduced a series of building energy codes and rating systems to assess and enhance the building energy performance. The purpose of this study is to develop a rating system for the building energy efficiency, based on in situ measurement. The system is intended for office buildings in China's cold zone. An evaluation framework, graphic dominant point, and principle of data collection and processing are illustrated in this paper. Three existing buildings were rated under the new rating system. The authors believe that the new system will contribute to a more accurate and comprehensive understanding for asset holders and occupants, that report on the extent to which energy efficiency buildings have been reached. Rating results are expected to be a reference for the retrofitting of existing buildings and the design of new buildings. In addition, the outlook for the rating system was also discussed.

Keywords: building energy efficiency; indoor environmental quality; rating system; actual performance; in situ measurement

---

1. Introduction

China is the country with the largest energy consumption worldwide, with a rate of 18% in 2010 [1]; in particular, the building energy consumption in China recently surpassed the US building consumption, and it is expected to increase significantly in the next decade, pushed by the continuous population and urbanization increase, and the improving living standards that are following the increasing urbanization rate [2]. The building sector is a major contributor to environmental degradation [3]. To preserve the environment and reduce building energy consumption in China, a series of measures has been implemented in order to promote building energy efficiency. The measures mainly consist of introducing and improving energy codes and design standards for new and existing buildings [4], and the energy evaluation of buildings.

China began monitoring its energy efficiency efforts in the early 1980s, in response to the continuous increase in the energy use of the residential sector [5], before expanding its efforts over a larger scope, leading to the introduction of a series of new building energy standards and codes [6–8]. These standards are mandatory at a national level and have a significant influence on the design phase of new buildings and the retrofitting of existing buildings. These standards defined the efficiency requirements of the building envelope, such as the minimum insulation of walls, roofs, and floors, and the thermal performance of windows, as well as HVAC systems. Energy certification standards [9,10] have also been introduced, in order to evaluate a building's energy consumption in its operational phase. However, whilst much attention has been paid to energy consumption due to the aforementioned measure, the indoor environmental quality of buildings is an issue that has been neglected [11].

Rating systems for sustainable building were developed in the 1990s, across the globe. These rating tools evaluate a building's environmental performance and pay much attention to energy consumption, as well as indoor environmental quality. The U.K. announced the first building environmental performance assessment system, known as BREEAM (Building Research Establishment Environmental Assessment Method) [12], and then developed countries proposed their own systems, such as the U.S.'s LEED (Leadership in Energy and Environment Design) [13], Japan's CASBEE (Comprehensive Assessment System for Building Environmental Efficiency) [14], etc. China issued the ESGB (Evaluation Standard for Green Building) [15] in 2006. LEED, as the most recognized building environment rating system, is also widely adopted in China. Major developers often undergo LEED assessment in order to demonstrate the improved environmental performance of their building assets, thus attracting international investors. These codes and rating systems play an important role in guiding the sustainable design and decision-making processes [16,17], and have a significant impact on building industry.

Buildings rated and certificated by energy codes, LEED, or ESGB, are expected to have a high energy efficiency performance and good indoor environmental qualities. However, studies show that the actual performance of these green buildings in China cannot achieve the energy efficient goal during their operational phase. A comparative study has shown that many LEED-certified buildings performed worse than their conventional counterparts [18]. Many studies show that the actual performance of certificated green buildings, does not support the hypothesis that they are superior in terms of aesthetics, serenity, lighting, ventilation, acoustics, or humidity, when compared with non-certificated ones [19,20].

The reasons for this are illustrated, as follows: (1) In China, most of the certificated energy efficient buildings or labeled green buildings cannot achieve green standards in their operation stage, due to the lack of mature technology and skilled workers [21]; (2) The point-based rating method in LEED and GBL, encourages designers to adopt as many sustainable strategies as possible in order to achieve a high enough score in the process of assessment, which does not directly lead to the better performance of buildings; (3) According to the existing rating systems, a building's energy performance during the operation phase is the result of simulation through theoretical calculation, based on codes or dynamic algorithms [22,23] which do not usually reveal the real behavior that an in situ measurement can show [24].

The purpose of this paper is to present a rating system for building energy efficiency, based on in situ measurement in China. The system is intended for office buildings in China's cold zone, during the operational phase. An evaluation framework, graphic dominant point, and principle of data collection and processing, are illustrated in this paper. Three existing buildings underwent one-year in situ research and measurement in order to collect quantitative data of their actual performance, and were assessed under the new rating system. The authors believe that the system will contribute to a more accurate and comprehensive understanding for assets holders and occupants, providing information on the extent to which a building's energy efficiency has been achieved, as well as revealing the actual indoor environmental quality of the buildings. In addition, the outlook for the rating system was also discussed.

2. Description of the Rating System

2.1. Evaluation Object

Relevant rating systems such as BREEAM, LEED, and GBL, are usually divided into categories such as quality of the site, resource consumption, environmental loads, indoor comfort, quality of service, and social and economic aspects [25]. Those categories are the main concerns and comprise the evaluation objects within a system. The advantage of such a system is that they account for various factors, comprehensively. However, the disadvantage is that it's too complicated. The authors believe that the main goal of rating systems is to reduce energy consumption and harmful impacts on environment, and that the development of buildings is intended to improve the comfort and health of the indoor environment. Thus, in this study, the evaluation object is limited to the building energy efficiency whose measurement parameter includes energy consumption and indoor environmental quality. Since the operation phase of a building has been reported to account for about 70%–98% of a building's energy use and greenhouse gas emissions, depending on the building's design and intended use [26,27], it is reasonable to assess a building's sustainability by focusing on the building energy performance during its operational phase. Therefore, energy consumption and indoor environmental quality should be based on in situ measurement.

Almost all of the rating systems have been designed to suit a territory. Evidence suggests that existing rating systems were developed for different local purposes, and are not fully applicable to all regions [28]. China has a vast territory and complex terrain. Climate significantly varies in different areas, due to geographical latitude, terrain, and other conditions. So, for different climatic conditions, the building energy efficiency requires a corresponding different approach. In order to clarify the scientific relationship between architecture design and climate, the Ministry of Construction of China divides China into five main climatic zones, and puts forward different design guides for each zone. Table 1 shows the climatic classification and climatic characters for each zone. This study mainly focused on buildings in China's cold zones, whose climate is characteristic of cold weather in winter and hot weather in summer, leading to a high energy consumption for heating and cooling. Various types of buildings differ in energy consumption and indoor environmental quality. Therefore, for the purpose of this study, the research designers only chose office buildings as a specific type for further research and assessment.

Table 1. Climatic classification and climatic characters in China.

	Climate Zones	Main Climate Index	Guides for Architecture Design
I	Severe cold zones	Average temperature in January $\leq -10\,^\circ$C; Average temperature in July $\leq 25\,^\circ$C	The building must meet the requirements of heat preservation in winter, anti-freezing and other requirements.
II	Cold zones	Average temperature in January $-10\sim0\,^\circ$C; Average temperature in July $18\sim28\,^\circ$C	The building must meet the requirements of heat preservation in winter, anti-freezing and other requirements.
III	Hot summer and cold winter zones	Average temperature in January $0\sim10\,^\circ$C; Average temperature in July $25\sim30\,^\circ$C	The building must meet anti-overheating, shading, ventilation and cooling requirements in summer. Anti-cold requirements should be taken into account in winter.
IV	Hot summer and warm winter zones	Average temperature in January $>10\,^\circ$C; Average temperature in July $25\sim29\,^\circ$C	The building must meet anti-overheating, shading, ventilation, cooling and anti-rainwater requirements in summer.
V	Temperate zones	Average temperature in January $0\sim13\,^\circ$C; Average temperature in July $18\sim25\,^\circ$C	The building must meet ventilation and anti-rainwater requirements in summer.

2.2. Evaluation Framework

The main purpose of this study is to develop a rating system for building energy efficiency, based on the actual performance of buildings during their operation phase. The stages of development are outlined in Figure 1.

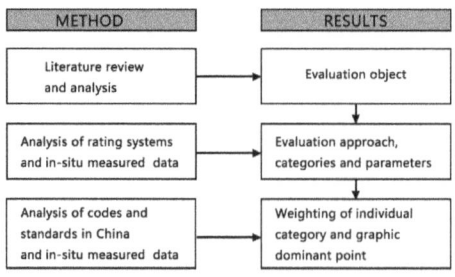

Figure 1. Work flow diagram.

2.2.1. Development of Evaluation Framework

In the first stage, as illustrated in Figure 1, the authors defined the evaluation object of the rating system, through a literature review and analysis.

In the second stage, the authors analyzed the existing rating systems under an evaluation framework. Compared to other rating systems such as LEED, BREEAM, and GBL, CASBEE uses a different system for assessing sustainability performance. Rather than relying upon a simple additive approach, CASBEE introduced the concept of Building Environmental Efficiency (BEE), and divided the system into two aspects: Q and L (Figure 2). Q stands for the building's environmental quality and L stands for the building's environmental loads, which is the harmful impact caused by the construction and operation of buildings. These two aspects are integrated into a two-dimensional system. The final assessment of the results depends on the coefficient levels of Q and L.

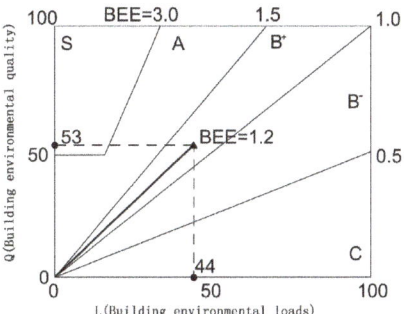

Figure 2. Diagram of CASBEE assessment.

The new rating system is focused on energy performance, as well as indoor environmental quality. Therefore, the two-dimensional system in CASBEE is chosen as a baseline for the rating framework, and modified (Figure 3) The rating result depends on two aspects of the building's performance. $(Q/L)_t$ stands for the building energy efficiency level and L stands for the total energy consumption. The author used L (total energy consumption) as a control parameter to prevent the possibility of increasing the total burden on the environment in the new rating system, in order to improve indoor environmental quality in the category rating.

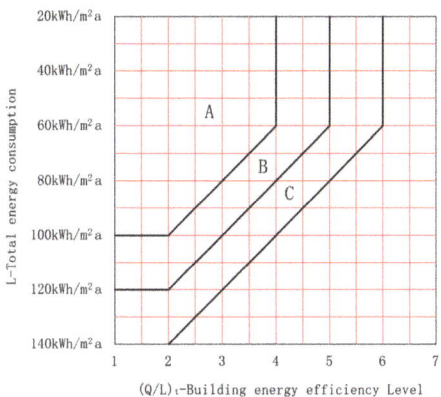

Figure 3. Diagram of final rating.

The systems are divided into four categories and every category is rated under a Q/L system. For office buildings, the authors believe that the key indoor environmental qualities affecting the occupants' feelings, health, and productivity, are thermal comfort, lighting and visual comfort, and other factors, including air quality, acoustic comfort, convenience, and maintenance of the building's appliances, hot water supply, etc., which are related to energy consumption. According to the statistics, in China's cold zone, the building energy consumption of office buildings consists mainly of heating energy consumption in winter, cooling energy consumption in summer, artificial lighting energy consumption, and other energy consumption which includes power equipment energy consumption (for elevators, fans, etc.), socket-equipment energy consumption (for daily office devices), and hot water production energy consumption, etc. [29].

The indoor air temperature, relative humidity, and indoor illumination are much more related to energy consumption. So, the data of the three is collected through in situ measurement, during the operational phase. Other indoor environmental qualities are measured through subjective questionnaires. Thermal comfort is measured by air temperature, indoor wind velocity, and relative humidity. In this study, the author took indoor air temperature as a parameter to measure the thermal comfort. In this paper, summer represents the period when the cooling system is occupied; winter represents the period when the heating system is occupied.

Therefore, the four categories consist of indoor temperature in winter/heating energy consumption, indoor temperature in summer/cooling energy consumption, indoor illumination/lighting energy consumption, and the satisfaction level/other energy consumption. Each category is assigned a score on a scale of 1 (excellent) to 7 (poor) (Figure 4). The evaluation framework and process of the rating system are shown in Figure 5.

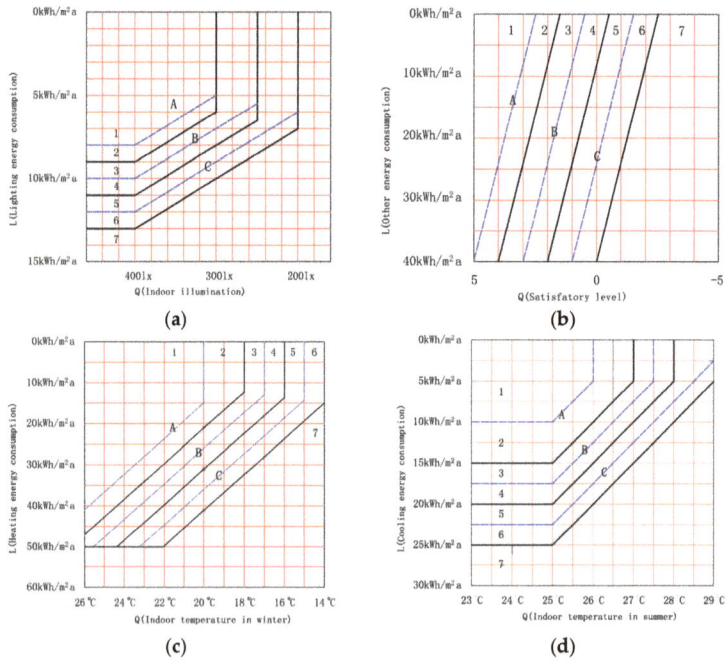

Figure 4. (**a**) Diagram of indoor temperature in winter/heating energy consumption rating; (**b**) Diagram of indoor temperature in summer/cooling energy consumption rating; (**c**) Diagram of indoor illumination/lighting energy consumption rating; (**d**) Diagram of satisfaction level/other energy consumption rating.

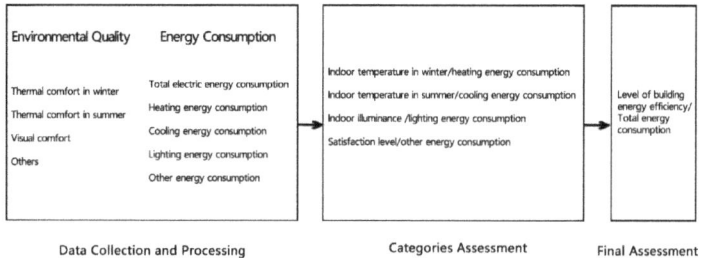

Figure 5. Diagram of evaluation framework and process.

2.2.2. Determination of Weighting and Graphic Dominant Point

In the third stage, after analyzing the codes, standards in China [30–32], and in-situ data, the authors define the weighting of categories and the graphic dominant point.

The final rating result depends on two parameters: $(Q/L)_t$ (building energy efficiency level) and L (total energy consumption). The rated building is placed on a scale from A (good) to C (poor), and if the performance of a rated building is worse than a C building, it won't be certified (Figure 3). The score of $(Q/L)_t$ is calculated as the sum of the scores obtained from each category, with corresponding weighting. According to relevant statistics of the data from office buildings in China's cold zone, heating energy consumption, cooling energy consumption, lighting energy consumption, and other consumption, account for 40%, 20%, 10%, and 30% of the total energy consumption, respectively [30,31]. Therefore, the weightings of the four categories are set as 0.4, 0.2, 0.1, and 0.3, respectively (Equation (1)).

$$(Q/L)_t = 0.4 \times (Q/L)_h + 0.2 \times (Q/L)_c + 0.1 \times (Q/L)_i + 0.3 \times (Q/L)_s \tag{1}$$

$(Q/L)_h$—Score of indoor temperature in winter/heating energy consumption rating
$(Q/L)_c$—Score of indoor temperature in summer/cooling energy consumption rating
$(Q/L)_i$—Score of indoor illumination/lighting energy consumption rating
$(Q/L)_s$—Score of satisfactory level/other appliance consumption rating
$(Q/L)_t$—Building energy efficiency level

The graphic dominant point of the diagrams is the basis of establishing a quantitative Q/L system rating. The values of Q and L of the graphic dominant point differ, according to the type of buildings and the climatic zone. Through referring to China's "Building Energy Standards" literature review and the result of in situ measurement, the graphic dominant point of each diagram can be identified, and thus the quantitative system of evaluation is established.

In this study, the graphic dominant points depend on the relevant standard values of indoor environmental quality and energy consumption, in individual categories. According to the architectural design code [10,11], the authors set the values for indoor environmental qualities: standard indoor temperature in winter value is 20 °C, standard indoor temperature in summer is 26 °C, and standard indoor illumination value is 300 lx [9,31]. Tables 2 and 3 show the heating energy consumption and non-heating energy consumption standard of a state institution office building in the Beijing region. The mandatory value and suggested value are stipulated in the standard, and an average value can be calculated and listed as the median value.

According to Tables 2 and 3, and recent studies and analyses of literature [30–32], values for heating energy consumption, cooling energy consumption, lighting energy consumption, and other energy consumption of office buildings, are determined and shown in Table 4. Thus, the graphic dominant point of each diagram can be determined. The authors then defined the diagram in Figure 4, based on the graphic dominant point, reference to the relevant literature and study in China [11,32], and their experience of green building design.

Table 2. Heating energy consumption standards of a state institution office building in the Beijing region (1 kgce = 3.695 kWh).

Heating Energy Consumption (kgce/m²a)	Large-Scale Urban Central Heating	Small-Scale Urban Central Heating	District Central Heating	Household Heating	Average Value
Mandatory value	9.8	10.3	13.8	11.1	11.25 ($\approx$42 kWh/m²a)
Median value					32 kWh/m²a
Suggested value	4.5	4.5	7.9	6.9	5.95 ($\approx$22 kWh/m²a)

Table 3. Energy consumption standards of a state institution office building in the Beijing region.

Energy Consumption (Heating Energy Consumption Excluded) (kWh/m²a)	State Institution Office Building (Class A)	State Institution Office Building (Class B)	Average Value
Mandatory value	45	70	58
Median value			49
Suggested value	30	50	40

Table 4. Building energy efficiency graphic dominant point for a public office building in a cold region.

Grade	Energy Consumption				
	Total Energy Consumption (kWh/m²a)	Heating Energy Consumption (kWh/m²a)	Cooling Energy Consumption (kWh/m²a)	Lighting Energy Consumption (kWh/m²a)	Other Energy Consumption (kWh/m²a)
A grade	62	22	10	6	24
B grade	81	32	15	8	26
C grade	100	42	20	10	28

2.3. Data Collection and Processing

Indoor environmental quality data is mainly collected through a temperature and illumination recording machine placed in monitoring points, and a subjective questionnaire. Temperature and illumination data are recorded through a natural year. TPJ-22 machines were used to record indoor illumination. Their measuring range is 0–20,000 lx and precision is ±5 lx. DT-171 machines were used to record indoor air temperature. Their measuring range is −40–70 °C and precision is ±1 °C. So, the indoor temperature in winter, indoor temperature in summer, and illumination of the building in working hours, can be collected. The principle of data collection is listed as follows. (1) The arrangement of monitoring points for temperature recording requirements: temperature monitoring points are distributed every 2000 m², the number of monitoring points of each story is not less than four, and the number of monitoring points in an office area and public area (the atrium, corridor, etc.) conforms to a ratio of 3:1; (2) The arrangement of monitoring points for illumination requirements: an illumination point is distributed every 1000 m² in an office area, and the number of monitoring points of each story is not less than two. The location of measuring points should be set in the office area at the height of the working plane, 1.5 m away from the exterior wall with windows; (3) Subjective questionnaire arrangement requirements: more than 50 effective subjective questionnaires should be collected for each rated building, and the object of the questionnaire should be chosen randomly, covering occupants who work in different areas within the building. The occupants were given a questionnaire which contained two parts: one for basic information of the person and one for the questions on satisfaction levels of the indoor environmental qualities. There were 12 questions in the latter part and related to the air quality, acoustic comfort, general feeling of the indoor environment, convenience of the building device, convenience and maintenance of the building, and hot water supply, which are related to other energy consumptions mentioned in Section 2.2.1. The scores of those questions are assigned on a scale of −5 (unsatisfactory) to 5 (satisfactory), and all of the questions have the same weighting. The indoor temperature in winter is the average indoor temperature of each monitoring point during winter. The indoor temperature in summer is the average indoor temperature of each monitoring point during summer. The indoor illumination is the average indoor illumination of each monitoring point during working hours (9 a.m.–6 p.m.) in a whole year.

Office buildings in China's cold zones are heated by a central heating system in winter, so heating energy consumption can be recorded by the heat flow meter installed in rated buildings, or the data provided by the district central heating station. The cooling of office buildings in the summer is supported by a central air-conditioning system whose energy consumption can be recorded through an electricity meter. The lighting energy consumption can be recorded through an electricity meter. Other energy consumption can be obtained by subtracting the cooling energy consumption and the lighting energy consumption from the total electricity consumption, which is recorded by the electricity meter. Therefore, the building's total energy consumption is the sum of the total electricity consumption, plus the heating energy consumption.

3. Rating Results and Discussion

Three existing office buildings underwent one-year of in situ research and measurement, in order to collect quantitative data on their actual performance and analysis under the new rating system. Table 5 shows the basic information of the rated buildings. The considerations for selection were: (1) the three projects are comparable in location, MIIT (Ministry of industry and information technology of PRC) is located in Beijing and the other two —TJDRC (Tianjin Development and Reform Commission) and LTB (Local Taxation Bureau of Nankai District)—in Tianjin, and both cities are cold zones in China's climatic partition; (2) the three buildings are all office buildings which house the government agency, just in different scales and sizes.

According to the data collection principle mentioned in this article, the authors obtain the annual data of energy consumption for heating, air conditioning, illumination, and total power consumption, and total energy consumption, as well as the average indoor temperature in winter and summer, indoor illumination, and other environmental qualities, based on a subjective evaluation. The data is shown in Table 6.

Table 5. Basic information of the case study buildings.

Project	MIIT	TJDRC	LTB
Architectural Appearance			
Typical Floor Plan			
Location	Xicheng District of Beijing	Heping District of Tianjin	Nankai District of Tianjin
Floor Area	62,700 m^2	29,300 m^2	7870 m^2
Building Story	6 stories on the ground, 3 stories underground	29 stories on the ground, 2 stories underground	6 stories on the ground, 1 story underground
Completion Time	2015	1997	2003
Ventilation Type	hybrid	hybrid	hybrid
Type of lamps	led	incandescent, fluorescent	led, fluorescent

Table 6. Data of energy consumption and environmental quality.

Project	Floor Area (Underground Parking Lot Area Is Not Included) (m²)	Heating		Cooling		Lighting			Other	Total Energy Consumption (kWh/m²a)
		Heating Energy Consumption (kWh/m²a)	Indoor Temperature in Winter (°C)	Cooling Energy Consumption (kWh/m²a)	Indoor Temperature in Summer (°C)	Lighting Energy Consumption (kWh/m²a)	Indoor Illumination (lx)	Satisfactory Level	Appliance and Other Consumption (kWh/m²a)	
MIIT	48,780	36.0	21.0	10.8	26.0	8.5	360	3.7	24.4	79.7
TJDRC	22,620	50.0	19.8	16.0	26.8	11.3	350	2.0	25.4	102.7
LTB	7870	38.0	19.2	14.0	26.4	13.5	390	3.1	30.5	96.0

3.1. Indoor Temperature in Winter/Heating Energy Consumption Rating

The indoor temperature in winter/heating energy consumption rating results of the three buildings are shown in Figure 6. The heating energy consumption of MIIT is 36.0 kWh/m²a, indoor temperature in winter is 21.0 °C, and the score is 5 (very close to 4). The indoor temperature is higher than the recommended design temperature, of 20.0 °C. Thus, there is a potential for the score of MIIT to be improved to 4, if the heating supply and the time of window-opening are reduced, leading to a reduction in heating energy consumption. The heating energy consumption of LTB is 38.0 kWh/m²a, indoor temperature in winter is 19.2 °C, and the score is 6. The thermal comfort of LTB is close to that of MIIT, but the energy consumption of LBT is much higher than that of MIIT, so the score of LBT is much worse than MIIT. The heating energy consumption of TJDRC is 50.0 kWh/m²a, indoor temperature in winter is 19.8 °C, and the score is 7, which is the worst of the three. The construction of TJDRC was completed in 1997, when the codes for the performance of buildings were not as strict as today. In order to maintain a comfortable indoor temperature in winter, the heating energy consumption must be very high. Also, there is little possibility of improving the rating score of TJDRC through optimizing the operation of buildings and the habits of its occupants.

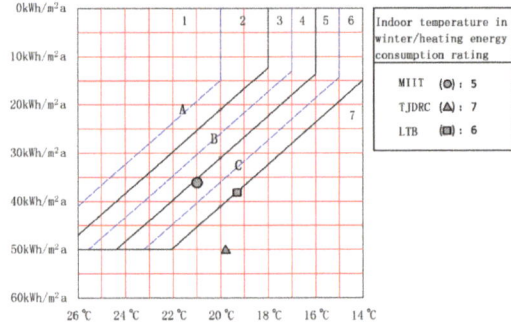

Figure 6. Indoor temperature in winter/heating energy consumption rating result.

3.2. Indoor Temperature in Summer/Cooling Energy Consumption Rating

The indoor temperature in summer/cooling energy consumption rating results of the three buildings are shown in Figure 7. The cooling energy consumption of MIIT is 10.8 kWh/m²a, indoor temperature in summer is 26.0 °C, and the score is 3. The thermal comfort of MIIT is good, and the energy consumption of cooling is low, so the overall score of MIIT is good. There is a possibility that the rating of MIIT can be improved to 2, if the natural ventilation time (especially at night) is prolonged, leading to reduction in the cooling energy consumption. The cooling energy consumption of TJDRC is 16.0 kWh/m²a, indoor temperature in summer is 26.8 °C, and the score is 6. The thermal comfort of TJDRC is close to that of MIIT, but the cooling energy consumption is much higher than that of MIIT, thus the score of TJDRC is worse than MIIT, by 2 points. The cooling energy consumption of LTB is 14.0 kWh/m²a, indoor temperature in winter is 26.4 °C, and the score is 5.

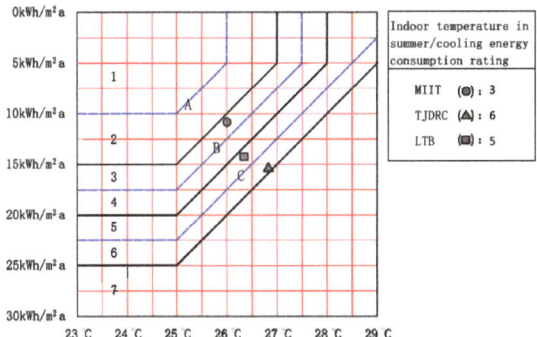

Figure 7. Indoor temperature in summer/cooling energy consumption rating result.

3.3. Indoor Illumination/Lighting Energy Consumption Rating

The indoor illumination/lighting energy consumption rating results are illustrated in Figure 8. The indoor illumination of MIIT is 360 lx, lighting energy consumption is 8.5 kWh/m²a and the score is 3. The indoor illumination of MIIT is comfortable and energy consumption is low. The rational layout design of MIIT, which provides an abundance of natural light, and the usage of energy saving lighting facilities, both contribute to lower lighting energy consumption. Thus, the rating result of MIIT is good. The indoor illumination of TJDRC is 350 lx, lighting energy consumption is 11.3 kWh/m²a and the score is 6. Although the indoor illumination of TJDRC is close to that of MIIT, its lighting energy consumption is much higher. So, the score is worse than MIIT, by 3 points. The indoor illumination of LTB is 390 lx, lighting energy consumption is 13.5 kWh/m²a, and the score is 7. The compact layout design and rich depth of LTB leads to bad natural lighting. The occupants of LTB are used to utilizing artificial lighting during the daytime to maintain a comfortable working environment, so the lighting energy consumption is higher than the other two. Optimizing the lighting facilities in LTB is unlikely to reduce energy consumption to a reasonable level.

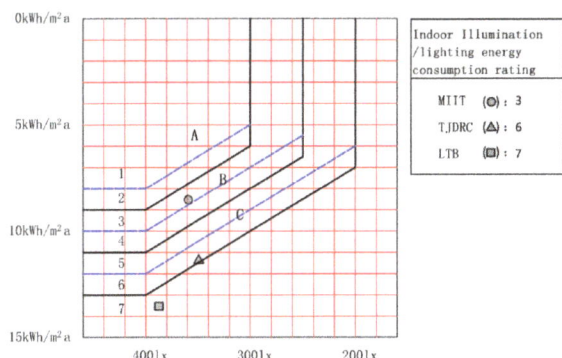

Figure 8. Indoor illumination/Lighting energy consumption rating result.

3.4. Satisfactory Level/other Energy Consumption Rating

The satisfactory level/other energy consumption rating results are illustrated in Figure 9. The questions in the subjective questionnaire involve an occupants' satisfaction level when considering indoor environmental qualities, such as thermal comfort, visual comfort, and other factors. When calculating the value of the satisfactory level, subjective assessments of thermal comfort in summer and winter, and visual comfort are excluded. So, the satisfactory level in this category stands for an occupants' assessment of other indoor environmental qualities relating to energy consumption. The satisfactory level of the MIIT is 3.7 and the correspondent energy consumption is 24.4 kWh/m²a. The satisfactory level of the TJDRC is 2.0 and the energy consumption is 25.4 kWh/m²a. The satisfactory level of the LTB is 3.1 and the energy consumption is 30.5 kWh/m²a. The three buildings scored 2, 4, and 3, respectively.

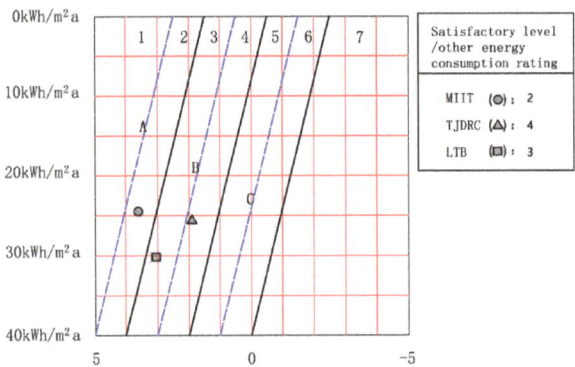

Figure 9. Satisfaction level/other energy consumption rating result.

3.5. Final Rating

Figure 10 shows the final rating results for the three buildings. The score of $(Q/L)_t$ of MIIT, TJDRC, and LTR, which are obtained through weighted calculations, are 3.5, 5.8, and 4.9, respectively.

The total energy consumption of MIIT is 79.7 kWh/m²a, and the building energy efficiency of MIIT is labeled as B grade. The total energy consumption of TJDRC is 102.7 kWh/m²a, and the total energy consumption of LTB is 96.0 kWh/m²a. TJDRC and LTB are not certified by the new rating system, due to their poor performance in energy consumption.

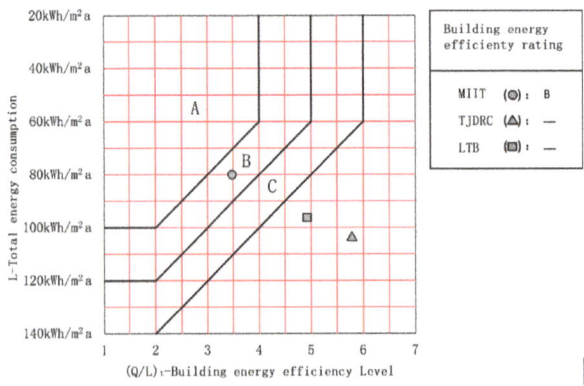

Figure 10. Building energy efficiency rating result.

4. Conclusions and Outlook

This article has presented a new rating system for building energy efficiency, and it is intended to evaluate office buildings in China's cold zone. The main novelty of the presented method is that the evaluation and rating is based on in situ measurement results of existing buildings, during their

Sustainability **2017**, *9*, 208

operational phase. The method was developed on the basis of the Q/L system of CASBEE, and a series of studies on relevant literature, rating systems, codes, and standards in China. The rating system considers the actual energy consumption and indoor environmental quality. Three occupied office buildings in Beijing and Tianjin underwent one year of in situ measurement and research. The collected data were processed and the buildings were evaluated using the new rating system. The result of MIIT is a GBL-certified building, rated as B grade under the new system, but it can be seen from the discussion that there is great potential for a better grade, through optimizing the occupation and operation of the building. The other two offices were not certified by the rating system because of their poor performance in energy consumption. There is a need to improve the building energy efficiency of these two buildings, by optimizing the operation, occupants' using habits, and maybe the retrofitting of the buildings.

The rating system is intended to provide a more accurate and comprehensive understanding of energy performance of a building to asset holders, occupants, and designers. It reveals the real energy efficiency and indoor environmental qualities that simulation in energy certification and existing rating systems can not show. Rating results under the new rating system, combined with design data of the buildings, can also be a reference for the retrofitting of existing buildings and the design of new buildings. It may inspire designers to make more climate-adapted decisions, instead of adopting strategies in order to meet relevant requirements under the existing certification or evaluation systems. In this study, only one type of building (office building) and one type of climatic context were taken into account, but the authors believe that through more research and study, the rating system can be expanded to a more complete level, under the framework and methodology that can serve a larger variety of buildings in all kinds of climatic zones in China.

Acknowledgments: This study was supported by the Project in the National Science & Technology Pillar Program during the Twelfth Five-year Plan Period (grant number 2013BAJ15B01) and National key research and development program during Thirteenth Five-year Plan Period (grant number 2016YFC0700206).

Author Contributions: Zhengnan Zhou designed research; Li Zhao completed Introduction section and literature research; all authors performed research and analyzed the data; all authors participated in writing the paper. All authors read and approved the final manuscript.

Conflicts of Interest: The authors declare no conflict of interest.

References

1. Energy Information Administration (EIA). International Energy Outlook 2014. Available online: http://www.eia.gov/outlooks/archive/ieo14/pdf/0484(2014).pdf (accessed on 25 January 2017).
2. Berardi, U. A cross-country comparison of the building energy consumptions and their trends. *Resour. Conserv. Recycl.* **2017**. [CrossRef]
3. Peuportier, B.; Thiers, S.; Guiavarch, A. Eco-design of buildings using thermal simulation and life cycle assessment. *J. Clean. Prod.* **2013**, *39*, 73–78. [CrossRef]
4. Li, J.; Shui, B. A comprehensive analysis of building energy efficiency policies in China: Status quo and development perspective. *J. Clean. Prod.* **2015**, *90*, 326–344. [CrossRef]
5. Long, W. China: Building and Energy Overview. In Proceedings of the Tongi-PolyU Student Seminar, Sino-German College of Applied Sciences, Tongji University, Shanghai, China, May 2005.
6. Ministry of Construction of the People's Republic of China. *Technical Specification for Energy Conservation Renovation of Existing Heating Residential Building (JGJ 129-2001)*; China Building Industry Press: Beijing, China, 2001.
7. Ministry of Construction of the People's Republic of China. *Design Standard for Energy Efficiency of Residential Buildings in Hot Summer and Warm Winter Zone (JGJ 75-2003)*; China Building Industry Press: Beijing, China, 2003.
8. Ministry of Construction of the People's Republic of China. *Design Standard for Energy Efficiency of Public Buildings (GB50189-2005)*; China Building Industry Press: Beijing, China, 2005.
9. Ministry of Construction of the People's Republic of China. *Standard for Building Energy Performance Certification (JGJ/T288-2012)*; China Building Industry Press: Beijing, China, 2012.

10. Ministry of Construction of the People's Republic of China. *Standard for Energy Consumption of Buildings (GB/T51161-2016)*; China Building Industry Press: Beijing, China, 2016.

11. Wong, S.; Abe, N. Stakeholders' Perspectives of a Building Environmental Assessment Method: The Case of CASBEE. *Build. Environ.* **2014**, *82*, 502–516. [CrossRef]

12. Silvestre, J.D.; de Brito, J.; Pinheiro, M.D. From the new European Standards to an environmental, energy and economic assessment of building assemblies from cradle-to-cradle. *Energy Build* **2013**, *64*, 199–208. [CrossRef]

13. Leadership in Energy & Environmental Design (LEED). Available online: http://leed.usgbc.org/leed.html (accessed on 25 January 2017).

14. Comprehensive Assessment System for Built Environment Efficiency (CASBEE). Available online: http://www.ibec.or.jp/CASBEE/english/overviewE.htm (accessed on 25 January 2017).

15. Ye, L.; Cheng, Z.; Wang, Q.; Lin, W.; Ren, F. Overview on Green Building Label in China. *Renew. Energy* **2013**, *53*, 220–229. [CrossRef]

16. Ando, S.; Arima, T.; Bogaki, K.; Hasegawa, H.; Hoyano, A.; Ikaga, T. *Architecture for a Sustainable Future*; Architectural Institute of Japan: Tokyo, Japan, 2005.

17. Cole, R. *Building Environmental Assessment Methods: A Measure of Success*; IeJC: California, CA, USA, 2013.

18. Newsham, G.; Birt, B.; Arsenault, C.; Thompson, L.; Veitch, J.; Mancini, S.; Galasiu, A.; Gover, B.; Macdonald, I.; Burns, G. Do green buildings outperform conventional buildings? *Indoor Environ. Energy Perform N. Am. Off.* **2012**, *1*, 1–71.

19. Gou, Z.; Lau, S.Y.; Shen, J. Indoor environmental satisfaction in two LEED offices and its implications in green interior design. *Indoor Built. Environ.* **2011**, *21*, 503–514. [CrossRef]

20. Paul Warren, L.; Taylor Peter, A. A comparison of occupant comfort and satisfaction between a green building and a conventional building. *Build. Environ.* **2008**, *43*, 1858–1870.

21. Li, Y.; Yang, L.; He, B.; Zhao, D. Green building in China: Needs great promotion. *Sustain. Cities Soc.* **2014**, *11*, 1–6. [CrossRef]

22. Desogus, G.; Mura, S.; Ricciu, R. Comparing different approaches to in situ measurement of building components thermal resistance. *Energy Build.* **2011**, *43*, 2613–2620. [CrossRef]

23. Buratti, C.; Moretti, E.; Belloni, E.; Cotana, F. Unsteady simulation of energy performance and thermal comfort in non-residential buildings. *Build. Environ.* **2013**, *59*, 482–491. [CrossRef]

24. Asdrubali, F.; Buratti, C.; Cotana, F.; Baldinelli, G.; Goretti, M.; Moretti, E.; Baldassarri, C.; Belloni, E.; Bianchi, F.; Rotili, A.; et al. Domenico Palladino and Daniele Bevilacqua. Evaluation of Green Buildings' Overall Performance through in Situ Monitoring and Simulations. *Energies* **2013**, *6*, 6525–6547. [CrossRef]

25. Bisegna, F.; Mattoni, B.; Gori, P.; Asdrubali, F.; Guattari, C.; Evangelisti, L.; Sambuco, S.; Bianchi, F. Influence of Insulating Materials on Green Building Rating System Results. *Energies* **2016**, *9*, 712. [CrossRef]

26. Scheuer, C.; Keoleian, G.A.; Reppe, P. Life cycle energy and environmental performance of a new university building: Modeling challenges and design implications. *Energy Build.* **2003**, *35*, 1049–1064. [CrossRef]

27. Ortiz, O.; Castells, F.; Sonnemann, G. Sustainability in the construction industry: A review of recent developments based on LCA. *Constr. Build. Mater.* **2009**, *23*, 28–39. [CrossRef]

28. Alyami, S.H.; Rezgui, Y. Sustainable building assessment tool development approach. *Sustain. Cities Soc.* **2012**, *5*, 52–62. [CrossRef]

29. Chen, H. The Status Quo and Countermeasures of Office Building Energy Utilization in Central Government Organs in Early Twenty-First Century. Ph.D. Thesis, School of Architecture, Tsinghua University, Beijing, China, 1 September 2008.

30. Ministry of Housing and Urban Rural Development & State Administration of Quality Supervision, Inspection and Quarantine. *Civil Building Design Standards*; China Building Industry Press: Beijing, China, 2016.

31. Building Energy Saving Research Center of Tsinghua University. *China Building Energy Saving Annual Development Report*; China Building Industry Press: Beijing, China, 2007.

32. Qin, Y.G. Green building planning and design guidelines and evaluation system. *China Sci. Technol. Achiev.* **2007**, *11*, 53–54.

Article

Integrated Sustainability Assessment of Public Rental Housing Community Based on a Hybrid Method of AHP-Entropy Weight and Cloud Model

Guangdong Wu [1],*, Kaifeng Duan [1], Jian Zuo [2], Xianbo Zhao [3] and Daizhong Tang [4],*

[1] School of Tourism and Urban Management, Jiangxi University of Finance & Economics,
    Nanchang 330013, China; kefee920729@163.com
[2] School of Architecture and Built Environment; Entrepreneurship, Commercialisation and Innovation
    Centre (ECIC), The University of Adelaide, Adelaide 5005, Australia; jian.zuo@adelaide.edu.au
[3] School of Engineering and Technology, Central Queensland University, Sydney, NSW 2000, Australia;
    b.zhao@cqu.edu.au
[4] School of Economics and Management, Tongji University, Shanghai 200092, China
*   Correspondence: gd198410@163.com (G.W.); tdzhong@126.com (D.T.)

Academic Editors: Umberto Berardi and Marc A. Rosen
Received: 9 February 2017; Accepted: 11 April 2017; Published: 13 April 2017

Abstract: As an essential part of a city, community is significant to the sustainable development of the city. At present, research on community sustainability assessment systems is relatively scarce. The existing community sustainability assessment systems often lack integrated consideration of community sustainability. For example, these systems especially place emphasis on the ecological and environmental aspects, but the economic and social aspects of sustainability are partially ignored. In order to comprehensively evaluate the sustainability of a community, this paper draws on the "participatory philosophy" and constructs an integrated assessment indicator system that includes five dimensions: environment; economy; society; institution; and culture. On this basis, a new hybrid evaluation method based on analytical hierarchy process (AHP)-entropy weight and the cloud model is proposed to evaluate community sustainability. This method combines AHP and the entropy weight method to determine index weight, thus making full use of their respective advantages. At the same time, it makes use of the superiority of the cloud model to transform qualitative remarks into quantitative representations and to reflect fuzziness and randomness. To verify the feasibility of this method, a case study is carried out on the "Minxinjiayuan" public rental housing community in Chongqing, China. The results show that the overall sustainability of the community lies between the "middle" and "good" level, and closer to the "middle" level. The level of the economic and social sustainability is higher than that of the environmental, institutional and cultural sustainability.

Keywords: AHP-entropy weight; cloud model; public rental housing community; sustainability assessment; indicator system

---

1. Introduction

Since the concept of "sustainable development" was defined in the Brundtland Report [1] in 1987, it has gradually been accepted by organizations and governments around the world [2] and spread to a variety of disciplines. The construction industry has significant impacts on the economy, society and natural environment due to its huge consumption of resources [3,4]. It is necessary to realize the transformation from traditional building to sustainable building [5]. Building sustainability assessment systems can help systematically evaluate the sustainability of the design, construction, operation and management stages of a building's whole life cycle [6]. It is one of the most important tools in promoting sustainable building development. Recently, more and more scholars have made an active exploration of building sustainability assessment systems and tools, and have obtained rich theoretical achievements [4,7–9]. Nevertheless, research on this aspect is still far from enough. Until now, the definition of sustainable building is not clear in the academic world [10–12]. However, in general, a sustainable building is considered to achieve balanced development in the dimensions of environment, economy and society [13–16]. There is a lack of comprehensive consideration of multidimensional sustainability indicators in the existing building sustainability assessment systems. Most of these systems focus attention on the ecological environment, especially construction energy-saving performance, while paying little attention to the economic and social aspects of sustainability [17–20].

In order to consider multiple dimensions of sustainability comprehensively, in recent years, more and more literature has discussed going beyond the research paradigm of single-building assessment and expanding the evaluation scale so as to fully consider the connection between buildings and people as well as the surrounding environment [10,21,22]. Wu defined the scope of the sciences of human settlements on five levels: globe; region; city; community; and construction [23]. As an essential part of a city, community is very important to urban development. The general sustainability development of the city depends on the sustainability level of urban communities [24]. For example, the development of community can help promote urban employment and improve the appearance of a city; community is closely related to the life of urban residents, so it is also the root of some social problems. The overall sustainability of a city is in doubt if its own components are not sustainable [24]. However, previous research on sustainability evaluation mainly concentrated on the macro city level [25,26] and the micro building level [27], while the research on the intermediate-level of community sustainability assessment (CSA) systems is still not enough [28,29]. So far, studies have shown that sustainable communities have a notable positive effect on house price [30]; environmentally friendly buildings in the community tend to attract property buyers and people are willing to pay more for them; residents in sustainable communities have a higher sense of wellbeing [31]; and they enjoy a better quality of life [25]. As the planning unit of urban development, community plays a significant role in city sustainable development. Thus, it is very important to conduct research on community sustainability assessment systems and tools [28,32].

Public rental housing is a specific product of the Chinese government to meet the housing demand of medium-low income groups in China. This new type of affordable housing appeared in 2010. Originally, it was a transitional form to meet the housing demand of the "sandwich layer" group [33], who neither satisfy the application standard for cheap rental housing or economically affordable housing nor can afford commercial housing. However, with the transformation of the Chinese affordable housing system, public rental housing projects have become a national strategy. By 2013, public rental housing had become the mainstream of affordable housing in China. Survey data in 2014 showed that, by the end of 2013, there were 14.25 million suites of public rental housing in China, of which newly built ones accounted for 94.7%. According to the Minister of Housing and Urban-Rural Development of the People's Republic of China, by the end of 2016 there were 10 million households living in public rental housing, and the monetization of public rental housing was also advancing. It can be predicted that in the near future, public rental housing projects will continue to flourish in China. Public rental housing community gathers medium-low income people and has a high level of population mobility. It has an inherent particularity compared to the traditional urban community [34,35]. The scale of the public rental housing community is larger than general urban community. A large number of residents from different professions live there. The living conditions in it are very complex. Hence, realizing sustainable development of the public rental housing community is a great challenge for the Chinese government. China has begun large-scale public rental housing construction only in recent years. It has not yet formed a sound theoretical system of the design, construction, operation and management of public rental housing community. Both theoretically and practically, the sustainability of the public rental housing community is a very important new issue. Research into sustainability assessment systems and tools of the public rental housing community is crucial to guide Chinese public rental housing toward sustainable development. It can also be used as a reference for the study of housing and community sustainability assessment in other countries. Existing CSA systems are mainly established by developed countries according to their national conditions. There are many limitations in their application in other developing countries [28,36]. Since sustainable communities have different meanings in different regions and environments [29], this paper attempts to establish a specific sustainability assessment indicator system, including multiple dimensions of sustainability, for the Chinese public rental housing community based on previous studies, relative policy analysis and evaluator scoring. In addition, this paper proposes a new hybrid method of analytical hierarchy process (AHP)-entropy weight and cloud model for the evaluation. The system and method can provide a new integrated perspective for sustainability assessment, and could be a theoretical reference for the research on sustainability evaluation systems and tools of China and other countries.

2. Literature Review

2.1. Community Sustainability Assessment System

The sustainability assessment system has been used in the construction industry for more than 20 years [37]. It was originated in Europe and North America and other developed countries [17,38]. After years of research and development, a variety of sustainability assessment systems and theories have been developed in the building environment, such as sustainable building rating systems, sustainable building certification systems, life cycle assessment methodology, sustainable building assessment technical guidelines, evaluation framework and checklists [39] etc. Relevant research shows that there are more than 600 rating systems for sustainability assessment available worldwide currently [40]. Among them, there are a lot of building evaluation systems developed by various organizations including the government [41] such as BREEAM (Britain), LEED (America), CASBEE (Japan), DGNB (Germany) and GBTool (Canada) etc. However, these assessment tools rarely have an integrated consideration of multiple dimensions of sustainability. Especially, most of them pay insufficient attention to the social and economic aspects of sustainability [17–20]. In order to make a more reasonable and comprehensive assessment of the multi-pillars of sustainability, it is necessary to expand the spatial boundary of the evaluation. For this reason, CSA or neighborhood sustainability assessment (NSA) has been paid more and more attention in the academic world [41]. In recent years, especially with the emergence of BREEAM Communities, LEED-ND, CASBEE-UD, etc., CSA and NSA have become hot topics in academic circles [42].

Most researchers tended to study the theory aspect of community or neighborhood sustainability assessment systems. They conducted deep research and comparisons of the types and evaluation criteria of different CSA or NSA systems to provide a general description of them. For example, Berardi compared BREEAM Communities, LEED-ND and CASBEE-UD and found that these evaluation systems lack a rational and comprehensive evaluation of the environmental, economic and social aspects of sustainability [28]. Reith and Orova conducted a detailed three-level comparison of five sustainability assessment systems (i.e., CASBEE-UD, the 2009 and 2012 versions of the BREEAM Communities, LEED-ND and DGNB-UD) [43]. The result indicated that DGNB-UD has done the best to consider the environmental, economic and social aspects of sustainability in a comprehensive and balanced way; CASBEE-UD differs from other evaluation systems in many respects due to its particular background; the BREEAM and LEED systems showed average results in main respects. In order to study the present situation of urban CSA systems, Haapio analyzed three typical systems (LEED-ND, BREEAM Communities and CASBEE-UD) [39]. He stated that sustainability evaluation systems should be connected with regional characteristics, and emphasized the importance of knowledge- and experience-sharing for the improvement of evaluation methods. Sharifi and Murayama critically and comprehensively analyzed seven NSA tools (i.e., LEED-ND, CASBEE-UD, BREEAM Communities, HQE2R, Ecocity, SCR and ECC) [29]. They pointed out that most of these systems did not perform well considering the coverage of social, economic and institutional respects of sustainability, and lacked mechanisms for local adaptability and participation. They also analyzed the feasibility of establishing a global standard for sustainability evaluation systems [32]. They focused on the evaluation results of different NSA systems in different environments and found that the evaluation results of the same evaluated projects are different in different NSA systems. They then proposed that the criteria and indices should be selected according to the specific environment of the neighborhood. Lin and Shih conducted a qualitative and quantitative study on the sustainability assessment systems of the internationally renowned countries and developed Asian countries [44]. They found that the NSA systems of many countries emphasize resources and energy but neglect the development of economy. The NSA systems of Asian countries had their particular characteristics compared with other countries. They also stated that it is necessary to ensure links between each indicator of the NSA system and public participation.

Additionally, there are some researchers concerned about the empirical aspect of CSA or NSA systems. They are trying to find the gap between the prospective design and practical application of the sustainability assessment systems. For example, Garde carried out a survey of 73 LEED-ND registered pilot projects in the United States [45] and studied the satisfaction degree of these projects to the standard of the evaluation system. He pointed out that the sustainable development of a community could not be guaranteed according only to LEED-ND standards, and that local and regional conditions should also be taken into account. Sharifi and Murayama analyzed the scorecard of 97 LEED-ND pilot programs [46]. They obtained the application frequency of evaluation criteria in these programs, and the results are basically consistent with Grade. Säynäjoki et al. found that some indicators of the existing NSA systems are not suitable for use in Finland [47]. Kyrkou et al. and Cable respectively studied the application rationality of LEED-ND in the English and German context [48,49]. They finally got similar conclusions with Säynäjoki et al. Komeily and Srinivasan studied a series of cases from the macro and micro levels of the application of NSA systems [50]. They pointed out that most of the existing systems tend to ignore the environmental characteristics of different neighborhoods and often attempt to establish a "one-size-fits-all" universal paradigm. They also put forward that NSA systems should consider the characteristics of different neighborhoods, such as local culture and the concept of residents. The evaluation systems of different neighborhoods should have a certain degree of specificity and diversity.

2.2. Public Rental Housing and Sustainability Assessment of Public Rental Housing Community

Public rental housing is an important form of affordable housing in China. It is an outcome of the livelihood policy implemented by the Chinese government to meet the housing demand of the medium-low income groups in China [34]. The affordable housing system is mainly formulated for low-income people in the society. Since there is a big gap between the supply of the government and the demand of the society, the Chinese government began to vigorously carry out the construction of public rental housing in 2010. In recent years, it has developed rapidly all over the country. With the rapid development of public rental housing, it has formed a new type of residence community composed of medium-low income groups. As a special product of the Chinese government to improve people's livelihoods, the public rental housing community has its own particularity compared with the traditional urban community. Although public rental housing is started in the form of rent, the tenants are allowed to purchase the houses after a few years of living in them. The renters and house buyers have formed a mixed case in the community [35]. Residents in public rental housing are a large number of medium-low income people such as migrant workers and newly graduated students. These people can only rely on temporary rental housing to solve the housing problem. Therefore, the population movement within public rental housing is relatively great. In addition, as one kind of affordable housing, the rent and house prices of public rental housing are lower than the market price level. At present, public rental housing projects have been growing rapidly throughout the country; however, the sustainability of these projects in environmental, economic and social aspects is not optimistic. For example, many cities manifested the phenomenon of public rental housing application rates being too low because of their remote locations, lack of supporting facilities, excessive introduction of market mechanisms and many other reasons [51]. Most of the public rental housing projects had serious impacts on the ecological environment regarding the use of traditional technology for design and construction [52]. The government mainly invests in the construction of public rental housing projects and it hasn't fully mobilized the enthusiasm of social forces [53,54]. All these problems are all not conducive to the sustainable development of public rental housing projects.

Since public rental housing has become a research hotpot in recent years in China, there are many research achievements about it. A number of similar concepts of public rental housing have been adopted in the global scope, such as social housing, public housing, affordable housing and social rented housing, etc. Sometimes these concepts can be replaced by each other [55]. To avoid overlooking the related literature of public rental housing, we do not specifically distinguish them herein. In the literature of sustainability of public rental housing, most researchers have only been concerned with the environmental, economic or social aspect. For example, Zhao et al. studied the impact on ecological environment of public rental housing projects by using traditional environmental impact assessment approach [52]. Hoppe and Chikamoto et al. explored strategies on how to reduce carbon emissions efficaciously by improving energy efficiency [56,57]. Li et al. analyzed the financial sustainability assessment and optimization of public rental housing projects through a case study of a public rental housing program in Nanjing [58]. Taiwo proposed qualitatively policy recommendations to encourage private institutions to participate in the construction of public housing through public-private partnerships (PPP) in Nigeria [59]. Peng and Fu analyzed the social sustainability of the public rental housing community from the perspective of residents and neighborhood committees within the community, and discussed a new governance mechanism for it [34]. Patulny and Morris investigated the effect of the government-introduced policy of social mix on the social sustainability of public rental housing programs by conducting a questionnaire survey [60]. In the literature about comprehensive evaluation of public rental housing projects, Li et al. assessed the integrated sustainability including environmental, economic and social dimensions of a public rental housing program from the perspective of complex ecosystem [55], and put forward some suggestions for improving the comprehensive sustainability of public rental housing. However, the research on the comprehensive sustainability of public rental housing community is still very sparse. The research on the integrated sustainability of public rental housing projects is just at the beginning stage and still has a lot of deficiencies. For instance, Carter and Chris believed that there was no reasonable weight allocation given to environmental, economic and social aspects in the sustainability assessment of British social housing projects and it failed to reflect the government's policy of sustainable development [61]. Therefore, this paper attempts to establish an integrated sustainability assessment system of public rental housing communities according to the characteristics of Chinese public rental housing communities and the existing literature about CSA systems, which is of great significance for promoting the sustainable development of Chinese public rental housing and providing reference for the establishment of CSA systems in other countries.

2.3. Research on Sustainability Assessment Index

Although there is no agreement on the definition and scope of "sustainable development" in academic circles [29], a traditional framework of sustainability assessment index systems can be divided into subsystems about environment, economy and society from the "triple bottom-line" perspective of sustainable development [62]. There are also scholars such as Valentin and Spangenberg, and Parris and Kates who emphasized the importance of incorporating an institutional dimension into the framework of sustainability assessment [63,64]. Spangenberg indicated that an institutional dimension could help facilitate the linkage between other dimensions of sustainability and be a supplement to them [65]. Turcu listed a series of indicators of sustainability assessment from dimensions of environment, economy, society and institution [22]. Such environmental sustainability indicators include energy use, water use, green open space etc.; economic sustainability indicators include business activity, house prices and housing affordability etc.; social sustainability indicators include a sense of community, crime and safety etc.; institutional sustainability indicators include local authority service and local partnership etc. In the integrated assessment of Chinese public rental housing projects, Li et al. [55] summarized some ecological sustainability indices such as reasonable design, energy saving, water saving, land resource conservation, green practices and environmental protection etc.; economic sustainability indices such as financial situation and budgeted-price measures etc.; social sustainability indices such as employment condition and home security etc. Yigitcanlar et al. [36] listed some environmental, economic and social indices according to the characteristics of the Malaysia community such as open space provision, education, public transportation, local service and affordable housing etc. In their paper about NSA tools, Yoon and Park [42] mentioned some environmental indices including pollution, air emission, water use and air quality etc.; economic indices including direct cost and indirect cost etc.; and social indices including health and safety and community development etc. In addition, scholars such as Wu et al. called for the inclusion of a cultural dimension in the evaluation system of a green community [66]. They argued that culture can act as a connecting and mediating factor for other dimensions of sustainable development through the creative sensitivity and aesthetic experience that the building provides. They then listed a number of indicators of cultural sustainability of green buildings, such as cultural vitality, cultural continuity, cultural diversity and so on. In general, environment, economy and society are considered as the three pillars of sustainability [29,67–69], but some scholars also suggest that institutional [41,63,64] and cultural dimensions [66,70] should be included in the sustainability evaluation system. Therefore, in order to make an integrated evaluation of the public rental housing community, the sustainability assessment indicators are selected according to these five dimensions by combining relevant literature and the characteristics of Chinese public rental housing.

3. Establishment of the Sustainability Assessment System of Public Rental Housing Communities

The sustainability assessment system of public rental housing communities is established on the foundation of the indicator-based approach. The indicators can provide information about the state or change of the system [37], so as to intuitively describe the sustainability level of public rental housing community. They play very important roles in the output evaluation of sustainability. The sustainability level indicates the sustainable development degree of the community. It is the overall assessment of the community resulting from summarizing the values of the individual indicators. The indicator can be used individually as part of a set, or in the form of a composite index, whereby individual indicators' scores are combined into a single number to represent the sustainability level. As we discussed in Section 2, we will respectively determine the corresponding indicators from the dimensions of environment, economy, society, institution and culture (see Figure 1).

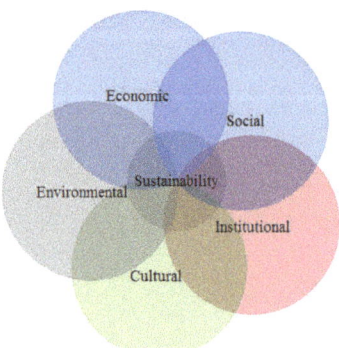

Figure 1. Five dimensions of sustainability.

In this paper, some important indicators of the sustainability assessment of public rental housing communities are extracted and summarized by referring to the relevant literature about sustainability assessment systems and public rental housing. We then analyzed some valuable policy information from the Chinese government and transformed it into the corresponding indicators by combining it with China's specific national conditions. One of the departure points of sustainability assessment is to help make or implement policy. As a result, it is necessary to involve the experts and policy makers to select the indicators. However, there is also a need to pay attention to the role of public participation in developing sustainability assessment indicators for a specific type of community. The sustainable development of a community should fully engage its end-users or target group from the very beginning [22]. It is more likely that if the target audience is allowed to participate in the conceptualization or development of the indicators, they will also use and appreciate the results [71]. Integrating the expert-led and resident-led ways of indicator development has been seen as salient to tapping into various levels of knowledge of sustainability, and thus a better way of evaluating sustainability [22]. Including the views of the stakeholders who are ultimately intended to benefit from the indicators can make the indicator system more effective [71] and more likely to cover the substantial issues associated with the sustainability of public rental housing communities. Based on this line of reasoning, we organized some experts and scholars in the field of sustainability assessment and public rental housing, some project managers of public rental housing, some administrators of government relevant department and some residents of public rental housing to score the importance of the indicators. The weight of their scoring is determined according to the authority and relevance of different types of personnel. We collected the weighted total scores of each indicator and then adjusted the indicators of higher scores according to the systematic and comprehensive principle to get the final sustainability assessment indicator system of public rental housing communities (see Figure 2). There are a total of 31 indicators in the integrated sustainability assessment system of public rental housing communities. Among them, there are seven indicators of environmental sustainability, six indicators of economic sustainability, eight indicators of social sustainability, four indicators of institutional sustainability and six indicators of cultural sustainability. The descriptions of each indicator are shown in Table 1.

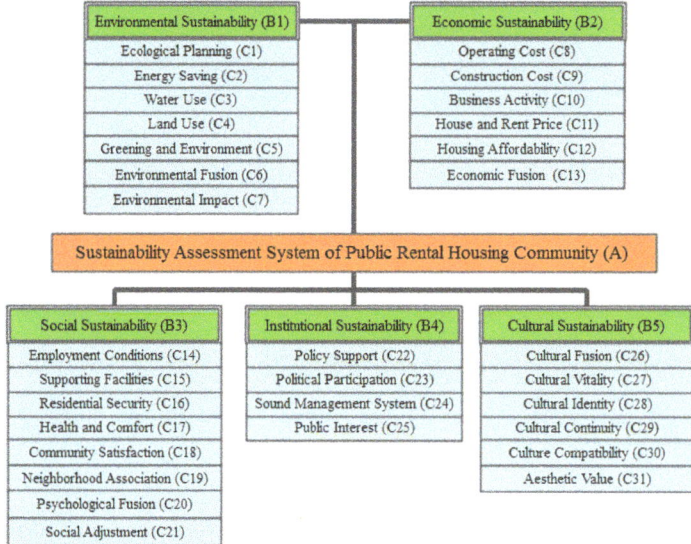

Figure 2. Sustainability assessment system of public rental housing communities.

Table 1. Description of each indicator.

Indicator	Indicator Description and Reference
Ecological Planning (C1)	There is a reasonable design through ecological identification and system planning and it makes full use of the natural conditions of the site [72,73].
Energy Saving (C2)	Energy saving of construction technology and community equipment, utilization of energy saving materials and considering recycling performance when selecting materials, etc. [55,73,74].
Water Use (C3)	Comprehensive utilization of different kinds of water resources, water-saving appliances and equipment, landscape irrigation ways, rainwater savings and utilization, etc. [22,55,75].
Land Use (C4)	Protection of local cultural relics, natural water systems and basic farmland, etc.; rational development and utilization of underground space; brownfield redevelopment; disposal and utilization of contaminated waste land, etc. [20,55,75].
Greening and Environment (C5)	Ratio of green space and plant diversity, etc. [55].
Environmental Fusion (C6)	Satisfaction of public space and public environment [76,77].
Environmental Impact (C7)	The impact of pollution, emissions, domestic waste, etc. on the environment [42].
Operating Cost (C8)	The cost of community operations and management [78].
Construction Cost (C9)	Total construction cost of the community [79].
Business Activity (C10)	Business activities within and around the community [22].
House and Rent Price (C11)	The relative house and rent price compared with the general level [22].
Housing Affordability (C12)	Housing affordability of community residents [22,36].
Economic Fusion (C13)	The situation of purchasing and renting, local purchase intentions, number of local relatives, etc. [80].
Employment Conditions (C14)	Employment opportunities, distance from the working place to the community, employment needs nearby the community, diversity of employment, etc. [55].
Supporting Facilities (C15)	The situation of schools, hospitals, public transportation and business, etc. nearby the community [36].
Residential Security (C16)	Personal privacy protection, fire prevention and security measures [22,36,55].
Health and Comfort (C17)	Indoor and outdoor air quality, thermal, sound and visual comfort, etc. [9].
Community Satisfaction (C18)	Residents' satisfaction with the community and the activity participation degree [81].
Neighborhood Association (C19)	Association with the surrounding communities and residents, interaction with friends in the community [76,77].
Psychological Fusion (C20)	Family identity, job satisfaction, housing satisfaction, community popularity, etc. [80].
Social Adjustment (C21)	Intention to settle in the community, the degree of discrimination, values of social reference, etc. [82].
Policy Support (C22)	Local government service level, tax and interest rate concessions, etc. [22].
Political Participation (C23)	Community residents' ability to participate in politics.
Sound Management System (C24)	Sound level of community management systems such as property supervision system.
Public Interest (C25)	Social security, health care, children's enrollment, public consultation, etc. [83].
Cultural Fusion (C26)	Master degree of local language, familiar degree of local customs, acceptance degree of local values, local dietary adaptation degree, etc. [80].
Cultural Vitality (C27)	The community has dynamic cultural activities and a compound pattern of land use [66].
Cultural Identity (C28)	The community can protect local history and the character of a place and can reflect collective memories. The residents have a sense of place, rootedness and belongingness [66].
Cultural Continuity (C29)	The community involves traditional practices, traditional craftsmanship and materials, and traditional architectural style such as vernacular architecture [66].
Culture Compatibility (C30)	Cultural diversity of the community; the community encourages cultural exchange and hosts different cultures; people with different backgrounds are respected and appreciated in the community [66].
Aesthetic Value (C31)	Aesthetic and cultural value of the buildings and landscape [66].

4. Assessment Approach

There are a lot of approaches be used in sustainability assessment, such as the fuzzy analytical hierarchy process (FAHP), the fuzzy comprehensive evaluation (FCE) method, principal component analysis (PCA) etc. However, these methods all have some insurmountable defects. For example, FAHP is a subjective method to determine weight, so it is easy to form a bias due to subjective factors.

FCE cannot solve the problem of the association of fuzziness and randomness in the evaluation process. PCA solves the problem of determining the evaluation weights, but it can lead to a loss of information. In order to conduct a rational evaluation on the assessment system established in Section 3, we put forward a new hybrid evaluation method that is suitable for the sustainability assessment of Chinese public rental housing community. It uses the AHP-entropy weight method to obtain the index weight, and then uses the cloud model to evaluate. This method can make full use of the respective advantage of the AHP and entropy weight method in determining weights. It can also make use of the qualitative evaluation information and transform it into quantitative evaluation data by using cloud model-related theories. The evaluation results can be expressed in the form of a cloud chart and provide guidance for managers and decision makers. Combined with the use of relevant calculation software, we can reduce the complexity of calculation and improve the efficiency and accuracy of sustainability evaluation.

4.1. Using AHP-Entropy Weight Method to Determine the Index Weights

The method to obtain weight can be divided into two categories: subjective weighting method and objective weighting method. The subjective weighting method includes the Delphi method, AHP etc.; the objective weighting method includes entropy weight method, variation coefficient method and so on [84]. AHP takes into account the experience and knowledge of experts and the intention and preference of decision makers. The ranking of index weights often has a high degree of rationality, but it has a defect of large subjective arbitrariness. Entropy weight can neither reflect experts' knowledge and experience nor decision-makers' opinions, but it can fully tap the information contained in the original data, so results have certain objectivity. According to the advantages and disadvantages of these two methods, we attempt to provide a unified method with AHP and entropy where entropy is adopted to complement the functions of AHP. Although no complete work is yet presented, the idea of combining information theory with AHP is not new. For example, Basak presented an example of utilizing entropy for selecting the most appropriate statistical model for the judgment data used in AHP [85]. The AHP-entropy weight method can help determine criteria weights both subjectively and objectively based on different types of assessing data and under variant levels of knowledge and experience [86]. In fact, for some important decision problems of high complexity, different types of people, including experts, decision makers or some other related personnel, are needed to participate in the evaluation. Since their knowledge background and preference differ, their understanding of the different aspects of the evaluation problems is also different. In the AHP evaluation process, the weighted arithmetic or geometric average is often used to synthesize the evaluators' opinion, which cannot reflect the difference between each evaluator and may cause bias in the evaluation results. Fortunately, the entropy weight method can reflect the uncertainty and difference of expert evaluation, so it has recently been used in conjunction with AHP by more and more researchers to get more scientific and comprehensive weight results in many fields [86,87]. On the basis of previous research achievements, the organic combination of AHP and the entropy weight method can be realized through the combined weight method [88]. Similar to the indicator selection, the determination of indicator weights in this paper also needs to integrate experts' and residents' understanding of sustainability to avoid ignoring some local issues and better reflect local priorities, values and needs of sustainability. We decide to continue drawing on the "participatory philosophy" [22] and have an overall consideration of the views of different stakeholders. The AHP-entropy weight method can better deal with variant levels of knowledge and experience from different types of evaluators. Therefore, this paper combines AHP with the entropy weight method, so as to get the weight comprehensively considering the subjective and objective factors.

4.1.1. Analytical Hierarchy Process (AHP)

AHP was proposed by American operations research expert Seaty in 1970s. It is a practical multi-objective decision-making method and can be combined with qualitative and quantitative analysis and solve the complex system problems composed of interrelated factors [89]. AHP divides the problem into different elements by analyzing the factors and their relationships. These elements are classified into different levels, and then the hierarchical structure is formed by these levels. At each level, according to a certain rule, the elements of the hierarchy are compared one by one, and then the judgment matrix is established. By calculating the maximum eigenvalue of the judgment matrix and the corresponding orthogonal feature vector, the weight of the element is obtained. On this basis, the weight of each level of elements can be obtained. AHP has a strong operability and it can fully consider the experts' experience and knowledge and decision-makers' preference, so it is used in many studies to get the weight of index.

Steps of AHP to obtain weight are as follows:

Step 1: Compare the importance of each indicator one by one according to the hierarchy structure of the indicator system. Then assign the relative importance value of the indices in the lower level by using the indices in the upper level as the benchmark and establish the judgement matrices. In order to make the judgement quantitative, we use the nine-point scale pair-wise comparison to score (as shown in Table 2).

Table 2. Relative importance scale.

Scale (a_{ij})	Meaning
1	Index x_i is as important as index x_j
3	Index x_i is slightly more important than index x_j
5	Index x_i is obviously more important than index x_j
7	Index x_i is strongly more important than index x_j
9	Index x_i is extremely more important than index x_j
2, 4, 6, 8	Middle value of the above adjacent judgments
Reciprocal	If $x_j/x_i = a_{ji}$, then $x_i/x_j = a_{ij} = 1/a_{ji}$

Step 2: Carry out the hierarchical single ranking. That is conducting the relative importance ranking of the lower-level evaluation indicators to the upper level. It is usually to calculate the maximum eigenvalue and the corresponding eigenvector of the comparative judgment matrix. The judgment matrices established according to Table 2 are all positive reciprocal matrices. Therefore, the maximum eigenvalues and the corresponding eigenvectors exist and are unique, and can be calculated by the Matlab or yaahp software. Then, through normalizing the eigenvectors, the weight of each indicator can be obtained. The calculation steps are as follows:

(1) Normalize the column vector of the comparative judgment matrix A, i.e., $A_{ij} = \frac{a_{ij}}{\sum_{k=1}^{n} a_{kj}}$.

(2) Sum of each line of A_{ij}, i.e., $V_i = \sum_{j=1}^{n} A_{ij}$ ($i = 1, 2, \ldots, n$).

(3) Standardize V_i to get Λ_i ($i = 1, 2, \ldots, n$), $\Lambda_i = \frac{V_i}{\sum_{i=1}^{n} V_i}$.

(4) Calculate the maximum eigenvalue of the judgement matrix λ_{max}, through the equation $A^*\Lambda = \lambda^*\Lambda$, λ_{max} can be obtained. $\lambda_{max} = \sum_{i=1}^{n} \frac{(A\Lambda)_i}{n\Lambda_i}$.

Step 3: The rationality of the weight of each index will directly impact on the correctness of the results. Therefore, in order to prevent the appearance of the judgement contrary to common sense in the process of assigning the relative importance values, we need to conduct the consistency test. The consistency test mainly includes the following 3 steps:

(1) Calculate the consistency index (CI), $\mathbf{CI} = \frac{\lambda_{max} - n}{n - 1}$.

(2) Determine the average random consistency index RI. Table 3 shows the average random consistency index of an n order matrix.

(3) Calculate the consistency ratio CR, CR = CI/RI. Only when CR < 0.1 can the judgment matrix pass the consistency test. Otherwise, it cannot meet the requirement and we need to score again.

Table 3. Average random consistency index RI.

Matrix Order (*n*)	1	2	3	4	5	6	7	8	9	10
RI	0	0	0.58	0.90	1.12	1.24	1.32	1.41	1.45	1.49

4.1.2. Entropy Weight Method

The conception of entropy was originally proposed by the physicist Rudolph Clausius. It was used to describe the irreversible phenomena of motion in thermodynamics. In 1948, American mathematician Shannon put it into information theory for the first time, and used it to represent the uncertain relationship between things and problems as a measure of uncertainty [90]. Entropy weight is a method using the value of information entropy to calculate the weight of each index according to their variation degree [91]. Entropy weight method can help avoid the interference of human factors to the weight of each evaluation index, so the evaluation results are more objective. By calculating the entropy of each index, the amount of information can be measured, so as to ensure that the indicators can reflect the vast majority of the original information.

In order to obtain the index weight comprehensively considering subjective and objective factors, in this paper, AHP and entropy weight method are used together. The steps of using entropy weight method to get weight are as follows:

Step 1: Establish judgement matrix D composed by m evaluation schemes and *n* evaluation indices.

$$D = (A_{ij})_{m \times n}, (i = 1, 2, \ldots, m; j = 1, 2, \ldots, n)$$

Step 2: Because of the differences of the evaluation index in the unit and property aspects, we need to carry out the standardized processing of matrix D to obtain the non-dimensional index matrix: $R = (r_{ij})_{m \times n}$, the standardized process is shown in Formulas (1) and (2).

If the evaluation index is a benefit indicator (i.e., the bigger the better), then

$$r_{ij} = \frac{A_{ij} - \min_j\{A_{ij}\}}{\max_j\{A_{ij}\} - \min_j\{A_{ij}\}} \tag{1}$$

If the evaluation index is a cost indicator (i.e., the smaller the better), then

$$r_{ij} = \frac{\max_j\{A_{ij}\} - A_{ij}}{\max_j\{A_{ij}\} - \min_j\{A_{ij}\}} \tag{2}$$

Step 3: According to the definition of entropy in the information theory, the information entropy of the *j*th evaluation indicator is:

$$E_j = -\frac{1}{\ln(n)} \sum_{j=1}^n P_{ij} \ln(P_{ij}), \ (j = 1, 2, \ldots, n) \tag{3}$$

In Formula (3), $P_{ij} = \frac{r_{ij}}{\sum_1^n r_{ij}}$, $E_j \in [0,1]$, if $P_{ij} = 0$, then define $\ln(P_{ij}) = 0$.

Step 4: Calculate the weight of each index through the information entropy:

$$\mu_j = \frac{1 - E_j}{n - \sum_{j=1}^n E_j} \tag{4}$$

From the above equation it can be drawn that the smaller the entropy value, the greater the entropy weight, the larger amount of corresponding evaluation index's information and the more important the indicator. By contrast, the greater the entropy value, the smaller the entropy weight, and the less important the indicator. On the basis of the index weights obtained by the entropy weight method, combining with AHP, the comprehensive weights of the sustainability assessment indices can be obtained. The step is as follows:

Step 5: Use AHP to get the preference vector of each evaluation index: $\Lambda_i = (\lambda_1, \lambda_2, \ldots, \lambda_n)$; then use the index weights μ_j determined by the aforementioned entropy weight method to revise the weights of each indicator Λ_i determined by AHP. In addition, then the comprehensive weight [88] of the *j*th evaluation index is:

$$\overline{\omega}_j = \frac{\mu_j \lambda_j}{\sum_{j=1}^n \mu_j \lambda_j} \tag{5}$$

4.2. Cloud Model

The cloud model was proposed by Li et al. in 1995 [92]. It is a model of reciprocal conversion between qualitative conception and quantitative representation formed by a specific structure algorithm based on the interaction between probability theory and fuzzy mathematics theory. The cloud model reflects the uncertainty of the concept in natural language as well as the linkage between randomness and fuzziness; it can constitute the mutual mapping between qualitative concept and quantitative data [92]. Since the cloud model can realize the conversion between uncertain linguistic information and quantitative concept, it is more objective than other methods and it can achieve less information loss [93]. It has been successfully applied in a lot of different fields, such as data mining [94], network security [95] and image segmentation [96].

In this paper, we proposed a series of indicators from different dimensions in a bid to improve the completeness in sustainability coverage. Some of the indicators are quantitative (e.g., construction cost), which can be easily measured, while there are also some qualitative indicators (e.g., community satisfaction) that are important to community sustainability. In the existing sustainability assessment systems and tools, these "soft indicators" are very difficult to evaluate since there is no standard reference for the evaluators. In general, the evaluators usually tend to express their views by fuzzy linguistic terms containing important information, which is hard to quantify. Fortunately, the cloud model is outstanding at dealing with this problem [93]. Hence, we attempt to use the cloud model to measure the sustainability of public rental housing community.

4.2.1. Cloud Definition

Let U be a quantitative domain composed of precise numerical data, and C is a qualitative conception related to U. x ($x \in U$) is a random number with stable trend of C, and the membership degree of x to C is $\mu(x)$ ($\mu(x) \in [0, 1]$). If:

$$\mu : U \rightarrow [0, 1], \ \forall \in U, x \rightarrow \mu(x)$$

Then the distribution of x in the quantitative domain U is called a cloud, which is made up of a number of cloud droplets [97].

4.2.2. The Digital Eigenvalues of the Cloud

In the cloud theory, three digital eigenvalues [93] of the cloud are used to reflect the overall characteristics of the conception, i.e., Expectation (*Ex*), Entropy (*En*) and Hyper Entropy (*He*). Expectation (*Ex*) is the most representative point of the qualitative conception C. Entropy (*En*) reflects the measurable granularity of C. It is determined by the randomness and fuzziness of the qualitative conception. The greater *En*, the greater fuzziness and randomness of the object. Hyper Entropy (*He*) measures the uncertainty of *En*, i.e., entropy's entropy. It reflects the condensation degree of the cloud droplets and is determined by the randomness and fuzziness of *En*.

4.2.3. Cloud Generator

The cloud generator is used to realize the reciprocal conversion between quantification and qualification in the cloud model theory [98]. The cloud generator can be classified into two types: positive cloud generator; and reverse cloud generator. The positive cloud generator can realize the transformation from a qualitative concept to a quantitative representation, which is a qualitative to quantitative mapping; it can output a series of droplets according to the digital eigenvalues of the cloud (*Ex*, *En*, *He*) and quantitatively express the qualitative concept through the uncertainty transformation of the cloud model. The reverse cloud generator can realize the transformation from a quantitative representation to a qualitative concept. It can transform a certain number of cloud drops to the three digital eigenvalues of the cloud (*Ex*, *En*, *He*). The processes of the positive cloud generator and the reverse cloud generator are shown in Figure 3.

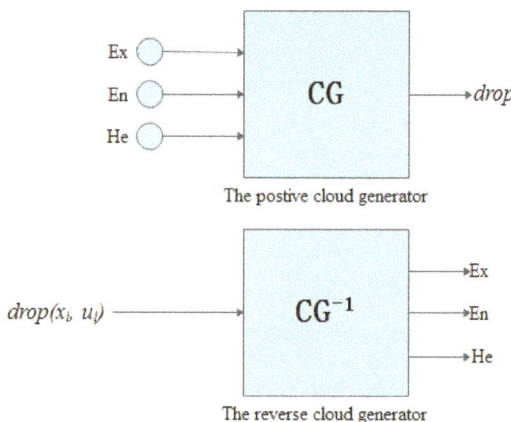

Figure 3. The positive cloud generator and the reverse cloud generator.

4.3. Integrated Sustainability Assessment of Public Rental Housing Community Based on the Cloud Model Theory

4.3.1. Establishment of the Evaluation Index System

We have established the integrated sustainability assessment index system of public rental housing community according to literature and policy analysis and evaluator scoring including five first-level evaluation indices (i.e., environmental sustainability, economic sustainability, social sustainability, institutional sustainability and cultural sustainability) and 31 second-level evaluation indices (see Figure 2).

4.3.2. Cloud Model Representation of Qualitative Comment Set

Determine the comment of each index to form a comment set V. Then divide the comment set V into five levels: {very bad, bad, middle, good, very good}. Among them, "very bad" and "very good" belong to the unilateral constraints; "bad", "middle" and "good" are middle segment comments, they belong to the bilateral constraints. For the bilateral constraint comments, we choose the symmetric cloud model to describe. The digital eigenvalues of the cloud model can be obtained by the following formula [99,100]:

$$\begin{cases} E_x = \frac{V_{max}+V_{min}}{2} \\ E_n = \frac{V_{max}-V_{min}}{6} \\ H_e = k \end{cases} \tag{6}$$

For the unilateral constraint comments, we use the semi cloud model to describe. The comments "very bad" and "very good" can be respectively described by "0" and "10". We select half of the corresponding symmetric cloud's entropy as their respective entropy [101]. In this formula, "k" is a constant, and it can be adjusted according to the uncertainty degree of the variables [102]. We assume that the corresponding theory domain of the comment set is [0,10], so the corresponding intervals and cloud model digital eigenvalues of each comment can be obtained as shown in Table 4.

Table 4. The corresponding intervals and cloud model digital eigenvalues of each comment.

Comment	Very Bad	Bad	Middle	Good	Very Good
Interval	(0,2]	(2,4]	(4,6]	(6,8]	(8,10]
Ex	0	3	5	7	10
En	1/6	1/3	1/3	1/3	1/6
He	k	k	k	k	k

4.3.3. Cloud Model Representation of the Second-Level Indices

The sustainability assessment indices are related to the viewpoints of experts and different stakeholders of public rental housing community. In order to improve public participation and have an overall consideration of sustainability, in this paper, the qualitative comments of each index are determined by delivering questionnaires to different types of evaluators. We use the reverse cloud generator [103] to get the cloud model digital eigenvalues (Ex, En, He) of each index.

4.3.4. Cloud Model Determination of the First-level indices

The second-level indices under each first-level index are basically independence of each other and the correlation between each index is very low. Thus, we can use the already determined cloud model digital eigenvalues of the second-level indices to determine the comprehensive cloud of the first-level evaluation indices. The following formula can be used [104]:

$$
\begin{cases}
Ex = \dfrac{Ex_1\omega_1 + Ex_2\omega_2 + \ldots + Ex_n\omega_n}{\omega_1 + \omega_2 + \ldots + \omega_n} \\[2mm]
En = \dfrac{\omega_1^2}{\omega_1^2+\omega_2^2+\ldots+\omega_n^2}En_1 + \dfrac{\omega_2^2}{\omega_1^2+\omega_2^2+\ldots+\omega_n^2}En_2 + \ldots + \dfrac{\omega_n^2}{\omega_1^2+\omega_2^2+\ldots+\omega_n^2}En_n \\[2mm]
He = \dfrac{\omega_1^2}{\omega_1^2+\omega_2^2+\ldots+\omega_n^2}He_1 + \dfrac{\omega_2^2}{\omega_1^2+\omega_2^2+\ldots+\omega_n^2}He_2 + \ldots + \dfrac{\omega_n^2}{\omega_1^2+\omega_2^2+\ldots+\omega_n^2}He_n
\end{cases}
\tag{7}
$$

In the formula, ω_i is the weight of each second-level index; (Ex_i, En_i, He_i) is the cloud model digital eigenvalues of each second-level index; n is the number of evaluation indices, $i = 1, 2, \ldots , n$.

4.3.5. Establishment of Comprehensive Cloud Model

There is a certain correlation between the first-level indices; the indicators will have an impact on each other. For example, environmental sustainability may have an impact on social sustainability and institutional sustainability may have an impact on economic sustainability. Therefore, it is necessary to carry out the comprehensive cloud computing in virtual cloud [105] when determining the comprehensive cloud model. The following formula can be used to integrate the cloud model of the five first-level evaluation indices into a more generalized cloud.

$$
\begin{cases}
Ex = \dfrac{Ex_1 En_1\omega_1 + Ex_2 En_2\omega_2 + \ldots + Ex_n En_n\omega_n}{En_1\omega_1 + En_2\omega_2 + \ldots + En_n\omega_n} \\[2mm]
En = En_1\omega_1 + En_2\omega_2 + \ldots + En_n\omega_n \\[2mm]
He = \dfrac{He_1 En_1\omega_1 + He_2 En_2\omega_2 + \ldots + He_n En_n\omega_n}{En_1\omega_1 + En_2\omega_2 + \ldots + En_n\omega_n}
\end{cases}
\tag{8}
$$

In the formula, ω_i is the weight of each first-level index; (Ex_i, En_i, He_i) is the cloud model digital eigenvalues of each first-level index; n is the number of evaluation indices, $i = 1, 2, \ldots , n$.

By using the digital eigenvalues of the comprehensive cloud model to draw the cloud chart of the comprehensive sustainability assessment of public rental housing community, we can get the specific information of the overall sustainability of public rental housing community. In this way, we use the AHP-entropy weight method to determine the weight of each indicator, and then use the cloud model theory to finish the comprehensive sustainability evaluation of public rental housing community. The specific process is shown in Figure 4.

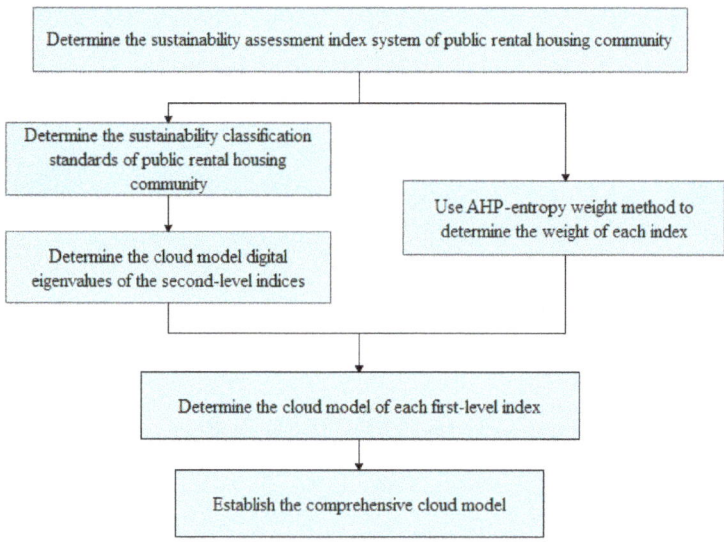

Figure 4. Sustainability assessment process of public rental housing community.

5. Case Study

As one of the national urban and rural comprehensive reform pilot areas, Chongqing plans and constructs the largest amount of public rental housing in China [106]. The public rental housing coverage of Chongqing is larger than other cities, and the development of public rental housing projects in Chongqing is also more mature than in other cities. Therefore, we select one of the earliest planning projects (the "Minxinjiayuan" community) as an example to carry out the integrated sustainability assessment, so as to verify the feasibility of the aforementioned method and provide a reliable reference for other similar projects.

5.1. Project Profile

The "Minxinjiayuan" public rental housing project began construction in 28 February 2010. It was the earliest public rental housing community of Chongqing. A lot of national leaders have visited and inspected there. The community was completed in 2012, and it has become a model of Chinese public rental housing. It is located in the northern new area of Chongqing: Yuanyang area. It has a total of 54 residential buildings, with a total construction area of 1.08 million square meters, and has a complete range of infrastructure and supporting projects. The "Minxinjiayuan" community has completed the residential occupancy for nearly five years, and has formed a relatively mature community culture. Like other public rental housing communities, it has many institutional problems. The already-formed culture in the community can influence the environmentally sound behaviors or individual and societal wellbeing to some extent. Thus, it is relatively suitable to use the assessment system with institutional and cultural dimensions to evaluate it. The integrated sustainability assessment of the community is of great significance to guide public rental housing towards sustainable development.

5.2. Determination of the Evaluation Index Weight

5.2.1. Using AHP to Determine the Subjective Weight of the Evaluation Index

We used a questionnaire to obtain index weight. We selected 10 Chinese experts and scholars in the field of public rental housing and sustainability assessment, 10 project managers of the design, construction, operation and management of the community, 10 administrators of relevant government department and 10 residents of the community, and conducted face-to-face questionnaires with them. Experts, scholars and government administrators have more authority in the theoretical determination of the index weight, but they do not have enough living and working experience compared with project managers and residents. In order to comprehensively take account of the authority, relevance and local contextual perspective, we conducted the same number of questionnaires with each kind of personnel. We then established the initial judgement matrices according to the recycling questionnaires. By using the yaahp software and the expert data aggregation method, we can get the subjective weights of the evaluation indices determined by AHP: λ_j = [0.0193 0.0522 0.0338 0.0505 0.0409 0.0534 0.0620 0.0407 0.0230 0.0427 0.0368 0.0699 0.0393 0.0336 0.0393 0.0316 0.0228 0.0175 0.0134 0.0276 0.0178 0.0222 0.0114 0.0165 0.0184 0.0426 0.0196 0.0370 0.0207 0.0167 0.0265].

5.2.2. Using the Entropy Weight Method to Determine the Objective Weight of the Evaluation Index

Same as above, we conducted another face-to-face questionnaire with each of the respondents. The respondents are the same as above, i.e., 10 Chinese experts and scholars in the field of public rental housing and sustainability assessment, 10 project managers of the design, construction, operation and management of the community, 10 administrators of government relevant department and 10 residents of the community. These 40 respondents scored respectively from 1–9 according to the importance of the 31 second-level indices. Then, according to the questionnaire data and Formulas (1)–(4), we can use the Matlab software to get the objective weights of the evaluation indices:

μ_j = [0.0491 0.0235 0.0060 0.0177 0.0126 0.0273 0.0530 0.0398 0.0310 0.0439 0.0427 0.0530 0.0181 0.0514 0.0227 0.0353 0.0471 0.0293 0.0162 0.0195 0.0040 0.0287 0.0687 0.0219 0.0453 0.0353 0.0361 0.0104 0.0427 0.0170 0.0505].

According to Formula (5), the final comprehensive weights are obtained: $\overline{\omega}_j$ = [0.0292 0.0376 0.0062 0.0274 0.0158 0.0447 0.1008 0.0498 0.0219 0.0575 0.0482 0.1136 0.0218 0.0531 0.0274 0.0342 0.0329 0.0157 0.0067 0.0165 0.0022 0.0196 0.0240 0.0111 0.0256 0.0461 0.0217 0.0118 0.0271 0.0087 0.0411].

5.3. Cloud Model Representation of the Second-Level Indices of "Minxinjiayuan" Community

We used the questionnaire survey method to obtain comments on each second-level index. To comprehensively consider the authority, relevance and local perspective, we conducted 50 face-to-face questionnaires with residents living in the community and experts in the field of public rental housing and sustainability assessment. Among them, there were 25 residents and 25 experts. Experts have a certain degree of authority when evaluating some indicators (e.g., ecological planning), but the residents score more rationally when evaluating some other indicators (e.g., community satisfaction) due to their living experience in the community. Therefore, we selected the same number of expert and resident respondents. We then collected the questionnaires and used the reverse cloud generator [103] to get the cloud model digital eigenvalues of each second-level index, the results are shown in Table 5.

Table 5. The weight and cloud model digital eigenvalues of each second-level index.

First-Level Index: B	Second-Level Index: C	Cloud Model Digital Eigenvalues (*Ex, En, He*)	Weight ω_i	Weight ω_{ij}
Environmental Sustainability B1	Ecological Planning C1	(5.4286, 0.8185, 0.3517)		0.0292
	Energy Saving C2	(5.5429, 0.8164, 0.3419)		0.0376
	Water Use C3	(5.6286, 0.9269, 0.2990)		0.0062
	Land Use C4	(6.6286, 0.9351, 0.3235)	0.2617	0.0274
	Greening and Environment C5	(5.9714, 0.9044, 0.1848)		0.0158
	Environmental Fusion C6	(5.7714, 0.8287, 0.3057)		0.0447
	Environmental Impact C7	(5.6000, 0.9024, 0.3943)		0.1008
Economic Sustainability B2	Operating Cost C8	(5.7714, 0.9392, 0.4137)		0.0498
	Construction Cost C9	(5.8286, 0.9494, 0.3288)		0.0219
	Business Activity C10	(5.8286, 1.0088, 0.4737)	0.3128	0.0575
	House and Rent Price C11	(6.2857, 0.8390, 0.2865)		0.0482
	Housing Affordability C12	(6.6286, 0.9699, 0.2309)		0.1136
	Economic Fusion C13	(5.8571, 0.9208, 0.2734)		0.0218
Social Sustainability B3	Employment Conditions C14	(5.6857, 0.9290, 0.2301)		0.0531
	Supporting Facilities C15	(5.8286, 0.8083, 0.3741)		0.0274
	Residential Security C16	(6.2857, 0.7162, 0.2599)		0.0342
	Health and Comfort C17	(6.9714, 0.7653, 0.1764)	0.1887	0.0329
	Community Satisfaction C18	(7.0000, 0.5729, 0.4486)		0.0157
	Neighborhood Association C19	(6.0571, 0.8819, 0.1281)		0.0067
	Psychological Fusion C20	(5.4286, 0.8083, 0.3273)		0.0165
	Social Adjustment C21	(5.4000, 0.8881, 0.2666)		0.0022
Institutional Sustainability B4	Policy Support C22	(6.2286, 0.8451, 0.2492)		0.0196
	Political Participation C23	(5.2286, 0.9883, 0.1682)	0.0803	0.0240
	Sound Management System C24	(4.8571, 0.9208, 0.3655)		0.0111
	Public Interest C25	(5.6286, 0.8369, 0.3273)		0.0256
Cultural Sustainability B5	Cultural Fusion C26	(4.8857, 0.6978, 0.1704)		0.0461
	Cultural Vitality C27	(5.7429, 0.7980, 0.2953)		0.0217
	Cultural Identity C28	(5.6857, 0.6384, 0.2609)	0.1565	0.0118
	Cultural Continuity C29	(5.5143, 0.9883, 0.3624)		0.0271
	Culture Compatibility C30	(5.5143, 0.7735, 0.3254)		0.0087
	Aesthetic Value C31	(5.5714, 0.7776, 0.3424)		0.0411

5.4. Cloud Model Determination of the First-Level Indices of "Minxinjiayuan" Community

By substituting the digital eigenvalues and weights of each second-level index under each first-level index into Formula (7) and conducting the comprehensive cloud computing, we obtained the cloud model digital eigenvalues of the five first-level indices as shown in Table 6.

Table 6. The cloud model digital eigenvalues of each first-level index.

First-Level Index	Cloud Model Digital Eigenvalues (*Ex, En, He*)
Environmental Sustainability B1	(5.7329, 0.8821, 0.3687)
Economic Sustainability B2	(6.1826, 0.9569, 0.2970)
Social Sustainability B3	(6.1363, 0.8287, 0.2553)
Institutional Sustainability B4	(5.5480, 0.8949, 0.2601)
Cultural Sustainability B5	(5.3888, 0.7728, 0.2687)

5.5. Establishment of the Comprehensive Sustainability Cloud Model of "Minxinjiayuan" Community

By conducting the comprehensive cloud computing of each first-level index in virtual cloud through Formula (8), we can obtain the cloud model digital eigenvalues of the integrated sustainability assessment of "Minxinjiayuan" community: (5.8953, 0.8793, 0.3015).

5.6. Determination of the Sustainability Level of "Minxinjiayuan" Community

In the finally gotten cloud model digital eigenvalues of the integrated sustainability assessment of "Minxinjiayuan" community, $He = 0.3015$. In order to compare the integrated cloud model and the corresponding cloud of each comment, we adjusted the value of k in Table 4, and took $k = 0.3$. We then input the integrated cloud model digital eigenvalues and the corresponding cloud model digital eigenvalues of each comment into the positive cloud generator, and used the Matlab software to draw the corresponding cloud charts as shown in Figure 5. From Figure 5, we can find that the overall sustainability of the community lies at a "middle" to "good" level and closer to a "middle" level. Therefore, the overall sustainability of this community needs yet to be improved.

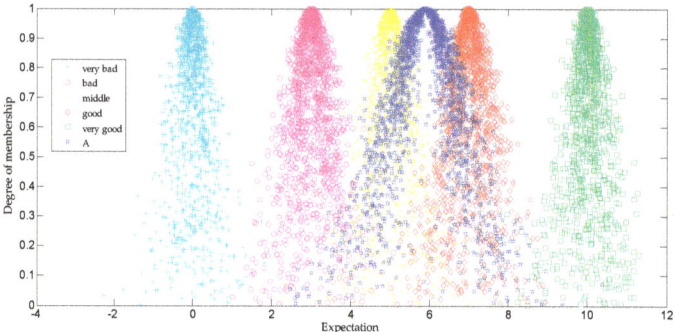

Figure 5. The cloud chart of the overall sustainability.

After that, we input the digital eigenvalues of the five first-level indices (i.e., environmental sustainability B1, economic sustainability B2, social sustainability B3, institutional sustainability B4 and cultural sustainability B5) and the corresponding digital eigenvalues of each comment into the positive cloud generator and used the Matlab software to draw the corresponding cloud charts as shown in Figures 6–10. It can be found that in Figures 6, 9 and 10 that the environmental, institutional and cultural sustainability of "Minxinjiayuan" community lies between the "middle" and "good" level, and closer to the "middle" level; while Figures 7 and 8 shows that the economic and social sustainability are closer to the "good" level. This means that the overall sustainability of "Minxinhuayuan" community lies between the "middle" and "good" level; in the pursuit of economic and social sustainability, the consideration of environmental, institutional and cultural sustainability is still insufficient. The level of economic and social sustainability is relatively higher than that of other dimensions, mainly because the aim of developing public rental housing is to improve the housing affordability of medium-low income groups and meet their housing demand. In addition, through the cloud model digital eigenvalues of each second-level index in Table 5, we can easily find that the scores of Sound Management System (C24) and Cultural Fusion (C26) are relatively low, while the scores of Community Satisfaction (C18) and Health and Comfort (C17) are relatively high. This information can provide guidance for the management and decision-making of the government and project administrators. Therefore, in the future, more attention should be paid to the environmental, institutional and cultural sustainability aspects in the design, construction, operation and management processes of public rental housing projects, such as improving the ecological planning, promoting the energy saving through the improving of technology, improving the management system of public rental housing community, promoting the cultural fusion of the community by organizing various activities etc.

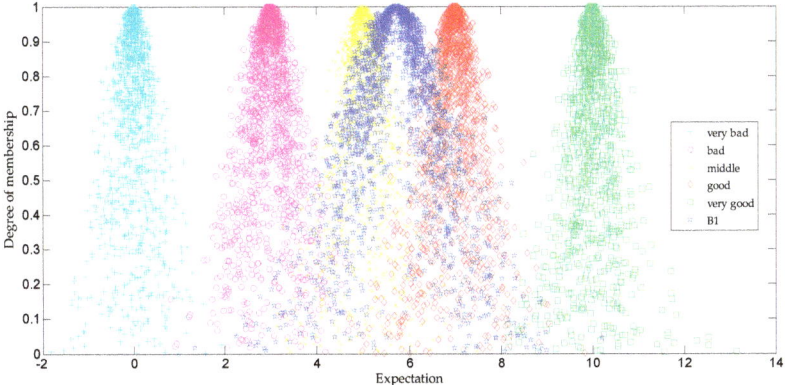

Figure 6. The cloud chart of the environmental sustainability.

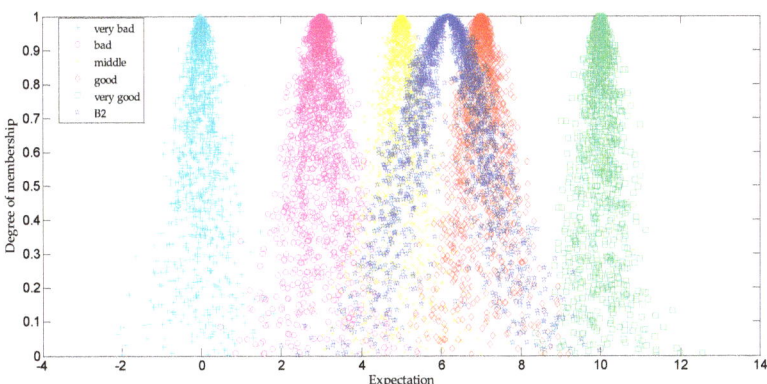

Figure 7. The cloud chart of the economic sustainability.

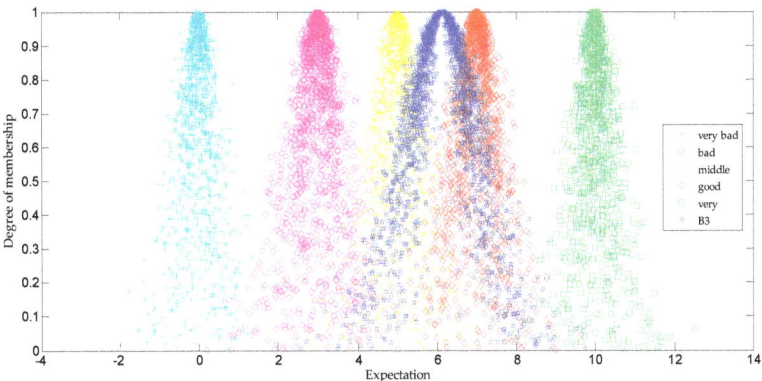

Figure 8. The cloud chart of the social sustainability.

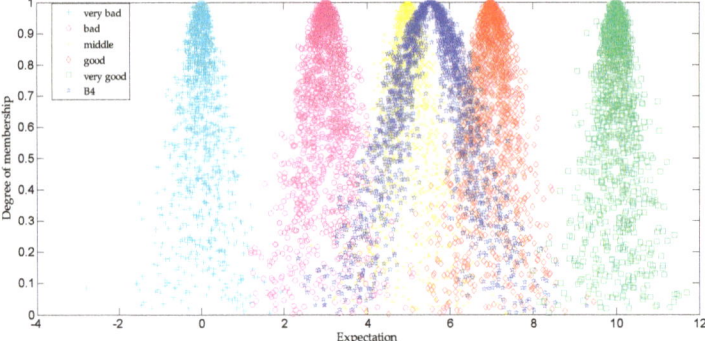

Figure 9. The cloud chart of the institutional sustainability.

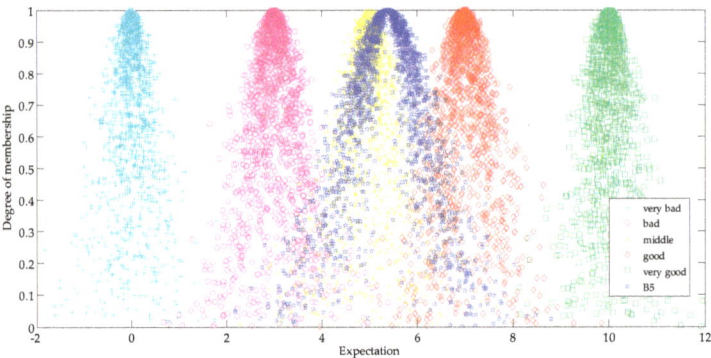

Figure 10. The cloud chart of the cultural sustainability.

6. Conclusions

This paper establishes an integrated sustainability assessment indicator system for Chinese public rental housing communities including environmental, economic, social, institutional and cultural dimensions by drawing on the "participatory philosophy". On this basis, this paper proposes a new hybrid evaluation method—that is, using AHP-entropy weight method to determine the weight of each evaluation index—and then using the cloud model theory to realize the transformation between qualitative comments and quantitative representations. In order to improve the degree of local participation and take regional characteristics into consideration, different types of people, including experts and scholars, project managers, government administrators and community residents, are asked to participate in the evaluation. The AHP-entropy weight method can determine the weight of each indicator under varying levels of knowledge and experience so as to help us to get a more scientific and comprehensive weight result. On the other hand, the cloud model has the superiority to convert between qualification and quantification and reflect fuzziness and randomness, so it provides a possibility for reasonably measuring some "soft indicators" that are difficult to evaluate in the existing assessment systems and tools. To verify the feasibility of this method, a case study is carried out on the "Minxinjiayuan" public rental housing community in Chongqing, China. We find that the overall sustainability of the community lies at a "middle" to "good" level and closer to a "middle" level; the level of economic and social sustainability is higher than that of environmental, institutional and cultural sustainability.

The index system proposed in this paper can help comprehensively consider multi-dimensions of sustainability and improve public participation of public rental housing community at the same time, while the method opens up windows of opportunity that address the needs to properly evaluate by different types of evaluators with varying levels of knowledge and experience and rationally measure both quantitative and qualitative indicators. The evaluation results are relatively intuitive and rational, at least to some degree. This paper can provide a new reference for the sustainability assessment of Chinese public rental housing community and the research on sustainability assessment systems and approaches. However, since sustainable development is a dynamic process which passes in time and depends on numerous parameters, there is no coincident conception of sustainability and the indicators were not unambiguously qualified. There are regional differences between different types of communities in different regions, so it is not appropriate to establish a universal indicator system. The index system established in this paper can supply a new integrated perspective for community sustainability assessment, while it is still far from enough to search a right direction for Chinese public rental housing communities towards sustainable development. The research on the CSA system is only in the initial stage. Pubic rental housing communities are also a very new phenomenon. Thus, exploration is still necessary into sustainability assessment systems and approaches to it. In future research, more consideration may need to be taken into the balance between completeness in sustainability coverage, adaptability and simplicity of operation, so that the system can be applied in other cases. For example, the mechanism for further utilizing the method proposed in this paper to more specific projects or other fields, and customizing a specific software package to run the method to improve operating efficiency could also comprise research points.

Acknowledgments: This study is supported by the National Natural Science Foundation of China (71561009 and 71310165), National Social Science Foundation of China (15BJY050), China Postdoctoral Science Foundation (2016M590605), Postdoctoral Science Foundation of Jiangxi Province (2016KY27), and Social Science Planning Foundation of Jiangxi Province (16GL32).

Author Contributions: Guangdong Wu conceived and designed the study, completed the paper in English, Kaifeng Duan participated in drafting the article and revised it critically for important intellectual content, Jian Zuo and Xianbo Zhao gave many good research advices and revised the manuscript. Daizhong Tang provided the relevant literature review and made a comprehensive English revision.

Conflicts of Interest: The authors declare no conflicts of interest.

References

1. World Commission on Environment and Development. *Our Common Future*; Oxford University Press: Oxford, UK, 1987.
2. Satolo, E.G.; Simon, A.T. Critical analysis of assessment methodologies for intraorganizational sustainability. *Manag. Environ. Qual.* **2015**, *26*, 214–232. [CrossRef]
3. Al-Nassar, F.; Ruparathna, R.; Chhipi-Shrestha, G.; Haider, H.; Hewage, K.; Sadiq, R. Sustainability assessment framework for low rise commercial buildings: Life cycle impact index-based approach. *Clean Technol. Environ. Policy* **2016**, *18*, 2579–2590. [CrossRef]
4. Kang, H.; Lee, Y.; Kim, S. Sustainable building assessment tool for project decision makers and its development process. *Environ. Impact Assess. Rev.* **2016**, *58*, 34–47. [CrossRef]
5. Elmualim, A.; Alp, D. Perception and challenges for sustainable construction in developing countries: North Cyprus case. *J. Civ. Eng. Architect.* **2016**, *4*, 492–500.
6. Li, W.; Ng, E. Assessing the sustainability of the built environment in mountainous rural villages in southwest China. *Mt. Res. Dev.* **2016**, *36*, 4–14.
7. Bendewald, M.; Zhai, Z. Using carrying capacity as a baseline for building sustainability assessment. *Habitat Int.* **2013**, *37*, 22–32. [CrossRef]
8. Alyami, S.H.; Rezgui, Y.; Kwan, A. Developing sustainable building assessment scheme for Saudi Arabia: Delphi consultation approach. *Renew. Sustain. Energy Rev.* **2013**, *27*, 43–54. [CrossRef]
9. Alyami, S.H.; Rezgui, Y. Sustainable building assessment tool development approach. *Sustain. Cities Soc.* **2012**, *5*, 52–62. [CrossRef]

10. Berardi, U. Beyond sustainability assessment systems: Upgrading topics by enlarging the scale of assessment. *Int. J. Sustain. Build. Technol. Urban Dev.* **2011**, *2*, 276–282. [CrossRef]

11. Cole, R.J. Changing context for environmental knowledge. *Build. Res. Inf.* **2004**, *32*, 91–109. [CrossRef]

12. Fowke, R.; Prasad, D. Sustainable development, cities and local government: Dilemmas and definitions. *Aust. Plan.* **1996**, *33*, 61–66. [CrossRef]

13. Ali, H.H.; Nsairat, S.F.A. Developing a green building assessment tool for developing countries—Case of Jordan. *Build. Environ.* **2009**, *44*, 1053–1064. [CrossRef]

14. Sahamir, S.R.; Zakaria, R. Green assessment criteria for public hospital building development in Malaysia. *Procedia Environ. Sci.* **2014**, *20*, 106–115. [CrossRef]

15. Yoon, S.W.; Lee, D.K. The development of the evaluation model of climate changes and air pollution for sustainability of cities in Korea. *Landsc. Urban Plan.* **2003**, *63*, 145–160. [CrossRef]

16. Ding, G.K.C. Developing a multicriteria approach for the measurement of sustainable performance. *Build. Res. Inf.* **2005**, *33*, 3–16. [CrossRef]

17. Berardi, U. Sustainability assessment in the construction sector: Rating systems and rated buildings. *Sustain. Dev.* **2012**, *20*, 411–424. [CrossRef]

18. Conte, E.; Monno, V. Beyond the buildingcentric approach: A vision for an integrated evaluation of sustainable buildings. *Environ. Impact Assess. Rev.* **2012**, *34*, 31–40. [CrossRef]

19. Sev, A. How can the construction industry contribute to sustainable development? A conceptual framework. *Sustain. Dev.* **2009**, *17*, 161–173. [CrossRef]

20. Berardi, U. Clarifying the new interpretations of the concept of sustainable building. *Sustain. Cities Soc.* **2013**, *8*, 72–78. [CrossRef]

21. Bourdic, L.; Salat, S. Building energy models and assessment systems at the district and city scales: A review. *Build. Res. Inf.* **2012**, *40*, 518–526. [CrossRef]

22. Turcu, C. Re-thinking sustainability indicators: Local perspectives of urban sustainability. *J. Environ. Plan. Manag.* **2013**, *56*, 695–719. [CrossRef]

23. Wu, L.Y. *Introduction to Sciences of Human Settlements*; China Architecture & Building Press: Beijing, China, 2011. (In Chinese)

24. Choguill, C.L. Developing sustainable neighbourhoods. *Habitat Int.* **2008**, *32*, 41–48. [CrossRef]

25. Alshuwaikhat, H.M.; Aina, Y.A. GIS-based urban sustainability assessment: The case of Dammam city, Saudi Arabia. *Local Environ.* **2006**, *11*, 141–162. [CrossRef]

26. Shen, L.Y.; Ochoa, J.J.; Shah, M.N.; Zhang, X. The application of urban sustainability indicators: A comparison between various practices. *Habitat Int.* **2011**, *35*, 17–29. [CrossRef]

27. Essa, R.; Fortune, C. Pre-construction evaluation practices of sustainable housing projects in the UK. *Eng. Construct. Architect. Manag.* **2008**, *15*, 514–526. [CrossRef]

28. Berardi, U. Sustainability assessment of urban communities through rating systems. *Environ. Dev. Sustain.* **2013**, *15*, 1573–1591. [CrossRef]

29. Sharifi, A.; Murayama, A. A critical review of seven selected neighborhood sustainability assessment tools. *Environ. Impact Assess. Rev.* **2013**, *38*, 73–87. [CrossRef]

30. Jayantha, W.M.; Wan, S.M. Effect of green labelling on residential property price: A case study in Hong Kong. *J. Facil. Manag.* **2013**, *11*, 31–51. [CrossRef]

31. Cloutier, S.; Larson, L.; Jambeck, J. Are sustainable cities "happy" cities? Associations between sustainable development and human well-being in urban areas of the United States. *Environ. Dev. Sustain.* **2014**, *16*, 633–647. [CrossRef]

32. Sharifi, A.; Murayama, A. Viability of using global standards for neighbourhood sustainability assessment: Insights from a comparative case study. *J. Environ. Plan. Manag.* **2014**, *58*, 1–23. [CrossRef]

33. Li, D.Z.; Guo, K.; You, J.; Hui, E.C.M. Assessing investment value of privately-owned public rental housing projects with multiple options. *Habitat Int.* **2016**, *53*, 8–17. [CrossRef]

34. Peng, X.B.; Fu, G.Q. Research on new community governance mechanism of public rental housing. *China Mark.* **2012**, *20*, 47–53. (In Chinese).

35. Deng, F. The characteristics and governance of public rental housing community. *Urban Probl.* **2012**, *8*, 73–79. (In Chinese).

36. Yigitcanlar, T.; Kamruzzaman, M.; Teriman, S. Neighborhood sustainability assessment: Evaluating residential development sustainability in a developing country context. *Sustainability* **2015**, *7*, 2570–2602. [CrossRef]

37. Häkkinen, T. Assessment of indicators for sustainable urban construction. *Civ. Eng. Environ. Syst.* **2007**, *24*, 247–259. [CrossRef]

38. Sev, A. A comparative analysis of building environmental assessment tools and suggestions for regional adaptations. *Civ. Eng. Environ. Syst.* **2011**, *28*, 231–245. [CrossRef]

39. Haapio, A. Towards sustainable urban communities. *Environ. Impact Assess. Rev.* **2012**, *32*, 165–169. [CrossRef]

40. Saunders, T. A Discussion Document Comparing International Environmental Assessment Methods for Buildings. Available online: http://www.prres.net/Proceedings/..%5CPapers%5CReed_International_Rating_Tools.pdf (accessed on 7 April 2017).

41. Komeily, A.; Srinivasan, R.S. A need for balanced approach to neighborhood sustainability assessments: A critical review and analysis. *Sustain. Cities Soc.* **2015**, *18*, 32–43. [CrossRef]

42. Yoon, J.; Park, J. Comparative analysis of material criteria in neighborhood sustainability assessment tools and urban design guidelines: Cases of the UK, the US, Japan, and Korea. *Sustainability* **2015**, *7*, 14450–14487. [CrossRef]

43. Reith, A.; Orova, M. Do green neighbourhood ratings cover sustainability? *Ecol. Indic.* **2014**, *48*, 660–672. [CrossRef]

44. Lin, K.W.; Shih, C.M. The Comparative Analysis of Neighborhood Sustainability Assessment Tool. Available online: http://journals.sagepub.com/doi/abs/10.1177/0265813516667299?ssource=mfr&rss=1 (accessed on 7 April 2017).

45. Garde, A. Sustainable by design: Insights from U.S. LEED-ND pilot projects. *J. Am. Plan. Assoc.* **2009**, *75*, 424–440. [CrossRef]

46. Sharifi, A.; Murayama, A. Neighborhood sustainability assessment in action: Cross-evaluation of three assessment systems and their cases from the US, the UK, and Japan. *Build. Environ.* **2014**, *72*, 243–258. [CrossRef]

47. Säynäjoki, E.; Kyrö, R.; Heinonen, J.; Junnila, S. An assessment of the applicability of three international neighbourhood sustainability rating systems to diverse local conditions, with a focus on Nordic case areas. *Int. J. Sustain. Build. Technol. Urban Dev.* **2012**, *3*, 96–104. [CrossRef]

48. Kyrkou, D.; Taylor, M.; Pelsmakers, S.; Karthaus, R. Urban sustainability assessment systems: How appropriate are global sustainability assessment systems? In Proceedings of the Plea 27th International Conference on Passive and Low Energy Architecture, Louvain-la-Neuve, Belgium, 13–15 July 2011.

49. Cable, F. Sustainable neighborhood rating systems: An international comparison. In Proceedings of the C.E.U. Climate Change and Urban Design Conference, Oslo, Norway, 14–16 September 2008.

50. Komeily, A.; Srinivasan, R.S. What is neighborhood context and why does it matter in sustainability assessment? In Proceedings of the International Conference on Sustainable Design, Engineering and Construction, Tempe, AZ, USA, 18–20 May 2016.

51. Lin, S.G. Study on the cold phenomenon of public rental housing: Based on the data analysis of Shanghai, Nanjing, Wuhan and Zhengzhou. *Price Theory Pract.* **2012**, *7*, 21–22. (In Chinese).

52. Zhao, J.; Zhang, K.R.; Zhang, B.; Xie, J. Public rental housing project for environment impact assessment: A case study of Xijiangyu area in Jinan city. *China J. Popul. Resour. Environ.* **2011**, *127*, 337–339. (In Chinese).

53. Jia, K.; Sun, J. Recommendations of using the PPP mechanism to provide cheap rental housing and public rental housing. *China State Financ.* **2011**, *15*, 43–45. (In Chinese).

54. Li, D.Z.; Chen, H.X.; Huang, Z.G.; Cui, M. Study on the incentive policy and its optimization of Chinese social capital participating in the construction of public rental housing. *Mod. Manag. Sci.* **2012**, *3*, 43–45. (In Chinese).

55. Li, D.Z.; Chen, Y.C.; Chen, H.X.; Guo, K.; Hui, E.C.M.; Yang, J. Assessing the integrated sustainability of a public rental housing project from the perspective of complex eco-system. *Habitat Int.* **2016**, *53*, 546–555.

56. Hoppe, T. Adoption of innovative energy systems in social housing: Lessons from eight large-scale renovation projects in the Netherlands. *Energy Policy* **2014**, *51*, 791–801. [CrossRef]

57. Chikamoto, T.; Kobayashi, Y.; Enomoto, J. Investigation of the amount change of the energy used by the equipment repair and the consciousness change in rebuilding and renovation of public rental housings. *AIJ J. Technol. Des.* **2013**, *19*, 243–248. [CrossRef]

58. Li, D.Z.; Chen, Y.C.; Chen, H.X.; Hui, E.C.M.; Guo, K. Evaluation and optimization of the financial sustainability of public rental housing projects: A case study in Nanjing, China. *Sustainability* **2016**, *8*, 330. [CrossRef]

59. Taiwo, A. The need for government to embrace public-private partnership initiative in housing delivery to low-income public servants in Nigeria. *Urban Des. Int.* **2015**, *20*, 56–65. [CrossRef]

60. Patulny, R.V.; Morris, A. Questioning the need for social mix: The implications of friendship diversity amongst Australian social housing tenants. *Urban Stud.* **2012**, *49*, 3365–3384. [CrossRef]

61. Carter, K.; Chris, F. Sustainable development policy perceptions and practice in the UK social housing sector. *Construct. Manag. Econ.* **2007**, *25*, 399–408. [CrossRef]

62. Kucukvar, M.; Tatari, O. Towards a triple bottom-line sustainability assessment of the U.S. construction industry. *Int. J. Life Cycle Assess.* **2013**, *18*, 958–972. [CrossRef]

63. Valentin, A.; Spangenberg, J.H. A guide to community sustainability indicators. *Environ. Impact Assess. Rev.* **2000**, *20*, 381–392. [CrossRef]

64. Parris, T.M.; Kates, R.W. Characterizing and measuring sustainable development. *Annu. Rev. Environ. Resour.* **2003**, *28*, 559–586. [CrossRef]

65. Spangenberg, J.H. Institutional sustainability indicators: An analysis of the institutions in Agenda 21 and a draft set of indicators for monitoring their effectivity. *Sustain. Dev.* **2002**, *10*, 103–115. [CrossRef]

66. Wu, S.R.; Fan, P.; Chen, J. Incorporating culture into sustainable development: A cultural sustainability index framework for green buildings. *Sustain. Dev.* **2015**, *24*, 64–76. [CrossRef]

67. Boyoko, C.T.; Cooper, R.; Davey, C.L.; Wootton, A.B. Addressing sustainability early in the urban design process. *Manag. Environ. Qual.* **2006**, *17*, 689–706. [CrossRef]

68. Martin, N.; Rice, J. Sustainable development pathways: Determining socially constructed visions for cities. *Sustain. Dev.* **2014**, *22*, 391–403. [CrossRef]

69. Martin, N.J.; Rice, J.L.; Lodhia, S.K. Sustainable development planning: A case of public participation using online forums. *Sustain. Dev.* **2014**, *22*, 265–275. [CrossRef]

70. Dessein, J.; Battaglini, E.; Horlings, L. *Cultural Sustainability and Regional Development: Theories and Practices of Territorialisation*; Routledge: Abingdon-on-Thames, UK, 2015.

71. Bell, S.; Morse, S. Breaking through the glass ceiling: Who really cares about sustainability indicators? *Local Environ.* **2001**, *6*, 291–309. [CrossRef]

72. Wang, Y.F.; Zhao, H.Y. A brief analysis on low-carbon urban planning about low-income residential area: Based on the study of wisdom city with low carbon. *Mod. Urban Res.* **2013**, *5*, 110–113. (In Chinese).

73. Ding, D.; Wang, C.J.; Zou, R. Energy-saving indemnificatory housing design of Jinan: A case study on Wenzhuang public rental housing. *J. Shandong Jianzhu Univ.* **2013**, *28*, 250–255. (In Chinese).

74. Pombo, O.; Allacker, K.; Rivela, B.; Neila, J. Sustainability assessment of energy saving measures: A multi-criteria approach for residential buildings retrofitting—A case study of the Spanish housing stock. *Energy Build.* **2016**, *116*, 384–394. [CrossRef]

75. Bragança, L.; Mateus, R.; Koukkari, H. Building sustainability assessment. *Sustainability* **2010**, *2*, 2010–2023. [CrossRef]

76. Chen, H.S.; Li, Z.G. Social integration of social housing communities in big cities of China: A case study of Guangzhou city. *City Plan. Rev.* **2015**, *39*, 33–39. (In Chinese).

77. Pan, Y.H.; Zhou, Z.H. Public rental housing community construction in the condition of urban fusion. *Chongqing Soc. Sci.* **2016**, *8*, 113–120. (In Chinese).

78. Du, J.; Zhao, X.L.; Li, D.Z. Comparison and evaluation of the main construction modes of Chinese public rental housing. *Mod. Manag. Sci.* **2013**, *7*, 88–90. (In Chinese).

79. Banani, R.; Vahdati, M.M.; Shahrestani, M.; Clements-Croome, D. The development of building assessment criteria framework for sustainable non-residential buildings in Saudi Arabia. *Sustain. Cities Soc.* **2016**, *26*, 289–305. [CrossRef]

80. Shi, X.B.; Xiong, J. Study on influence factors and city integrating of peasant workers under the family perspective. *Popul. Dev.* **2014**, *20*, 42–51. (In Chinese).

81. Yuan, W.; James, P.; Yang, K. Community sustainable development indicator systems in China: A case study of Chongming County, Shanghai. *Geogr. Res.* **2003**, *22*, 484–494. (In Chinese).

82. Zhou, H. Measurement and theoretical thinking of social integration of floating population. *Popul. Res.* **2012**, *36*, 27–37. (In Chinese).

83. Wang, G.X.; Luo, E.L. A study on the current situation of peasant migrants' social integration in Shanghai. *J. East China Univ. Sci. Technol. (Soc. Sci. Ed.)* **2007**, *22*, 97–104. (In Chinese).

84. He, Y.B.; Sun, L.; Qin, W. Study on risk sharing of PPP projects based on AHP and entropy method. *Proj. Manag. Technol.* **2016**, *14*, 35–41. (In Chinese).

85. Basak, I. On the use of information criteria in analytic hierarchy process. *Eur. J. Oper. Res.* **2002**, *141*, 200–216. [CrossRef]

86. Al-Aomar, R. A combined ahp-entropy method for deriving subjective and objective criteria weights. *Int. J Ind. Eng. Theory Appl. Pract.* **2010**, *17*, 12–24.

87. Freeman, J.; Chen, T. Green supplier selection using an AHP-Entropy-TOPSIS framework. *Supply Chain Manag.* **2015**, *20*, 327–340. [CrossRef]

88. Zhu, J.M.; Liu, L.; Meng, K.; Gui, A.Q. The supply and demand matching of taxi resources in different time and space based on AHP-entropy: Taking Shanghai as a case. *J. Taiyuan Norm. Univ. Nat. Sci. Ed.* **2016**, *1*, 52–58. (In Chinese).

89. Amiri, M.P. Project selection for oil-fields development by using the AHP and fuzzy TOPSIS methods. *Expert Syst. Appl.* **2010**, *37*, 6218–6224. [CrossRef]

90. Zeng, X.Q.; Chen, J.G.; Lv, F. Risk assessment of BIPV project investment based on Entropy-Topsis. *Sci. Technol. Manag. Res.* **2015**, *35*, 31–35. (In Chinese).

91. Wu, Y.P. Environment impact assessment of shale gas development based on cloud model. *Environ. Prot. Sci.* **2016**, *42*, 79–85. (In Chinese).

92. Li, D.Y.; Meng, H.J.; Shi, X.M. Membership clouds and membership cloud generators. *J. Comp. Res. Dev.* **1995**, *32*, 15–20.

93. Li, L.; Fan, F.F.; Ma, L.; Tang, Z.R. Energy utilization evaluation of carbon performance in public projects by FAHP and cloud model. *Sustainability* **2016**, *8*, 630. [CrossRef]

94. Feng, Y.Q.; Wang, H.L.; Cao, M.K. Intelligent decision support system based on cloud model. In Proceeding of the 2006 Chinese Control and Decision Conference, Tianjin, China, 27 July 2006; pp. 1081–1084.

95. Zhang, J.; Zhang, J.A.; Sun, P. Trust evaluation model based on cloud model for C2C electronic commerce. *Comput. Syst. Appl.* **2010**, *19*, 83–87.

96. Qin, K.; Xu, K.; Liu, F.; Li, D. Image segmentation based on histogram analysis utilizing the cloud model. *Comput. Math. Appl.* **2011**, *62*, 2824–2833. [CrossRef]

97. Li, D.Y.; Han, J.W.; Shi, X.M.; Chan, M.C. Knowledge representation and discovery based on linguistic atoms. *Knowl. Based Syst.* **1998**, *10*, 431–440. [CrossRef]

98. Zhao, H.R.; Li, N.N. Risk evaluation of a UHV power transmission construction project based on a cloud model and FCE method for sustainability. *Sustainability* **2015**, *7*, 2885–2914. [CrossRef]

99. Ding, H.; Wang, D. The evaluation method of water eutrophication based on cloud model. *Acta Sci. Circumstantiae* **2013**, *33*, 251–257. (In Chinese).

100. Wang, Y.C.; Jing, H.W.; Zhang, Q.; Yu, L.Y.; Xu, Z.M. A normal cloud model-based study of grading prediction of rockburst intensity in deep underground engineering. *Rock Soil Mech.* **2015**, *36*, 1190–1193. (In Chinese).

101. Liao, L.C.; Fan, L.J.; Wang, P. Method of evaluating organizational performance based on cloud theory. *Syst. Eng.* **2010**, *1*, 99–104. (In Chinese).

102. Huang, M.Y.; He, X. Evaluation of ecological security of land in Anhui province based on normal cloud model and entropy weight. *Soils* **2016**, *48*, 1049–1054. (In Chinese).

103. Li, D.Y.; Du, Y. *Artificial Intelligence with Uncertainty*; National Defence Industry Press: Beijing, China, 2005. (In Chinese)

104. Xu, Y.X.; Wang, H.Y. Evaluation of airport service quality cloud model based on AHP-entropy weight method. *Value Eng.* **2016**, *2*, 7–10. (In Chinese).

105. Qin, D.Z. A comprehensive evaluation for network security risk assessment based on the cloud model. *Netw. Secur. Technol. Appl.* **2011**, *7*, 29–32. (In Chinese).

106. Wang, H.X. Research on predicament and countermeasure of property management in Chinese public rental housing: Taking Chongqing as an example. *Constr. Econ.* **2016**, *37*, 71–74. (In Chinese).

Article

Assessment of Alternative Scenarios for CO_2 Reduction Potential in the Residential Building Sector

Young-Sun Jeong

Korea Institute of Civil Engineering and Building Technology, 283 Goyangdae-Ro, Ilsanseo-Gu, Goyang-Si, Gyeonggi-Do 10223, Korea; sunj74@kict.re.kr; Tel.: +82-31-9100-108; Fax: +82-31-9100-361

Academic Editor: Umberto Berardi
Received: 19 December 2016; Accepted: 28 February 2017; Published: 10 March 2017

Abstract: The South Korean government announced its goals of reducing the country's CO_2 emissions by up to 30% below the business as usual (BAU) projections by 2020 in 2009 and 37% below BAU projections by 2030 in 2015. This paper explores the potential energy savings and reduction in CO_2 emissions offered by residential building energy efficiency policies and plans in South Korea. The current and future energy consumption and CO_2 emissions in the residential building were estimated using an energy–environment model from 2010 to 2030. The business as usual scenario is based on the energy consumption characteristic of residential buildings using the trends related to socio-economic prospects and the number of dwellings. The alternative scenarios took into account energy efficiency for new residential buildings (scenario I), refurbishment of existing residential buildings (scenario II), use of highly efficient boilers (scenario III), and use of a solar thermal energy system (scenario IV). The results show that energy consumption in the residential building sector will increase by 33% between 2007 and 2030 in the BAU scenario. Maximum reduction in CO_2 emissions in the residential building sector of South Korea was observed by 2030 in scenario I. In each alternative scenario analysis, CO_2 emissions were 12.9% lower than in the business as usual scenario by the year 2030.

Keywords: scenario analysis; CO_2 reduction; residential buildings; long-range energy alternative planning (LEAP) model

1. Introduction

Since the 1992 Earth Summit in Rio de Janeiro, parties to the United Nations Framework Convention on Climate Change (UNFCCC) have developed strategies, policies, and measures to mitigate climate change and to reduce their respective greenhouse gas emissions, both within and outside the Kyoto Protocol agreement. It was noted that the greenhouse gas effect has caused the average temperature of the Earth to increase by 0.74 °C over the past century. Climatologists and environmental scientists say that if the earth's average temperature increases by over 2–3 °C due to global warming, immense changes could occur and the human civilization may have to face severe damage. For this reason, international societies continually emphasize discussions and agreements on the importance of combating global warming, but no concrete outcome has yet been realized [1]. However, the global CO_2 emissions are continually increasing because of various human activities. The increase in CO_2 emissions has been attributed largely to the enormous consumption of fossil fuels for electricity production, transportation, industry and building operation, as well as the destruction of forested regions.

The building sector, including housing, constitutes 30%–40% of the society's total energy demand and must be prioritized in order to reach a sustainable society within a reasonable period [2]. According to the report of International Energy Agency (IEA), CO_2 emissions in the building sector, including indirect emissions from the use of electricity, account for almost 30% of global CO_2 emissions [3]. Accordingly, global warming and increased CO_2 emissions have elicited the greatest amount of interest from the building sector.

The world is striving to reduce global carbon intensity by increasing the energy efficiency of buildings and by strengthening building energy efficiency policies. Recently, potential CO_2 emission reductions in the building sector have been widely investigated. The IEA analyzed the energy savings and the potential impact of global warming on buildings by developing energy efficiency technologies in the building sector [3]. Radhi asserted that the energy design measures and building envelope codes, such as thermal insulation, thermal mass and double glazing in building envelopes, are important in coping with global warming [4,5]. Gaterell and McEvoy suggested that climate change could have a considerable impact on the performance of energy efficiency measures and energy policies applied to existing dwellings in a case study [6]. Jun Li investigated the potentials of energy savings and CO_2 reductions offered by the implementation of building energy efficiency policy scenarios in China [7]. Yu et al. assessed the long-term impacts of building codes on building energy consumption and CO_2 emissions using the Global Change Assessment Model. This study found that building energy codes would reduce energy consumption in Chinese buildings by 13%–22% depending on building code scenarios [8].

According to a report by the Third National Communication of the Republic of Korea [9], primary energy consumption in South Korea reached about 243.3 Mtoe (million tons of oil equivalent) in 2009. South Korea imported 96.4% of its total energy consumed in 2009. With regard to final energy consumption by sector, the building sector accounted for about 19.6% of overall consumption. Total CO_2 emissions reached 607.6 Mton CO_2 (million tons of CO_2 equivalent) in 2009, representing a 105% increase since 1990. This ranked South Korea ninth in the world in terms of CO_2 production. The annual increase rate of CO_2 emissions was 3.9% from 1990 to 2010, which was the top among the Organization for Economic Cooperation and Development (OECD) member nations.

The South Korean government announced at the Copenhagen climate change conference in 2009 its goal to reduce the country's CO_2 emissions by up to 30% below the business as usual (BAU) projections by 2020. Various policies and measures for reducing greenhouse gases are being rapidly established and implemented in South Korea. For the residential building sector, a 27% CO_2 emission reduction target below BAU has been established [10,11]. The Paris Agreement was adopted as a post-2020 climate regime at the 21st Conference of Parties (COP21) in the United Nations Framework Convention on Climate Change in Paris, France (2015). South Korea has declared the establishment of a plan to reduce CO_2 emissions by 37% by 2030. Accordingly, the South Korean government has been demanded to provide a measure of how to achieve this greenhouse gas reduction goal and corresponding strategy in building sector.

In South Korea, an action plan was established for green building activation toward low-energy and low-carbon green construction and zero-energy buildings in order to meet the country's CO_2 reduction goals by 2020. South Korea has concentrated its support on achieving energy efficiency in new and existing buildings, and has been continuously strengthening its energy policies for buildings. These efforts can help reduce CO_2 emissions and the fossil fuel consumed for energy in the South Korean building sector.

Therefore, the assessment of alternative scenarios for CO_2 reduction potential is a very important topic for fundamental study in South Korea in order to achieve the goal of CO_2 mitigation in the post-2020 climate regime and pursue sustainable development. In this paper, we estimate and predict energy consumption and associated CO_2 emissions in South Korea's residential building sector. Based on scenario analysis, we also assess the potential for CO_2 emission mitigation offered by the implementation of residential building energy efficiency policies in South Korea.

2. Methodology

2.1. 'Long-Range Energy Alternative Planning (LEAP) Model

This study used an accounting- and scenario-based modelling platform called 'long-range energy alternative planning' (LEAP) system to assess the impacts of alternative scenarios for energy consumption and CO_2 emissions in the residential building sector.

LEAP is an energy–environment modelling tool for energy policy analysis, alternative energy technology analysis and climate change mitigation assessment, which was developed at the Stockholm Environment Institute (SEI). The central concept of LEAP is an end-use driven scenario analysis. LEAP contains a full energy system accounting framework, which considers both demand- and supply-side technologies and which accounts for the total system impacts. The LEAP software tool is used to analyze current energy patterns and simulate alternative energy futures, along with environmental emissions, under a range of user-defined assumptions. LEAP emphasizes the detailed evaluation of energy use and CO_2 emissions within the context of integrated energy and environmental planning for each 'what if' scenario or combination of scenarios [12].

Several studies on energy consumption and CO_2 emissions have been conducted in various energy sectors using the LEAP model. Bose et al. used LEAP to estimate the energy consumption pattern and environmental emission levels in the transport sector of Delhi city [13]. In California, LEAP was used for energy forecasting and for identifying energy scenarios [14]. The energy and CO_2 emissions in the passenger transport sector of Rawalpindi and Islamabad were analyzed using the LEAP model [15]. Tao et al. published a study quantitatively describing China's low-carbon economic development level in 2050 based on the LEAP model with three kinds of scenarios [16]. The Taiwan LEAP model was used to compare future energy demand and supply patterns, as well as CO_2 emissions, for several alternative scenarios of energy policy and energy sector evolution [17]. In South Korea, the LEAP model was used to analyze future energy consumption in the electricity generation sector and to assess the environmental and economic impacts of renewable energy planning using alternative scenario investigations [18–20]. There have not been any studies assessing CO_2 emissions and reduction potential in the building sector using the LEAP model. The LEAP model can analyze the reduction potential of energy consumption and CO_2 emissions in each demand sector, including industry, transport, buildings and others.

In this study, the LEAP model as a building energy–environment model was used to analyze and forecast energy consumption and its related CO_2 emissions under alternative strategies (scenarios) for the residential building sector in South Korea.

2.2. Background of South Korea's Residential Building Sector

To develop the building energy–environment model and scenarios, we first studied building types, building stock and the historical trends of energy consumption in the residential building sector. South Korea is made up seven metropolitan cities, including Seoul, and nine local governments within a total land area of 99,392km². It is located in a temperate climate zone with a moderate altitude. It is cold and dry in the winter and hot and humid in the summer due to the influence of the north Pacific anticyclone under conditions of high temperature and humidity.

There were major changes in residential building types between 1990 and 2010. In 1990, apartment buildings accounted for 22.7% of total residential buildings; detached houses constituted 66.0%; low-rise townhouses 8.4%; and other types made up the final 2.8%. However, in 2010 multi-family housing accounted for 71.0% of South Korea's residential buildings. Apartment buildings with five stories or more accounted for 58.4% of residential buildings, whereas detached houses made up 27.9% [9]. As of 2010, there were about 13.6 million houses and 17.2 million households. It is evident that currently the most common building type is multi-family housing such as apartment buildings and townhouses. According to the construction statistics in Korea, the number of houses built per year for the past five years ranged from about 460,000 to 600,000 [21].

Figure 1 illustrates the final energy consumption in residential building sector. As for the final energy consumption by sector, the energy consumption of the residential building sector was 21.2 Mtoe in 2010, accounting for 10.8% of total national energy consumption and 56.9% of the energy consumed in the building sector, which is a very high proportion [22]. Residential buildings consumed 21.3 Mtoe of final energy in 2012 because use of natural gas continued to increase for space heating, water heating and cooking. In 2012, natural gas accounted for roughly 48% of total residential building final energy consumption (Figure 1). The penetration of electricity is still 25% of total energy used by residential buildings. Electricity is widely used for lighting and for powering household appliances. Oil fuel has been used for space heating in the form of kerosene and for cooking in the form of liquefied petroleum gas (LPG). Oil has decreased to an annual average growth rate of about –7.2%. Because of the penetration of district heat system in urban areas, district heat energy consumption represented 7.3% of the total energy used by the residential building sector. The use of oil is not common but is still used in the Korean buildings, mostly for space heating, water heating and cooking. Space heating, water heating and space cooling roughly accounted for 70% of residential energy consumption.

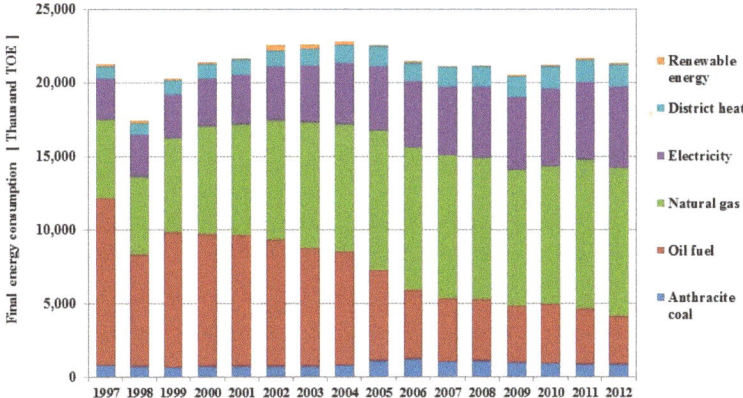

Figure 1. Final energy consumption in residential building sector, 1997–2012.

2.3. Basic Assumptions and Assessment Model Structure

A country's total CO_2 emission is influenced by many factors including economic growth, population, energy prices, industrial structure, weather and the development and distribution of energy-saving technologies. The business as usual (BAU) scenario forecasts these preconditions and reflects the results before estimating CO_2 emissions. The base year data set was developed using statistics from relevant government agencies. The building energy–environment model used in this study is built on current accounts and future projections for the 20-year period 2010–2030. Energy consumption and CO_2 emissions from residential building sector have been analyzed for the time span 2010–2030.

A key assumption relies on activity data such as economic growth rate, oil price, population and number of households, all of which are used to forecast energy demand of residential sector. The major socio-economic indicators based on the BAU scenario are presented in Table 1 [21–24]. We assume that South Korea's population will peak at 49,340,000 persons in 2018, and then decline until 2030. The economic growth rate at the national level is 6.3% in 2010 and will decline to 2.24% in 2030. Oil prices reflected long-term oil price fluctuation by reference to the national energy plan (2008–2030) [24]. The number of households will increase to 19,871,000 households in 2030 because of increase of single-person households. The number of single-person households has more than doubled in the past 10 years. Total final energy consumption increased from 181.4 Mtoe in 2007 to 257.1 Mtoe in 2030, recording an increase rate of approximately 41.7%. These socio-economic assumptions are used as a major driving force for residential buildings and energy service within the building sector. The total number of residential buildings will increase from 12,980,000 units in 2007 to 15,759,000 units in 2030, an increase of approximately 21.4%. The key assumption variables and energy consumption forecasting reflects the national energy basic plan [24], energy statistics and energy balance [21,22].

Table 1. Major socio-economic indicators.

Item	Unit	2007	2010	2020	2030
Economic growth rate	%	5.1	6.3	3.66	2.24
Oil price	USD/bbl [a]	96.0	91.4	70.0	82.0
Population	Thousand	48,456	48,874	49,326	48,635
Number of households	Thousand	16,417	17,152	19,012	19,871
Number of residential buildings	Thousand	12,980	13,603	15,078	15,759
Total final energy consumption	Mtoe [b]	181.4	193.8	225.4	257.1

[a] USD/bbl: US dollars per barrel of oil; [b] Mtoe: million tonnes of oil equivalent.

General information and basic assumptions for estimating energy consumption and CO_2 emissions of residential buildings are as follows:

- Time period: 20 years (2010–2030)
- Base year: 2007
- Energy end use in residential buildings: space heating, space cooling, cooking, lighting, electrical appliances
- Current accounts and future projections (from 2010 to 2030) of existing residential buildings and energy consumption of the residential building sector in South Korea were determined in a survey database in this study model

The structure and framework of the assessment model is presented in Figure 2. This building energy–environment model consists of four parts: input and assumption, assessment model, scenarios and result and forecast. The result and forecast part shows the annual output projection of energy consumption and CO_2 emissions according to the BAU scenario and alternative scenarios. The data from socio-economic assumptions and the number of residential buildings are used as inputs for the building energy–environment model to create the residential building stock data and detailed building energy model (profile of residential building's energy end-use). The residential building stock data consisted of new building data after base year (from 2008) and existing building data before the base year (by 2007). The detailed building energy model is comprised of five sectors: space heating, space cooling, cooking, lighting and appliances.

The main key issue is the representation of the expansion of residential building stock data for the number of residential buildings used in this model. We collected historical statistics about residential buildings, such as yearly numbers of residential buildings and new constructions between 1985 and 2010. After 2010, the forecast of number of households and the assumed population growth were used to calculate the total number of residential buildings to 2030. Particularly, residential building growth is strongly linked to household growth in Figure 3. We assumed that the lifespan of a residential building to be 40 years after construction and apply the demolition rate of 2.3% from the construction statistics [21,23]. The demolition rate means that 2.3% of the remaining building stock in any given year retires in the following year. A total residential building stock consists of new residential buildings and existing residential buildings (Figure 3). The number of existing residential buildings will decrease from 12,105,000 houses in 2010 to 7,601,000 houses in 2030. On the other hand, the number of new residential buildings will increase from 1,498,000 houses in 2010 to 8,159,000 houses in 2030, because the new residential building is the cumulative value of the number of residential building built after the base year.

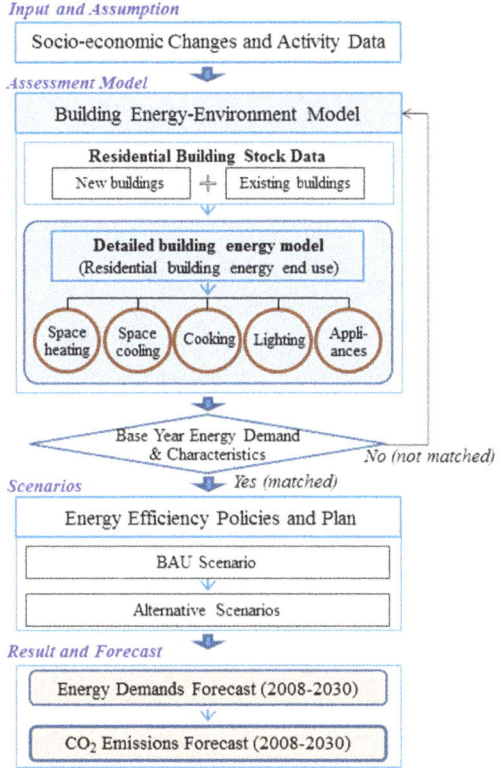

Figure 2. The structure of the assessment model. BAU: business as usual.

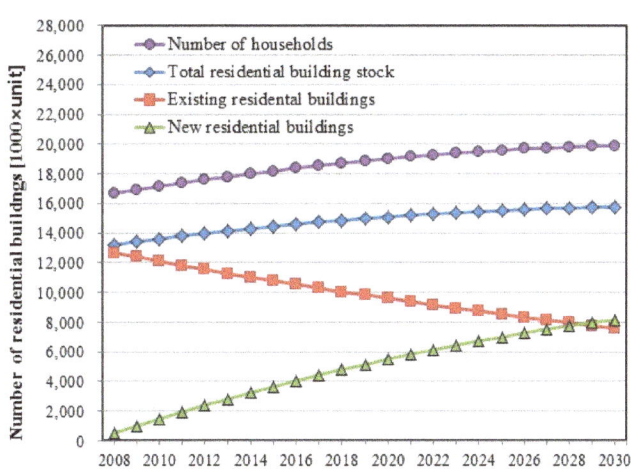

Figure 3. Projected number of residential buildings—total residential building stock and number of households in South Korea, 2008–2030.

The second key issue in this assessment model is to determine the energy service required for end-use energy in buildings by residents. The composition and scope of analysis with regard to energy service were divided into the space heating sector including hot water, space cooling, cooking, lighting and home electricity use. In addition, energy technology was created by collecting relevant data including data from the boiler, air conditioner, cooking devices, lighting and home appliances. All data are reflected on the analysis model. Energy sources in this model are separated into coal, oil, natural gas, district heat (heat), electricity and renewable energy.

The assessment model with LEAP model must match the national energy statistic and the characteristics of the end-use energy of residential buildings in the base year. If the result of assessment model did not match the base year's energy consumption data, we calibrated the detail-building energy model and assumption data. The baseline case of residential building energy is determined in BAU scenario using this assessment model. The BAU scenario is composed of the current accounts and future projection from 2008 to 2030. This structure of model allows us to predict the energy consumption and CO_2 emissions and to apply the alternative scenarios for CO_2 reduction potential in the residential building sector.

The key variable used in the analysis to calculate CO_2 emissions is the specific CO_2 emissions factor by energy source. This is because CO_2 emissions show a large difference depending on the emission factor, even if the same amount of energy is consumed. Table 2 presents the CO_2 emission factors for calculating greenhouse-gas emissions in Korea. This study used the factor provided by the guideline [25] by Intergovernmental Panel on Climate Change (IPCC) as the CO_2 emissions factor of fossil fuel when calculating CO_2 emissions. The annual CO_2 emission factor from the Korea Power Exchange was used as the electricity factor and its value was presented by the Korea's Ministry of Environment for district heat [26].

Table 2. CO_2 emission factor in this study.

Energy Source	CO_2 Emission Factor (Ton CO_2/Toe)
Coal anthracite	4.314
Natural gas	2.343
Kerosene	2.995
Liquefied petroleum gas (LPG)	2.633
Electricity	5.456
District heat	2.681

3. Scenarios and Data Framework

3.1. Business As Usual (BAU) Scenario

The baseline case of the residential building sector is determined in the BAU scenario using the assessment model of this study. The BAU scenario refers to the CO_2 emissions estimate under the assumption shown in Section 2.3 that the tendency of social and economic growth will continue in the future after a basic year, and that technological efficiency will also continue to improve based on patterns seen from the past to the present.

Assessment results of the BAU scenario are shown in Table 3 and Figure 4. Total final energy consumption in residential buildings in 2007 is reported at 19.88 Mtoe. This shows a 5.6% error compared to 21.07 Mtoe, which was the final energy consumption in 2007 reported by Korea Energy Statistics [22]. The energy output of the BAU scenario in 2010 was 21.19 Mtoe, whereas the final energy output from Korea Energy Statistics was 21.18 Mtoe. Results of the BAU scenario during the period 2007–2010 are quite similar to the figures presented by Korea Energy Statistics [22]. The increase in the amount of energy expected to be consumed in 2030 was over 33% in the BAU scenario. On the basis of the final energy consumption in 2007 from Table 3, space heating accounted for about 67.5%, which is the largest proportion of energy consumption in residential buildings. Space heating accounts for most of the energy consumption and is a key factor in CO_2 emissions of residential buildings. Space heating energy consumption is expected to increase 16.0% in 2030 compared to 2010. It was found that the energy consumption from home electrical appliances accounted for 17.5% of the total energy consumption in 2010. This rate is seen to increase by 4.8% from 2010 to 2030. In the BAU scenario, energy consumption continuously increased by 124.8% during the period 2010–2030. Figure 4 gives the demands of the energy source in the BAU scenario for the period 2007–2030. In 2030, the maximum energy consumption is expected to be come from natural gas (57.2%), electricity (31.0%) and district heat (10.3%). Natural gas and district heat are used for space heating in South Korea's residential buildings. Natural gas increases by 148.6% from 2010 to 2030. Electricity is mostly used to operate home electrical appliances and lighting in households. Electricity consumption will rise by 179% by the year 2030. The energy consumption output of the BAU scenario was projected using the conventional trends (population, household and efficiency), the energy use patterns of residential buildings, the economic situation and the energy policy.

Table 3. Results of energy demand by energy end-use, BAU scenario (Mtoe [a], %).

Energy End Use	2007	2010	2015	2020	2025	2030
Space heating	13.43 (67.5)	14.12 (66.7)	14.80 (65.0)	15.55 (64.1)	16.13 (62.7)	16.38 (61.9)
Space cooling	0.36 (1.8)	0.45 (2.1)	0.60 (2.6)	0.75 (3.1)	0.87 (3.4)	0.89 (3.3)
Cooking	1.78 (9.0)	1.84 (8.7)	1.89 (8.3)	1.80 (7.8)	1.93 (7.5)	1.94 (7.3)
Home electrical appliance	3.31 (16.6)	3.71 (17.5)	4.32 (19.0)	4.91 (20.3)	5.52 (21.5)	5.90 (22.3)
Lighting	1.00 (5.0)	1.06 (5.0)	1.14 (5.0)	1.13 (4.7)	1.25 (4.9)	1.34 (5.1)
Total	19.88 (100)	21.19 (100)	22.75 (100)	24.24 (100)	25.70 (100)	26.44 (100)

[a] Mtoe: million tons of oil equivalent, calculated from this study using the LEAP model.

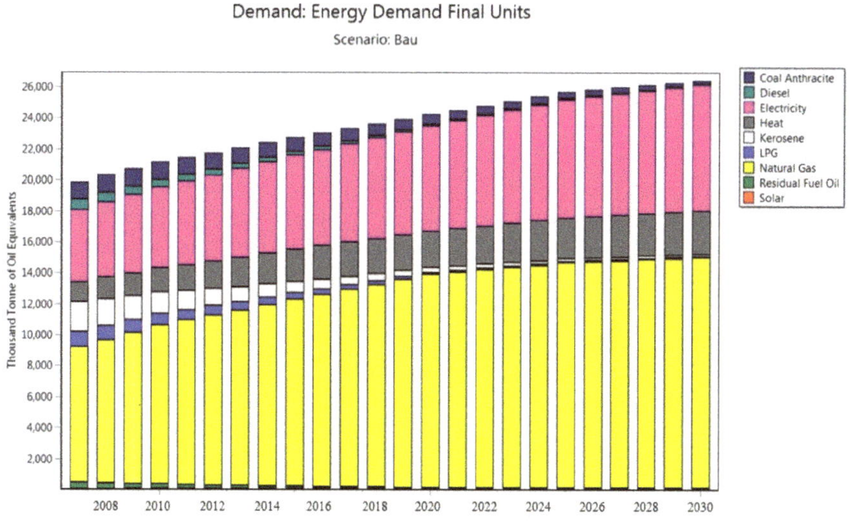

Figure 4. Annual final energy consumption in BAU scenario.

Table 4 shows the output projections of space heating energy in BAU scenario. It is shown that heating energy will increase by about 22% from 14.12 Mtoe in 2010 to 16.38 Mtoe in 2030. The annual rate of increase of space heating energy is 4.1%, which is the mean value for the time horizon. Natural gas, among the different heating energy sources, was estimated to increase from 61.8% in 2010 to 79.2% in 2030. Among the fossil fuels, anthracite and oil fuel are projected to decrease significantly from 26.0% in 2010 to 2.3% in 2030. The results of heating energy using the BAU scenario were analyzed to reflect the tendency with regard to an increased number of houses, the expanded pipe network of natural gas in a compact housing district, the tendency to prefer clean energy, and alternative fuels using natural gas and district heat. The Korean government promoted district heating, which uses high efficiency equipment that utilizes a combined heat and power (CHP). The use of CHP equipment can improve energy use efficiency by producing heat and power simultaneously [27]. Energy sources used in district heating in Korea were coal, oil, liquefied natural gas (LNG) and wastes. Heat from waste incineration accounted for about 21% and heat from the electricity generation using LNG and coal accounted for more than 70% [28,29]. After completion of the BAU scenario, energy and CO_2 reduction potential of residential buildings were compared using the alternative scenarios.

Table 4. Output projection for space heating energy by energy source type, BAU scenario (Mtoe [a], %).

	2007	2010	2015	2020	2025	2030
Anthracite coal	1.11 (8.3)	1.17 (8.3)	0.9 (6.1)	0.66 (4.2)	0.44 (2.7)	0.24 (1.5)
Natural gas	7.36 (54.8)	8.73 (61.8)	10.39 (70.2)	11.89 (76.5)	12.65 (78.4)	12.97 (79.2)
District heat	1.29 (9.6)	1.55 (11.0)	2.11 (14.3)	2.33 (15.0)	0.17 (16.4)	2.78 (17.0)
Oil fuel	3.60 (26.8)	2.51 (17.7)	1.20 (8.1)	0.46 (2.9)	0.17 (1.0)	0.13 (0.8)
Renewable energy	0.07 (0.5)	0.07 (0.5)	0.08 (0.5)	0.09 (0.6)	0.09 (0.6)	0.10 (0.6)
Total	13.43 (100)	14.12 (100)	14.80 (100)	15.55 (100)	16.13 (100)	16.38 (100)

[a] Mtoe: million tons of oil equivalent; calculated from this study using the long-range energy alternative planning (LEAP) model.

3.2. Description of Alternative Scenarios

There are four alternative scenarios based on the implementation of residential building energy efficiency policies and plans [23,24,30–34] and technologies of the South Korean government: energy efficiency for new residential buildings (scenario I), refurbishment or renovation of existing residential buildings (scenario II), use of highly efficient boilers (scenario III) and use of a solar thermal energy system for heating spaces and water (scenario IV). The details of each scenario are shown in Table 5.

3.2.1. Scenario I

According to the IEA's report, the building envelope and the good design of a building play a substantial role in determining the heating and cooling load for a desired indoor temperature [3]. It is estimated that the space heating and cooling accounted for 39% of the residential building sector's CO_2 emissions in 2007. Building envelopes, including walls, floors, ceilings, windows and doors are very important elements in determining heating and cooling demand.

Table 5. Description and main conditions of alternative scenarios.

Scenario	Description	Main Condition
Scenario I	Energy efficiency for new residential buildings	- Object: New residential buildings - Heating energy efficiency: 40% - Penetration rate: 60% by 2020, 100% by 2025
Scenario II	Refurbishment of existing residential buildings	- Object: Existing residential building stock - Heating energy efficiency: 20% - Penetration rate: 8% by 2020, 20% by 2030
Scenario III	Highly efficient boilers	- Object: Total residential buildings that use gas boilers - Energy efficiency of the boiler: more than 87% - Penetration rate: 30% by 2015, 60% by 2020, 100% by 2030
Scenario IV	Solar thermal energy system for heating space and water	- Object: Total residential building stock - The supply of green-house with solar thermal heating system - Heating energy saving: 50% - Penetration rate: 7.6% by 2020, 10% by 2030

It is possible to construct residential buildings with heating energy consumption reduced by over 40% by applying an energy-efficient design, using high-efficiency insulation technology as well as high-efficiency window technology [23]. South Korea's major construction companies also report that apartment buildings can be constructed with 30%–40% reductions in energy consumption by promoting housing brands [35–37]. These energy-saving, sustainable houses can be supplied in numbers reaching about 1,684,000 by 2020. South Korea is pursuing a policy that residential buildings will require energy levels 30% lower than the current average in residential buildings from 2012 and will meet a passive house levels using high insulation, airtightness, heat recovery ventilation systems and various energy-saving technologies from 2017. Since 2009, the thermal insulation standards of building envelopes have been intensified to meet the passive house standard by 2017. All new residential buildings constructed after 2025 must likewise be constructed as energy-efficient buildings that do not demand any fossil fuel energy. It is a long-term roadmap set by the government. Scenario I includes the above-mentioned contents and is based on the green building activation plan for long-term building energy efficiency by the government.

3.2.2. Scenario II

The energy saving effect of reducing heat loss from buildings through energy retrofits for the existing residential building stock is expected to be huge. In OECD countries, most of the building stock was constructed before the 1970s (around 60% of the residential dwellings) and has very high space heating requirements. Refurbishing or renovating these buildings offers the largest abatement of potential heating energy demand [3].

The South Korean government is driving the project to transform the existing housing stock into energy efficient green homes [30]. To improve the energy efficiency of these buildings, an action plan for green building activation stipulates the continuation of retrofit programs for buildings and supply projects for green remodeling of buildings. Through the old housing renovation project, the government has a plan to retrofit 280,000 dwellings (existing housing) over 15 years until 2016. The government is promoting improvement of the energy efficiency of the existing buildings through the enactment of 'the act on the promotion of green buildings' [30]. The government introduced a building energy certification system that encourages people to select a more energy efficient building by attaching building energy certificates in building sales or rental processes. A government-funded green building remodeling program is operated by a green remodeling creation center to support the interest of cost US$0.25 million spent on energy improvements in 2015 [38]. In addition, from the 2012 housing budget, the Korean government spent about USD$66.1 million on repairing deteriorated public rental houses, and about USD$26.7 million on repairing houses belonging to socially vulnerable people.

Retrofitting residential buildings with energy efficiency improvements can result in up to 20% space heating energy savings. Houses with energy-saving, eco-friendly housing repair works are expected to make up about 8% of the total existing residential building stock in 2020, reaching 20% in 2030. South Korea is in the process of promoting the contents of this policy plan. Scenario II includes the above-mentioned contents.

3.2.3. Scenario III

Improved energy efficiency for the energy supply and demand parts within buildings can be considered the biggest factor for reducing CO_2 emissions. Heating energy in residential building stock is generally supplied by a boiler for which natural gas is used as the energy source. Multi-family housing with over 20 families will require the installation of a high efficiency boiler with over 87% heating energy efficiency from 2010 [31].

Natural gas consumption increased by 5.2% annually from 2002 to 2007 and it is estimated that gas consumption of households will increase by an annual average of about 2.5% by 2022 [32]. We assume that the distribution of high efficiency boilers among the different natural gas boilers will increase from 11% in 2009 to 30% in 2015, 60% in 2020 and 100% in 2030. This plan is applied to new and existing residential buildings. This assumption is consistent with the historical trend of spread of high efficiency boiler in housing and long term natural gas supply and demand program.

3.2.4. Scenario IV

Since a solar thermal energy system is relatively more efficient and economically more feasible than alternatives, this new and renewable energy facility offers a large distribution potential. In addition, the IEA has declared solar technology a major measure in preparing for sustainable energy properties and as an efficient measure for reducing CO_2 emissions [3]. A basic plan for new and renewable energy was set up to raise the percentage of new and renewable energy in primary energy from 2.6% in 2008 to 11% in 2030 [31]. The South Korean government is promoting a policy to raise the renewable energy distribution from the current 2.4% in 2007 to 11% in 2030 [23,31].

South Korea plans to supply the renewable energy system to one million dwelling houses by 2020, particularly to new residential buildings and the existing housing stock [33]. Although the solar thermal energy system is now being used as a renewable energy facility that effectively produces heating energy, the system supplies only about 50% of the heating energy required for residential buildings [39]. We assume that the installation of solar thermal energy system will be increased linearly up to 1,576,000 housings by 2030. In this scenario, residential buildings with solar thermal energy systems for heating will account for 1.05% of total residential building stock in 2010, 7.6% in 2020 and 10% in 2030.

4. Scenario Analysis Results and Discussion

The final energy consumption, CO_2 emissions, invested amount cost and CO_2 reduction potential in the alternative scenarios were analyzed, respectively and compared with the outcomes of the BAU scenario.

4.1. Energy Consumption and CO₂ Emission

Table 6 shows the annual energy consumption projection using the assessment model of this study based on each alternative scenario (scenarios I–IV). Energy consumption in 2030 is projected to show a 25.2% increase in scenario I, a 31.1% increase in scenario II, a 33.1% increase in scenario III, and a 45.9% increase in scenario IV, relative to 2007. The energy reduction effect is shown to be highest in scenario I among all the alternative scenarios.

Table 6. Annual output projection of energy consumption in alternative scenarios (Mtoe [a]).

	2007	2010	2015	2020	2025	2030
Scenario I	19.88	21.16	22.57	23.68	24.60	24.89
Scenario II	19.88	21.17	22.68	24.07	25.44	26.08
Scenario III	19.88	21.17	22.47	23.55	24.70	25.15
Scenario IV	19.88	21.20	22.99	24.73	26.33	27.18

[a] Mtoe: million tons of oil equivalent; calculated from this study using the LEAP model.

The time-horizon variation of global warming potential for each alternative scenario is shown in Table 7. According to a publication released by the South Korean government, total CO_2 emissions in 2007, which was used as the base year, were 610.5 Mton CO_2. The residential building sector accounted for 11.5% of emissions, with 70.47 Mton CO_2. In 2007, CO_2 emissions in the BAU scenario were 65.99 Mton CO_2, about 6.4% less than the 70.47 Mton CO_2 reported by the national CO_2 emission statistics. In 2010, CO_2 emissions in the BAU scenario were 70.14 Mton CO_2, about 3.1% lower than 72.40 Mton CO_2 reported by the national CO_2 emission statistics. This is significant because the energy consumption and CO_2 emissions in the real residential building sector were realistically reproduced and modeled by using the preconditions and variables collected in this study and through the BAU scenario. The data obtained are seen to have significant utilization value.

Table 7. CO_2 emission potentials according to scenarios (Mton CO_2).

	2007	2010	2015	2020	2025	2030
BAU scenario	65.99	70.14	72.08	71.46	71.12	73.07
Scenario I	65.99	70.10	71.60	70.06	68.41	69.08
Scenario II	65.99	70.08	71.90	71.02	70.48	72.19
Scenario III	65.99	70.10	71.42	69.83	68.79	70.06
Scenario IV	65.99	70.12	71.59	70.45	69.81	71.54

According to the CO_2 emissions results in the BAU scenario, CO_2 emissions in the residential building sector are projected to continually increase until 2030. Energy consumption in the residential building sector is expected to increase by about 33% from 2007 to 2030, and CO_2 emissions are expected to increase by about 10.7%. As seen from the estimates on space heating energy consumption, this is due to the fact that consumption is expected to be transferred to low CO_2 energy sources while the consumption of high CO_2 fossil fuel is expected to decrease. The district heating system is expected to be supplied and used more, although the total energy consumption is expected to increase. In addition, continual efficiency improvements of the boiler and lighting devices are determined to be a key factor for this.

Through building energy efficiency planning in residential buildings after 2007, CO_2 emissions were found to decrease in all scenarios. As each scenario reflects the energy efficiency in the residential buildings, CO_2 emissions are expected to drop by 2030 in all alternative scenarios when compared to the BAU scenario. The CO_2 emission in scenario I increased from 65.99 Mton CO_2 in 2007 to 69.08 Mton CO_2 in 2030. In the case of scenario I, since an energy-efficiency scenario for new residential buildings is being driven, CO_2 emissions are seen to maintain their level in 2020. In scenario II, with energy retrofitting of the existing buildings, CO_2 emissions increased from 70.08 Mton CO_2 in 2010 to 72.19 Mton CO_2 in 2030. Scenario III, which uses a high efficiency gas boiler, showed the lowest CO_2 emissions among all alternative scenarios from 2010 to 2020. Scenario III yielded projections of 68.79 Mton CO_2 in 2025 and 70.06 Mton CO_2 in 2030. According to scenario IV, with regard to the introduction of solar thermal energy systems for heating energy, the CO_2 emissions were found to increase by 8.4% in 2030. The energy consumption in scenario IV increases by 36.7% from 2007 to 2030, but CO_2 emissions are projected to become relatively lower. This is because the renewable energy that is to be used as heating energy produced through the solar thermal energy system was evaluated as emitting zero CO_2.

4.2. Cost

This study analyzed the discounted cumulative total costs for energy efficiency measures from 2007 to 2030 for each scenario. The results of the investment cost identified by the assessment model are shown in Table 8. All costs are shown in 2007 values. The investment includes the initial investment, maintenance cost and energy cost according to the scenario. Because the initial investment amount on solar system is quite significant, the 2030 cost in scenario IV is higher by about 16.4% compared to the BAU scenario.

Table 8. Results in terms of costs according to scenarios (in millions, $USD).

	2007	2010	2015	2020	2025	2030
BAU scenario	15,291	14,088	11,280	9131	7444	5909
Scenario I	15,291	14,084	11,263	9113	7426	5890
Scenario II	15,291	14,098	11,303	9177	7499	5969
Scenario III	15,291	14,081	11,185	8955	7254	5722
Scenario IV	15,291	14,125	11,973	10,212	8524	6876

4.3. CO_2 Emission Reduction Potentials

Table 9 shows the amount of CO_2 removed in each alternative scenario in 2007, 2010, 2015, 2020, 2025 and 2030. By 2030, the amount of CO_2 removed in each alternative scenario from highest to lowest is as follows:

Energy efficiency for new residential buildings (scenario I) > use of high efficient boilers (scenario III) > use of a solar thermal energy system for heating spaces and water (scenario IV) > refurbishment of existing residential buildings (scenario II)

Table 9. CO_2 emission reduction potentials according to scenarios (Mton CO_2).

	2007	2010	2015	2020	2025	2030
Scenario I	0.0	0.04	0.48	1.40	2.71	3.99
Scenario II	0.0	0.06	0.18	0.44	0.64	0.88
Scenario III	0.0	0.04	0.66	1.63	2.33	3.01
Scenario IV	0.0	0.02	0.49	1.01	1.31	1.53

The CO_2 emissions reduction in 2030 in scenario I is the highest at 3.99 Mton CO_2. When the reduction effect was applied by 2020, the reduction through the use of a high-efficiency gas boiler (scenario III) was found to be the highest among the alternative scenarios at 1.63 Mton CO_2 in 2020. The reduction potential achieved by supplying the solar thermal energy system (scenario IV) was found to be 1.01 Mton CO_2 in 2020, and is expected to decrease to 1.53 Mton CO_2 by 2030. According to the accumulated CO_2 reduction potential in all scenarios, the reduction potential was 0.16 Mton CO_2 in 2010, 4.48 Mton CO_2 in 2020 and 9.41 Mton CO_2 in 2030. This amount is equal to a reduction potential of about 12.9% compared to the CO_2 emission by 2030 in the BAU scenario.

The unit reduction cost of scenario III, having the lowest CO_2 emission levels among all the alternative scenarios was minus (−) 62.3 USD/ton of CO_2 by 2030. Thus, scenario III is seen to have the most cost-effective measure. Because the solar thermal energy system (scenario IV) has significantly higher initial installation and maintenance costs, its projected unit reduction cost in 2030 was found to be 629.5 USD/ton of CO_2.

5. Conclusions and Policy Implications

A major goal of improved building technologies and building energy policies is the reduction of CO_2 emissions, which is also the primary goal of energy efficiency and carbon policies. The results obtained from the BAU scenario in estimating energy consumption and CO_2 emissions in the residential building sector were based on the energy consumption characteristics of the current residential building sector and socio-economic development potential. The alternative scenarios were established based on energy-saving technologies and green building policy initiatives. This study provides insights into the trends in energy consumption and CO_2 emissions in the residential building sector of South Korea.

This study focuses on both potential energy savings impacts and CO_2 emission mitigation of the energy efficiency measures within residential buildings. We suggest the building energy–environment model using LEAP software. We developed it as a flexible tool for assessing the ability of the green-building strategies to achieve desired CO_2 reductions goal. The results show that the CO_2 emissions of residential buildings will have a significant impact on the building's energy efficiency and on its energy usage.

CO_2 emissions in the residential building sector are seen to increase from 65.99 Mton CO_2 in 2007 to 71.46 Mton CO_2 in 2020 and 73.07 Mton CO_2 in 2030, translating to a 10.7% increase compared to 2007 in the BAU scenario. This is because energy consumption continually increases as the population and the numbers of dwellings increase. In particular, the energy consumed for heating energy was found to be the highest at 61.9–67.5%. Efficient heating energy technology is seen to be the more cost-effective measure for energy consumption and CO_2 emission reduction.

This study analyzed the environmental and economic impact of energy technologies from the South Korean government's energy efficiency and carbon policies. These technologies are capable of introducing a number of highly efficient new buildings, with energy retrofitting of existing buildings, high-efficiency gas boilers and solar thermal systems on the residential buildings through alternative scenarios by using the building energy–environment model. These alternative scenarios could help reduce the residential building sector's energy consumption and its CO_2 emission. The CO_2 reduction amount potential by alternative scenarios was 12.9% compared to the potential of the BAU scenario by 2030. This CO_2 emissions reduction potential is significant in terms of the country's total CO_2 emissions because it represents the combined effect of the building sector's energy efficiency and the power sector's decarbonization.

However, there remains technological, economic and institutional uncertainty with regard to the introduction of these technologies in future residential building markets. To overcome such limitations, technological supply systems or policies need to be promoted at the national level. It is also necessary to establish a long-term comprehensive plan and prepare a system for implementing such plans to activate the construction of low-energy green buildings by linking the plan to a long-term national CO_2 reduction goal. Only when energy efficiency technologies in residential buildings are considered along with the measures to supply these technologies to the housing construction markets can these technologies be helpful in CO_2 emission reduction in the residential building sector.

Acknowledgments: The author is grateful for the support of the Korea Institute of Civil Engineering and Building Technology (Key R&D project No. 2014-0047).

Conflicts of Interest: The author declares no conflict of interest.

References

1. Kim, H.K. *The Right Way to Know about Green Growth*; Nanam Publishing House: Gyeonggi-Do, Korea, 2011.
2. Erlandsson, M.; Bog, M. Generic LCA-methodology applicable for buildings, constructions and operation services-today practice and development needs. *Build. Environ.* **2003**, *38*, 919–938. [CrossRef]
3. International Energy Agency (IEA). *Energy Technology Perspectives 2010: Scenarios & Strategies to 2050*; International Energy Agency: Paris, France, 2010.

4.   Radhi, H. Evaluation the potential impact of global warming on the UAE residential buildings—A contribution to reduce the CO_2 emissions. *Build. Environ.* **2009**, *44*, 2451–2462. [CrossRef]

5.   Radhi, H. Can envelope codes reduce electricity and CO_2 emissions in different types of buildings in the hot climate of Bahrain. *Energy* **2009**, *34*, 205–215. [CrossRef]

6.   Gaterell, M.R.; McEvoy, M.E. The impact of climate change uncertainties on the performance of energy efficiency measures applied to dwellings. *Energy Build.* **2005**, *37*, 982–995. [CrossRef]

7.   Li, J. Towards a low-carbon future in China's building sector—A review of energy and climate models forecast. *Energy Policy* **2008**, *36*, 1736–1747. [CrossRef]

8.   Yu, S.; Eom, J.; Evans, M.; Clarke, L. A long-term, integrated impact assessment of alternative building energy code scenarios in China. *Energy Policy* **2014**, *67*, 626–639. [CrossRef]

9.   Korean Government. *Korea's Third National Communication under the United Nations Framework Convention on Climate Change*; Korean Government: Seoul, Korea, 2011.

10. Korean Government. *Greenhouse Gas Reduction Targets by Sectors and Years*; Korean Government: Seoul, Korea, 2011. (In Korean)

11. Korean Government. The National Roadmap to Achieve the National Greenhouse Gas Emissions Reduction Target. Available online: http://me.go.kr/home/web/board/read.do?pagerOffset=0& maxPageItems=10&maxIndexPages=10&searchKey=&searchValue=&menuId=286&orgCd=&boardId= 339265&boardMasterId=1&boardCategoryId=&decorator= (accessed on 21 October 2016). (In Korean)

12. Stockholm Environmental Institute (SEI). Long-Range Energy Alternative Planning System-User Guide for LEAP, Web Version for LEAP 2015. Available online: http://www.energycommunity.org (accessed on 7 February 2017).

13. Bose, R.K.; Srinivaschary, V. Policies to reduce energy use and environmental emissions in the transport sector: A case of Delhi city. *Energy Policy* **1997**, *25*, 1137–1150. [CrossRef]

14. Ghanadan, R.; Koomey, J.G. Using energy scenarios to explore alternative energy pathways in California. *Energy Policy* **2005**, *33*, 1117–1142. [CrossRef]

15. Shabbir, R.; Ahmad, S.S. Monitoring urban transport air pollution and energy demand in Rawalpindi and Islamabad using leap model. *Energy* **2010**, *35*, 2323–2332. [CrossRef]

16. Tao, Z.; Zhao, L.; Changxin, Z. Research on the prospects of low-carbon economic development in China based on LEAP model. *Energy Procedia* **2011**, *5*, 695–699. [CrossRef]

17. Yophy, H.; Jeffrey, B.Y.; Chieh-Yu, P. The long-term forecast of Taiwan's energy supply and demand: LEAP model application. *Energy Policy* **2011**, *39*, 6790–6803.

18. Shin, H.; Park, J.; Kim, H.; Shin, E. Environmental and economic assessment of landfill gas electricity generation in Korea using LEAP model. *Energy Policy* **2005**, *33*, 1261–1270. [CrossRef]

19. Jun, S.; Lee, S.; Park, J.W.; Jeong, S.J.; Shin, H.C. The assessment of renewable energy planning on CO_2 abatement in South Korea. *Renew. Energy* **2010**, *35*, 471–477. [CrossRef]

20. Park, N.B.; Yun, S.J.; Jeon, E.C. An analysis of long-term scenarios for the transition to renewable energy in the Korean electricity sector. *Energy Policy* **2013**, *52*, 288–296. [CrossRef]

21. Korean Statistical Information Service Database Portal. 2014. Available online: http://kosis.kr/eng (accessed on 30 September 2016).

22. Korea Energy Economics Institute. Year of Energy Statistics 2013. Available online: http://www.keei.re.kr (accessed on 30 September 2014).

23. *The Action Plan for Green Building Activation (Government Report/2009/11)*; Korea Ministry of Construction and Transportation: Seoul, Korea, 2009. Available online: http://www.greengrowth.go.kr/?p=38696&cat=35 (accessed on 30 September 2016). (In Korean). (In Korean)

24. Prime Minister's Office; MOSF; MEST; MOFAT; MKE; ME; MLTM. *The 1st Korean National Energy Basic Plan (2008–2030)*; Korean government: Seoul, Korea, 2008. (In Korean)

25. International Panel on Climate Change (IPCC). *IPCC Guidelines for National Greenhouse Gas Inventories*; International Panel on Climate Change (IPCC): Hayama, Japan, 2006.

26. Korea Ministry of Environment. Greenhouse Gas and Energy Target Management Scheme (Notification No. 2011-29). Available online: http://eng.me.go.kr (accessed on 30 August 2013).

27. Park, S.; Lee, K.; Yoo, S. Economies of scale in the Korean district heating system: A variable cost function approach. *Energy Policy* **2016**, *88*, 197–203. [CrossRef]

28. Korean Government. *The Fourth Framework for the District Energy Supply*; Korea Ministry of Trade, Industry & Energy: Seoul, Korea, 2014. (In Korean)
29. Homepage of Korea District Heating Corporation. Available online: http://www.kdhc.co.kr (accessed on 9 February 2017).
30. Korean Government. *The Act on the Promotion of Green Buildings*; Korea Ministry of Land, Transport and Maritime Affairs: Seoul, Korea, 2012. (In Korean)
31. Korean Government. *Construction Standard and Performance of Eco-Friendly House (Notification No. 2010-421)*; Korea Ministry of Construction and Transportation: Seoul, Korea, 2010. (In Korean)
32. Korean Government. *The 9th Plan for Long Term Natural Gas Supply and Demand Program*; Korea Ministry of Knowledge Economy: Seoul, Korea, 2008. (In Korean)
33. Korean Government. *Third New and Renewable Energy Technology and Dissemination Program*; Korea Ministry of Knowledge Economy: Seoul, Korea, 2008. (In Korean)
34. Korea Ministry of Knowledge Economy. *1 Million Green Home Distribution Projects*; Korea Ministry of Knowledge Economy: Seoul, Korea, 2009. (In Korean)
35. Kim, S.G. Zero energy house (ZENER HEIM) case study. *Rev. Archit. Build. Sci.* **2010**, *54*, 48–54.
36. Won, J.S. DAELIM ECO house technology development status and prospects. *Rev. Archit. Build. Sci.* **2012**, *56*, 18–25.
37. Lee, M.J. Planning and implementation of Korea's first zero energy housing complex. *Rev. Archit. Build. Sci.* **2014**, *58*, 47–53.
38. Korea Ministry of Land, Infrastructure and Transport. Green Remodeling and Support Projects for Buildings. Available online: http://www.greenremodeling.or.kr/support/sup1000.asp (accessed on 30 September 2016). (In Korean)
39. Lee, D.W. Overview and status of solar thermal systems. *Mag. Soc. Air-Condit. Refrigerating Eng. Korea* **2011**, *40*, 5–10.

 *sustainability*

Article

Multicriteria Spatial Decision Support Systems for Future Urban Energy Retrofitting Scenarios

Patrizia Lombardi, Francesca Abastante, Sara Torabi Moghadam * and Jacopo Toniolo

InterUniversity Department of Regional and Urban Studies and Planning (DIST),
Polytechnic University of Turin, 39 Viale Mattioli, 10125 Turin, Italy; patrizia.lombardi@polito.it (P.L.);
francesca.abastante@polito.it (F.A.); jacopo.toniolo@polito.it (J.T.)
* Correspondence: sara.torabi@polito.it; Tel.: +39-011-090-7467

Received: 31 March 2017; Accepted: 13 July 2017; Published: 18 July 2017

Abstract: Nowadays, there is an increasing concern about sustainable urban energy development taking into account national priorities of each city. Many cities have started to define future strategies and plans to reduce energy consumption and greenhouse gas emissions. Urban energy scenarios involve the consideration of a wide range of conflicting criteria, both socio-economic and environmental ones. Moreover, decision-makers (DMs) require proper tools that can support their choices in a context of multiple stakeholders and a long-term perspective. In this context, Multicriteria Spatial Decision Support Systems (MC-SDSS) are often used in order to define and analyze urban scenarios since they support the comparison of different solutions, based on a combination of multiple factors. The main problem, in relation to urban energy retrofitting scenarios, is the lack of appropriate knowledge and evaluation criteria. The latter are crucial for delivering and assessing urban energy scenarios through a MC-SDSS tool. The main goal of this paper is to analyze and test two different methods for the definition and ranking of the evaluation criteria. More specifically, the paper presents an on-going research study related to the development of a MC-SDSS tool able to identify and evaluate alternative energy urban scenarios in a long-term period perspective. This study refers to two Smart City and Communities research projects, namely: DIMMER (District Information Modeling and Management for Energy Reduction) and EEB (Zero Energy Buildings in Smart Urban Districts).

Keywords: multicriteria spatial decision support system (MC-SDSS); criteria definition; criteria ranking; urban energy scenarios

---

1. Introduction

Today, there is a large concern about green building design and the reduction of greenhouse gas emissions in cities. Indeed, the highest amount of energy usage belongs to cities, accounting for 32% of global final energy consumption, and it is expected that this number will increase in the near future due to the growing urban population [1]. A further element of concern is related to the age of the existing buildings stock since most of them are dated back to the 1970s, leading to low energy performances. Consequently, appropriate retrofitting strategies are needed due to the low demolition rate of existing buildings, in order to make successful energy savings targets.

With this in mind, many cities started to define future strategies and plans to reduce energy consumption and greenhouse gas emission [2]. Policies and urban energy scenario development require the consideration of a territorial approach and the analysis of a large stock of buildings and their energy performances [3], rather than the analysis of single building energy efficiency improvement [4].

Cities are dynamic living organisms that are continuously evolving, requiring integrated, collaborative, and inclusive multiple stakeholders and multiple criteria decision processes [5].

Therefore, developing urban energy scenarios for energy transition is a time consuming and delicate decision process that requires a very large number of data and information [6].

Geographic Information Systems (GIS) are recognized as being key players against those tasks mainly due to the extent of required data/information and the presence of multiple stakeholders and criteria with conflicting interests and objectives. GIS can support evaluations and decision processes on the urban scales about the complexity of the related energy strategies scenarios [7], being able to integrate different subsystems and database. Interestingly, GIS can support the decision processes related to the definition of energy urban scenarios identifying critical zones with the use of colored maps [8]. This purpose requires geographical data visualization of the alternative scenarios, producing thematic maps and performing spatial operations [9]; in this sense, a spatial decision support system (SDSS) consist in a system devoted to support the decision processes in spatial problems [10].

In order to properly manage the decision processes related to the definition of urban energy scenarios, multicriteria decision analysis (MCDA) can be applied to consider multiple stakeholder's point of views, as well as the multiple aspects of the problem in exam. Indeed, MCDA is proved to be a powerful methodology able to consider different aspects of complex situations and to provide priority rankings both in term of alternative scenarios and qualitative/quantitative decision criteria [11].

The synergetic capabilities of SDSS and MCDA are recognized since they can potentially enhance both spatial decision processes, helping to reach a consensus [12]. Accordingly, the Web-based Multicriteria Spatial Decision Support System (MC-SDSS) extends the SDSS tool to include not only the GIS capabilities but also MCDA [13]. One of the main advantages of the MC-SDSS is that they allow the stakeholders expressing their preferences with respect to decision criteria and/or alternative scenarios using GIS-based procedures, which provide feedback, increasing the trust in the results. Moreover, the MC-SDSS are powerful visualization tool through which the maps become *'visual indices'* offering solutions to the planners to change and optimize the conditions [14].

This paper presents an on-going research related to the development of a MC-SDSS able to provide and evaluate alternative energy urban scenarios in a long-term period perspective. The research study specifically refers to the following two smart urban energy projects: the European DIMMER project (District Information Modeling and Management for Energy Reduction) [15] and the National Smart City and Communities EEB project (Nearly Zero-Energy Buildings in Smart Urban Districts) [16].

The methodological steps involved in this study are: (1) data collection and integration; (2) criteria definition and ranking; (3) scenarios development and evaluation. In particular, the paper focuses on the test of two different methods for the definition and ranking of the decision criteria which are required for delivering and assessing the urban energy scenarios: the Measuring Attractiveness by a Categorical Based Evaluation Technique (MACBETH) [17] and the "Playing Cards" method [18].

The paper is organized as follows: the next section provides an overview of both MCDA and SDSS, including the approaches used to define and rank the evaluation criteria to be used in the decision analysis. Section 3 describes the definition of the decision criteria adopted in the DIMMER and EEB projects, while Section 4 highlights the strengths and weaknesses of the proposed approaches. Finally, Section 5 presents the conclusions and the future development of the research.

2. Methodological Theoretical Framework

MCDA and SDSS are, nowadays, recognized as fundamental tools to define and analyze urban energy retrofitting scenarios since they are able to compare different solutions, based on the combination of multiple factors and criteria [13].

SDSS can be considered as an interactive computer system for assisting the user(s) (i.e., single or group) to efficiently perform decision processes [19]. In this sense, the SDSS is able to visually support the stakeholders during different focus groups and workshops to understand how the criterion trade-offs evolve when one or several decision parameters change [20].

The SDSS acquires, manages and stores the geo-referenced data performing the analysis of spatial problems. Moreover, it provides an interactive environment for performing effective visual activities thanks to the visual interface, which enables a dynamically-interactive session in a real-time exchange of information between the user and the system to support the stakeholders through all decision phases [19]. According to [21] the SDSS should be able to:

- Provide mechanisms for the spatial data input;
- Allow representation of the spatial relations and structures;
- Include the analytical techniques of spatial and geographical analysis; and
- Provide output in a variety of spatial forms, including maps.

The Multicriteria Spatial Decision Support Systems (MC-SDSS) are part of a larger field of SDSS [22]. In the framework of MC-SDSS, two interrelated instruments coexist: the GIS, whose main role is supporting in data storage, management, visualization of maps, and analyzing the decision problems; and the MCDA, which provide a full range of methods for structuring decision problems, and for designing, evaluating, and prioritizing alternative decisions [13].

In the following Sections 2.1 and 2.2 the main features of both MCDA and SDSS will be highlighted.

2.1. The Multicriteria Decision Analyses (MCDA)

The MCDA are valuable and increasingly widely-used approaches able to help decision-makers (DMs) in making decisions in a structured and intuitive way [11,23]. Despite the diversity of MCDA, the basic ingredients are the following: a finite or infinite set of actions (alternative, solutions, options), a number of decision criteria, and at least one DM or stakeholder. In general terms the MCDA are considered powerful tools able to support decision-making processes where there is a choice to be made between competing alternatives or criteria. Over the years, the MCDA proved to be particularly useful for urban planning, where a complex and inter-connected range of environmental, social, and economic issues must be taken into consideration and where objectives are often competing, making trade-offs unavoidable.

Given the large number of available MCDA approaches, it is necessary to select the most suitable method for the specific decision context [24]. In this paper, we choose to apply two different MCDA methods, respectively: the "Measuring Attractiveness by a Categorical Based Evaluation Technique" (MACBETH) [17] and the "Playing Cards" methods [18]. The choice of applying the two aforementioned methods for the definition and ranking of the decision criteria, which are required for delivering and assessing the urban energy scenarios, is due to a number of reasons.

First, despite the differences existing between the two methods, both of them are considered simple methodologies and easy to be understood, even by those who are not experts in the decision processes [11]. Second, they are able to help DMs in handling values that cannot be easily quantified, involving qualitative judgments Hence, real-life applications show that when one asks the DM what importance he wishes to assign to each decision criterion, he/she expresses his/her preferences spontaneously, without knowing neither the range of the scale nor the procedure used to encode this scale [25]. However, in order to obtain relevant information (output) it is crucial that the output takes into account both the nature and the encoding [26]. This opens a significant debate regarding how to translate qualitative judgements into numerical values, which must reflect the relative importance of the selected evaluation criteria [27]. The MACBETH and the "Playing Cards" methods proved to be relevant in this debate [25]. Third, the technical parameters involved in the two methodologies can be interpreted in an easy way, allowing a simplification of the problem. The results obtained from their application are lists of k-best actions expressed in numerical values to be analysed further by the people involved [17,18]. Finally, the MACBETH method can be supported by the so-called M-MACBETH software, which is compatible with the way of reasoning of the inquired people and with their meaning of useful results. Sections 2.1.1 and 2.1.2 briefly describe the main characters of the MACBETH and the "Playing Cards" methods. (For a comprehensive analysis of the MACBETH and "Playing Cards" methods please refer to [11,28]).

2.1.1. The MACBETH Method

The MACBETH method is a structured MCDA that was developed in the early 1990s. It is based on the additive value model and requires only qualitative judgments about differences of value to help an individual, or a group, quantify the relative attractiveness of the actions or criteria. Starting from the qualitative judgments requested to the stakeholders, the MACBETH method allows the construction of quantitative values model supporting the interactive learning process about the problem in exam. In this sense, it is able to reduce the "cognitive discomfort" [28] that could arise in the stakeholders when they are asked to express their preferences in a numerical scale. The MACBETH methodology can be divided into three main application phases: model structuring, model evaluating and analyzing the results.

Model Structuring: During the structuring phase, the options to be evaluated and their performances, as well as the values of concern need to be identified and structured in the form of a tree, generally referred to as a "value tree", offering an organized visual overview of the various concerns at hand.

Model evaluating: After structured the model, MACBETH involves a series of pairwise comparisons, where the stakeholders are asked to specify the difference of attractiveness between all of the alternatives with respect to the criteria. In order to fill in the pairwise comparison matrices, the semantic categories described in Table 1 are used.

Table 1. Semantic categories of the MACBETH method, Source [17].

Categories	Description
Extremely	Extreme preference of the criterion/option A over the criterion/option B
Very strongly	Very strong preference of the criterion/option A over the criterion/option B
Strongly	Strong preference of the criterion/option A over the criterion/option B
Moderately	Moderate preference of the criterion/option A over the criterion/option B
Weakly	Weak preference of the criterion/option A over the criterion/option B
Very weakly	Very weak preference of the criterion/option A over the criterion/option B
Not at all	No difference in terms of preference

Analysing the results: Once the model has been structured and filled in, the MACBETH method provides very clear results in the form of ranking allowing identify the attractiveness of the problem's criteria and alternatives.

The MACBETH method has been applied in a number of case studies related to different fields [29,30]. However, in the emerging field of energy planning, very few examples of application are available in literature. An interesting application is provided by Burton and Hubaceck [31]. The two authors used the MACBETH approach for assessing and comparing eight renewable energy technologies at differing scales, using an official definition of renewable energy provided by the UK government. In particular, the study highlighted the advantages and disadvantages of a number of different renewable energy technologies, concluding that the MACBETH method constitutes a useful support in handling values that cannot be easily quantified. In their study, the authors proved that the decisions reached following the use of the MCDA are likely to be more effective than those realized by using only financial methods; however, this result is reached on the basis of a high conflicting process among stakeholders over the values and weights to be explicated in a MCDA application.

Although this study has been inspired by the work developed by Burton and Hubaceck, in the present paper the MACBETH method is used for defining decision criteria to be adopted in the development of urban energy scenarios rather than comparing different energy technologies on the base of established decision criteria. Furthermore, in this application of the MACBETH method consensus among the stakeholders is reached inside focus groups, while Burton and Hubaceck approached the problem with single interviews.

2.1.2. The "Playing Cards" Method

The "Playing Cards" method is a semi-structured participative procedure suitable to support group discussion. It allows the stakeholders involved to think about and express the way in which they wish to hierarchize the different criteria in a specific context. One of the major advantages of the "Playing Cards" method is the ease of application. This method in fact, consists in associating a "card" with each criterion. Moreover, the stakeholders have a set of "white cards" available, the use of which depends on specific needs. The application of the procedure is very simple: (1) the stakeholders are asked to order the "cards" according to the importance of the criteria (from the last important to the most important one) providing a complete pre-order. If some criteria have the same importance, the stakeholders should build a subset of cards holding them together; (2) according to the fact that the importance of two successive criteria in the ranking can be more or less close, the stakeholders are asked to insert the "white cards" between two successive "cards" (the greater the difference between the mentioned weights of the criteria, the greater the number of white cards) providing a final ranking of the importance of criteria; (3) the final ranking of criteria is converted into weights according to Simos' algorithm. The fact that the stakeholders involved have to handle the cards in order to rank them allows a rather intuitive understanding of the aim of this procedure [32].

Unfortunately, few applications of this method are available in literature [25,33,34]. Mention has to be made to the study provided by Bottero et al. [33], which proposed an innovative application of the "Playing Cards" method in connection with ELECTRE III [33] in order to compare five urban requalification projects. Although the topic is different and is not related to the energy context, this study constituted an interesting reference highlighting a number of benefits of the "Playing Cards" method, as follows: it is interactive, easy to be understood and accepted by the stakeholders involved. In the application of the "Playing Cards" method, Bottero et al. [33] promoted an individual discussion with the stakeholders. In the present study, on the contrary, the method is applied directly inside a focus group in order to inform the stakeholders and stimulate the discussion. In the urban energy retrofitting context, the present study constitutes one of the first examples.

2.2. Methodological Steps of a MC-SDSS

From a methodological viewpoint, the process needed to define and assess urban scenarios includes the three following phases [19,35]:

1. *Intelligence phase*: the decisional context analysis for structuring and identifying the decision problem should be provided in this phase. Both relevant decision criteria and alternative scenarios should be established, identified and assessed in this phase. The process model includes: (i) data collection and integration; (ii) criteria definition; and (iii) scenario definition;

2. *Design phase*: once the alternative scenarios are defined, it is necessary to carefully choose the most appropriate MCDA method in order to structure the decision model and the evaluation matrix (criteria and alternatives matrix);

3. *Evaluation and Choice*: the selected MCDA method will assess and evaluate the alternative scenarios. During this phase, a sensitivity analysis is suggested in order to examine the consistency of the obtained outcomes and the robustness of the model.

The scenarios definition, therefore, constitutes the final step of a MC-SDSS tool development. In the context of this research project, scenarios analysis is adopted to understand future energy consumption patterns, considering possible refurbishment actions in the built environment. These refurbishment actions consist of: diminishing the energy needs of the building (e.g., window replacement, insulation of the opaque envelope), increasing of the heating system efficiency (e.g., boiler replacement, control improvement), or the use of renewable energy resources on-site (e.g., solar thermal plant or solar photovoltaic (PV) plant installation). Moreover, an attempt was made in this study to introduce different participative scenarios based on the feasibility of retrofit measures, taking into account the influence of socio-economic demographic variables and the capability and desire to invest in renovation measures.

3. Identifying a Coherent Set of Criteria for the MC-SDSS

In this section, a suitable set of criteria to be included in the MC-SDSS for urban energy retrofitting scenarios (from now-on named "Dashboard") will be presented. This set derives from a collaborative work developed in two different projects: the European project DIMMER and the National Smart City and Communities project Zero Energy Buildings in Smart Urban Districts (EEB). A short explanation of these two projects is provided below, together with the methodologies used for selecting and ranking the final criteria based on focus groups [36]. It is notable to say that the energy consumption reduction and the energy efficiency regulations proposed by the EU legislation were not considered as decision criteria, but as a final objective and target of each scenario. In fact, the recent Second Report on the State of the Energy Union [37] describes the state of the art of energy transition to secure and low carbon sources: adapting and updating existing local energy grids, such as in the DIMMER project, this objective has been enforced. Moreover, the EU has determined a new plan for energy efficiency, setting several policy targets, known as the "20-20-20" in order to reduce greenhouse gas emissions by 20% from 1990 levels [38]. In both mentioned projects, a predictive "what-if" scenarios approach has been taken into account, which are often short/medium term [39]. This approach investigates what will happen on the condition of some specified actions for future development [39]. Therefore, each scenario is defined taking into account the EU targets with the aim at reducing, at a minimum, 20% of total energy consumption.

3.1. The Criteria Set in the DIMMER Project

DIMMER (2013–2016) is a European project coordinated by the Politecnico di Torino, which received funding from the European Union's Seventh Program for Research, Technological Development and Demonstration under grant agreement no. 609084.

DIMMER consists of a software system destined to energy managers and public authorities to monitor district energy data as well as simulate and implement energy management policies and scenarios at district level. Moreover, thanks to DIMMER, we started to develop the Dashboard, which aims at supporting energy decision processes at a district-scale of intervention.

In order to test and validate the DIMMER innovative system and the Dashboard, both public and private buildings included in urban districts are considered in two different cities: Turin (Italy) and Manchester (The United Kingdom—for more details please refer to the project's website www.dimmerproject.eu).

During the DIMMER project, we started to define and rank the decision criteria to be used to develop urban energy scenarios. Starting from this, a coherent set of criteria, reflecting the concerns relevant to the decision problem has been identified. The criteria considered in the present application were selected based on the relevant international literature and on the requirements coming from the DIMMER project (Table 2).

Table 2. Description of the considered criteria (DIMMER project).

Aspect	Criteria	Literature	Description	Unit
Economic	Investment costs	[40]	Investment costs related to refurbishment of buildings (efficiency investment) and new energy sources (infrastructure investment).	Euro
	Payback Period (PBP)	[41]	Performance measure used to evaluate the efficiency of an investment or to compare the efficiency of a number of different investments.	Years
Environmental	Reduction of the CO_2 emissions.	[36]	Reduction of the CO_2 pollutant emissions.	Percentage
Technical	Reduction of the energy requirement	[34]	Percentage of reduction of the energy requirement due to the buildings' intervention (coat insulations and windows).	Percentage
	Resilience of the energy system.	[34]	Ability of soak up economy and physical shocks of the energy system.	Ordinal

The Ranking of the Criteria Based on MACBETH Approach

The structured method MACBETH [17] was applied with the aim of providing a ranking of evaluation criteria. Three focus groups have been organized with the participation of real stakeholders, including: representatives of the builders' associations, developers, designers, representatives of administrations' offices and academic experts (energy and economic evaluations). The M-MACBETH software facilitated the application of the method.

According to the MACBETH method, a series of questions related to the criteria under examination have been posed to the stakeholders involved. They were asked to answer according to the semantic categories described in Table 1 starting from their personal opinion and knowledge and taking into account their area of expertise. The questions were of the type:

(1a) Looking at the criteria under examination in Table 2, rank them from most preferred to least preferred.

(1b) According to the rank so far provided, to what extent do you prefer one criterion to another?

Example: I strongly prefer the criterion "investments' costs" over the criterion "running costs" and I weakly prefer "running costs" to the criterion "resilience of the energy system".

In order to obtain an output in form of numerical ranking, we inserted the answers provided by the stakeholders in the M-MACBETH software that is able to translate the semantic categories into numerical judgments according to the MACBETH method [17]. During this phase, some judgmental hesitations and/or disagreement appeared among the stakeholders about which MACBETH category better reflected the difference of attractiveness. In such cases, a discussion within the group has been stimulated in order to reach the consensus.

The overall criteria ranking resulting from the MACBETH applications during the focus groups are presented in Table 3.

Table 3. Final ranking of the considered criteria.

Criteria Ranking	Scores (%)
Investment costs	30
Payback period (PBP)	27
Reduction of the energy requirement	23
Reduction of the CO_2 emissions	18
Resilience of the energy system.	2

During the focus groups, the business operators emphasized the need for an economic viability of the investment, while the representatives of the public authorities advocate a reduction of the CO_2 emissions. However, the results highlighted the higher preference given to the economic aspects compared with the environmental ones, as one can notice in Table 3 (Investments costs 30% and PBP 27%). The criterion "resilience of the energy system" was not considered important for the definition of future energy scenarios.

Additional suggestions emerging from the discussion among the stakeholders are: the demand for a more flexible and participative approach for ranking the criteria; and the need to consider additional social criteria and urban planning aspects.

3.2. The Criteria Set in the EEB Project

The EEB is a National project coordinated by ST-Microelectronics [42] and funded by the Ministry of Innovation. The project aims at exploring energy consumption patterns at the urban-scale providing a methodology for evaluating different urban energy retrofitting scenarios based on multi-criteria analysis in the context of sustainable urban planning. In the framework of the EEB project, a focus group involving real stakeholders has been established in order to test the Dashboard. As for the

DIMMER project, the criteria considered in the present application have been selected on the basis of both the relevant literature review, as it is presented in Table 4 and the specific requirements deriving from the EEB project. Finally, as suggested by the previous focus group organized in the context of the DIMMER project (see Section 3.1), we included social, architectural, and technical criteria in the analysis (Table 4).

Table 4. Description of the considered criteria (EEB project).

Aspect	Criteria	Literature	Description	Unit
Environmental	Global emissions CO_2	[36,43,44]	Measure the equivalent emission of CO_2, which is avoided by the examined action.	Tons/year
	Local emissions ($NO_X + PM_{10}$)	[43]	Direct impact on the health of the community and an indirect impact on the social state of the community.	Ordinal scale
Economic	Payback period (PBP)	[41]	Performance measure used to evaluate the efficiency of an investment or to compare the efficiency of a number of different investments.	Years
	Investment cost	[40]	Investment costs related to refurbishment of building (efficiency investment) and/or new heating system (infrastructure investment).	Euro
	Socio-economic feasibility	[45]	The economic capability and willingness of the people.	Number
	Maintenance costs	[46]	Running fixed and variable costs due to maintenance of the heating system (does not take into account fuel costs).	Euro
Technical	Reliability	[36,47]	Efficiency of the technology and the requalification result.	Ordinal scale
	Technical life	[44]	Durability of the whole strategy in relation to the service life of each retrofit measure.	Years
Social	Social acceptability	[47,48]	The perception of the people related to specific impacts due to the refurbishments.	Ordinal scale
	Local Job creation	[49]	Potentiality of creating job and better regularity of the employee.	Man-day/ordinal scale
	Architectural Impact	[49]	The visual and architectural impact of refurbishments in the existing built environment.	ordinal scale

Table 4 shows the list of criteria used in EEB project. This is a longer list compared with the one used in the DIMMER project. In this list, a number of relevant additional criteria have considered as follows: (1) "local emissions" is crucial, but is often ignored due to a lack of available data; (2) the "reliability" criterion has been inserted in order to consider the technical feasibility of the possible energy projects at the urban level; and (3) we took into account a number of social aspects. It is proved they are definitely fundamental criteria for people's acceptance of energy changes [34]. Therefore, they need to be considered in the SDSS, in order to better guide the design of future urban energy transition scenarios.

The Ranking of the Criteria Based on Playing Card Method

To define the importance of the criteria during the EEB project we decided to apply the "Playing Cards" method [18]. As described in Section 2, the "Playing Cards" method is a semi-structured participative procedure, which differs from the MACBETH approach previously applied.

Operatively, the "Playing Cards" method has been here applied during a focus group organized in Turin (Italy) whose purpose was to discuss and rank the most important criteria to be further implemented in the Dashboard. The stakeholders involved in this focus group belong to the following categories: designers, representatives of the public administrations, experts in SDSS development, expert in visualization tool, building administrators, and academic experts (i.e., energy, economic evaluations, and urban planning).

During this focus group, the stakeholders were divided in three heterogeneous groups of work. First, each group received a set of cards: each card represented a decision criterion. Second, the groups were asked to rank the cards according to their preferences. Third, we asked them to think about the fact that the importance of two successive criteria can be more or less close. Therefore, we invited the stakeholders to introduce the white cards between two successive cards according to the logic "the grater the number of white cards, the greater the difference between the mentioned weights of the criteria" [25]. Then, each group provided a rank of criteria. Finally, the three ranks were showed in a plenary session. Differently from the approach used for the Macbeth application, in this case the stakeholders were forced to discuss about the rank in order to obtain a consensual rank of criteria (Table 5).

Table 5. Final results coming from the "Playing Cards" method.

Rank	Subset of Ex-Equo	Number of Cards	Positions	Non-Normalize Weights	Normalized Weights	Total [2]
1	Architectural Impact	1	1	1	1316	132
2	White cards	3	(2,3,4)	-	-	-
3	Local Job creation	1	5	5	6579	658
4	White cards	1	(6)	-	-	-
5	Reliability	1	7	7	9211	921
6	White cards	2	(8,9)	-	-	-
7	Socio/economic feasibility + Local emissions	2	10,11	10,5	13,816	2763
8	White cards	1	(12)	-	-	0
9	Investment costs	1	13	13	17,105	1710
10	Payback Period	1	14	14	18,421	1842
11	Global emissions CO_2	1	15	15	19,737	1973
SUM			76 [1]			100

[1] This sum does not include the positions of the white cards (in brackets). [2] The total column reports the normalized weights multiplied for the number of cards of each position.

From Table 5 it emerges that some of the criteria included in Table 4 have been removed by the stakeholders during the discussion since they were considered unimportant for the analysis. In particular, the "social acceptability" has not been considered as a crucial aspect due to several reasons: (1) the construction phases are usually very short and, therefore, they do not constitute an inconvenience; and (2) the stakeholders believed that the possible inconveniences occurring during a construction phase are unavoidable and uncontrollable. On the contrary, both the "maintenance costs" and the "technical life" criterion have been considered as relevant criteria, but only in association with the "payback period" criterion.

During this exercise, the stakeholders questioned the calculation methods of the social aspects with particular reference to the "local job creation". This is probably one of the reasons why the social aspects are partially neglected. Similarly, the "architectural impact" has been considered to not be fundamental from the stakeholders involved since this kind of impact is, nowadays, reduced thanks to international and national norms. On the contrary, the economic and environmental aspects have been considered much more important than the technical and social ones. In particular, the local and global emissions have been generally considered as crucial. The correlation with human health in a specific area will have to take into account the actual concentration of those pollutants in the district environment (air) [43] and to propose a risk methodology for the augmented potential risk created.

4. Discussion

The MACBETH approach proved to be a well-structured method able to organize the evaluation criteria according to a robust and well-accepted methodology. Hence, the use of the M-MACBETH software has facilitated the ranking of the criteria, considering the preference of the stakeholders involved. A positive aspect of this method is the pair-wise comparison approach, which has proved to be quite intuitive and easy to be understood. On the contrary, the negative aspect of this method is the lack of appropriate knowledge of the relationships between the input and the output of the model. In other words, the way data are processed is not clear, resulting in a "black box" for the stakeholders.

On the other side, the "Playing Cards" method showed to be a flexible method able to stimulate the discussion among the stakeholders involved in the focus group. Thanks to these characteristics, the method is useful to support decisions with subjective criteria. Moreover, the stakeholders perceived the "Playing Cards" method as a very intuitive and engaging method, able to support discussion on the criteria involved and useful for ranking them according to their preferences.

Regarding results, both the two MCDA methods highlighted that the most important criteria for the development of energy urban retrofitting scenarios are related to both economic and environmental aspects. On the other hand, the social aspects proved to be difficult to be taken into account.

Table 6 summarizes the main differences between the two approaches, emerged during their application in the DIMMER and EEB projects.

Table 6. The comparison between two approaches.

	MACBETH Approach	Playing Card (Simos Approach)
Selecting and Weighting Methods	Guided (ordinal scale)	Subjective (subjective scale)
Participation Structure	Participative approach structured through the use of a dedicated software	Semi-structured participative based on free discussion
Approach	Participants are asked to pair-wise compare the importance of criteria through worksheets	Participants are asked to rank the cards according to their personal knowledge and background
Importance ranking	Scales can vary from 0 (equal importance) to 5 (absolutely more important)	Rank importance position by inserting a set of cards "white cards" between colored cards
Stakeholders acceptance	Black box	Intuitive and entertaining

5. Conclusions

This paper has illustrated two different methods for defining and ranking the decision criteria required for assessing urban energy scenarios: (i): the Measuring Attractiveness by a Categorical Based Evaluation Technique (MACBETH) and (ii) the "Playing Cards" method. The two approaches have been applied to two research Smart City projects, DIMMER and EEB, related to the definition of a Spatial Decision Support System (SDSS), the Dashboard.

Although differences exist among the two approaches and outputs, as highlighted in Section 4, both the methods have been useful in order to identify a sensible set of criteria and their ranking. These are required for delivering appropriate, stakeholders-based scenarios and policies for energy demand reduction at urban and district scales. Both the MACBETH and the "Playing Cards" methods are stakeholder-based approaches, i.e., they are based on stakeholders' preferences. The application of the two approaches from a very earlier phase of a decision process may help to achieve effective outcomes, since the definition and ranking of the criteria strongly influence the final results.

Finally, it is important to underline that the application of both the MACBETH and the "Playing Cards" methods presented in this paper represents a validation step [50] aiming at verifying whether the key issues have been appropriately considered in the decision making process [51] and testing the model by using experimental or real data in order.

In conclusion, this study is only one-step toward the goal of developing future urban energy scenarios through the development of the Dashboard. This will support DMs to deliver retrofitting GIS-based alternative scenarios. In particular, the main advantages of the Dashboard in the field of urban energy planning can be summarized as follows: to allow the participative processes; to give a visualization opportunity for the decision process in specific areas; to consider multiple criteria (e.g., economic, environmental, technical and, particularly, social aspects); to manage and store a very large amount of georeferenced data; to illustrate results requested by users according to different spatial forms (e.g., maps, graphs); to show the distribution of buildings' geometrical characterization and buildings' energy consumption. The next steps of this research include both the definition of the urban scenarios and the development of a second focus group to choose the "best" urban energy scenario.

Acknowledgments: The authors of this study wish to acknowledge the contributions of a number of colleagues institutions involved in the EU VII Framework Program projects, named "DIMMER-District Information Modeling and Management for Energy Reduction" funded from the European Union's Seventh Program for Research, Technological Development and Demonstration under grant agreement no. 609084, and an on-going National Cluster Smart City and Communities project, named "EEB-Zero Energy Buildings in Smart Urban Districts" funded by National Operational Program for Research and Competitiveness 2007–2013 (PON R and C), CTN01_00034_594053.

Author Contributions: Although the paper is the result of a joint effort of all authors, Patrizia Lombardi has supervised and revised the whole work and developed Sections 4 and 5; Francesca Abastante has developed Sections 2.1 and 3.1 and co-edited Sections 1, 3.2 and 4; Sara Torabi Moghadam has written Sections 1, 2.2 and 3.2; and Jacopo Toniolo has supported the delivery of both Sections 3.1 and 3.2 with technical inputs presented in Tables 2–4.

Conflicts of Interest: The authors declare no conflicts of interest.

References

1. International Energy Agency (IEA). *Energy Technology Perspectives 2016—Towards Sustainable Urban Energy Systems*; International Energy Agency (IEA) Publications: Paris, France, 2016.
2. Howard, B.; Parshall, L.; Thompson, J.; Hammer, S.; Dickinson, J.; Modi, V. Spatial distribution of urban building energy consumption by end use. *Energy Build.* **2012**, *45*, 141–151. [CrossRef]
3. Torabi Moghadam, S.; Mutani, G.; Lombardi, P. Gis-based energy consumption model at the urban scale for the building stock. In *JRC Conference and Workshop Reports, Proceedings of the 9th International Conference Improving Energy Efficiency in Commercial Buildings and Smart Communities, Frankfurt, Germany, 16 March 2016*; Bertoldi, P., Ed.; European Union: Luxembourg, 2016; Volume EUR 27993 EN, pp. 56–63.
4. Fracastoro, G.V.; Serraino, M. A methodology for assessing the energy performance of large scale building stocks and possible applications. *Energy Build.* **2011**, *43*, 844–852. [CrossRef]
5. Lombardi, P.; Ferretti, V. New spatial decision support systems for sustainable urban and regional development. *Smart Sustain. Built Environ.* **2015**, *4*, 45–66. [CrossRef]
6. Torabi Moghadam, S.; Delmastro, C.; Lombardi, P.; Corgnati, S.P. Towards a new integrated spatial decision support system in urban context. *Procedia Soc. Behav. Sci.* **2016**, *223*, 974–981. [CrossRef]
7. Caputo, P.; Costa, G.; Ferrari, S. A supporting method for defining energy strategies in the building sector at urban scale. *Energy Policy* **2013**, *55*, 261–270. [CrossRef]
8. Chalal, M.L.; Benachir, M.; White, M.; Shrahily, R. Energy planning and forecasting approaches for supporting physical improvement strategies in the building sector: A review. *Renew. Sustain. Energy Rev.* **2016**, *64*, 761–776. [CrossRef]
9. Arciniegas, G.; Janssen, R.; Omtzigt, N. Map-based multicriteria analysis to support interactive land use allocation. *Int. J. Geogr. Inf. Sci.* **2011**, *25*, 1931–1947. [CrossRef]
10. Chakhar, S.; Martel, J.-M. Towards a spatial decision support system: Multi-criteria evaluation functions inside geographical information systems. *Ann. Du Lamsade* **2004**, *2*, 97–123.
11. Figueira, J.; Greco, S.; Ehrgott, M. *Multiple Criteria Decision Analysis: State of the Art Surveys*; Springer: Berlin, Germany, 2005.
12. AbuSada, J.; Thawaba, S. Multi criteria analysis for locating sustainable suburban centers: A case study from Ramallah governorate, Palestine. *Cities* **2011**, *28*, 381–393. [CrossRef]
13. Malczewski, J. Gis-based multicriteria decision analysis: A survey of the literature. *Int. J. Geogr. Inf. Sci.* **2006**, *20*, 703–726. [CrossRef]
14. Jankowski, P.; Andrienko, N.; Andrienko, G. Map-centred exploratory approach to multiple criteria spatial decision making. *Int. J. Geogr. Inf. Sci.* **2001**, *15*, 101–127. [CrossRef]
15. DIMMER. District Information Modelling and Management for Energy Reduction. Available online: www.dimmerproject.eu (accessed on 24 February 2017).
16. EEB. Zero Energy Buildings in Smart Urban Districts (EEB). Available online: www.smartcommunitiestech.it (accessed on 23 February 2017).
17. Bana e Costa, C.A.; De Corte, J.M.; Vansnick, J.C. Macbeth: Measuring attractiveness by a categorical based evaluation technique. In *Wiley Encyclopedia of Operations Research and Management Science*; Cochran, J.J., Ed.; Wiley Online Library: Hoboken, NY, USA, 2010.

18. Simos, J. L'evaluation environnementale: Un processus cognitif Negocie. These de doctorat. In *DGF-EPFL, Lausanne*; Presses Polytechniques et Universitaires Romandes: Lausanne, Switzerland, 1990.
19. Malczewski, J. *Gis and Multicriteria Decision Analysis*; Wiley: Hoboken, NJ, USA, 1999; p. 392.
20. Chakhar, S.; Martel, J.-M. Enhancing geographical information systems capabilities with multi-criteria evaluation functions. *J. Geogr. Inf. Decis. Anal.* **2003**, *7*, 47–71.
21. Densham, P.J. Spatial decision support systems. *Geogr. Inf. Syst. Princ. Appl.* **1991**, *1*, 403–412.
22. Ferretti, V. Integrating multicriteria analysis and geographic information systems: A survey and classification of the literature. In Proceedings of the 74th Meeting of the European Working Group "Multiple Criteria Decision Aiding", Yverdon, Switzerland, 6–8 October 2011.
23. Roy, B.; Slowinski, R. Question guiding the choice of a multicriteria decision aiding method. *EURO J. Decis. Process.* **2013**, *1*, 69–97. [CrossRef]
24. Abastante, F. Multicriteria decision methodologies supporting decision processes. *Geoing. Ambient. Mineraria GEAM* **2016**, *149*, 5–18.
25. Figueira, J.; Roy, B. Determining the weights of criteria in the electre type methods with a revised simos' procedure. *Eur. J. Oper. Res.* **2002**, *139*, 317–326. [CrossRef]
26. Keeney, R.L.; Raiffa, H. *Decisions with Multiple Objectives—Preferences and Value Tradeoffs*; Cambridge University Press: Cambridge, UK, 1993.
27. Mousseau, V. Eliciting information concerning the relative importance of criteria. In *Advances in Multicriteria Analysis. Nonconvex Optimization and Its Applications*; Pardalos, P.M., Siskos, Y., Zopounidis, C., Eds.; Kluwer Academic Publishers: Dordrecht, The Netherlands, 1995; Volume 5, pp. 17–43.
28. Fasolo, B.; Bana e Costa, C.A. Tailoring value elicitation to decision makers' numeracy and fluency: Expressing value judgments in numbers or words. *Omega* **2014**, *44*, 83–90. [CrossRef]
29. Bana e Costa, C.A.; Correa, E.C.; De Corte, J.M.; Vansnick, J.C. Facilitating bid evaluation in public call for tenders: A socio-technical approach. *Omega* **2002**, *30*, 227–242. [CrossRef]
30. Bana e Costa, C.A.; Oliveira, M.D. A multicriteria decision analysis model for faculty evaluation. *Omega* **2012**, *40*, 424–436. [CrossRef]
31. Burton, J.; Hubacek, K. Is small beautiful? A multicriteria assessment of small-scale energy technology applications in local governments. *Energy Policy* **2007**, *35*, 6402–6412. [CrossRef]
32. Maystre, L.; Pictet, J.; Simos, J. *Methodes Multicriteres Electre—Description, Conseils Pratiques et Cas D'application a la Gestion Environnementale*; Presses Polytechniques et Universitaires Romandes: Lausanne, Switzerland, 1994.
33. Bottero, M.; Ferretti, V.; Figueira, J.R.; Greco, S.; Roy, B. Dealing with a multiple criteria environmental problem with interaction effects between criteria through an extension of the electreiii method. *Eur. J. Oper. Res.* **2015**, *245*, 837–850. [CrossRef]
34. Wang, J.-J.; Jing, Y.-Y.; Zhang, C.-F.; Zhao, J.-H. Review on multi-criteria decision analysis aid in sustainable energy decision-making. *Renew. Sustain. Energy Rev.* **2009**, *13*, 2263–2278. [CrossRef]
35. Simon, H.A. *The New Science of Management Decision*; Harper & Brothers: New York, NY, USA, 1977; p. 175.
36. Beccali, M.; Cellura, M.; Mistretta, M. Decision-making in energy planning. Application of the electre method at regional level for the diffusion of renewable energy technology. *Renew. Energy* **2003**, *28*, 2063–2087. [CrossRef]
37. European Commission. *Second Report on the State of the Energy Union*; Commission Communication; European Commission: Brussels, Belgium, 2017.
38. European Commission. *Energy Efficiency Plan 2011*; Commission Communication; European Commission: Brussels, Belgium, 2011.
39. Börjeson, L.; Höjera, M.; Dreborg, K.H.; Ekvall, T.; Finnveden, G. Scenario types and techniques: Towards a user's guide. *Futures* **2006**, *38*, 723–739. [CrossRef]
40. Becchio, C.; Ferrando, D.G.; Fregonara, E.; Milani, N.; Quercia, C.; Serra, V. The cost-optimal methodology for the energy retrofit of an ex-industrial building located in northern Italy. *Energy Build.* **2016**, *127*, 590–602. [CrossRef]
41. Volvačiovas, R.; Turskis, Z.; Aviža, D.; Mikštienė, R. Multi-attribute selection of public buildings retrofits strategy. *Procedia Eng.* **2013**, *57*, 1236–1241. [CrossRef]
42. ST-Microelectronics. Available online: www.st.com (accessed on 25 March 2017).

43. Jovanović, M.; Afgan, N.; Radovanović, P.; Stevanović, V. Sustainable development of the Belgrade energy system. *Energy* **2009**, *34*, 532–539. [CrossRef]

44. Giaccone, A.; Lascari, G.; Peri, G.; Rizz, G. An ex post criticism, based on stakeholders' preferences, of a residential sector's energy master plan: The case study of the Sicilian region. *Energy Effic.* **2017**, *10*, 129–149. [CrossRef]

45. Mutani, G.; Vicentini, G. Buildings' energy consumption, energy savings potential and the availability of renewable energy sources in urban spaces. *J. Civ. Eng. Arch. Res.* **2015**, *2*, 1102–1115.

46. Cavallaro, F.; Ciraolo, L. A multicriteria approach to evaluate wind energy plants on an Italian Island. *Energy Policy* **2005**, *33*, 235–244. [CrossRef]

47. Ertay, T.; Kahraman, C.; Kaya, İ. Evaluation of renewable energy alternatives using Macbeth and fuzzy Ahp Multicriteria methods: The case of Turkey. *Technol. Econ. Dev. Econ.* **2013**, *19*, 38–62. [CrossRef]

48. Theodorou, S.; Florides, G.; Tassou, S. The use of multiple criteria decision making methodologies for the promotion of res through funding schemes in Cyprus, a review. *Energy Policy* **2010**, *38*, 7783–7792. [CrossRef]

49. Dall'O, G.; Norese, M.; Galante, A.; Novello, C. A multi-criteria methodology to support public administration decision making concerning sustainable energy action plans. *Energies* **2013**, *6*, 4308–4330. [CrossRef]

50. Landry, M.; Malouin, J.; Oral, M. Model validation in operations research. *Eur. J. Oper. Res.* **1983**, *14*, 207–220. [CrossRef]

51. Tsoukias, A. From decision theory to decision aiding methodology. *Eur. J. Oper. Res.* **2007**, *18*, 138–161. [CrossRef]

MDPI AG

St. Alban-Anlage 66

4052 Basel, Switzerland

Tel. +41 61 683 77 34

Fax +41 61 302 89 18

http://www.mdpi.com

Sustainability Editorial Office

E-mail: sustainability@mdpi.com

http://www.mdpi.com/journal/sustainability

www.ingramcontent.com/pod-product-compliance
Lightning Source LLC
Chambersburg PA
CBHW041138120626

46547CB00020B/3034